SCOTTISH OFFICE LIBRARIES
RETENTION
Control No. A3
Date 3/10/91
Shelfmark

SCOTTISH INDUSTRIAL POLICY

SERIES : 4

Editors : Neil Hood and Stephen Young

THE SCOTTISH FINANCIAL SECTOR

Paul Draper, Iain Smith,
William Stewart and Neil Hood
for the University Press

EDINBURGH

© Paul Draper, Iain Smith,
William Stewart and Neil Hood 1988

Edinburgh University Press
22 George Square, Edinburgh

Printed in Great Britain by
Redwood Burn Ltd, Trowbridge

British Library Cataloguing
in Publication Data
The Scottish financial sector—
(Scottish industrial policy series; no.4)
1. Financial institutions—Scotland
I. Draper, P.   II. Series
332.1′09411   HG186.G7
ISBN 0 85224 550 5

FOREWORD

I am pleased to have been asked to write a few words about the Strathclyde Business School's Project on the Scottish Financial Sector. At a time of immense change in our financial markets, including growing internationalisation, the detailed study undertaken by the Business School will, I hope, provide the platform for those in the Scottish financial sector to identify new opportunities, focus on the necessary skills and technology and develop further its range of services. Specialised institutions such as those long established in Scotland have a major role to play in building up the capability and capacity of the UK financial sector as a whole, especially in terms of facing up to the tremendous challenges in today's market. I am delighted that, along with the Scottish Development Agency and the Committee of Scottish Clearing Bankers, the Bank has been able to play a positive role in advancing this worthwhile project.

R. Leigh-Pemberton

Bank of England

CONTENTS

Foreword	v
Preface	ix
Acknowledgements	x
List of Tables and Figures	xi
Introduction	1
1. HISTORICAL AND ECONOMIC PERSPECTIVE	3
2. FINANCIAL FLOWS AND EMPLOYMENT IN THE FINANCIAL SECTOR IN SCOTLAND	24
3. SCOTTISH FINANCIAL MARKETS	46
4. THE SCOTTISH CLEARING BANKS	68
Appendix. The Deposit-Taking and Lending Activities of the Scottish Clearing Banks	111
5. RETAIL DEPOSIT INSTITUTIONS	131
6. OTHER BANKING AND DEPOSIT INSTITUTIONS	162
7. INSURANCE FUNDS AND INSURANCE BROKING	191
8. INVESTMENT MANAGEMENT	245
9. PUBLIC VENTURE CAPITAL	278
10. INNOVATION IN FINANCIAL MARKETS AND INSTITUTIONS	295
11. SUMMARY	307
12. CONCLUSIONS	328
Bibliography	337
Index	342

PREFACE

The need for a volume that surveyed the markets and institutions that comprise the Scottish financial sector as a whole has long been felt. Despite such a need there was considerable reluctance to undertake a volume of this type given the difficulties and expense of acquiring information together with the rapid rate of change that made material redundant and irrelevant all too quickly. The generositity of the SDA, the Bank of England and the Scottish Clearing Banks – Bank of Scotland, the Royal Bank of Scotland plc and Clydesdale Bank plc – in funding this research made it possible for the book to be written. A condition of the sponsorship was a requirement for speedy completion, a condition that we have endeavoured to satisfy and which has influenced, in places, the nature of the book. The volume represents an attempt at analysing the Scottish financial sector. It collects together, for the first time, material on the many financial institutions currently operating in Scotland and endeavours to assess their significance and future prospects.

The volume is in every sense a joint work although Iain Smith, as the projects research assistant, must be singled out for his herculean efforts at assembling material, interviewing and chapter writing. Wherever possible the drafts were circulated to interested parties for comment, clarification and discussion before rewriting and editing. The last section of the last chapter deserves a comment of its own. It is different from the rest of the book and deliberately provocative. It puts forward a number of actions that should be discussed and examined with a view to promoting the well-being of the sector. It reflects a view of the Scottish financial sector as of August 1986 that we believe is substantiated by the material in this volume. Inevitably opinions will vary on the acceptability of this view and our suggestions. We hope this volume represents the beginning of a long and fruitful analysis of the Scottish financial sector and it is in this spirit that this programme of action is offered.

P. R. Draper
   Dept of Accounting and Finance
I. W. Smith
   Dept of Economics
W. J. Stewart
   Dept of Economics
N. Hood
   Dept of Marketing
   University of Strathclyde, October 1986

ACKNOWLEDGEMENTS

Many individuals and institutions have helped in the writing of this book. Our thanks are due to those we interviewed and to those others who gave or offered their help. We would also like to record our gratitude to those who commented on the many drafts that we sent out. We have attempted to listen to and understand the arguments put forward. Inevitably some comments we have ignored, misinterpreted or misunderstood. Our apologies are proffered. If we have omitted any names from the following list of institutions and individuals to whom we are indebted it is through oversight alone: Airdrie Savings Bank, Alexander Stenhouse, Alliance Trust, Asset Services (Paisley), Association of Investment Trust Companies, Association of Scottish Life Offices, Bacon & Woodrow, Grant Baird, Bank of America, Bank of England, Bank of Ireland, Bank of Nova Scotia, Bank of Scotland, Banque Nationale de Paris, British Linen Bank, Clydesdale Bank, Clydesdale Bank Pension Fund, Credit Lyonnais, Dunfermline Building Society, Edinburgh Financial & General Holdings, FS Assurance, Max Gaskin, General Accident, Halifax Building Society, Highlands and Islands Development Board, Investors in Industry, Ivory & Sime, Lloyds Bowmaker Finance, David Locke, Manufacturers Hanover Trust Co., Morgan Grenfell (Scotland) Ltd, Murray Johnstone, National Association of Pension Funds, National Savings Bank, National Westminster Bank, Postel Pension Fund, Roger Tym & Partners, Scottish Amicable, Scottish Equitable, Scottish Life Assurance, Scottish Mutual, Scottish Provident, Scottish Widows, Mike Smith, Standard Chartered Bank, Standard Life, Strathclyde Regional Council Pension Fund, The Building Societies Association, The Committee of London Clearing Bankers, The Committee of Scottish Clearing Bankers, The Economist, The Institute of Bankers in Scotland, The Royal Bank of Scotland, The Scottish Stock Exchange, Unit Trust Association, Walter Scott & Partners, WM Company.

We also made use of the MSC's National Online Manpower Information System (NOMIS), programmed and developed at the Department of Geography, University of Durham, by R. Nelson and P. Dodds.

For her patient help in the preparation of the text we wish to thank Irene Nugent. Finally we should like to record our thanks to our families who have had to live with the preparation of this book. It has not always been easy!

Professor Hood is now on secondment to the SDA as Director of Locate in Scotland. The views he expresses here are personal and are not a reflection of official policy.

LIST OF TABLES AND FIGURES

Chapter 1. Historical and Economic Perspective
Table 1.1. Early Scottish banking innovations   p.15
Table 1.2. History of financial services in Scotland   p.22
Chapter 2. Financial Flows and Employment in the Financial Sector in Scotland
Table 2.1. Government/Regional Transfers 1974/75: 1977/78 average £m at 1978 survey prices   p.26
Table 2.2. Purchase or alteration of dwellings, including average weekly mortgage payments   p.30
Table 2.3. Sources of income in Scotland and the UK. Average weekly income over two-year period and percentage distribution of sources   p.31
Table 2.4. Average weekly expenditure (£) over a two-year period on life assurance and other savings and investment   p.32
Table 2.5. Regional location quotients for MLHs 860, 861 and 862 and percentage of Great Britain MLH 860–862 total employment, 1981   p.34
Table 2.6. National and regional growth rates of MLH 860–862 total employment, 1971–81   p.36
Table 2.7. Growth rates of total employment in insurance, banking and other financial institutions, in Scotland and other regions of Great Britain, 1971–81   p.36
Table 2.8. Changes in male and female financial employment in Scotland, 1971–81, selected years   p.39
Table 2.9. Employment in MLHs 860, 861 and 862 by Scottish Financial Centres, 1971 and 1981   p.41
Table 2.10. Employment and employment changes in division 8 in Great Britain, 1981–85, selected activities   p.43
Chapter 3. Scottish Financial Markets
Table 3.1. Scottish members of the Stock Exchange   p.52
Table 3.2. Stockbroker services available in Scotland   p.54
Chapter 4. The Scottish Clearing Banks
Figure 4.1. Senior management structure of the Royal Bank of Scotland plc (the clearing bank) as at 1 October 1985   p.86
Figure 4.2. Ownership of the three Scottish clearing banks   p.95
Table 4.1. Balances of the three Scottish clearing banks and their subsidiaries, as at 1975, 1980 and 1985   p.74
Table 4.2. Number of accounts at London and Scottish clearing banks   p.75

List of Tables and Figures

Table 4.3. Scottish and London clearing banks, sources and distribution of banking funds (UK residents)   p.78
Table 4.4. Number of Scottish clearing bank branches, 1975 to 1985   p.80
Table 4.5. Scottish clearing bank groups: UK staff   p.84
Table 4.6. Overseas representation of the Scottish clearing banks   p.90
Table 4.7. Scottish and London clearing banks' profits before taxation (historic cost)   p.99
Table 4.8. Scottish and London clearing bank accounts data for 1975, 1979 and 1985   p.100
Table 4.9. Annual profitability and resource data: percentage ratios   p.101
Table 4.10. Scottish and London clearing banks' sterling deposits: analysis by type, 1975, 1980, 1984, and 1985   p.112
Table 4.11. Scottish and London clearing banks: sterling deposits from UK residents – outstanding by sector, 1978, 1981 and 1985   p.114
Table 4.12. Deposit growth: Scottish and London clearing banks, building societies and the TSB, 1975–85   p.114
Table 4.13. Scottish clearing bank groups' deposits by outstanding maturity, August 1985   p.116
Table 4.14. Scottish clearing bank groups' advances to UK residents by outstanding maturity, August 1985   p.116
Table 4.15. Scottish clearing banks and their subsidiaries – advances and acceptances: total facilities outstanding and percentage utilisation, 1983–85   p.119
Table 4.16. Advances to UK residents in sterling and other currencies   p.122

Chapter 5. Retail Deposit Institutions

Figure 5.1. TSB structure prior to incorporation   p.134
Figure 5.2. TSB structure after incorporation   p.134
Table 5.1. TSB group principal subsidiaries   p.132
Table 5.2. Trustee savings banks' deposits and branches 1970–85   p.135
Table 5.3. TSB Scotland: six-year financial summary   p.137
Table 5.4. Building society flow of funds in Scotland, 1975 to 1985   p.144
Table 5.5. Regional distribution of loans and owner occupation in 1979 and 1985   p.146
Table 5.6. The housing stock and tenure pattern in Scotland 1966 to 1984, and distribution of the housing stock by tenure in Great Britain, December 1984   p.147
Table 5.7. Number of building societies in Scotland and Great Britain, 1900 to 1985   p.149
Table 5.8. Regional concentration of building societies, end 1984 (BSA members only)   p.149
Table 5.9. Building society representation in Scotland 1984–85   p.150
Table 5.10. Building society and bank branching in Scotland 1975–84   p.152
Table 5.11. Building society and bank personal savings and house purchase loans, 1975–84   p.154

List of Tables and Figures

Table 5.12. Personal sector liquid assets: market share (%) p.155

Chapter 6. Other Banking and Deposit Institutions

Table 6.1. Scottish merchant banks p.168

Table 6.2. National Savings Bank statistics p.186

Chapter 7. Insurance Funds and Insurance Broking

Figure 7.1. The British insurance and pensions market p.193

Table 7.1. Worldwide net premium income of British insurance companies, 1984 p.194

Table 7.2. Territorial analysis of General Accident's general business premium income and underwriting results, 1984 and 1985 p.196

Table 7.3. Intercompany comparisons of general insurance business, three-year averages, 1978–85 p.198

Table 7.4. Overall trading profit of worldwide general insurance, 1979–84 p.198

Table 7.5. Trading results of top three companies writing general insurance business, 1976, 1981, and 1984–85 p.200

Table 7.6. Worldwide underwriting: General Accident's premium income and operating ratios for one-year insurance p.202

Table 7.7. The revenue account of a life assurance company p.206

Table 7.8. The balance sheet of a mutual life assurance company p.206

Table 7.9. Expenditure on media advertising p.212

Table 7.10. Long-term business investments at end 1984 and 1985. Market value (£ million) p.216

Table 7.11. Staff of the Scottish Amicable Assurance Society as at 1 June 1986 p.219

Table 7.12. Concentration ratios of leading groups' worldwide OLT premium income, 1983 p.225

Table 7.13. Mobility among life insurance companies measured by size of OLT funds, 1929, 1968, and 1983 p.226

Table 7.14. Ordinary insurance business of the Scottish and UK insurance offices 1971–84 (£ million) p.229

Table 7.15. A sample of selected UK insurance companies' commission expenditure as a proportion of their new premium income for 1985 p.233

Chapter 8. Investment Management

Figure 8.1. Relationship of investment fund managers to investment vehicles p.246

Table 8.1 Assets of UK investment institutions (£ million) p.247

Table 8.2. Funds under management p.248

Table 8.3. Scottish fund management activity p.249

Table 8.4. Composition of funds under management p.251

Table 8.5. Joint ventures marketing investment expertise internationally p.255

Table 8.6. Unit trust performance p.257

List of Tables and Figures

Table 8.7. Growth in the investment trust market   p.261
Table 8.8. Geographical spread of trust assets   p.263
Table 8.9. Investment trust performance   p.264
Table 8.10. Pension fund management in Scotland   p.267
Table 8.11. Fund management charges   p.269
Table 8.12. Unit trust trusteeships   p.271

Chapter 9. Public Venture Capital

Table 9.1. SDA investment profile   p.282
Table 9.2. HIDB contribution to project cost   p.286
Table 9.3. HIDB receipts and payments account 1976–77 to 1983–84   p.288
Table 9.4. Grants and loan assistance approved 1974–83 at 1983 prices   p.289

Chapter 11. Summary

Table 11.1. Other financial institutions' sources of funds (£ million)   p.325

INTRODUCTION

The intention of this book is to outline and explain the past, present and future development of capital markets and financial intermediation in Scotland. Chapter 1 provides a short history of financial markets and institutions in Scotland and explores the causes of financial development before examining the benefits that have flowed from the existence of a regional financial sector and capital market. A principal function of the capital market is to transfer funds from those economic units such as households which have a surplus of savings to those economic units such as companies which have a deficit of savings. These financial flows between economic units and financial institutions are explored in chapter 2 together with the impact of the financial sector on employment.

The transfer of funds between economic units is achieved in two different ways. Savings surplus units, typically households, may purchase directly the financial claims issued by savings deficit units such as companies or the government, a process facilitated by the existence of financial institutions acting as brokers and informants with the purpose of bringing both parties together. Most direct sales of financial securities take place through the medium of the Stock Exchange and this is considered in chapter 3. Besides new issues the stock market provides a market for existing securities. The sale of such securities provides liquidity by enabling savers to realise their holdings easily when they need to and is an important aid to the investment process. It is carried out primarily through intermediaries such as stockbrokers. The role of these intermediaries is also examined in the chapter.

The transfer of funds between savers and lenders is also effected by financial institutions selling their own securities, termed indirect claims, to ultimate lenders and using the proceeds from these sales to purchase securities from ultimate borrowers. The function of the financial institution is to act as an intermediary standing between the ultimate borrowers and lenders in the economy providing more attractive terms to both parties than would otherwise be possible. As economies grow they experience an increase in the relative importance of indirect as compared with direct financing in the economy. The economy experiences a growth of financial sophistication through the use of financial intermediation.

The financial intermediaries operating in Scotland are considered in chapters 4 to 9; chapters 4, 5 and 6 cover deposit institutions, chapters 7 and 8 discuss investment institutions and chapter 9 examines the role of government agencies with intermediary functions.

The Scottish clearing banks are the most important deposit-taking insti-

Introduction

tutions in Scotland and are discussed in chapter 4. They occupy the central place in the Scottish financial sector through the payments clearing system and their borrowing and lending activities. Although generally thought of as retail banks they participate in both retail and wholesale markets and carry out a range of other financial service activities. It is largely because of their presence that Scotland has a distinctive financial sector. The domestic and international banking operations of the Scottish clearing banks are examined together with their performance, the competition they face and their response to new technologies.

Chapter 5 deals with the two other main retail deposit institutions operating in Scotland, the Trustee Savings Bank and the building societies as well as the only independent savings bank in Scotland, the Airdrie Savings Bank. These institutions collect the bulk of their deposits in the retail market from individuals. Their lending business is more specialised than that of the clearing banks. The operations and recent performance of the TSB and the building societies in Scotland are reviewed and possible changes to their business in the light of recent legislation are considered.

Other deposit and banking institutions present in the Scottish financial sector including merchant banks and international banks, specialist retail banks, finance houses and the National Savings Bank are considered in chapter 6.

Chapter 7 covers the Scottish life assurance offices, general insurance and insurance broking. It examines their operations, investments and the competition they face. Chapter 8 considers the role of investment fund managers in the Scottish financial sector and in particular their importance as managers of unit trusts, investment trusts and pension funds. The provision of development capital from public sources, notably the Scottish Development Agency and the Highlands and Islands Development Board, is examined in chapter 9.

The importance of innovation and regulation in the financial sector is a strong theme that emerges from these chapters. This issue is taken up in chapter 10 and particular attention is paid to the impact of developments in communications on the need for geographical centralisation; the impact of increased competition arising from the relaxation of regulatory constraints; and the effects of technological developments on financial institutions.

A summary of the Scottish financial sector's development and the key issues affecting its future are examined in chapter 11. Chapter 12 presents some conclusions and suggestions for action.

1

HISTORICAL AND ECONOMIC PERSPECTIVE

Scotland's historic role in the provision of financial services is often forgotten. A Scotsman was responsible for founding the Bank of England in 1694 and in the following year the Bank of Scotland was established in Edinburgh. The innovations introduced by Scotland's bankers were important and numerous and resulted in the spread of Scottish banking practices, and indeed bankers, throughout the world. Scottish banking ascendancy peaked in the late nineteenth century to be followed by years of stagnation and decline. The rise and fall of Scottish banking supremacy holds lessons for today. Scotland was a poor country dwarfed both in size and power by its neighbour. Yet, economic necessity coupled with a high degree of literacy and a freedom from regulation enabled it to innovate and provide services that were the envy of the world. Our concern is not, of course, with the glories of the past but rather to extract from the past lessons for the future so as to provide pointers for the conditions required to allow a resurgence of banking and financial innovation in Scotland. This chapter endeavours to identify both salient features that explain the development of a financial sector in Scotland and the dominance of Edinburgh within it, and the role and benefit that Scotland derives from its financial sector.

A number of major themes are discernible in the development of the Scottish financial sector. Most notably the competitive environment that prevailed and its associated regulatory framework; the demand for intermediation and the level of economic development; entrepreneurial talent and the dynamism of the economy; and a variety of locational factors that have influenced the development of Edinburgh as the premier centre within Scotland and have contributed to its continued existence as an alternative financial centre to London.

The presence or absence of these factors today provides indicators of the ability of the Scottish financial sector to survive and thrive in the changing conditions of present day financial markets as well as emphasising the advantages and benefits to be derived from a growing and expanding financial sector. Regional financial institutions may improve the flow of information in financial markets and reduce the cost of information with benefits to producer and consumer alike. In short, regional financial centres can reduce market imperfections and offer significant advantages to the regional and national economy.

Historical and Economic Perspective

Development of the Scottish Financial Sector

The development of the Scottish financial sector has not been independent of events elsewhere. Scotland is part of the UK monetary union and has been affected by developments outside its own boundaries. For this reason it would be misleading to consider Scotland as a separate financial system although it exhibits many of the characteristics of such a system. Scotland's financial sector is more than an odd assortment of institutions. It displays, to some degree, both of the essential features that Revell (1973) suggests a financial system must display; it consists of a network of financial links between economic units and it is a superstructure erected on the basis of the real wealth of the community. However, as the following chapters will document, the financial links are far from complete whilst the superstructure is erected on the basis of the real wealth of both Scotland and the UK-wide community.

Scotland's institutions undoubtedly fulfil some or all of the functions of a financial system. They bring savers and borrowers together allowing the transfer of resources between savings surplus economic units such as households, and savings deficit economic units such as firms or the government. The institutions do little saving and capital formation for themselves but exist to channel funds from surplus to deficit units. They exercise this function in a multiplicity of ways but their essential characteristic is one of transforming assets in such a manner as to make them more attractive. Large borrowings by corporations are transformed into smaller, more marketable securities that individuals can easily trade. Financial intermediaries provide a variety of services that make financial claims more attractive to savers. Financial intermediaries benefit from economies of scale and provide specific expertise in dealing with both borrowers and lenders as well as providing the advantages of risk reduction through diversification which allow the transformation process to be accomplished at minimum cost.

The financial claims that intermediaries may offer are many and varied. Scottish institutions are concentrated in particular areas of the financial market and it is of interest to explore methods by which the range of claims could be extended whilst at the same time the purpose of a financial system, to both allocate savings in an economy to ultimate users in such a manner that the highest level of satisfaction is attained and to provide a payments mechanism, is best achieved. This purpose may be accomplished both by widening financial markets in which investment opportunities compete so as to stimulate the formation of savings and its pooling, and by effecting payments and transferring savings between places and through time. Kindleberger (1974) suggests that the financial system is made more efficient by the development within it of financial centres:

> Banking and financial centres perform a medium of exchange function and an interspacial store of value function. Single payments between

separate points in a country are made most efficiently through a centre, and both seasonal and long run surpluses and deficits of financial savings are best matched in a centre.

The Role of the Banks

The earliest financial institutions to develop were the banks and their early history provides numerous instances of the importance of entrepreneurial talent and the competitive environment with its associated regulatory framework. The founding of the banks illustrates clearly how the pressures of economic development acted to produce financial innovations. Checkland (1975) suggests that Scottish banking creativity was a product of economic necessity coupled with a general cultural background in which responsibility and the work ethic were important, a high degree of literacy in the population and historical accident which denied the Bank of England the monopoly which it was able to exercise in England. The early period of Scottish banking was free of oppressive regulation and the competitive ethos was dominant. Prior to the creation of the public banking companies transactions were conducted with coin or negotiable bills of exchange issued by the major merchants and exchangeable for coin at some stated time in the future. The bills traded at a discount to their redemption value, a discount that varied with the prosperity of the domestic economy. Expansion sucked in more imports with a consequent increase in the number and value of bills of exchange and led ultimately to an outflow of coin creating problems for the domestic economy. So long as holders of bank notes were content to use them as money the issue of notes by banks provided a solution to these problems of an expanding economy. The need for such notes to finance trade led to the foundation of the major public banks, the Bank of Scotland and the Royal Bank in 1695 and 1727 respectively. The issue of notes was not, however, restricted to the public banks. Anyone was free to issue notes and profit from their issue.

The early history of the banks highlights the reasons for the rise of Edinburgh and the connections with London. Both banks had strong early connections with London and with the men of wealth and influence in Scotland's capital. The Bank of Scotland was promoted jointly by residents of Edinburgh and London and was governed from both Edinburgh and London. The arrangements proved unworkable, and the Bank early on centralised control in Edinburgh and the London connection was largely broken. The Royal Bank's foundation and early existence was intimately connected with the Scottish Whigs and their connections to the Westminster government. The Bank maintained strong links with London and was the recipient of the profitable business of remitting customs receipts to the capital. It was Edinburgh based as a result of its links with politics. Edinburgh offered connections and wealth; invaluable commodities to the early banks.

Historical and Economic Perspective

In contrast to the public banks set up in response to the needs of a rapidly growing economy the private banks of the period to 1750 were typically merchants who provided elements of banking services. They did not issue their own bank notes but did discount bills and transmit money. Coutts, an Edinburgh merchant, for example, transmitted the Scottish Excise to London. The private banks, in consequence of their merchant origins, were particularly prominent wherever substantial trade took place, notably in Edinburgh and Glasgow.

The role of economic growth in promoting financial innovation is also clearly visible in subsequent Scottish banking history. The rise of the provincial banks was in response to rapid economic growth. In many ways the provincial banks were the natural successors to the private banks. They were founded in response to the needs of trade and largely funded on the profits of that trade. The economic rise of Glasgow thus coincided with its emergence as a financial centre although its promise was never to be completely realised. Unlike New York, which in consequence of its economic growth emerged as the US financial centre, despite the early role of Philadelphia in financial innovation and development, Glasgow was not able to shake the supremacy of the Edinburgh banks. However, the Glasgow banks survived despite the united attempts by the Edinburgh public banks to put them out of business although as it transpired their close connections with the Glasgow tobacco lords and their limited aspirations meant that their success was limited. Edinburgh

> was still the centre for the nobility and landed men, and for the law courts and the church. . . . It was upon Edinburgh that landed savings converged, as did landed borrowings, still the largest elements in the nation's credit transactions. . . . the public banks had learned that the interests of both lay in mutual aid against interlopers, operating through a pact of amity. The Glasgow banks were never to achieve this solidarity. (Checkland 1975)

Outside Edinburgh and Glasgow a number of banking companies were formed and became dominant on the basis of their intimate knowledge of local conditions. The difficulty for merchants in operating cash accounts from Edinburgh, primarily due to their inability to establish credit-worthiness through poor communications with the capital, created a demand for a source of cheap bank credit in the provinces. Notes were issued and circulated locally by the banking companies, viewed with much chagrin by the Edinburgh banks as a competitive attack on their business despite their unwillingness or inability to extend their own banking services to the provinces. (Relations between the bank companies themselves varied from harmony to hostility most often caused by attempts to increase note circulation at the expense of each other.) However by 1770 a 'provincial' note exchange was established in Edinburgh and the two public banks, who had already secured such an arrangement between themselves some twenty years earlier, extended the exchange by agreeing to accept the notes of the banking companies. Significantly, this ensured Edinburgh retained and strengthened its status over Glasgow as the most important banking centre in Scotland. Munn (1981) comments that 'the note exchange played an important part in developing the stability which was such an important feature of the Scottish banking system' and 'was a permissive factor in business expansion.'

The banking companies also assisted the growth of practices which ensured the success of Scottish banking, not only through their own localised actions but by stimulating the Edinburgh banks to adopt branching and extend their influence in an effort to suppress provincial competition. Deposit-taking was developed enabling loan demand to be met beyond the limitations of capital which was scarce in Scotland. Various factors conspired to cause the decline of the banking companies and in particular the scale of economic activity. Their replacement by a new banking structure (the joint stock bank) is an illustration of the ability of the system to evolve to meet changing needs and requirements within an environment where regulation was undoubtedly desirable but not synonymous with restriction, and competition was unprecedented.

The provincial banks were, in the main, small in terms of both nominal and paid up capital. Whilst a potential force their limited regional basis precluded them from having a major economic impact. Of potentially much greater historical significance was the formation of the British Linen Bank. Chartered in 1746 to carry on linen manufacture and allowed also to bank, the bank could have been the forerunner of a much closer involvement of the banks with industry and trade. Its early years however were primarily noteworthy for its lack of success in the linen trade causing it to turn to the trade of banking. Early initiatives for bringing together manufacturing and finance thus came to nought.

The economic prosperity of Glasgow continued to provide challenges to Edinburgh's banking supremacy. The abortive challenge from the joint stock companies based in Glasgow (1830–50) provides an interesting example of the impact of legislation on the financial sector. The early history of the sector owes much to the competitive ethos and lack of regulation in the founding and running of the banks. It is true that the privilege of a Charter was restricted and in its early years the Bank of Scotland was accorded a monopoly, but competitive forces remained. Private and joint stock banks were formed and provided strong and effective competition since the ability to issue notes was not restricted until the Bank Acts of 1844–45. The Bank Acts preserved the Scottish note issue but introduced strict gold backing and denied any new bank the right of note issue. The 1845 Act did not provide for the lapsing of Scottish note issues when banks amalgamated as was the case in England but it effectively put a stop to new bank formation since any new bank required the co-operation of the Bank of England in providing it with notes, a co-operation that was not always forthcoming. 'The differences imposed by law on the Scottish and English systems in 1844/5 were a powerful influence in keeping them separate' (Checkland 1975). It has also been suggested by Gaskin (1965) that the note issue ability of existing Scottish banks prevented their expansion in England because of the threat of political attack in such circumstances from the English banks. During this decade agreement between the banks was also much improved so that by 1850 there was 'fairly firm agreement about rates' (Checkland 1975). The elements of a comfortable oligopoly and absence of competition were now in place.

A number of authors have found it useful to draw a distinction between regulation and supervision. The Bank Acts went beyond what was required for supervision and indeed as two spectacular bank failures in the second half of the century illustrate were not totally effective in this role. The Bank Acts failed to provide the benefits of 'constructive legislation' that Robbins and Terleckyj (1960) note so helped New York but were rather regulatory strait-jackets that discouraged banking innovation in Scotland and confirmed Edinburgh in its role as the banking capital despite the trading prosperity of Glasgow.

> Throughout its history, Scotland, in spite of the swing of commercial and industrial predominance to the west, and the accompanying banking initative there, has had a single financial centre. The system of rate control and unanimity among general managers, largely emanating from Edinburgh, thus became a Scottish banking tradition. (Checkland 1975)

An unseen consequence of this lack of competition was the relative decline in the Scottish banks relative to the English ones. The Scottish banks were locked into a system with high barriers to entry, agreed rates and an unwillingness to innovate. The amalgamation movement that swept the English banking scene and created larger, stronger units by-passed the Scottish banks so that the early advantages and innovations pioneered by the Scottish banks were lost. Changes were delayed until after the First World War when stakes in several of the banks were acquired by the London banks and the Royal Bank acquired Drummonds, Williams, Deacons and Glyn, Mills and Co. These changes were not dramatic. Ownership changed but there was little intervention in the policies of subsidiaries. It was not until the 1950s that the Bank of England's policy of preventing further bank mergers was challenged and major changes in the structure of Scottish banking took place.

The period before the Bank Acts and the decades following represent the high point of Scottish financial innovation. The intermediation requirements of small savers led to the establishment of the savings banks, later to become the trustee savings banks which provided a means for small savings to be accumulated which could later be transferred to the major banks.

Started in 1810 the idea gained rapid acceptance so that by 1835 legislation was needed allowing them to lend to the government or invest through trustees. The savings banks have continued to provide services to small savers and by responding to rising incomes and the extension of banking habits to a large sector of the population have become largely indistinguishable from other clearing banks.

Risk Capital and the Rise of the Stock Exchange

Shareholdings in large concerns such as the banks had been a feature of economic life for many years before the establishment of a stock exchange. The stock exchange, however, was significant in improving the marketability and liquidity of investments thus greatly increasing their attractiveness. The London Stock Exchange was founded in 1773 and by 1815 there is evidence that stockbrokers were trading in Edinburgh although a Stock Exchange was not opened until 1844. In that year exchanges were opened in both Edinburgh and Glasgow followed by Aberdeen the following year and exchanges in Dundee and Greenock later on in the century. The establishment of the exchanges is interesting not only for the financial innovation it heralded, but also for the dynamism of the Scottish economy, the competitive spirit and entrepreneurial talent that was displayed. The establishment of exchanges in both Edinburgh and Glasgow was marked by restricted membership and strict commission levels. The response of those excluded was to set up rival exchanges in both cities. Profit opportunities combined with an absence of restrictive legislation allowed entrepreneurs to give free reign to their ideas and energies. There was a willingness to embrace entrepreneurial risk and a desire for early involvement with possible profitable innovations.

The history of the Exchanges have been documented by Thomas (1973) and Mitchie (1981) and it is interesting to note the method of dealing between brokers without, in general, the benefit of jobbers. Jobbers provided the London Exchange with the ability to handle large issues and the system was ideally suited for its main business, transactions in national and international stocks. Regional markets did not have the same ability to handle large transaction volume but the absence of a jobbing system significantly reduced the costs of operation. Regional markets provided a relatively low cost quotation for local established companies, such as the banks and insurance companies, as well as providing a means of financing new enterprises. There can be little doubt that the Scottish Exchanges provided a means of raising speculative capital whether for domestic railways, coal mines and steel companies or for overseas, particularly American, investment. The investment trust movement was one of the beneficiaries of this surplus of local funds indicative of the increasing sophistication of financial markets and Scottish intermediary skills. Mitchie (1981) notes that in addition to being markets in local companies, the regional exchanges were also recognised for distinct specialisations. Glasgow (second only to London in size) was the mining exchange attracting business from throughout the country. 'There was . . . a separation between London and the local stock exchanges, not only geographically, but also in the type of securities in which they traded.' 'The London and provincial stock exchanges were both useful and necessary, but different in the functions they performed.'

A variety of booms in particular sectors of the market led to large short term increases in new issues by the market. The average size of new issue was fairly small however, and the actual capital raised in Scotland modest. Figures quoted by Thomas (1973) indicate that the cost of new issues was substantial, perhaps ten per cent for the usual size of provincial issue but that these costs were probably less than half those of a quotation for such a company in the much bigger London market. Requirements for quotations became progressively more stringent but even so it appears that exchange committees were often flexible and allowed quotation without too much difficulty. The Scottish exchanges were of considerable value to the smaller companies. Capital was easily raised for the creation or extension of any business offering a reasonable possibility of substantial profits.

The decline in the markets was a consequence of several contributory factors. Most important was a significant reduction in the stocks trading on the markets as a result of the World Wars that saw the liquidation of a large proportion of UK overseas investments. This was added to by the reorganisation of the railroads in 1921 which at a stroke reduced the number of railroad companies from 51 to 21, whilst amalgamations in the banking industry and nationalisation of railway and steel firms after 1945 led to further declines. Offsetting these reductions was the introduction of new companies to the exchanges although increasing regulatory control on corporate business may have served to reduce the formation of new Scottish enterprises. However, whilst Glasgow boomed in the inter-war years the pattern was increasingly of a drift south, a consequence of the increase in size of companies which required more active trading and benefited from the increased marketability that the London jobbing system conferred, more diffuse share ownership and for a time the rules of the exchanges that did not allow the division of commission with agents. Unfortunately such a drift, once established, becomes difficult, if not impossible, to stop. The markets did not grow as rapidly as might be expected and there was a consequent failure to secure economies of scale. Increased volume of business both improves marketability and allows a reduction in the cost of transactions. It increases the ability of the exchange to absorb large share issues which offer improved facilities and lower costs to companies raising capital. The result was the amalgamation of the exchanges with a concentration on Glasgow, which in turn has become part of the wider organisation based in London. Opportunities to provide local firms with capital on better terms than might otherwise be possible were thus lost, although the rise of the Unlisted Securities markets in London may have gone some way to filling the small company gap.

The Growth of Insurance

Innovation in the insurance market also followed the lead of London. The earliest insurance business in Scotland was associated with marine and fire underwriting. As a provincal port of growing importance in the eighteenth century Glasgow required a local source of insurance for overseas merchant connections. A number of insurance companies were established in Edinburgh and Glasgow early in the nineteenth century. The predominantly wooden buildings of that period, prone to severe fires, the worst of which burned for three days and destroyed a considerable number of tenements and other buildings, provided a ready market for fire insurance and led to the arrival of competitors from London and elsewhere, attracted by the high premiums on offer and engaging in substantial price cutting. As the insurance business developed, the companies extended their activities into other areas and progressively developed the scale and markets open to their business. Growth was helped by rising incomes, legislation which induced a demand for particular types of insurance such as employer liability and the entrepreneurial ambitions of the managers which induced several of the companies to move into developing overseas markets. Access to local capital through the regional security markets and permissive legislation in this area of business also contributed to their growth.

Cockerell and Green (1976) have suggested that lack of technical development and the unimpressive profitability of annuity and life business worked against the growth of the life assurance market before the mid-eighteenth century. It was during this period that the Equitable Life Assurance Society came to be founded in London and pioneered the scientific selection, rating and valuation of all types of life business including long term. The Equitable concentrated its operations on the London market although other London offices sought more widespread business. The Scottish Widows' Fund and Life Assurance Society was established in Edinburgh in 1815 to corner the regional market. The annals of the Scottish Widows' Fund states that

> it was owing to the prosperity of the Equitable, which in 1809 had accumulated nearly 4.5 million of invested capital and had more than 8 million of assurances, that the promoters of the Scottish Widows' Fund were induced to take the bold step of adopting the mutual system, under which the whole profits should be divided among the policy holders, instead of the proprietary system, which was almost universal at that time among other assurance companies, and under which the profits were assigned to those who subscribed the capital of the concern.

Cockerell and Green (1976) note that the life assurance market was not untouched by the speculative promotions arising from the joint-stock company booms of the early nineteenth century and that many of the proprietary companies set up failed but 'the Scottish companies enjoyed an obvious advantage in their home market, and they rapidly became a strong recognizable section of the life assurance industry.' This was in large part due to the mutual structure which the Scottish companies had adopted. In similar fashion to banking the market for life assurance and the educating of the community to its benefits were extended by competition through the branch system, and by innovations such as group schemes and the introduction of industrial life assurance, although these were not peculiar to Scotland. However, by the later nineteenth century the Scottish offices were in the vanguard of developing overseas markets and were particularly influential in North America while legislation there was favourable. Business was also found in the British colonies and early participants were the Scottish Amicable in the West Indies (1845) and South America, and the Colonial Life Assurance Company throughout the British Dominions (1846), an office which had close links and later amalgamated with Standard Life.

The Scottish proprietary insurance companies involved in fire, marine, accident and life assurance were not, however, unaffected by the processes of amalgamation and association. This reflected the trend towards large composite offices in order to extend connections or to stabilise profits through business diversification and necessitated the ability to pay high prices to secure the additional profitable business. Raynes (1964) has suggested that the arrival of the insurance broker and the economies he could offer through transacting all classes of insurance also favoured concentration. There is little doubt that the wealth of the English insurance companies was responsible for the disappearance of many Scottish companies. Very few companies were purchased because of financial weakness in their business. General Accident of Perth is one of the Victorian accident offices which grew up to meet new types of daily risks and remains a notable exception as the only large Scottish composite group in existence and the only independent survivor of that period. Concentration never reached the extent of the banking system partly due to the need for re-insurance and partly to the lack of legislative barriers to the promotion of new companies during periods of market expansion. The same legislative structure provided no opposition to the purchase of Scottish insurance companies and the continued existence of a strong regional life assurance sector must owe much to their mutual constitution.

The experience of running insurance companies was also instrumental in setting up the investment trusts that rose to prominence in the last two decades of the nineteenth century. Holmes Ivory, for example, moved from insurance into founding investment trusts and his family went on to establish the Ivory & Sime management group. The investment trusts enabled the prospering middle classes to invest in securities with reduced risk, as a result of their diversification and management, and to reap the benefits of more profitable opportunities provided by overseas investment. Substantial sums, for the period, were placed in these markets reflecting the surplus funds generated by the industrial successes of Glasgow, Edinburgh and Dundee and furthering the opportunity to foster financial expertise. The insurance companies provided the training ground for individuals to gain experience in such investment and awakened prospective managers to the untapped markets for such intermediation.

The Development of Financial Centres

Locational advantages for both insurance companies and investment trusts are not so strong as to require their siting in Edinburgh. The success of General Accident illustrates the ability of provincial insurance companies to thrive, as indeed does the continued existence of the Alliance Trust in Dundee, a centre particularly active in the nineteenth-century pioneering of overseas investment through specialist investment vehicles, initially in land and mortgage activity as well as stock market paper. However, location at the financial centre does offer advantages of easy and fast communications and hence lower information costs both between intermediaries and companies and with their customers, as well as external economies which reduce the costs of doing business. Robbins and Terleckyj (1960) in their study of New York identify three kinds:

1) those that spring from the high degree of financial specialisation among individuals and firms;
2) those that come from joint facilities set up by groups of financial firms;
3) those resulting from services provided by other industries such as printing.

These advantages of course accrue in even greater measure in London although the continued existence of bank clearing in Edinburgh based on the regional nature of most of their business provides an important external economy that probably could not be matched in London. The most serious threat to the dominance of a region as a financial centre is according to Robbins and Terleckyj (1960) more rapid economic growth in other geographic areas. Within Scotland Edinburgh faces little challenge from this cause but in the context of the UK the South-East represents a continuing centre of greater economic growth. Indeed this may have always been the case and suggests that regional forces, primarily Scottish bank clearing, have been an important influence for the continued existence of a Scottish financial sector and provided the necessary base on which a financial sector can develop.

Other important factors may have stemmed from the regional distinctness of Scotland from the rest of the UK. Scotland, for example, has its own system of laws and education. The existence of co-partnery in Scottish law permitted the formation of large partnerships. The exclusion of Scotland from legislation protecting the Bank of England enabled the financial sector in Scotland to develop independently of the constraints suffered by institutions in England.

The literacy of the population has already been remarked upon and it was from such origins that a considerable desire to improve the education of the workforce stemmed. The Institute of Bankers was founded in 1875, the first organisation in the world devoted to banking education, and the Faculty of Actuaries, although started in 1856, eight years later than the English equivalent, was the first to receive a Royal Charter in 1868. It functions both as a professional examining body and a learned society.

At a less congratulatory level the Scottish institutions were also amongst the first to combine to secure mutual benefits and restrict competition. The banks provide a number of examples, some of which have been previously mentioned, whilst the fire offices came together as early as 1829 to agree rates. Scottish institutions early on perceived the benefits of cartel arrangements and reducing competition.

The ossification of the banking sector in the 1850s not only protected the existing banking institutions but also allowed the development of other intermediaries. The Scottish banks ignored opportunities for expansion into England and were slow to adopt new banking innovations. The small size of the Scottish banking system with its multiplicity of branch offices resulted in comparatively high operating costs and consequently higher interest rates to the average borrower and lower rates to depositors. Gaskin (1965) argues that the differences were small and in any event were less important than differences in availability. He suggests that small borrowers in Scotland were better served than in England but admits that facilities for larger business borrowers were inferior. The problems are two-fold, the absolute size of the advances required by some companies and the movement through their accounts. The swings of payments through a big account may cause difficulties to a small bank.

The early rise of the Scottish banks was based on the needs of the local economy. In a period of expansion the domestic monetary system was inadequate and the banks provided a means of overcoming such difficulties. Not only did the banks meet local needs but they also pioneered techniques that were subsequently adopted by others. The cash credit introduced by the Royal Bank in 1729 was a means of 'lending on character backed by personal guarantee' (Gaskin 1965). The concept was subsequently extended and has become known as the overdraft. Table 1.1 provides an insight into the range of banking innovations that were pioneered in Scotland. Banking legislation effectively killed further innovation and at the same time protected existing participants against competition both from within and without. Protected as they were there was no need to rationalise, reduce costs or even dramatically expand. The Bank Acts appear to have been a turning point in which entrepreneurship and innovation were abandoned by

Table 1.1. Early Scottish banking innovations.

Cash Credit	Lending on character backed by personal guarantee (Royal Bank). Similar to an overdraft with interest charged on daily balance. Interest paid on credit balance.	1729
Exchange Rate Stabilisation	Purchase and sale of Edinburgh and London bills to stabilise exchange rate:	
	Bank of Scotland	1700
	Royal Bank	1730
Interest-bearing Deposits	Time deposits for 6 or 12 months (Bank of Scotland)	1731
Note Acceptance	Bank of Scotland – Royal Bank	1751
Branch Banking	Earlier attempts were unsuccessful (Bank of Scotland)	1774
Savings Bank	Accumulation of very small savings	1810
Institute of Bankers	Education	1875

Source: Checkland (1975).

the Scottish banking industry. Mitchie (1981) suggests that size was an important indication of security to investors in banks so that existing concerns flourished while new companies found it difficult to become established. Ownership might change but until the post-war period there was no real threat to the oligopoly. Threats from the larger English clearers were neutralised by their ownership involvement and by the attitude of the Bank of England to any takeovers. It is only in the recent past that significant changes in ownership have been considered, changes that would expose the Scottish banks to much stronger competition and possibly threaten the continued existence of Edinburgh as a banking centre.

It is ironic that the conservatism and stability of the banking system with its base in Edinburgh forced entrepreneurs to look for opportunities in other spheres and provided a justification for the location in Edinburgh of other financial activities. Edinburgh provided external economies to financial intermediaries, economies that might not have existed with a less protected banking network and might, in consequence, have resulted in the majority of these intermediaries locating in London. It is apparent that regulation and restriction constitute a double-edged sword. Regulation protected Edinburgh as a financial sector and enabled financial service growth but at the same time it acted as a barrier to innovation which could have provided an alternative strategy for strengthening the regional financial centre. A highly innovative centre could provide a successful basis for growth although innovations are easily imitated and such a strategy can only be successful in the long term if there is a continuing sequence of innovations. Nor are regulation and innovation necessarily incompatible. Indeed an important challenge for administrators is to regulate to protect investors against fraud (but not their own greed) whilst at the same time providing a dynamic environment encouraging growth and innovation. This is possibly more of a requirement for regional financial centres than national ones which benefit from their size, position and capacity.

Edinburgh and London

The relationship of Edinburgh to London is a question of considerable interest. The public banks from their earliest years had strong London connections both as a source of capital and political influence. Bills drawn on London were an important source of trade finance whilst London also played an important role as a reserve centre for the banks. Government securities were held so that in times of stress they could be sold for gold in London. The development of the London discount market made it possible to lend money profitably and yet retain high liquidity, reinforcing the importance of London. Other reasons for connections with London may easily be adduced. The migration of Scottish business south has persuaded the banks of the need for London offices that can retain some or all of this business within the bank. At the national level the Bank of England slowly expanded its role within the UK. The Bank Acts of the first half of the nineteenth century which centralised the Enlish note issue forced the Bank to become the ultimate source of liquidity for the banking system. It exercised control through changes in the discount rate and open market operations as well as developing the technique of general guarantee so that by the Baring crisis of 1890 the Scottish banks were subscribing to a guarantee fund as a means of preventing widespread collapse. By this century the Bank constituted an important element of control over the Scottish banking system. External economies have also been important in centring new financial activity in London. The industrial decline of the Scottish economy has been mirrored by the financial decline indicating the role of economic growth in the development of financial intermediation, as well as the loss of dynamism in the regional economy and reduction in entreprenurial activity from whatever causes.

Thus the development and continued existence of Edinburgh as a financial centre has been aided by the factors working to concentrate banking activity and by the early historic factors connected with Edinburgh's political role. Once established economies of scale in clearing and the ability to economise on working balances by centralising operations tend to maintain a financial centre. The rise of Glasgow as a centre of manufacturing could have affected this pre-eminence since local credit markets have decided advantages in dealing with small firms in an area. However, regional government continued to centre on Edinburgh, providing profitable opportunities whilst legislation and the unhelpful attitude of the Bank of England tended to preserve the status quo.

The Benefits Conferred by Scottish Financial Institutions

It has been taken as axiomatic that Scottish institutions benefit Scotland. Before proceeding further it is important that we should examine the relationships between institutions and the Scottish economy with some degree of care. The relationship may be usefully considered from at least three perspectives, the consumer, the local institutions and the economy. For the Scottish consumer, both domestic and industrial and borrowers and lenders, concern is centred on the range of financial services that are obtainable within the region. The domicile of the managers or the owners is of little concern except in so far as it affects the consumer's ability to secure finance or find investment outlets. Locally based institutions may provide securities or funds that would not otherwise be obtainable or provide services at a cost lower than that attainable from other institutions. The position of the institutions is somewhat different. A Scottish domicile or management may confer particular advantages, informational, marketing or managerial. It may also involve certain costs. Viewed from the perspective of the Scottish economy the clearest advantage accruing from the existence of indigenous institutions is the employment created by head offices. Witnesses to the Monopolies Commission Report on the Royal Bank (1982) noted that whilst the three Scottish clearing banks offered similar services to their retail customers they differed greatly in their diversification into other services. The witnesses suggested that one reason for the Clydesdale Bank's lack of diversification was that it was constrained to make use of the facilities of its parent. If this assertion is correct the benefits to employment of Scottish domicile or ownership are increased. Other advantages are more difficult to quantify but economic benefits would flow if indigenous institutions increased the local availability of funds and financial instruments, although in a financial system as integrated as that of the UK the likely benefits are small.

Two concerns stand out from this discussion. For the consumer it is the range of financial services and intermediaries available that matter and not its origin. For the economy it is the domicile of the firm and its management that is of concern since this is related to employment, growth and other benefits. It is therefore necessary to explore the advantages of being based in Scotland. Such an exploration is one of the themes of the chapters on individual institutions. It is not the purpose here to duplicate this but rather to consider the costs and benefits from a wider perspective. The most obvious advantage of Scottish institutions is their ease of access to local markets. Regional institutions may have a degree of knowledge of local conditions that can only be learnt by close involvement with customers and companies. Communications are improved and information costs reduced.

The value of this information should not be underestimated. The location of regional offices by American banks in Aberdeen, Edinburgh and Glasgow clearly demonstrates the need for local information in finding new opportunities, assessing risk and meeting the needs of existing clients. Such benefits are not acquired at zero cost, the cost of the regional network being but one of the expenditures involved in acquiring local knowledge and information.

Arguments in favour of locally based institutions are frequently based on beliefs that institutions closely involved with the local community may at times grant credit to clients even though strict commercial assessment of the risk does not warrant it. Before accepting this argument it is necessary to consider whether it is likely that such lending does take place and if it does whether it is ultimately to the benefit of the local community. It is also worth considering if such lending requires an indigenously owned institution or merely any institution with a high degree of local involvement irrespective of the domicile of its owners or management.

For small loans, local managers generally have some degree of discretion and may be persuaded to advance funds. These are not, however, the projects of prime concern here. Large projects generally require approval from head or regional office and it is questionable whether any such office would sanction sizeable loans on non-commercial grounds except under very unusual circumstances. A typical example that is quoted, is when failure to support an ailing company by a bank would bring down a large number of the company's suppliers who are also customers of the bank. Bank support in such situations generally stems not from altruism but from commercial considerations: the effect on the bank of losses accruing to a number of its substantial customers. For Scottish based companies Scottish banks are more likely to be bankers to the local suppliers of the ailing company than those based in London or elsewhere. The important consideration is not the domicile of the bank but its involvement with the local community. Any institution involved in lending to a web of clients will be concerned about the knock-on effects of its actions.

If this argument is misplaced and Scottish banks and institutions are involved in lending or providing other services at times on a non-commercial basis (the continued existence of Loganair was suggested in the Monopolies Commission Report on the Royal Bank as an example, although its subsequent disposal rather weakens the argument) then, in the short term, employment and services in local communities may benefit. In the longer term such policies have costs for the lender which will ultimately be reflected in their profits and accounts. Non-commercial lending, whilst sometimes socially desirable, is not the function of most private sector institutions and in the longer term will weaken their capital base and abilities to expand and grow with long run consequences for employment and the economy.

Local involvement does not necessarily imply subsidised lending. If capital markets are imperfect so that funds are not simply allocated by price (the interest rate) but also by availability, then regional involvement may be a method of increasing the availability of funds to firms that would otherwise find it difficult. There is considerable agreement that firms with good prospects and opportunities find it easy to raise funds. The difficulties face those with the less desirable prospects, in particular small firms with short financial histories, uncertain prospects and little equity capital. Banks and others are often unwilling to provide fixed interest finance since in the absence of adequate equity the fixed interest security bears the risk of the venture. In the absence of special credit institutions, intermediaries sponsored and supported by government to fill gaps in the capital market, recourse must be had to providers of equity capital and there may be an unwillingness to help smaller firms because of the costs of resolving uncertainty about their future prospects. Regional involvement by institutions can reduce the information costs attached to appraising such situations. Branch managers can assess the management, products and assets of the company from a position of local knowledge and experience.

Local knowledge is not only a method of reducing the information costs of companies and individuals interested in borrowing funds but also of increasing the ability of intermediaries to raise funds. A branch network enables institutions to attract funds that might otherwise be inaccessible. The development of building society networks is an example of attempts to tap such funds. Arguments could be made for a regional stock market, specialising in small, low-cost issues for which investors are provided with the minimum of information necessary to assess risk and prevent fraud. The regional exchanges of the past appear to have fulfilled just such a function.

The reduction in information-cost argument together with other factors such as the demands of customers for easily accessible and convenient facilities is important for exploring the development of branch networks. The argument does not suggest that Scottish domicile is a necessary attribute although it is conceivable that it confers distinct and significant marketing advantages. Indeed it has been suggested to us by industry marketing experts that the Scottish reputation for caution and thriftiness in financial matters results in increased sales. It is on such arguments that the advantages of location in Scotland of such institutions as insurance companies must be based. With the majority of their business and investments in the rest of the UK or overseas it is unlikely that there are any significant informational cost advantages attached to their siting in Scotland. Indeed distance from the major capital markets may impose additional costs on the institutions although such costs are likely to be small and falling. Their present location is a consequence of their history rather than locational advantages although it is almost certainly true that there are no substantial advantages attached to any other location and possibly external diseconomies such as higher labour costs and less congenial surroundings. The regional economy benefits through the employment created at head offices but other benefits are much less tangible. Connections between Scottish companies and institutions at board level are noticeable and it is possible that considerable advantages stem, as a result of the consequent information flows, from such inter-relationships.

The Insurance Society of Edinburgh (quoted in the Monopolies Commission Report on the Royal Bank, 1982) analysed changes in the numbers of professionally qualified staff since the time of the middle sixties when many of the insurance companies in Edinburgh were taken over by others with headquarters in the South. In offices still headquartered in Edinburgh the proportion of professionally qualified staff to total staff was similar to that in 1965. On the other hand the number of qualified staff in Edinburgh in composite companies whose headquarters were outside Edinburgh had fallen by about 34 per cent while the number of total staff had shown virtually no change. The Monopolies Commission Report on the Royal Bank notes that the removal of headquarters functions also had an indirect effect on a wide range of professional services such as those provided by lawyers, accountants, data processors and printers. These services depend for their survival on proximity to the headquarters of a number of large organisations.

Survival of the Scottish Financial Sector

Acceptance of the information-cost and marketing arguments as favouring locally based institutions brings to the fore a second question of whether these advantages are strong enough for the local institutions to survive current changes in financial markets. Two factors are of prime importance in evaluating the threat: the sector's ability to innovate and the competition posed by other institutions. There is little doubt that the comfortable oligopoly enjoyed by the Scottish banks for a long period is no longer as profitable or so unassailable. Increased integration of financial markets and institutions has been an important and continuing trend despite the introduction of new financial instruments and the rise of new institutions. There has been greater recognition of the similarities between institutions; they compete for the same pool of savings and offer similar services of diversification and management to savers despite differences in their markets. The mortgage market and the greatly increased competition between banks and building societies provides an example of the process and it would be surprising if the distinctions between the two types of institutions did not blur in the coming years with current changes in legislation and other pressures for integration.

In the capital markets as a whole reduced regulation and attacks on restrictive practices have opened up financial markets to a wider range of institutions and allowed greater integration in the activities of market participants. Increased competition from overseas has also been an important factor with an influx of institutions into the UK and much-improved access for both borrowers and investors to overseas markets. The geographical segregation of financial markets is no longer possible. The Scottish banks face competition in both their retail and commercial markets. The building societies have successfully attacked the retail saving markets whilst other banks have made inroads into the market for commercial and industrial loans. Other parts of the Scottish financial sector have been subject to similar forces and there is little doubt that competitive forces in the sector have strengthened. It is not at all clear that the local institutions are able to stand up well to this increase in competition although there have been some encouraging signs of stronger financial groups beginning to emerge as well as much greater attention being paid to the marketing of financial services.

The past few years have witnessed two significant events in Scottish banking, the bid for the Royal Bank by non-Scottish banks and the sale by Barclays of their holding in the Bank of Scotland. Both events have strengthened the Scottish banking sector. The Monopolies Commission ruling on the Royal Bank has forced it into a long overdue integration of its English subsidiaries, acquired pre-War, into a UK network, and to develop its merchant banking activities. The sale of the Bank of Scotland holding by Barclays to a Scottish life office paves the way for the eventual emergence of a financial conglomerate able to offer a wide range of financial services. Equally, of course, the sale allows Barclays to enter the Scottish market directly and to seek the more profitable banking business. The deal has increased potential competition in the sector.

In addition to increased competition, the sector has also witnessed considerable innovation in the recent past. Detailed analysis of the implications of these innovations are discussed in a subsequent chapter but some general observations are in order here. In the past the Scottish institutions have not always been at the forefront of recent financial innovations. They have preferred a lower key, wait and see, approach. Many arguments can be made for such conservatism particularly with regard to current changes in the City. However, the Scottish institutions have largely missed out on the growth and profits of other recent innovations as a result of such policies so that, for example, their involvement in unit trusts and insurance linked funds until recently has been minimal despite a large investment management sector. Their record has been poor with little or no involvement in futures, options and unlisted securities and is a cause for considerable concern. It suggests that on past trends the Scottish sector may be slow to adopt new innovations with the inevitable consequence of a decline in the financial sector's importance relative to London and overseas markets.

Conclusions

Although no attempt has been made at a comprehensive analysis of the development of the Scottish financial sector a number of important factors stand out. The needs of the economy for financing trade coupled with a substantial rate of economic growth was an important determinant of bank-

Table 1.2. History of financial services in Scotland.

	Banking	General Insurance	Life Assurance	Fund Management	Stockbroking
1980	Electronic banking Mergers and consolidation Merchant banking Acquisition of finance houses	Takeover and mergers	Unit Trusts Move into non-insured pension business	International fund management Pension fund investment Unit Trusts	Decline of regional brokers Incorporation into UK Exchange Amalgamation of regional Exchanges
1950	Acquisition of stakes by London banks	Rise of General Accident			
1900	Banking stability Institute of Bankers			Development of overseas expertise Investment Trusts	Development of Glasgow as a specialist market
1850	Challenge of Glasgow banks		Colonial Life set up for overseas business		Glasgow and Edinburgh Stock Exchanges
1800	Savings Bank Rise of Provincial Banks	Emergence of rate agreements	Scottish Widows founded		Stockbroking
	The Royal Bank		Friendly Society Life Office		
1700	Bank of Scotland				

Sources: Checkland (1975), Mitchie (1981), Raynes (1964), Thomas (1973).

Conclusions

ing innovation. The absence of regulation and the flowering of entrepreneurial activity led to notable financial innovations in banking and subsequently in the development of other financial intermediaries. Table 1.2 indicates some of the more important historical landmarks in the sector. Depression in the regional economy was mirrored by a loss of entrepreneurial talent in financial activity and left a sector strongly skewed to the older established forms of intermediation.

The benefits to Scotland from the presence of financial intermediaries stem mainly from two sources: their impact on employment and growth, and their role in reducing capital market imperfections. Head Offices create employment and have spin-off benefits to a wide range of professional services. Local knowledge both reduces the information costs of companies and individuals interested in borrowing funds, and increases their ability to raise funds.

The survival of the Scottish institutions depends on their ability to respond to the greatly increased competition in financial markets as a result of current changes brought about by deregulation and other forces. An important part of meeting competition is their ability to innovate, and on past performance their future would not look secure; although more recently there have been encouraging signs of increased attention being paid to marketing and innovation.

2

FINANCIAL FLOWS AND EMPLOYMENT IN THE FINANCIAL SECTOR IN SCOTLAND

The previous chapter has traced the historical influences on the development of the Scottish financial sector. The present chapter addresses itself to an investigation of the current financial flows and financial sector employment in Scotland as a means of assessing the present status of Scotland as a regional financial sector in the context of the UK.

Central and Regional Financing

Despite the existence of its own distinct financial sector and the issue by its Banks of their own notes, Scotland is part of the UK currency union and exchange rate changes between the component parts of the union or of one component of the union against non-union members are inconceivable. Interest rates and money supply targets are determined outwith Scotland and reflect the common monetary policy of the UK. For a time in the 1960s Scottish banks were subject to different Special Deposit requirements compared to English banks indicating that some differentiation is possible although it is not clear whether this was the intention of the authorities (Gaskin 1965) or simply a consequence of the liquidity reserve ratios of Scottish banks differing from those in England. Financial flows within the UK are, therefore, not determined by those influences which would normally affect flows between countries. Borrowing and lending activity is dictated by other characteristics which may provide certain advantages for the key financial centre, London. These advantages – economies of scale, specialisation, excellent communications and proximity to more active competitive markets – may make London the natural and increasingly dominant financial centre. Financial centres outside London have a greater handicap to overcome before they can appeal to saving and lending institutions as an attractive location in which to operate. Improvements in technology may improve this appeal by allowing information to be rapidly disseminated to the regions but as with many developments it is a double-edged weapon encouraging, because of its cost, even more concentration. The combination of a financial, commercial and government centre in one location represents a potent combination for organising borrowing and lending operations; the issue of, and markets in, government financial instruments provides a particularly attractive feature in conditions where large government borrowing is the norm.

There are, however, attractions in favour of regional financing which may offer advantages to counteract these pressures. Lack of local knowledge of firms and markets may mean that those operating in the central market may underestimate the scope for profitable lending in the regions because of lack of information. As a result better risk assessment particularly with regard to new and growing enterprises crucial for regional growth may exist in a regional centre. The existence of regional offices for many London-based institutions in centres such as Edinburgh may offer support for these points.

A stronger commitment to the region expressed by the granting of financial support for locally based enterprises, especially in times of financial stringency, encourages the use of regional financial institutions. Lower costs of operation attracting institutions away from the central location may be a further potent force improving the performance and attraction of regional institutions.

The handicap faced by Scotland as a financial centre is reduced by its distinctive banking system, the presence of major life offices in the country and a significant investment trust and investment management presence all of which provide the base for a competing financial centre. Interviews with financial institutions located in Scotland also suggest, in some instances, a strong preference by firms located in Scotland for dealing with locally represented institutions.

The linkage between the UK financial system and Scotland is enhanced by two other important features of the Scottish economy: the open nature of the economy and the external ownership of many Scottish companies producing in Scotland. The Scottish input/output tables for 1979 indicate that some 69 per cent of GDP is exported with approximately two-thirds going to the rest of the UK. Imports accounted for a similarly large proportion of inputs. The financial sector may be less open and the input/output tables suggest that for inter-industry demand 37 per cent is provided by imports whilst for final consumer demand it is 35 per cent.

A significant proportion of Scottish output is controlled from outside Scotland so that Scotland is not the natural location in which to arrange financing or the provision of other financing services. The increasing non-Scottish ownership of firms in Scotland would tend to enhance this feature, with consequent implications for the provision of non-financial services such as accounting and legal services (Ashcroft et al. 1986).

The role of the regional financial centre is even more important if the region also faces an adverse balance of payments with the rest of the country. Whilst in the short run these payments imbalances are automatically financed through the financial system, without the traditional means to secure balance of payments adjustment – exchange and interest rate changes – and with relative regional wage and price level adjustment difficult to secure within a national market, the solution ultimately falls on the level of income and unemployment as a means of reducing continuing deficits or else requires a dependence on transfer payment through the government sector. The latter may do little to secure long-term adjustment if expectations are not influenced in a favourable direction, encouraging the development of locally based economic activity.

One source of flows into Scotland is the fiscal transfers between the government sector and the region. Despite the importance attached to regional policy over the years there is no official series of statistics measuring the overall cash flows between the government and the regions. Figures dealing with particular categories of expenditures are available, but no attempt to cover all expenditures and revenues has been made because of the difficulties associated with allocating some public goods expenditures to the regions – defence, overseas services, prison expenditure, debt service interest. Similar problems arise with tax revenues which are difficult to allocate to the region where the tax liability accrues rather than where it is paid because of the existence of multi-regional companies where tax is paid at headquarters for the whole company.

Table 2.1. Government/regional transfers 1974/75–1977/78. Average £m at 1978 survey price.

	Scotland	Total Regions	%
Current Expenditures			
Regionally relevant current expenditure	4417.0	40051.1	11.0
National expenditures and trade in regionally relevant expenditures	596.7	9247.1	6.5
Total current expenditure	5013.7	49298.2	10.2
Taxation	4487.2	50975.6	
Net current flows	526.5	−1677.4	
Capital Expenditures			
Regionally relevant capital expenditure	1159.4	9489.3	12.2
National expenditures and trade in regionally relevant expenditures	23.9	267.5	8.9
Total capital expenditures	1183.3	9756.8	12.1
Net current plus capital flows	1709.8	8079.4	21.2
Per Capita Transfers (£)			
Current flows	101.4	−30.0	
Net flows	329.4	144.7	

Source: Short (*SJPE*, June 1984).

Fortunately an estimate of such flows has been made by Short (1984) which gives some idea of the magnitudes involved and their importance for Scotland (table 2.1). In the table regionally relevant current expenditures are those made in a region for that region – expenditures on wages and salaries, goods and services and national transfer payments to that region where the benefits accrue exclusively to that region. National expenditures and trade in regionally relevant expenditures are those expenditures of a public good nature where the benefits do not fall exclusively to one region. They are allocated in proportion to a region's population. The regional taxation receipts have been determined as far as possible according to the original location of the liability to tax. Having deducted the tax flows from current expenditure an estimate of net current flows is achieved.

A similar distinction between regionally relevant and national expenditures is made with regard to capital expenditures to provide an estimate of overall net cash flows between the government and the regions. These figures relate to 1974/75 to 1977/78 averages and are recorded at 1978 prices. A per capita estimate is also provided which gives a better perspective on the issue. As might have been predicted the figures show that Scotland is a substantial net recipient on both current and capital account for the years for which the estimate was made. The Scottish figure amounted to net flows of £329.4 per capita exceeded only by Northern Ireland and significantly in excess of the £5.5 for the North West and £60.4 for the South East. Of the net current and capital flows Scotland accounted for 20 per cent of the total.

Since the Public Sector Borrowing Requirement (PSBR) was substantial in those years all regions received some transfer when capital transactions are taken into account. What the figures do not show is the sources of the borrowing which enabled the PSBR to be financed. Assuming some increase in holdings of government debt in all regions the net flows are reduced. These figures only show the first round impact of the regional transfers. Since regional expenditures are subject to large leakages the continuing benefit from these transfers is likely to be reduced. They nevertheless highlight the importance of the government sector in reconciling financial flows, an influence many times greater than a concentration on simply regional policy would suggest. Although there would have been some degree of arbitrariness in the allocation figures, on the basis of the estimates provided by Short it is clear that Scotland secures a significant net inward flow of funds from the government sector.

Input/Output Tables for Scotland

One source of information on the links between the financial sector and the rest of the Scottish economy is provided in the input/output tables for 1979. However, the measurement of output adopted, using the national income accounts convention, means that output is significantly under-recorded in the financial sector because of the treatment of interest payments. These are regarded as transfer payments and are recorded against the sectors ultimately paying and receiving the interest. This implies that the substantial net income obtained by the financial sector arising from the difference between interest rates on borrowing and lending is not attributed to the banking, insurance and finance sector.

This element of under-recording appears to have fallen more heavily on the Scottish financial sector than for the UK as a whole. Comparing Scottish banking output with UK output for that sector suggested that Scotland accounted for only four per cent of UK output. This relatively small proportion is almost certainly due largely to the different interest and charging methods employed by the Scottish banks. Scottish banks relied more heavily on net interest income. Interest charges were higher but other charges were lower than the national average. This is not reflected in the output measure because of the treatment of interest in the tables. Despite this limitation on the measurement of output the input/output tables provide some indication of the extent of the linkages within the Scottish economy and with the rest of the UK. On the input side there is a limited dependence on the rest of the Scottish economy and significant links exist with only a few sectors such as printing, construction, postal and telecommunications. Significant expenditures occurred with the rest of the Scottish financial sector, but these were not as large as expenditures with the rest of the UK, suggesting that links with London are more important than links with the rest of the Scottish financial sector. Exports from the sector apparently accounted for less than 10 per cent of Scottish financial output.

The output figures for this sector must be used with caution. Certainly if value added as estimated in the input/output tables and official statistics are used as a measure of output they seriously underestimate the contribution of the industry and would tend to cast unjustified doubt on the wisdom of expanding output in that sector as a means of increasing employment opportunities. The tables confirm that the sector faces competition from the rest of the UK in providing financial services.

Flow of Funds

Another means of assessing the importance and significance of the financial sector is through a flow of funds statement. The flow of funds statement provides information on the sources of national income – consumption, investment, government expenditure, exports and imports. These present their own problems in a regional context particularly with the treatment of government expenditure of a public goods nature. Exports and imports of goods and services are also difficult to establish for a region operating within a currency union with no obligation to record transactions with other entities within the currency union and with exports and imports likely to be routed through ports in other parts of the country.

The main component of a flow of funds table is concerned with financing of the surpluses and deficits which arise for the sectors which are distinguished showing the institutions and instruments undertaking the financing. Separating out transactions relating to Scotland in these financial flows is not possible. Whilst there are some institutions such as the banks with a strong Scottish orientation, there are others whose major activities are concerned with the wider national and international markets – insurance and assurance companies, investment and unit trusts. The separation of flows of funds between Scotland and the rest of the UK would prove impossible to determine without detailed investigation at the organisation level. The Scottish Life Offices derive 85–90 per cent of their premium income outside Scotland. Similarly there are flows between residents of Scotland and financial intermediaries and markets not represented in Scotland so that the preparation of a complete flow of funds statement for Scotland is not possible since such figures are not available on a regional basis. Some general indication of the significance of the Scottish financial sector can be provided on a partial basis by noting developments in parts of the sector which have a large Scottish content and/or where there are figures available.

A recent survey by the Bank of England of funds under management indicated that Scottish based firms controlled £10675 million. Of this £10305 million was managed on behalf of UK residents and £370 million for overseas residents. This represented some 9.6 per cent and 1.3 per cent of the UK totals respectively. These figures do not provide comprehensive coverage of all funds under management, but only funds under management for clients. The substantial funds managed by Scottish based firms on their own account are not included in the picture. These figures almost certainly underestimate the importance of the Scottish sector in funds under management in the UK (see chapter 8).

The building societies provide figures showing the flow of funds into and out of building society offices in Scotland. These figures highlight certain significant trends, in particular their success in attracting deposits. By the end of 1984 these had grown to £5547 million. This compares with deposits held by the personal sector at Scottish clearing banks of £4265 million at the same date. In 1978 the equivalent figures were £2141 million and £2051 million respectively. On the lending side the trend towards owner occupation in Scotland is highlighted by the fact that in most recent years Scotland has been a net recipient of flows for house purchase.

The growing importance of the housing sector in Scotland is further shown from the Family Expenditure Survey figures in table 2.2 which record that while expenditure on purchase or alterations of dwellings, including mortgages, is still less than the national average, as a percentage of the national average it has increased. This suggests that there is still further scope for expansion in expenditure in the housing sector. Proposed changes in legislation are likely to mean an even more significant role for the building societies in the Scottish financial sector.

The banking system represents the major distinctive element in the Scottish financial system with its widespread local representation which provides financial services for all sectors of the economy. The location of their head offices in Scotland represents a major source of influence on financial development in Scotland. Their role in the Scottish system is changing to the extent that they are becoming less Scottish as they extend their activities to a wider constituency. The necessity of a significant presence in London where the major financial markets are located and the need to respond in their borrowing and lending activities to the competitive pressures exerted on them by developments elsewhere in the financial system are also significant. The recent establishment of the combined Committee of London and Scottish Clearing Bankers is another straw in the wind.

Table 2.2 Average weekly payment (£) for purchase or alteration of dwellings, including mortgage payments.

	Scotland	UK	Scotland as % of UK
1974/75	1.52	3.21	47
1975/76	1.61	3.69	44
1976/77	2.02	4.12	49
1977/78	2.78	4.63	60
1978/79	3.83	6.45	59
1979/80	6.69	8.83	76
1980/81	7.04	10.82	65
1981/82	7.17	12.28	58
1982/83	7.54	12.44	61

Source: Family Expenditure Survey.

The key role of the banks is based on their dominance of the payments mechanism which provides them with a natural link to all economic units and a basis on which to build a more extensive financial relationship. This role is under threat as competitors are developing payments mechanisms and offering competing facilities. There is particular pressure from the foreign banks as they seek to service the growing foreign company presence in Scotland or exploit some comparative advantage in a specialist sector in the market.

The nature of the flow of funds has changed over the years in response to changed regulations, competitive pressures and consumer demands. Major factors affecting the flow of funds include the costs of undertaking financial transaction, both information and transactions costs. The lower the costs the more likely are asset holders to transact. Costs will be affected by competition in the markets and the attitude of the authorities to the regulation of the market. One of the effects of competition and lower costs after the October 1986 changes in Stock Exchange rules is expected to be higher turnover in the financial markets. Innovation in both instruments and markets by varying the basic ingredients of income, liquidity and risk attracts more funds to the market to meet some latent demand or overcome some hindrance to participation. By improving the functioning of markets or

Table 2.3. Sources of income in Scotland and the UK. Average weekly income (£) over two-year period and percentage distribution of sources.

	Scotland						UK					
		Source of Income (%)						Source of Income (%)				
	Household income	Wages & salaries	Self-employed	Invest-ments	Social Security	Other	Household income	Wages & salaries	Self-employed	Invest-ments	Social Security	Other
1970/71	34.92	75.1	5.2	4.1	10.4	5.2	37.04	74.1	6.9	3.8	8.8	6.4
1971/72	37.13	76.4	5.0	2.8	11.4	4.4	40.63	74.7	6.6	3.3	9.0	6.7
1972/73	43.20	75.2	6.2	3.3	10.8	4.5	46.16	74.5	6.4	3.2	9.1	6.8
1973/74	52.15	73.7	7.3	3.8	10.3	4.9	53.73	72.9	7.1	3.4	9.2	7.4
1974/75	63.60	76.0	5.0	3.8	10.5	4.7	65.87	73.8	6.4	3.5	9.5	6.8
1975/76	74.68	78.1	3.4	3.0	10.7	4.8	77.59	73.9	5.4	3.3	10.1	7.3
1976/77	85.00	74.4	5.0	3.4	11.8	5.4	87.64	72.6	5.6	3.0	11.0	7.8
1977/78	100.44	71.9	6.5	3.9	11.6	6.1	99.46	71.8	5.4	2.9	11.6	8.3
1978/79	114.45	73.4	5.9	2.8	11.4	6.5	113.24	71.7	4.8	2.7	12.1	8.7
1979/80	126.46	75.0	4.4	2.3	12.6	5.7	134.08	71.4	5.2	2.9	12.1	8.4
1980/81	146.79	70.5	7.2	2.7	13.9	5.7	157.80	69.5	5.8	3.5	12.6	8.6
1981/82	162.29	68.0	7.3	2.9	15.1	6.7	172.11	67.3	6.0	3.9	13.5	9.3
1982/83	167.51	68.2	4.3	3.1	17.1	7.3	182.09	65.9	6.3	3.8	14.4	9.6

Source: Family Expenditure Survey.

introducing new markets a wider appeal is achieved and both liquidity and attractiveness to savers and borrowers increased. Meeting the need for diversification has become more important in recent years because of variable nominal and real interest rates and volatile nominal and real exchange rates together with rapidly changing expectations concerning both.

For Scotland it is important that the financial sector meets the demands of savers, investors and wealth-holders in order to generate economic activity. This involves not only creating desirable products and services but also marketing them effectively. However, given the performance of the economy in Scotland over the years this does not provide a basis for expecting rapid growth in the financial sector. Using Family Expenditure figures the average household income in Scotland is consistently less than the national average (table 2.3). Of that income a higher proportion is received from wages and salaries and social security payments than the national average. Given this outcome it is interesting to note that expenditure on life assurance, including endowment, mortgage endowment policies and on pension and superannuation funds deducted by employers, is comparable to the UK average levels in absolute terms and has been higher in recent years (table 2.4). It may be that endowment assurance is a preferred instrument for

Table 2.4. Average weekly expenditure (£) over a two-year period on life assurance[1] and other savings and investment.[2]

	Scotland		UK	
	Life assurance	Savings & investment	Life assurance	Savings & investment
1970/71	1.23	0.53	1.28	0.89
1971/72	1.31	0.51	1.44	1.83
1972/73	1.52	0.65	1.65	1.95
1973/74	1.93	0.73	1.91	1.25
1974/75	2.28	1.27	2.30	1.19
1975/76	2.59	1.76	2.66	1.11
1976/77	2.96	1.28	3.02	1.15
1977/78	3.46	1.19	3.45	1.18
1978/79	4.14	1.43	3.90	1.55
1979/80	4.71	1.48	4.55	2.18
1980/81	5.37	1.72	5.36	2.84
1981/82	6.10	—[3]	5.95	3.21
1982/83	6.93	—[3]	6.47	2.98

1. Life assurance premiums, including industrial policies, mortgage endowment policies, contributions to pensions and superannuation funds deducted by employers.

2. Purchases of savings certificates and bonds, premium bonds, stocks and shares, unit trusts, deposits in savings banks, building societies, SAYE contributions.

3. Sampling error greater than 50%.

Source: Family Expenditure Survey.

financing house purchase in Scotland compared to the rest of the UK. Under 'other savings and investment', covering such items as savings certificates and bonds, premium bonds, stocks and shares, unit trusts, building society deposits, savings bank deposits and SAYE contracts, Scottish figures are generally lower although the sample size presents problems of interpretation. Overall such figures do not suggest a domestic base for rapid future growth in the financial sector, although not all financial activity is directly related to income levels and income growth.

If the Scottish financial sector is to achieve growth it must be through attracting institutions, markets and their related servicing activities to Scotland against UK competition. The existing financial institutions and the ancillary professional skills and services provide a strong base on which to build. The predicted growth in the international financial services market provides the opportunity. The ability to choose the appropriate areas to match the skills and opportunities will determine the success.

Financial Sector Employment in Scotland

An important feature of a strong regional financial centre is the contribution made to employment within the region and the potential contribution to future employment growth. The most comprehensive and accurate sources of recent data on employment and employment trends in the Scottish financial sector is the 1981 Census of Population and earlier statistical series compiled by the Department of Employment (DE). The information that can be gleaned from looking at the Census figures is somewhat dated. Data from the 1984 Census is not yet available. Subsequent UK Labour Force Surveys and employment estimates present regional figures for banking, insurance and finance at a highly aggregated level[1] only, which is of no practical use for our purposes. The main constraint placed upon an analysis of employment in the Scottish financial sector therefore is derived from a lack of up-to-date statistical data which can only be overcome by obtaining figures directly from the institutions concerned, but this would entail a separate major study in the nature of Gaskin (1980). This section is therefore mostly confined to a discussion of the employment trends in the Scottish financial sector over the period 1971 to 1981 highlighting the more important changes that have taken place as well as looking at the importance of financial sector employment in Scotland relative to the rest of Great Britain, and for individual Scottish centres.

Employment in the financial sector in Scotland is provided by a wide variety of financial institutions and by other organisations carrying out finance-related activities. For official statistical purposes this data is available under two different classifications, Order XXIV of the 1968 Standard Industrial Classification (SIC) and Division 8 of the 1980 SIC. Order XXIV is broken down into a number of Minimum List Headings (MLH) including insurance, banking and bill discounting and other financial institutions,[2] and

Table 2.5. Regional location quotients for MLHs 860, 861 and 862, and percentage of Great Britain MLH 860–862 total employment, 1981.

	South East[1]	London	East Anglia	South West	West Midlands	East Midlands	Yorks & Humberside	North West	North	Wales	Scotland	GB
MLH 860 Insurance	1.06	1.82	1.39	1.14	0.71	0.52	0.64	0.88	0.36	0.50	0.81	—
MLH 861 Banking and bill discounting	0.79	2.12	0.60	0.86	0.60	0.65	0.68	0.95	0.68	0.66	0.91	—
MLH 862 Other financial institutions	0.85	2.05	0.58	0.87	0.85	0.67	1.07	0.68	0.68	0.67	0.63	—
MLH 860–862	0.94	2.15	0.95	1.02	0.72	0.63	0.76	0.93	0.67	0.63	0.87	—
Percentage of GB Employment in MLH 860–862												
%	15.5	33.9	2.9	7.0	6.4	4.1	6.3	10.2	3.4	2.6	7.7	100.0
Total employment	119641	262427	22167	53788	49772	32049	48474	79052	26086	20339	59402	773197

1. South East excludes London.

Source: Department of Employment.

figures are available for the period 1971 to 1981. The 1981 Census information has also been presented in terms of the new 1980 SIC. For consistency, and to avoid confusion, the 1968 SIC is used throughout this section, other than where more recent UK financial employment data is used to provide a more up-to-date estimate of total Scottish employment. The three MLHs of insurance, banking and other financial institutions contain most of the financial sector employment in Scotland. Other MLH categories under Order XXIV such as advertising and market research, and other business services, which would include computing, almost certainly have some connection with the activities of finance. However, since it is impossible to quantify this component in terms of employment they are not treated here as being part of the Scottish financial sector.[3]

At September 1981 employment in banking, insurance and finance in Scotland stood at 59402, which amounted to a 7.7 per cent share of the Great Britain total, and accounted for 3.0 per cent of all employment in Scottish industry and services. The Scottish share of 7.7 per cent fell below her 9.3 per cent share of total employment in industry and services in Great Britain, a feature that is found in all regions but London, and reflects the high concentration of financial employment – 34 per cent – in the Greater London area. In addition to London, four further regions had a relatively higher representation of financial sector employment than did Scotland in 1981 – the South East, East Anglia, South West and North West. This can best be seen by looking at the location quotients given in table 2.5 for MLH 860 to 862. A location quotient compares a region's share of employment in a particular industry with the national share of employment in that industry. If the location quotient is equal to 1.0 then the region's share of employment in the industry is the same as the national share, but if it is less than 1.0 the industry is under-represented in the region, while if it is greater than 1.0 the industry is over-represented.[4] Ignoring the very high values for London, it would appear that Scotland has high relative employment levels in insurance although behind the regions of East Anglia, the South West and North West, and in banking where only the North West has higher relative employment (outside London). Scotland has low relative employment in the Other financial institutions category.

The main problem with the location quotient is that it is a ratio of two values; as such it tells us nothing about the absolute importance of regional financial employment. Figures for the regional share of employment in insurance, banking and finance in 1981 are provided at the bottom of table 2.5. Outwith London and the South East, which together account for almost 50 per cent of the total, Scotland has the second largest concentration of financial sector employment (7.7 per cent) behind the North West (10.2 per cent).

Regional growth rates of financial sector employment from the early 'seventies to the early 'eighties are given in table 2.6. Fastest growth has

Table 2.6. National and regional growth rates of MLH 860–862 total employment, 1971–81 (1971 = 100).

	South East[1]	London	East Anglia	South West	West Midlands	East Midlands	Yorks & Humberside	North West	North	Wales	Scotland	GB
1976	124	104	128	131	110	112	107	100	104	103	110	109
1981	158	110	150	167	128	133	126	115	123	115	121	125

1. Excludes London.
Source: Department of Employment.

Table 2.7. Growth rates of total employment in insurance, banking and other financial institutions, in Scotland and other regions of Great Britain, 1971–81 (1971 = 100).

	Insurance MLH 860				Banking MLH 861				Other financial institutions MLH 862			
	Scotland	Other regions[1]	South East[2]	London	Scotland	Other regions[1]	South East[2]	London	Scotland	Other regions[1]	South East[2]	London
1976	94	101	121	86	127	116	122	121	107	118	146	104
1981	99	114	153	89	137	139	146	127	149	147	221	115

1. 'Other regions' comprises all standard regions of Great Britain except Scotland, South East and London.
2. South East excludes London.
Source: Department of Employment.

taken place in the South West, South East and East Anglia and the traditional centres for finance, London, Scotland and the North West, have performed relatively poorly. It is likely that the two southern regions have been the beneficiaries of the movement of head office activities out of London, including the relocation of large life assurance companies, in search of staff and accommodation economies and a pleasant working and living environment. Scotland has had less success in either attracting or generating financial employment. The change in Scottish employment at MLH level over the same period is compared with the trend in London, the South East and the remaining standard regions (as a group) in table 2.7.

Employment in the insurance sector in Scotland declined over the 'seventies before rising, by 1981, to virtually the same level as ten years earlier. London also suffered a loss of jobs in insurance, but by proportionately more. In contrast the insurance totals rose in the other UK regions with the South East outstripping the provinces by a substantial margin.

Strong growth in banking employment is a feature of all the regions but again the South East and other regions have created jobs at a faster rate than in Scotland, despite an early advantage due to a build-up of staff in the National Savings Bank in Glasgow, peaking in 1976 and subsequently declining. Employment in other financial institutions in Scotland has more than kept pace with growth in other regions and has grown faster than the Scottish banking total. However, this sector accounted for only 10 per cent of financial employment in Scotland in 1971, rising to 12 per cent in 1981. The contribution of other financial institutions to total sector employment in the South East in 1981 was about 16 per cent after dramatic growth over the previous ten years.

The regional pattern and trends of financial employment in Great Britain suggest that Scotland has not performed particularly well. Scotland's share of total financial sector employment fell from 7.9 per cent to 7.7 per cent between 1971 and 1981. While this decline is not as great as for London, almost all other regions have increased their share. Financial sector employment has risen fastest in the South East (excluding London) and probably reflects a strong regional economy with expanding markets, excellent communications, the desire of new financial enterprises to reduce risk and establish themselves close to potential markets and large pools of skilled labour, and the attractions of short distance transfer from London to lower cost locations offering employees a high quality life-style.

Insurance

Under the general heading of insurance, MLH 860 combines employment in the fields of general and long-term insurance and insurance broking thus including a wide spread of different insurance activities. In Scotland employment in these activities is provided both by Scottish based companies and by non-Scottish companies which have set up branch or regional offices. Gaskin

(1980) has observed that the greater part of Scottish insurance employment is in non-Scottish companies and it is true that virtually all of the large general and life assurance offices are represented in Scotland, most often with regional headquarters in Glasgow or Edinburgh and branches in other cities and towns. The large international insurance broking firms are also represented. There are nine Scottish life assurance companies, of which six are headquartered in Edinburgh and three in Glasgow, and one Scottish general insurance company, General Accident, which is based in Perth but which also has a large office in Glasgow. These insurance companies account for most of the employment provided by Scottish based insurance institutions. Gaskin put the share of Scottish head office employment within the MLH total at between one-fifth and one-quarter, although there are grounds to believe that currently a ratio of between one-quarter and one-third would be a more accurate estimate.

Insurance employment in Scotland (MLH 860) at September 1981 amounted to almost 22000, accounting for over one-third of total financial sector employment. This figure was marginally below the total recorded in 1971 which would suggest that Scottish insurance employment followed a level trend over the 1970s. Closer examination of the Department of Employment's figures, however, reveals a sharp decline between 1971 and 1972 followed by a fairly level trend to 1978. As can be seen from table 2.8, male employment declined over this period but was offset by a rise in female employment. Much the same change occurred in the Great Britain totals. Both the Scottish and Great Britain figures show a fairly substantial rise in male employment between 1978 and 1981, the next year for which DE data is available. Given the surprising reversal of the trend it may be worth bearing in mind the possibility of a discrepancy between the presentation of DE figures for 1981 and earlier years.

A static trend in employment does not necessarily mean that insurance markets have failed to grow but could indicate changes both in the nature of employment and employment productivity. Gaskin (1980) attempted to set the trends in both employment and insurance output over the 'seventies alongside one another in order to provide a 'qualified view on productivity changes in the recent past' and concluded 'it is clear from all comparisons of output growth and employment that the productivity of labour in the insurance industry has increased during the last decade, in Scotland as in Britain.'[5]

The biggest influence on rising productivity was almost certainly the introduction of work measurement programmes and computerisation. The computer has had an impact not only on staffing levels required to process and service increased volumes of insurance policies but also on the structure of insurance employment. The decline of traditional male policy preparation and servicing work has been matched by the increased numbers of women employed in data processing and in secretarial work. Table 2.8

Table 2.8. Changes in male and female financial employment in Scotland, 1971–81 selected years.

	1971	1973	1976	1978	1981
MLH 860 Insurance					
Male	12615	11227	11052	10885	11428
Female	9612	9659	9861	9945	10493
of which Female part-time	1535	1497	1726	1767	1812
MLH 861 Banking					
Male	10172	10372	11201	11652	11034
Female	11486	13040	16654	18387	19073
of which Female part-time	1075	1081	2257	2863	3722
MLH 862 Other financial institutions					
Male	2316	2451	2367	2610	3174
Female	2643	2795	2921	3293	4200
of which Female part-time	384	392	510	593	917
Total MLH 860–862					
Male	25103	24050	24620	25147	25636
Female	23741	25494	29436	31625	33766
of which Female part-time	2994	2970	4493	5223	6451

Figures for Female part-time are included in those for Female.
Source: Department of Employment.

shows that this increased use of female labour, between 1971 and 1981, has mainly been in part-time employment.

Banking

By far the largest proportion of Scottish financial employment is now to be found in the banking sector. In 1981 just over half the employment represented by MLH 860 to 862 was in banking, a total that had grown, in marked contrast to insurance, by 37 per cent over the previous decade. Banking in Scotland is conducted by the three Scottish clearing banks, the TSB, the National Savings Bank and a small group of 'other' banks which include branches of English clearing banks, merchant banks and international banks. The Scottish clearers' share of banking employment was about 80 per cent in 1981, or some 24500 employees,[6] clearly having a significant influence over both the banking and financial sector employment totals. Employment in the Scottish clearing banks is dealt with in more detail in chapter 4. We confine ourselves here to a general assessment of sector trends between 1971 and 1981. The figures in table 2.8 for banking employment show that the number of female staff has grown rapidly to account for just over 63 per cent of total employees by 1981. Male employment, on the other hand, has shown only a small increase and peaked in 1977. The computer has also tended to displace more male employees in the lower clerical grades sector than female employees, while providing a greater number of new posts for women in data processing. Part-time women employees have shown the fastest rise, from almost 5 per cent of total employment in 1971 to 12 per cent by 1981, an average yearly increase of 13 per cent. (There is very little male part-time employment in banking.) Overall, the employment growth was similar to that for Great Britain, although female staff numbers, in particular part-time, grew faster in Scotland with male employment increasing more slowly than at national level.[7]

While banking employment totals in Scotland show a significant rise between 1971 and 1981 much of the growth took place in the first five years of the period. The decline in NSB employment (over 1500 between 1976 and 1981), owing much to computerisation, was not entirely offset by the growth in TSB staff, which was in the process of change from a savings bank to a retail bank, and the banking staff of non-indigenous institutions. The expansion in bank staff, however, was higher over the second half of the period.

The very large increase in bank employment appears to have occurred at a time when the workload has risen substantially, particularly in the payments system. There are indications, however, that the expansion of work has more than kept pace with increased staff numbers and Gaskin (1980) has suggested that a comparison of the growth rates of Scottish clearing bank staff and money transmissions work between 1972 and 1979 gives figures of 4 per cent and 7 per cent respectively, which implies rising labour productivity. As in insurance, productivity gains have been achieved through work measurement programmes and efficiency drives at branch and head office level and computerisation.

The computer was first introduced in the 1950s but its importance was not fully recognised, nor did its use become widespread until the 1970s when more powerful machines and programs became available providing a means to cope with an increased volume of business. These developments have continued into the 'eighties with large investment in cash dispensers, counter terminals and the increased use of automated payments in the retail banking sector, spurred on by the continuing growth in money transmission and the desire to avoid a sustained growth in staff numbers.

Other Financial Institutions

MLH 862, 'Other financial institutions' is a catch-all category which gathers together the very diverse range of institutions and operators not included in the insurance and banking sectors. The most important of these, in employment terms are the building societies, the finance houses, stockbrokers, investment trusts and factoring companies. The contribution that these individual institutions make to the Scottish financial sector is perhaps measured less by total employment numbers than by the financial functions they perform. Nevertheless at September 1981 they together accounted for 12.4 per cent of total financial employment and showed the fastest rate of growth between 1971 and 1981, increasing at an average of 4.0 per cent per annum.

Other Financial Institutions

It is probable that much of this growth was due to the building society expansion in the 'seventies in Scotland, which, as a region, was underbranched relative to the rest of the UK. Table 2.8 shows that both male and female employment recorded growth over the period. It is not possible here to take a more detailed look at employment in the different groups of MLH 862 and the interested reader is referred to Gaskin (1980).

Finally, it is worth recognising that overall growth in Scottish financial employment has, rather strikingly, been largely confined to woman employees and many of the new posts created have been part-time. This can clearly be seen by bringing MLH 860, 861 and 862 together at the foot of table 2.8. In 1971 more men than women were employed in finance but the static trend in male employment coupled with the rapid growth in female labour substantially reversed this position by 1981.

The Geography of Financial Employment

The presence of a number of large Scottish-based financial institutions in Edinburgh serving markets both within and outwith Scotland has meant that the capital city has traditionally been seen as the centre of the Scottish financial sector. This role has been enhanced by the decision of many non-Scottish institutions to set up their regional headquarters in Edinburgh. There are, however, a number of important indigenous institutions and incomers based in Glasgow and Scotland's two other major cities of Aberdeen and Dundee are also, or were at least in the near past, seen as centres for specialist skills which serve wider markets. Perth forms another centre for financial activity owing much to the presence of one of Scotland's largest and most internationally-orientated institutions, General Accident.

Table 2.9. Employment in MLHs 860, 861 and 862 by Scottish financial centres, 1971 and 1981.

	Edinburgh 1971	Edinburgh 1981	Glasgow 1971	Glasgow 1981	Dundee 1971	Dundee 1981	Aberdeen 1971	Aberdeen 1981	Perth 1971	Perth 1981
MLH 860	5682	5781	5890	5814	925	738	1056	1161	1413	1635
MLH 861	3622	5845	2700	4184	627	864	963	1644	391	423
MLH 862	1551	2098	1506	1495	178	344	199	389	37	117
Total MLH 860-862	10855	13724	10096	11493	1730	1946	2218	3194	1841	2175

Source: Department of Employment.

Employment figures for MLH 860, 861 and 862 are given in table 2.9 for the five centres at September 1981. In total they account for 55 per cent of Scottish financial employment. Edinburgh has the highest employment total and is ahead of Glasgow in banking and in 'Other financial institutions'. This reflects the city's primacy as the major banking and financial centre outwith London, with, most importantly, the headquarter presence of Scotland's two largest banks (and more recently TSB Scotland) and the branches of many of the international banking institutions that maintain a presence north of the border. Glasgow has the Clydesdale Bank and important divisional branches of the Royal Bank of Scotland and Bank of Scotland but a larger part of the employment total is branch rather than headquarter staff, although the total is clearly boosted by the numbers employed at the NSB headquarters. Insurance employment is higher in Glasgow, probably due to the presence of non-Scottish general insurance companies and broking firms.

Dundee has the lowest financial employment total and has suffered most from the decline in insurance employment over the 'seventies. It is probable that there has also been some fall in investment trust employment. In contrast, Aberdeen has shown the fastest growth between 1971 and 1981, clearly arising from the oil-related expansion of the city and regional economy. In particular, banking has shown an impressive rate of growth. A comparison of the employment growth rates of Edinburgh and Glasgow over the same period shows that Edinburgh has been more successful at generating jobs. This may be, in part, a reflection of differing local and regional economic growth, or the nature of financial employment itself. As Gaskin observed 'The trends favouring head office employment, relative to branch offices, are definitely present in all the financial institutions.' Edinburgh may therefore have benefited from the higher complement of institutional headquarters, both indigenous and regional. It is very difficult to assess how important these factors have been in the more recent past or will be in the future.

Employment in the 'Eighties

It is unfortunate that Scottish financial sector employment figures are not available for more recent years. General observation and discussion would indicate that employment has continued to grow, but it is difficult to reach any degree of precision as to number or trends and we can, at best, only make some estimate (or informed guess). One starting point would be to look at how financial employment has grown in Great Britain between 1981 and 1985. Division 8 of the 1980 Standard Industrial Classification provides the Activity levels which most closely correspond with MLH 860–862 (1968 SIC). These are presented in table 2.10 for 1981 and 1985 and the percentage change over the period is also given.

Total financial employment in Great Britain has continued to increase in the 'eighties at a rate of 3 per cent per year. If we assume, and this may not altogether be an unreasonable assumption given that both Scottish and national employment growth rates were similar in the 'seventies, that Scottish totals increased at the same rate as for Great Britain, direct financial sector employment in Scotland in 1985 would have been just over 67000. It must be remembered, however, that the Great Britain figures are themselves Department of Employment estimates. Table 2.10 indicates that insurance employment has risen in recent years and discussions with insurance companies in Scotland suggest that staff numbers have had to rise to cope with large increases in the volume of business which has more than matched systems improvements.

Table 2.10. Employment and employment changes in Division 8 in Great Britain, 1981–85 selected activities.

Activity	Total employment (1000s) 1981	1985	% change
8140 Banking	360.9	393.7	9.1
8250 Insurance	223.6	246.7	10.3
8150 Other financial institutions	104.1	132.0	26.8
8310 Activities auxiliary to banking/finance	18.6	24.7	32.8
8320 Activities auxiliary to insurance	65.9	76.9	16.7
Total 8140–8320	773.1	874.0	13.0

Source: Department of Employment.

It is less certain, however, whether banking employment in Scotland has grown as fast since 1981 as it may have done in the rest of Great Britain. Scottish clearing bank employment accelerated in the latter half of the 1970s but has slowed markedly in the 1980s (see chapter 4) most probably as a result of the benefits starting to flow from the introduction of new money transmission technologies. The banks have also instituted branch rationalisation programmes and, in general, have sought to achieve and maintain tight control over branch and head-office staffing levels which are a major source of costs. While this is also a feature of banking in England, the relatively greater dominance of the bank employment totals by the Scottish clearing banks has most likely meant slower growth in banking employment in Scotland. Our estimate of the total numbers of bank staff in Scotland in 1985 largely from published accounts is as follows:

Scottish clearing banks	25300
TSB	2900
NSB	3000
Other Banks	1000
Total	32200

If this estimate is correct then total numbers estimated to be employed in the Scottish financial sector would be reduced to around 65000. The heterogeneous nature of the Other financial institutions category make it impossible to estimate with any accuracy changes in employment and for this reason the 3 per cent growth figure for the UK as a whole would seem appropriate.

Conclusions

Although we are unable to provide detailed figures on the flow of funds in Scotland the available data does allow us to draw a number of important conclusions. Short's work on regional transfers suggests that Scotland is a major beneficiary on both current and capital account of government financial flows. The Scottish input/output tables are limited in their usefulness but do indicate significant linkages between the financial and printing, postal and telecommunication and construction sectors as well as important linkages with London. Recorded financial exports were small despite major insurance activity in Scotland mainly for non-Scottish customers. Examination of financial transfers at the institutional level provides an interesting although incomplete picture of financial activity. Fund management and insurance is carried out for clients throughout the UK and to a lesser extent for world markets. The relatively under-developed housing sector in Scotland results in a significant flow of funds into Scotland from the rest of the UK, whilst the banking industry is characterised by its small, but expanding role in international markets and its increasing importance in the UK banking scene.

The financial sector in Scotland is a significant provider of employment. There has been continuing growth in the years 1971–81, but the rate of growth has generally been less than for most other regions during the period with the result that Scotland's share of total financial employment in Great Britain has fallen. The major growth has been in the banking sector and in the other financial institutions category. Employment in the insurance sector has been virtually static over the eleven years. In all sectors there has been a trend towards greater female part-time employment, especially in the banking sector. As expected Edinburgh provides most employment particularly in the headquarters operations, but there is also substantial employment in Glasgow. The increase in Aberdeen over the years 1971–81 has been most marked. To the extent that this has been oil-related the current problems facing that industry will have an adverse effect.

The overall prospects for continuing growth in employment must be good to the extent that the demand for financial services continues to expand and Scottish institutions respond to the changes in the market. Substantial increases in employment are largely dependent on attracting business from outside Scotland reflecting existing major dependence of Scottish financial institutions on the UK, and particularly South East, markets.

NOTES

1. Division 8 of the 1980 Standard Industrial Classification, which includes non-financial activities.
2. There are seven MLHs contained in Order XXIV: 860 Insurance, 861 Banking and bill-discounting, 862 Other financial institutions, 863 Property owning and managing, 864 Advertising and market-research, 865 Other business services, 866 Central offices not allocable elsewhere.
3. In so far as finance-related activities support employment in businesses covered by these classes then this can be seen as a further important contribution of a regional financial centre. See Gaskin (1980) for a discussion of MLH 865, Other business services in Scotland.
4. For example insurance accounted for 1.11 per cent of total industry and service employment in Scotland in 1981 and 1.37 per cent for Great Britain. The location quotient is given by $1.11/1.37 = 0.81$, implying under-representation in Scotland.
5. Considerable difficulties arise with any attempt to measure insurance output – see Gaskin.
6. Estimate of Scottish-based employees, i.e. after deducting allowance for staff employed in England from total employees.
7. The figures for Great Britain are influenced by London where, as recognised by Gaskin, the nature of the banking operations provides an above-average proportion of men (51 per cent in 1981).

3

SCOTTISH FINANCIAL MARKETS

The Nature and Function of Financial Markets

Financial markets are a mechanism for the exchange of financial assets such as money, bonds, equity or other securities yielding a monetary return. Such assets offer investors a range of securities with different terms and conditions. Trading in these securities may be concentrated in one location or dispersed across many locations. The issue of mortgages and assurance policies is generally dispersed whilst equity trading is predominantly concentrated in one location, the Stock Exchange.

The Stock Exchange enables a trade in secondhand securities to take place. The initial issue of a financial asset – a new issue of a company security, the granting of a mortgage or the issue of an assurance policy – is a 'primary' transaction and the issue of all financial assets involve such a transaction. A minority of asset types, primarily equities and bonds, are subsequently traded between owners who are not associated with the original issuers. Such trades are termed secondary transactions and take place in secondary markets. Not all securities are so traded. Mortgages, insurance policies and bank loans are rarely traded in secondary markets although it would be possible, if such securities were suitably standardised, for trade to occur.

The economic function of primary capital markets is to bring savers and borrowers together. Without such markets every economic unit would have to be financially self sufficient and would be limited in their capital expenditure to their own savings with a consequent loss of choice in their consumption and investment decisions. The trade of already existing financial assets in the secondary markets imparts a liquidity to these assets which they would not otherwise have. Without a secondary market the initial purchaser of a financial asset would have to keep it until maturity with the result that investors' portfolios would be frozen in their composition. Secondary markets allow investors to make portfolio adjustments and hence improve the flow of resources into primary securities.

The desirable benefits consequent upon the existence of primary and secondary markets do not of course require their existence in every financial centre. To attain the full benefits it is only necessary for investors to have access to such markets. The advent of rapid telecommunications has led to the increasing internationalisation of secondary markets with the Eurodollar market providing a prime example. Regional and even national markets have been increasingly eclipsed by international markets offering a wider variety of securities and able to make trades in a greater quantity of securities. These advantages may not be secured at zero cost to all participants. The large company may benefit from the economies of scale offered by deep markets, as indeed may the substantial investor able to acquire assets in large blocks rather than penny lots, but the smaller company and investor may be faced with higher costs as organisations geared to raise hundreds of millions or buy stocks for investors costing tens of millions find it expensive to operate at the lower end of the market. Smaller companies and investors may find the traditional routes to raising or investing funds effectively blocked by increasing costs.

One answer to the higher costs faced by smaller companies and investors is a greater use of the services of financial intermediaries. Financial intermediaries stand between the ultimate borrower in the economy, frequently companies wishing to raise large sums of money for expansion, and the ultimate lenders: the households and small investors. Intermediaries operate by acquiring the securities of borrowers, generally too large to be easily sold, and issuing their own 'indirect' securities to savers. Because of their size the intermediaries offer advantages of risk reduction, economies of scale and flexibility to savers. The indirect securities they offer are more attractive to small savers than the offerings of companies. Examples of such securities are legion; bank and building society deposits, unit trust units and assurance policies providing some of the more obvious. Although a part of Scotland's financial markets, the role and importance of these 'indirect' securities is more conveniently appraised in the context of the issuing institution (see chapters 4–9).

Regional Stock Markets

In contrast to the indirect securities issued by financial institutions both Government and public company securities are issued direct to private and institutional investors by means of an Offer for Sale or an alternative method of introduction to the Stock Exchange. The Stock Exchange is based in London but maintains a floor in Glasgow, a remnant of the merger of the independent Glasgow, Edinburgh, Aberdeen and Dundee Exchanges into the Scottish Stock Exchange in 1964. The Scottish Exchange was itself part of the Federation of Stock Exchanges in Great Britain and Ireland before the merger in 1973 of all Exchanges into one body. The present Stock Exchange represents the culmination of a long process of consolidation on London and decline of the regional markets.

Historically,[1] London always monopolised the market for government stock although its participation in other areas of the market was often very limited. The unique jobbing system of the London Exchange evolved to cater for a substantial turnover in a small number of standard securities and made it 'a poor market for the shares of anything but the largest enterprises or the most active of stocks' (Mitchie 1981). The London and Scottish markets evolved to meet differing needs, the former for government and other large securities while the latter met the needs of regional joint stock enterprises for small issues, limited turnover and a variety of issues. Discussing the period before 1900 Mitchie writes

> In isolation, the London Stock Exchange gives the impression of an obsession with overseas investment and large corporations but, when its function is examined, it is seen to be a part of a wider market in which the areas it neglected were looked after in other locations.

The decline of local enterprises with their nationalisation or merger into national companies resulted in the replacement of small, local shares with a substantial number of shares with uniform characteristics ideally suited to the facilities offered by the London Exchange. The mergers in which many companies engaged were motivated by the desire to secure product market advantages and economies of scale and their effects have been accentuated with the diminution of the Scottish industrial base and the movement of corporate headquarters to the South. With the movement of companies to London local knowledge and interest in a firm was no longer important whilst national awareness of a company removed the need for local market facilities. The requirement for provincial exchanges largely disappeared so that the Scottish Exchange has become an ancillary floor to London offering nothing in the way of additional services. There is now a national securities market which includes all potential buyers and sellers of securities and which functions through several marketplaces which are designed to facilitate transactions.

Marketplaces include both the formal Stock Exchange marketplaces such as the Scottish floor and the informal, outside the Exchange, such as the Over the Counter market (OTC) where buying and selling is telephone based and does not involve any face to face contact. Dealing in any company traded on the Stock Exchange can take place on the Glasgow floor and much of the trade is in major UK stocks together with some gilt dealing. Turnover of the local floor represents a small part of total stock market activity in the UK and is estimated to involve, per day, 1500–2000 individual deals with between £8 and £10 million of equity bargains and accounting for about 12 per cent by volume of the turnover of the whole Stock Exchange. Turnover by value is much lower (2–3 per cent).[2] The Glasgow floor is a part of the Stock Exchange, operated as a convenience to regional members and providing Stock Exchange services such as settlement. Although the Glasgow floor is a geographically distinct marketplace it functions as part of an integrated system so that whilst securities can be delivered to Glasgow and cheques paid by Glasgow as part of the settlement procedure, the settlement is computer based and covers the whole of the UK. Similarly, other services may be provided by the Scottish Unit but they are provided in Glasgow as a convenience to members although the services may originate in London or elsewhere. Thus, applications for quotation for securities may be made to the Glasgow Unit but its only role is to act as a liaison with the specialised Stock Exchange departments. A subsequent quotation is on the Stock Exchange irrespective of where the application originated or where the majority of deals are done.

The passing of the independent regional Exchanges into history has not been achieved totally without cost. Use of the London Exchange offers investors and companies a wider and deeper capital market together with economies of scale resulting from concentration on one main market. Trading in the majority of stocks has become cheaper and easier. Unfortunately the loss of the local markets may also have lost some important regional skills. Mitchie argues that

> the disappearance of the local markets and the accompanying centralisation removed more than the separate geographical components of a national capital market. It also destroyed the personnel and the institutions that had been important in encouraging small joint stock enterprise and in providing a market for their securities. This the London Stock Exchange was not designed to do and the British capital market was, consequently, poorer as a result.

Besides the loss of business from the decline of the local Exchanges, local stockbrokers, banks and merchant banks, accountants, solicitors and other activities have suffered since a financial marketplace generates additional business for many other local firms and institutions.

This argument, of the losses inflicted by the decline in local markets, is not without its problems. It ignores the question of causation. In part, at least, the decline in formation of small joint stock enterprises caused the decline in the regional markets. The decline in the regional industrial base was probably as large a contributory factor as the economies of scale offered by the London Exchange to larger companies.[3] The argument also ignores the improvements in communication that have been a feature of the last century. Such improvements have introduced regional companies to a larger investing audience and at the same time largely removed from many companies the constraint of geographical concentration. National distribution is easily obtained with few barriers to the company wherever it is situated. The argument also ignores the improvements in the facilities of the London market that have taken place. Most important, perhaps, from the perspective of replacing the capital raising function of the local markets, has been the setting up of the Unlisted Securities Market and the provision for small company issues.

It is unlikely that the effects of the loss of an independent local Exchange can ever be satisfactorily resolved. Regional stock markets at their height were relatively cheap and effective methods of raising capital but this coincided with the existence of a substantial group of active and wealthy investors in the market. This source of capital has been largely cut off by the tax advantages associated with investing through institutions although the introduction of Business Expansion Schemes is prompting new interest in small companies whilst some institutions do provide capital for new enterprises. The markets were also largely devoid of regulation making it easier for new businesses to raise capital. Information was often poor and inadequately disseminated and the result was the not infrequent collapse of the more speculative enterprises. Investors required local knowledge to sift the worthy and potentially successful from the merely hopeful or even fraudulent. All of these conditions have now passed. Minimum standards of information are generally required and the information is widely disseminated. It is unlikely that an independent Scottish market could have provided significant advantages over the London Exchange unless it had struck out in new directions to promote small regional companies: allowing new issues and the trading of companies which provide only a bare minimum of information on the principle of caveat emptor could have provided a useful service to the smaller company enabling it to secure access to equity capital with low issue costs, or the introduction of trade in new types of securities increasing the choice available to investors might also have been successful. However, such radical innovations were not characteristic of the independent regional markets in their later years.

The existence of a Scottish floor provides a compromise between an independent regional stock market and a single London based national market. Prices on the floor reflect the levels prevailing in the UK as a whole, a consequence of the possibilities of arbitrage between Glasgow and London together with the duty of stockbrokers, wherever they are located, to endeavour to secure the best terms for their clients.[4] Some 60–70 per cent of business comes by telephone from brokers outside Scotland.[5] The Scottish floor enables capital to be raised locally, imparts additional liquidity to small Scottish stocks, provides benefits to other local financial companies and heightens local awareness of stock market investment with a consequent impact on, and interest in, share ownership.

Regional Stockbrokers and Jobbers

Similar arguments can be made for regional stockbrokers and jobbers. Although not financial institutions within the conventional use of the term, they are important intermediaries that promote the efficient functioning of capital markets by facilitating the purchase and sale of securities. It has been conventional to identify stockbrokers and jobbers as single function organisations; stockbrokers acting as agents for investors in the buying and selling of securities, and jobbers acting as principals and providing a market making capacity[6] in which they smooth the flow of purchases and sales by buying and selling from or for their own stock (book) of securities. Since the removal of minimum commissions in October 1986 this distinction has been redundant with the market having moved from single capacity (separate broking and jobbing firms) to dual capacity in which brokers may also be dealers (market makers) in securities. Broking and jobbing firms are able to integrate the two functions and any firm can now carry out both jobbing and broking functions.

In 1985 there were thirteen firms of stockbrokers and two firms of jobbers based in Scotland, a reduction from the twenty-six brokers, one jobber and one dual-capacity firm operating in 1975 although the number of individual members had shown a small increase over the same period.[7] The decline in the number of brokers in Scotland reflects the trend towards concentration in the industry although recent links with other institutions and stockbrokers are now bringing new partners into the Exchange, as table 3.1 reveals. The decline in the number of firms in Scotland is graphically illustrated by the numbers trading on the Scottish floor. The floor when commissioned in 1972 provided places for 108 members of 25 brokers and three jobbers (including dual-capacity firms). In March 1986 six broking firms had a physical presence whilst several others used telephone links to the two jobbers. Employees of the Exchange had halved to 15, although the figure in the early 'seventies was inflated by staff acquired as the result of the merger of the local Scottish Exchanges.

The two firms of jobbers (or market makers as they are now more correctly termed) currently operating in the Glasgow market, Aitken Campbell & Co. and R. A. Maclean & Co., between them cover all the 'market leaders'. The jobbers deal in and hold shares on their own account. Until the switch to dual capacity jobbers could not deal directly with the public nor charge commission. Their profits arise from buying and selling securities for a 'turn', the difference between the purchase and sale price. Jobbers (market makers) maintain a book of securities and provide a market smoothing function ensuring that sales and purchases, of a reasonable size, can be made in the majority of companies. Aitken Campbell is quoted as being prepared to make prices in amounts of up to £250000 although the average deal in equities is in the £200–£500 range, indicating their important role in encouraging small investors. In addition to servicing institutional deals the two Glasgow jobbers are important in servicing private client business. They make a market in the shares of large actively traded companies but do not have the capability to deal in very large quantities. Their main activity is in moderate sized deals in these shares. Aitken Campbell also deals in gilts and is the only Gilt market maker outside of London. Dealing in small companies is often unprofitable since it may require jobbers to hold stock for extended periods of time. Jobbers prefer dealing in companies which have an active two-way market but may deal in less active companies in order to foster a name for providing dealing services in a specialised area. County Bisgood, a London-based jobber, is

Table 3.1. Scottish members of the Stock Exchange.

	Branches	Scottish members	Inter-relationships
Bell, Lawrie, MacGregor & Co.	Edinburgh Dumfries	19 1	independent – 25% of equity sold to Bank of Scotland and 2 trusts
Campbell Neill	Glasgow Inverness London	12 1	Hoare Govett – Security Pacific Bank
Carswell & Co.	Glasgow	5	independent
Chalmers Ogilvie & Co.	Dundee	3	Joined Stirling Hendry (Glasgow) 1986
Greig Middleton & Co.	Glasgow London	9	Formed from the merger of R.C.Greig (Scotland) and Middleton & Co. (London)
Horne & Mackinnon	Aberdeen	2	independent
Laing & Cruickshank	Glasgow London	7	Mercantile House. L & C acquired McNally & Montgomery (London) who had taken over Wilson Scott (Glasgow)
Murray W.M.	Aberdeen	2	independent
Parsons & Co.	Glasgow Edinburgh Aberdeen Dundee London	20 3 3 3	20% held by Postel and J.Capel (owned by H.K.& S. Bank). Joined Allied Provincial Securities 1986
Penney Easton & Co.	Glasgow Edinburgh Stirling Perth London	16 4 2 1	S.N.Penney & McGeorge merged with a London firm to become Penney, Costello, Carlebach. Then merged with Easton Goff (Glasgow) which had amalgamated with J.Watson Smith.
Speirs & Jeffrey	Glasgow	12	independent
Stirling Hendry (inc. A.C.Anderson & Co.)	Glasgow	15	independent
Torrie & Co.	Edinburgh	5	Dunfermline firm that joined Mansfield firm, subsequently moved to Edinburgh
Wishart Brodie	Edinburgh	7	Joined Laing & Cruickshank 1986
Wood Mackenzie & Co.	Edinburgh London	28	Hill Samuel
Scottish members with non-Scottish firms			
A.J.Bekhor	Edinburgh	1	
Capel Cure Myers	Edinburgh	2	
Stockjobbers			
Aitken Campbell	Glasgow	8	Union Discount
Maclean (R.A.) & Co.	Glasgow	9	independent

Table excludes other UK partners, overseas offices and stockbrokers operating in Scotland with non-Scottish partners.

Compiled March-August 1986 with the assistance of the Glasgow unit of the Stock Exchange.

often quoted in this context since prior to October 1986 it was prepared to deal in any USM stock irrespective of the profitability of such dealing. The two Scottish jobbers provide a similar service for Scottish stocks. By maintaining a book, encompassing all Scottish companies, the jobbers make it possible to deal in Scottish companies and improve the marketability of the smaller firms.[8] Aitken Campbell has announced that in the future it intends 'to concentrate on Scottish stocks . . . [and] will establish a niche for ourselves in the market.'[9] It is undertaking to make a market in all Scottish stocks. Specialisation by sector is not the only possibility. The Scottish jobbers, for example, provide a dealing facility that specialises in smaller quantities of stocks. Although the dealing process is often presented as a *de facto* acceptance of quoted prices, the jobbers are open to offers and will negotiate prices on deals. All large deals are negotiated but on the London floor most other deals do not offer this flexibility since the business available does not make it worth the firms' while to negotiate. Regional jobbers may be more prepared to negotiate on smaller deals and therefore offer brokers a more attractive service.

The existence of the regional floor does not formally depend on the existence of jobbers (market makers) but without them it is unlikely that it would continue. In their absence brokers would have to deal with London and might equally well use their own offices.

Besides their function of acting as agents for investors stockbrokers also provide a variety of services to their customers. Table 3.2, adapted from *Scottish Business Insider* July 1986 provides a summary of their services. Wood Mackenzie, the largest of the Scottish brokers,[10] currently functions in three main areas: sales and distribution, research, and corporate finance. Sales, primarily to institutional clients, cover UK equities, gilts, futures and options. Both overseas stocks and overseas clients are also covered and account for some 20 per cent of equity commission. Research, a major factor in Wood Mackenzie's growth, is directed at institutional sales and concentrates on a number of major sectors. A consequence of its expertise has been its entry into business publications and consultancy, an activity that has been growing rapidly (30 per cent per annum) and currently earns about one and a half million pounds.[11] The strength in research and sales has led the firm into corporate finance and it offers, from London, advice and sponsorship for new issues, underwriting and capital raising through placings, and advice on mergers and acquisitions. In short, it provides many of the advice functions of a merchant bank and indeed has joined with Hill Samuel to provide a wider range of services in the future. An interesting omission from the present range of services has been the absence of institutional fund management. Although supporting private client investment the firm does not offer fund management services unlike many of the larger London brokers. This may reflect its regional origins since many Scottish investment institutions express reservations about dealing through an

Table 3.2. Stockbroker services available in Scotland.

	Number of private clients	Minimum advisory portfolio	Other services
A.J.Bekhor & Co.	1000	no min.	ABCDEFG
Bell, Lawrie, MacGregor & Co.	n/d	no min.	ABCDEFGHIJK
Campbell Neill & Co.	10000	30000	ABCEFGHIKL
Capel-Cure Myers (Edinburgh)	850	variable	ABCDEFGHIJKLM
Carswell & Co.	2000	no min.	ACFGHL
Greig Middleton & Co.	12000	5000	AFG
Laing & Cruikshank	3000	no min.	ABCDEFGHIJKLM
Parsons & Co.	20000	no min.	ACEFGHIJK
Penney Easton & Co.	n/d	no min.	ACDEFGHIJK
Speirs & Jeffrey	5000	no min.	AFGHIJK
Stirling Hendry (inc. A.C.Anderson & Co.)	12500	no min.	AFGHIJK
Torrie & Co.	n/d	no min.	FGKL
Wishart, Brodie & Co.	3-4000	no min.	ABCDEFGHIJKLM
Wood Mackenzie & Co.	n/d	*	ABCEFGHIJKL

n/d not disclosed; * figures currently being revised.

Other services: A In-house financial planning; B Own unit trusts; C Corporate finance; D Newsletters; E Research; F Portfolio management; G Unit and investment trust advisory services; H Advice on life and pensions business; I Inheritance tax advice; J School fee plans advice; K Capital Gains Tax advice; L Advice on other investments such as options, traded options, Eurobonds, gold coins, etc.; M Financial futures information.

Source: Compiled from 'The mists begin to clear as Big Bang approaches' (R.Perman 1986).

organisation that is also a competitor.

Other Scottish stockbroking firms do not typically offer such a wide range of services or at least in such depth. Parsons is generally considered to be the second largest firm but with less than a third of the number of staff (115 to 375 approximately) it is very much smaller. Like Wood Mackenzie it has a substantial list of corporate clients (predominantly Scottish) but its major strength is its private client network (15–20000). It also offers insurance broking, pension and tax planning services as well as managing an investment trust. Parsons has linked with the London brokers James Capel and Postel, the Post Office pension fund, as part of a regional broking network, Allied Provincial Securities, consisting of eight brokers with 25 offices run from the Parsons office in Glasgow. The cash from the shareholdings sold to Capel (20 per cent) and Postel (20 per cent) is to be used for investment in computer systems and expansion. Allied will concentrate on private client business as well as researching and specialising in regional stocks. Other

Scottish stockbrokers such as Campbell Neill have also linked with London brokers, the attraction to Hoare Govett of its link with Campbell Neill apparently being the private client network. Penney Easton has followed a somewhat different path. The company has sold the 'back office' embracing the administrative side of the firm to Broker Services Ltd, a new company formed by Barclays Bank and the computer services firm NMW. Broker Services will provide administrative services to other brokers. Penney Easton has been freed to 'get on with the job of advising our clients and managing their funds – the income generation side of the business not the administrative side'.[12] The absence of any major link-up between the Scottish banks and the brokers remains a mystery. Bell Lawrie has sold 25 per cent of its equity to the Bank of Scotland and two investment trusts but the Bank's involvement is small. A considerable part of the business of the brokers emanates from the banking network (as much as a third according to some estimates) and many brokers are concerned about competition for this business. Several Scottish brokers would be severely affected by any significant changes in current practice. Generally the smaller brokers are less orientated to institutional business and the research that it demands, and more organised to serve the needs of their large private client base. The existence of regional brokers fosters the growth of private client networks and also provides a pool of skills that may be used by local companies. Research on local companies may improve marketability whilst corporate finance skills may assist in bringing new firms to the market as well as providing advice on a range of financial activities. Regional brokers offer services to local companies that may not otherwise be so readily available.

New Issues

Capital issues by Scottish companies have been in decline for a number of years. In the last six years, since the beginning of the 1980s, only nine Scottish companies have requested a full listing and nineteen an introduction on the Unlisted Securities Market (USM).[13] The USM in that same period has grown to 337 companies (December 1985) despite a considerable number of mergers, takeovers and other deaths. The figures highlight both the dearth of small Scottish companies coming forward and the insignificance of the Scottish institutions for primary issues. The majority of issues have been handled by a London based institution sometimes in association with a Scottish institution. This is not a new trend. Thomas (1973) notes that between 1946 and 1968 there were over 1000 Scottish new issues but that in no more than a dozen issues a year was a provincial broker sole broker and then only for small placings and introductions.

Quotation on the USM or on the Stock Exchange involves meeting demanding disclosure requirements that generally involve companies in considerable additional costs, since they require well-functioning accounting procedures. Managers are subject to greater scrutiny by the press and investors and may be subject to increased pressure to look at short term rather than long term prospects. It is also likely that the shares of existing shareholders will be valued more highly for tax puposes causing potential tax problems for the owners whilst if a considerable portion of the equity is sold the possibility of an unwelcome takeover bid also exists. To set against the problems associated with quotation there are some important advantages notably the ability of existing shareholders to readily realise part of their investment, easier access to new finance and to make acquisitions, and the improved trading status conferred by a quotation. Listing on the USM is possible if companies that have traded have had a three-year trading record (five years for the Exchange), 10 per cent of the equity is held in public hands (25 per cent for a full listing on the Stock Exchange (LSE)), and companies have a minimum capitalisation of around £0.5 million (according to most brokers) although there is no formal minimum market capitalisation (£5–10 million is commonly estimated as the minimum capitalisation although the formal minimum is only £0.7 million on the LSE). The average cost of a USM introduction for the period 1980–85 was £70000 (no allowance for inflation).[14] Costs for any individual company will vary according to the nature of the company's business and the need for capital reorganisations, preparation of profit forecasts and asset valuations. The main saving of the USM against the listed market is in the reduced advertising requirements so that savings in the region of £30000–£60000 might be expected.[15] Once quoted the continuing requirements of both the USM and full listing are similar. The USM is 'strongly regulated' in an attempt to provide adequate protection to investors and maintain their confidence.

The costs and requirements of quotation on the Stock Exchange (including the USM) are substantial. Although it was anticipated, when the USM was started, that it would provide the major means for small companies to raise capital, its disclosure and information requirements are enough to deter many smaller companies. The result has been the emergence of a third-tier market, the over-the-counter (OTC) market, outside the controls and requirements of the Stock Exchange and catering for smaller and new businesses. The market was born in 1972 when M.J. Nightingale (now Granville & Co.) started matching shares in large unlisted companies (buyers and sellers are matched at identical share prices and commission of one-and-a-quarter per cent is charged). Subsequently Harvard Securities acted as a market maker in speculative shares (outside the LSE) primarily for private investors and in 1983 started bringing companies to the OTC market. There are currently around 15 market makers (Wilmot 1985) dealing in OTC stocks. Transactions are carried out by licensed dealers who may buy and sell for their own account as well as deal directly with investors. The market is fragmented and telephone based but the procedures for buying and selling are similar to those operated by stockbrokers. The main differences arise with respect to the way in which shares are quoted and the nature of the stocks traded. Quotes may relate to a jobbing market in which the licensed dealer acts as a principal by keeping a book and buying and selling accordingly; on a matched bargain basis in which the desires of willing buyers and sellers are matched; and a negotiable price basis in which the dealer negotiates with potential buyers and sellers to try and establish a price at which a transaction can be completed.

The majority of OTC-quoted companies are new or emerging businesses with in most cases less than three years audited accounts. Dealings in OTC stocks is of a high risk nature since the market provides equity finance at an early stage in a company's development. The cost of coming to the market is not insignificant since the trade association, the British Institute of Dealers in Securities (BIDS) to which all the major active market makers except Granville & Co. are affiliated, imposes listing and prospectus requirements. Firms involved in an OTC issue must pay fees to external accountants, solicitors and professional advisers as well as produce and print a prospectus. Licensed dealers making issues are normally jealous of their reputations and will vet a company seeking a quote. However, there have been complaints from shareholders about the lack of information provided by some OTC companies after quotation and there may be grounds for regulation to force disclosure. There is inevitably a conflict between the reluctance of management to spend time on producing suitable information and the needs of investors to make informed decisions. It should not be the intention to protect investors from risk since it is the purpose of equity investment to bear the risk of an enterprise. The aim must be to provide enough information to protect the reputation of the market and the pockets of investors from fraud, but not so much that its production is a very real cost and deterrent to the entry of new companies.

OTC activity in Scotland has been small. Guidehouse, a specialist London issuing house, forged links in 1984 with a Leeds investment management company, Capital for Companies, with a view to offering an OTC market in the north of England, whilst at the same time linking with Glasgow-based Penney Easton & Co. and a London pensions consultancy, Richards, Longstaff, to coordinate the specialist services they offer. Edinburgh licensed dealers Clarke Farquharson and Partners were responsible for an OTC offer of Chieftain Industries, a Livingston-based company developing heat pumps. A number of Scottish stockbrokers such as Parsons' corporate division have also been active in this area.

The Future

Although much has been written on the effects of the change in Stock Exchange commission scales on the financial services industry relatively little has been written on the effect on the Scottish floor and regional stockbrokers. The immediate effect has been to accelerate the trend to mergers of existing firms but a number of other effects will slowly percolate through the industry.

The causes of the changes are buried in the recent history of the Exchange. Technological, political and economic pressures were all instrumental in bringing about changes.[16] The technological pressures were apparent from developments in the OTC market in the US and the Eurobond market in London. In the US the National Association of Securities Dealers Automated Quotation system (NASDAQ) provided immediate on-screen information of bid and offer prices supplied by market makers in all parts of the US, whilst in the Eurobond market, market makers bid and offer prices were displayed internationally on Reuter monitor screens and dealings were carried out by telephone. It appeared that there was no need for a central market place. The threat posed by Automated Real Time Investments Exchange (ARIEL) a decade earlier had re-emerged and was altogether more difficult to deal with.

Political pressures stemmed from the conditions of the Restrictive Trade Practices (Services Order) 1976 which required the Stock Exchange to register its Rules and Regulations and led to the identification by the Office of Fair Trading (OFT) of seventeen restrictions on trade. Legal battle was joined and the Stock Exchange and the Restrictive Trade Practices Court prepared cases. Further pressure arose from the investigations of the Wilson Committee together with the Conservative Government's belief in competition. The case of the Office of Fair Trading focused on the major restrictive practices, most notably the rules fixing minimum commission, and after several years of argument and delay this led to the agreement by the Stock Exchange to dismantle the rules prescribing minimum scales of commission.

Economic pressures arose from the increasing internationalisation of the securities markets. It became apparent that other markets, such as the Eurobond market, functioned effectively without the division between jobbers (market makers) and brokers (retailers). At the same time the London jobbing system was coming under economic pressure as the size and volume of transactions increased reflecting the growing dominance of the institutions and resulting in a fall in the number of jobbers.

Almost no new Stock Exchange firms entered the UK industry from the Second World War until the present although there were splits and mergers between existing firms. In economic terms there have been no serious restrictions on entry to the industry. The capital and skills required could easily have been obtained. The restrictions on entry stemmed from the self regulatory nature of the Exchange, governed by a Council composed predominantly of its own members and requiring a vote of the membership to change the Exchange's deed of settlement. The result was the increasing isolation of the Exchange and its failure to respond to changing needs and requirements. Difficulties faced by Stock Exchange firms in obtaining new capital restricted the growth of existing firms and caused a dramatic fall in the number of jobbers since the capital available to jobbers for maintaining a book failed to increase at the same rate as the size of institutional deals. Mergers were only a partial answer. The ability to restrict entry to the Exchange was reflected in the commission scales. Charges were not related to differences in brokers costs. Institutional business was excessively profitable and this led to extensive non-price competition offering investors research and elaborate sales presentations. The reduction in the ability of jobbers to handle large deals also encouraged the growth in 'put-through' deals in which a broker sells a block of stock for an institutional client directly to another institutional client and, when negotiated, the deal is put through a jobber. It is only a small step from such deals to leaving out of the transaction the jobber, and perhaps the broker, altogether. The computer system ARIEL, set up in 1972 by the Accepting Houses, did exactly that although it never attracted a large share of the market. More recently, the merchant bank Robert Fleming set itself up as an off-exchange market maker, dealing directly with investors in 31 quoted electrical stocks. It is believed to have gained 10 per cent of the market. Also important has been the growth in London of foreign brokers and investment bankers who, although they do little trade in the majority of UK equities, dominate London trading in US shares and Eurobonds and are increasingly important in dealings in the larger UK companies.

Foreign investment houses have gained an increasing portion of UK investment business, growth that was encouraged by the abolition of Exchange Control. At the same time transaction costs involved in purchasing UK equities have encouraged the spread of American Depositary Receipts (ADR). Shares of leading British companies are purchased by American banks and registered in their name. A Deposit Receipt is then issued against these shares and this receipt can be traded on the New York markets without further payments of stamp duty. This method of purchasing UK equities considerably reduced the costs of dealing. It is estimated that as much as 62 per cent of the trade in ICI in the second half of 1984 was in US markets and that ADRs as a whole accounted for 7 per cent of the turnover in the 100 major stocks.[17] American brokers were making a market (broking and jobbing) in the shares of the largest British companies outside the Stock Exchange. Total turnover between London member firms in all overseas securities in 1982 was £2.4 billion, while that by US brokers and banks in US equities alone on behalf of UK clients was approximately £10.7 billion. The growth of ADR business poses a serious threat to the Stock Exchange and there is force to the argument that the Exchange could not become a competitive international marketplace until the tax was reduced. It remains to be seen whether the reduction to half a per cent together with the tax on converting securities to ADRs is sufficient.

The decision to end minimum commission effectively killed the single capacity system. To remain viable brokers in a highly competitive environment needed to match a high percentage of buying and selling orders within their own organisations. If a complete match could not be achieved they would take the unplaced surplus for their own account or sell short. But if brokers were allowed to take stock for their own account, the jobbers would demand permission to deal direct with members of the public and single capacity would cease to exist. In addition, the Bank of England made proposals for the gilt-edged market which required future participants to have substantial financial resources.

Hand in hand with the move from minimum commission and single capacity have come changes in ownership and technology. The changes in ownership reflect the increased need for capital of member firms and the desire of other financial institutions, particularly the banks, to acquire a stake in the broking industry. Market making, especially in gilts, requires substantial resources whilst the removal of minimum commissions will reduce the ability of some firms to survive unaided. Coupled with a boom year (1985/86) for the Exchange, resulting in very high exit prices for member firms, the result has been a significant change in the ownership of broking and jobbing firms.[18] The technological changes largely centre on improvements in communications and the provision of information. For some years the Stock Exchange has provided the Teletext Output of Price Information by Computer (TOPIC) and this has been extended to provide a system similar to that of NASDAQ. Stock Exchange Automated Quotations (SEAQ) provide 'representative' bid and offer prices, taken from market makers' quotes, to members of the public. It also provides a more detailed service to broker/dealers giving information on bid and offer prices together with the amounts and the names of the participants.[19] The Exchange is also developing a Market and Trading Information System which will allow the automatic execution of small orders with significant cost savings. In parallel with the development of information systems the Exchange has introduced a central settlement system, TALISMAN, which has greatly simplified the settlement procedure. Further improvements in the system are planned, including links with the Clearing House Automatic Payment System (CHAPS).

The full impact of these changes on existing firms is as yet unknown. Suffice to say that the larger firms may take positions from time to time but smaller firms may continue in their traditional role as agents for private investors.[20] A number of specialist firms may also be set up offering discount brokerage and other such services. American experience in 1975 on the introduction of negotiated commissions is of particular interest. By 1977 institutional customers were paying on average only 67 per cent of the fixed commission rate on orders between 1000 and 10000 shares. Ninety per cent of individual orders experienced an increase in rates charged. Dealers specialising in providing research to institutions were particularly badly hit. Most of the firms went out of business or merged with other firms.[21] The lower levels of commission charged in the UK make it less likely that the effects will be so drastic here but commission income per transaction will undoubtedly be reduced although the reduced costs of trading will almost certainly lead to an increase in the volume of transactions.

A common criticism of the new structure is the concentration of power in the hands of a few large firms of broker/dealers. These firms, it is argued, will be interested primarily in the larger domestic and multinational companies and this will lead to a neglect of smaller, including Scottish, companies. It will no longer, it is claimed, be possible to allow the current levels of cross subsidisation of services to smaller stocks. However, not all participants in the market will be very large firms. Many firms may see benefits in specialising in particular areas of the market. Under the new structure they will be able to reinforce their dealing capacity by acting as principals in these smaller companies and it is quite probable that the marketability of many smaller stocks will be improved. There may be a loss of the subsidy presently given as a result of cross subsidisation from other activities, but at the same time, increased competition, greater specialisation and improved information and communication facilities including automatic execution, suggest that this subsidy will not be necessary.

In sum, the changes facing stock market firms as the Exchange modernises its practices and procedures are substantial. The firms are squeezed between the effects of rule book changes, which will reduce their receipts from carrying out purchases and sales, and the increased competition resulting from improved information systems and more and financially stronger competitors both within and outside the Exchange. To survive the firms must both reduce their costs and innovate so as to increase the volume of their sales. At present large institutional customers are provided with a package of services including advice, brokerage and research. Some or all of these service can be unbundled and charged for separately. There may also be scope for increasing the efficiency of operations, introducing new products and improving their marketing effort and many firms are currently making efforts in one or all of these directions.

Of the Scottish brokers Wood Mackenzie, with its orientation to research, would appear, from American experience, to be the most vulnerable. However, it has already unbundled some of its research and built up a substantial income from this aspect of its business. It has also been active in trading in international equities, a market that is already highly competitive and in which the current changes should help UK broking firms. The smaller Scottish broking firms with their extensive private client network are unlikely to suffer in the short term. Indeed, on the basis of American experience they may even benefit. In the longer term more aggressive competition from the larger stockbrokers through share shops and the offer of comprehensive financial planning and advice services, as well as from other financial institutions such as the banks, may be expected to affect their business. More aggressive marketing to the private sector, coupled with a Government committed to giving the personal sector a greater role and to encouraging private investment through Personal Equity Plans and other such devices, may be expected to expand the total market share so that whilst provincial stockbrokers will almost certainly lose market share in the private client area, the overall effect may be one of little change.

The introduction of SEAQ may be of real benefit to Scottish market makers as their quotations will be brought to the attention of a wider audience. At present, it is common for Scottish brokers to check both Glasgow and London prices but for London brokers to ignore prices on the regional floors. The SEAQ system will bring the quotations of provincial market makers to the attention of London brokers and may in consequence increase the flow of transactions to them. Given the lower costs of regional firms compared to those based in London, it should be possible for the firms, both jobbers and dealers, to operate on smaller margins and increase their proportion of the UK market. Improved information systems should work to the advantage of regional firms since it will give them immediate access to the whole UK market and enable them to take advantage of lower settlement and staff costs.

The changes in the structure of the market institutions and the introduction of SEAQ, which will provide much improved information on prices to institutions, raises the question of whether a trading floor is necessary. Brokers maintain that face-to-face dealing is easier and more pleasant than using the telephone and that the advantages are particularly apparent when there are very large volumes of transactions. Economic considerations suggest that telephone communication is cheaper than maintaining a floor position. Companies are freed from geographical restrictions which impose substantial costs on them and this suggests that there is likely to be a move away from the floor, particularly for smaller issues where transactions are relatively few and prices do not change rapidly. Large companies may continue to be dealt in on the floor although even here the move of business away from the floor will undermine the economics of maintaining a floor position.[22] The Scottish floor will be subject to two conflicting pressures. The increased competition from London-based brokers and institutions will move business away from Glasgow but at the same time the regional floor can provide many of the benefits of personal dealing without the cost of maintaining the same elaborate staffing.

Substantial changes are also possible in the new issue of securities. At present most listed companies use a merchant bank and a stockbroker as company advisers. New issues are organised by the merchant bank with the broker handling the sales. In the US new issues are normally syndicated through a group of investment banks, one bank taking the role of lead manager. The banks buy for their own account the whole issue and then sell it at a higher price to investors.[23] The banks act as underwriters to the issue.

Their activities in the new issue market are an extension of their market making function and it may be expected that this approach to new issues will become more significant in the UK. In principle, under the US system competition between investment banks keeps the costs of new issues very low but figures in Smith (1977) suggest that the advantages may be exaggerated. Costs in excess of 15 per cent for small issues are reported falling to 4 per cent for very large issues. For the UK, figures provided by Merrett, Howe and Newbould (1967) and Davis and Yeomans (1974) are higher for small issues but fall considerably with larger issues. Given the difficulty of cross-comparisons because of the effects of size, it is to be doubted if the advantages are enormous. Both systems have substantial fixed costs which greatly increase the cost of small issues whilst the difficulty of estimating an appropriate value for the firm is the same. The American system potentially benefits from competition between investment bankers to take the issue, the UK system from the reduced conflicts of interest since the investment banker determining the price is not also the purchaser of the stock.

It is unlikely that the changes in the new issue market will have a substantial impact on Scottish brokers and institutions. Wood Mackenzie, through its links with Hill Samuel, will be placed to offer investment banking services on the US pattern but the other Scottish brokers are too small to be substantially involved in large issues. Opportunities will exist for them to build on their current specialisations, most obviously in Scottish stocks and to compete in other less popular areas of the market. The current internationalisation of security markets may also offer opportunities to combine traditional investment skills in overseas markets with raising capital on the UK market for overseas companies. Small American companies might be more cheaply funded in the UK than in the US, a reflection of the differences in relative size. A modest issue in the US may be of considerable size in the UK and more cheaply handled in consequence.

Outside the Stock Exchange the outlook for the OTC market is favourable although the recent decision by the Stock Exchange to create a Third-Tier Market may have a dramatic effect on competition. The attraction of the relatively unfettered and low cost market to small, young, growing firms is manifest whilst the effects of the Business Expansion Scheme (BES) are such as to suggest that the market will expand greatly. The 1983 BES scheme replaced an earlier unsuccessful scheme and offers investors tax relief on equity investments in unquoted (including OTC) companies. Investments must be held for at least five years and may be either direct investment in a company or through a BES-approved fund which pools investors' money and invests in a number of suitable companies. Direct investment in OTC companies has already helped the market and it is possible that prices reflect, in part, the value of the tax relief, raising doubts about their future level. However, many BES funds have made investments in small companies which lack any active market in their shares and it is to be expected that at the end of the five-year holding period many investors will expect these companies to seek a listing on the USM or secure a quote on the OTC so as to improve their marketability. At present, Scotland is unlikely to benefit from any such increase in activity. There is no reason, however, why Scottish institutions should not be active in extending the OTC market. Several BES funds are managed from Scotland, although the BES scheme has proved difficult to apply in Scotland, and providing some of their investments prove profitable it should be possible for Scottish institutions to offer OTC facilities. Whilst it would be rash to suggest that American experience will be repeated here, and it is necessary to discount the more optimistic estimates that suggest that the market in ten years time will offer quotes on 4000–5000 companies with 50–100 market makers,[24] it is likely that the market will grow significantly and, given its telecommunications basis, could easily involve Scottish institutions as both market makers and issuing houses.

Prospects

An assessment of the likely shape and nature of the equity market in Scotland in the next five to ten years is fraught with danger. Rapid changes in the structure and organisation of UK markets make it difficult to predict the likely position and exacerbate attempts at forecasting. Secondary trading in securities for private clients looks set to be an area of growth but existing participants will have to compete for business more energetically than in the past. Existing private client networks will provide an element of stability but it is unlikely that customer loyalty will be too strong if faced with attractive offers from well known London brokers or increased direct marketing of brokerage services through separate share shops, banks and other intermediaries. The methods of sales and distribution currently being experimented with are numerous including both department stores and electronic viewdata systems and whilst not all will succeed it is unlikely that none will be successful. The majority of Scottish brokers have little experience of marketing their services and may find it difficult to be effective competitors. On the institutional side only Wood Mackenzie and to a lesser extent Parsons, Campbell Neill and Bell, Lawrie, MacGregor appear to be significantly involved and American experience would suggest that there is some danger of reduced business in this area. New issue activity could be a growth area but there will be strong competition for business and given the traditional orientation of many Scottish brokers to private clients and their consequent lack of expertise it is unlikely that most brokers will participate in this business. Wood Mackenzie and Parsons appear the most likely beneficiaries. An expansion of OTC activity in Scotland is to be expected since several institutions are interested in this area and the market, being telephone based, can as easily function here as elsewhere. The Scottish floor is likely to decline in importance as will the London floor. Its rapid obsolescence is inevitable given the introduction of improved dealing and information facilities, as well as limited automatic execution[25] which will greatly reduce its usefulness. It appears destined for extinction within five years. The Scottish jobbers may well flourish as market makers and could be joined by others. Wood Mackenzie has announced its intention to act as a market maker in both bonds and selected areas of the equity market, although it is unlikely to use the Glasgow floor.

The face of stockbroking will be very different in ten years time and although many existing Scottish firms may survive their share of the market will be greatly reduced. Marketing and the offer of a higher level of service to clients will be more significant than at present and some of the brokers do not have the financial muscle to compete effectively.

Scotland has been absent from the newer, fast-growing markets dealing in options, futures and other similar securities. Up to the present trading in these securities has been concentrated in London and there is little reason to expect that to change. The presence of American institutions in London provides it with a pool of investors who are experienced in dealing in these financial innovations. Skills and experience exist in London which it is difficult to find elsewhere. It is conceivable that new securities markets could develop elsewhere in the UK given the importance of telecommunications in these markets, but the initiation of markets requires resources, manpower and experience which most regional centres do not have. It would be possible for enterprising firms to commence trading in mortgage paper, for example, with standardised securities and a guarantee system but its unlikely that most regional firms have either the skills or the financial strength. It should be possible for Scottish firms to participate in these markets but it is unlikely, on present trends that the markets would be based anywhere but in London. The Eurobond market provides a useful example. Although the market is telephone based more than 450 foreign banks have found it desirable to have offices in London. Part of this may be explained by the need for an office in the European time zone but there also appears to be a locational factor that is difficult to explain but nevertheless present. There is no reason to believe that new security markets must be centred in London but until the pressure for innovation comes from outside the City they are unlikely to be situated elsewhere.

NOTES
1. For a discussion of the relationships between regional stock markets and London see W. A. Thomas (1973) and R. C. Mitchie (1981).
2. Estimates from W. B. Carmichael (1985) and from *The Stock Exchange Quarterly*.
3. Evidence for this view is attested by the continuing importance of the Birmingham floor in providing a market in small local issues. The main business of Birmingham is in the shares of small Midlands engineering companies.
4. Carmichael (1985) suggests that Scottish brokers always check the prices in both Glasgow and London before dealing.

5. The Glasgow floor benefited from the closure of the Manchester floor and now provides a market in a number of companies based or held primarily in the North of England. This has generated a considerable volume of extra business for the floor.
6. Market makers have the function of maintaining a two-way price in the securities in which they deal. They actively maintain a book of securities which enables them to make unmatched trades. The size of their book depends on their view of a company's prospects and market sentiment, and may be adjusted by appropriate changes in their bid and offer prices.
7. 156 Scottish voting members in 1975, 170 in 1985.
8. Carmichael (1985) states that the two firms of jobbers in the Glasgow market, Aitken Campbell & Co. and R. A. Maclean & Co., 'have made a firm committment to make a market in any Scottish based company coming either to full listing or to the U.S.M.'. Under Stock Exchange rules every security must have two jobbers. Jobbers can take on new securities in which they intend to deal without difficulty, but the two-jobbers rule may make it difficult to shed the less attractive securities. Jobbers once they accept a security are committed to act as dealers in that security and their compliance is checked by the Stock Exchange surveillance department.
9. W. Carmichael quoted in 'The mists begin to clear as Big Bang approaches' (Perman 1986).
10. Turnover approached 5 per cent of the UK equity market in 1985 compared to 2 per cent in 1986. There is some debate as to whether Wood Mackenzie is any longer a Scottish broker. It has offices in London as well as overseas and its business in dealing, sales and distribution, and corporate finance are all London-based. Edinburgh is responsible for settlement, private clients and research.
11. Wood Mackenzie had a major involvement in computing, particularly performance appraisal. This has been floated off as a separate company based in Edinburgh and currently employing more than 300 people.
12. Murdo Tolmie quoted in Perman (1986).
13. Alastair Balfour (1985).
14. Placing costs ranged from £68000–£188000 on average whilst Offers for Sale ranged from £212000–£1.25 million, depending on the amount raised. (Peat Marwick *USM Quarterly Survey* April 1985). Research by Davis and Yeomans (1974) on new issues on the London Stock Exchange indicates that both the size of the issue and the size of the Company are important determinants of the cost of an issue.
15. Cucksey and Medland (1984).
16. This section draws heavily on J. Dundas Hamilton (1986) and articles in *The Stock Exchange Quarterly*.
17. *Financial Times* 21 February 1985 and Dundas Hamilton (1986).
18. For a discussion of the changes and a table showing participation in UK Stock Exchange firms see *Bank of England Quarterly Bulletin*, December 1985.
19. For the purposes of display on SEAQ stocks traded on the Exchange are divided into four separate categories: alpha stocks, which are the most actively traded; beta stocks, which are less actively traded; and gamma and delta stocks, which are relatively inactive. Market makers must show firm, continuous two-way prices in alpha and beta stocks through SEAQ. All trades in alpha stocks are published immediately on TOPIC. The prices of gamma and delta stocks may be representative rather than firm.
20. Some commentators have argued that all brokers must become market makers to survive, because firms offering agency services akin to those of the traditional

Notes

broker will have to use a market maker for non-matched deals and hence will have higher costs than firms that can carry out both functions in-house. Whilst this is almost certainly true for large deals in frequently traded issues, for the less frequently traded stocks there is likely to be much greater specialisation with only one or two firms wishing to make a book in any particular security. In such stocks all brokers, whether market makers or not, may have to shop around for stocks they do not specialise in so that the investor will continue to require an agent who is in contact with other brokers and knows who is currently trading in what. 'By late September 1986 only 35 Stock Exchange firms had registered as market makers in equities – leaving the overwhelming majority of the 244 member firms committed primarily to old-style dealing as exclusive agents for investors' (*Financial Times* Survey, 'The City Revolution', 27 October 1986).

21. For a discussion of the effects of the removal of minimum commission charges in the US see Dundas Hamilton (1986), S. Smidt in Polakoff *et al.* (1981), and *The Economist* 'New York's Dummy Run', 16 August 1986.
22. Spicer & Pegler Associates ('Future of Stockbroking in Scotland', briefing paper for the SDA, 8 May 1985) suggests that 80–90 per cent of business by value will move off the London floor. It expects the impact on the Scottish floor to be less. Orders for SEAQ equipment as of December 1985 suggest that in October 1986 there will be 64 market-making firms using SEAQ compared to 15 jobbing firms in the Stock Exchange. Of these market makers 26 are requiring some facilities on the floor and the remainder are operating directly from their offices.
23. The arguments with respect to rights issues are somewhat different. American companies are not required to offer their existing shareholders new issues in proportion to the old shares held. Some American stockbrokers argue that UK companies are made worse off because of the need to issue securities below the current share price and that this system should change (*The Times*, 31 January 1986). Such a view is misconceived since the rights offering does not affect the real plant and equipment owned by the company. The firm may choose to issue a greater number of shares at a lower price or a few at a high price. As long as rights are exercised there is no cost to the company. Indeed, if setting a low price removes the need for expensive stand-by arrangements it may be beneficial to offer rights at a low price.
24. See, for example, Wilmot (1985).
25. The issue of automatic execution raises many strong feelings. That it is possible has been demonstrated by the Cincinnatti Exchange which is totally electronic, but doubts remain about the advantages of such a system. Power cuts are a perennial problem of computer systems but more important perhaps are fears relating to the security of such systems. Automatic execution could enable firms to take orders beyond their financial capacity with possibly disastrous consequences for other members who are not protected from the default of a fellow member. Small trades automatically executed do not raise such fears since potential losses are manageable but there is real concern over automatic execution of very large deals. Fears such as these suggest that the move to full automatic execution will be slow with members gaining experience and building in safeguards. Pressure for such schemes will stem from their cost advantages, benefits which will increase as manpower increases in price.

4

THE SCOTTISH CLEARING BANKS

The Scottish clearing banks form a separate and distinct group of commercial banks in the United Kingdom. The three banks – Bank of Scotland, the Royal Bank of Scotland and the Clydesdale Bank,* the latter owned by the Midland Bank, are among the most important financial institutions in Scotland providing through their extensive branch networks for the general deposit-taking, lending and money transmission needs of the economy. Both Bank of Scotland and the Royal Bank of Scotland have their head office in Edinburgh, while Clydesdale Bank is based in Glasgow. The Royal Bank has 864 branches with over 500 in Scotland. This compares with the Bank of Scotland's 550 and Clydesdale's 370 branches, virtually all in Scotland. The Royal Bank employs just under 17000 staff with about half in Scotland. Bank of Scotland employs 9500 and Clydesdale 7000. In balance sheet terms the Royal Bank of Scotland is almost twice the size of Bank of Scotland and about five times the size of Clydesdale Bank. At September 1985 the total assets of the Scottish clearing banks amounted to £15.1 billion. Those of the six London clearing banks amounted to £141 billion.[1]

The most basic function of any financial system is to facilitate payments of all kinds in the economy. Without an efficient payments mechanism the financial system would have great difficulty in performing its borrowing, lending and other functions. Responsibility for the operation of the payments mechanism in the UK falls on the Bank of England, the London and Scottish clearing banks and the Northern Ireland banks.[2] Together these banks (excluding the central bank) can be considered the principal retail banks in the UK.

The Scottish clearing banks carry out the vast bulk of the cash distribution and money transfer activities in Scotland but, fundamental though this is, they have an equally important role to play as financial intermediaries, channelling funds from those in surplus to those who wish to borrow. This

* As this book was in press it was announced that the Midland is to sell the Clydesdale to the National Australia Bank (NAB). The sale should free the Clydesdale from some of the constraints it has laboured under in recent years arising from the Midland's problems elsewhere, but raises interesting questions about the motivation and future strategy of the NAB in this acquisition. For one of the author's views on the takeover see the finance section of the Fraser of Allander Quarterly Commentary, vol. 13 no. 1 (August 1987).

Introduction

facilitates the effective accumulation and efficient allocation of capital in the Scottish economy, though their activities are by no means confined to Scotland, or indeed the UK. The Scottish clearing banks are involved in both retail and wholesale deposit-taking and lending. They meet the payments and liquidity requirements of their depositors through non-interest bearing current accounts. Other less liquid funds are attracted through a variety of interest-bearing retail deposit accounts. Retail lending involves the Scottish banks in overdraft and instalment loans to persons, house purchase finance, and overdraft and term loans to small businesses.

Wholesale business involves the banks in taking large deposits for a variety of terms and at higher rates of interest than those on deposit accounts, deploying liquid funds in money market instruments and making large term loans. Banks therefore cater for the needs and requirements of big business as well as those of other financial intermediaries. The Scottish banks are not heavily involved in the wholesale deposit market although they do make use of these deposits to finance their loans. The majority of their loans are financed by retail liabilities but shortages or surpluses of funds arising from retail activities are accommodated through the wholesale deposit market. In both retail and wholesale deposit markets borrowers generally want access to funds for long periods. In contrast, all other things being equal, lenders want to hold liquid deposits. The result is that banks must engage in maturity transformation since the average maturity of their loans is considerably greater than that of their deposits. In addition, individual loans are frequently larger than individual deposits and while banks, by holding a well diversified portfolio, can limit the risk attached to making loans they cannot remove it altogether. Because of the size, risk and maturity transformation that they carry out the banks obtain a higher return on the funds they lend than they offer for the funds that they borrow. This margin goes to cover their expenses of operation and provide a profit.

An important role of a financial system is to facilitate the flow of funds between different sectors of the economy, for example between the personal sector and the company sector. This role has long been carried out by the banks. Bain (1981) comments that

> the banks are the general deposit-takers and lenders in the economy; taken as a whole they show no sector preference or specialisation. But they are more than this, for they are also the residual lenders in the economy. It is to the banks that borrowers turn for funds, when they either cannot or do not wish to raise them elsewhere.

Of course, there is no guarantee that the banks will make a loan to a potential borrower. Nevertheless, the Scottish clearing banks play a very important role in Scotland both as residual lenders and as general deposit-takers and lenders.

The Scottish clearing banks undertake the important task of providing a payments mechanism throughout Scotland and between Scotland and the rest of the UK. They compete in Scottish and UK financial markets to secure surplus cash and savings through the issue of appropriate liabilities, and to secure growth by the purchase of profitable loan assets thereby providing finance for economic activity. Banking forms the major part of the operations of the three banks, but they have over the years established a number of subsidiary and associate companies to provide their customers with a wide range of complementary and ancillary financial services. These have in recent times been a growing part of their business.

In the five sections of chapter 4 the three Scottish clearing banks are examined in detail. Domestic banking operations; international banking operations; ownership, competition and performance; new directions and new technologies are all considered. In addition, a perspective of the Scottish clearing banks is provided together with our conclusions. An appendix to the chapter provides additional material on the deposit-taking and lending activities of the Scottish clearing banks. The merchant bank and finance house activities of the three banks are not considered in this chapter[3] but are dealt with in chapter 6.

Domestic Banking Operations

The domestic banking operations of the Scottish clearing banks are included under three separate headings: money transmission; deposit-taking and lending; and branching and employment.

Money Transmission

The key factor that distinguishes the clearing banks from other banking and deposit-taking institutions in the UK is their dominance of the payments system. Methods of payment take a variety of forms but by far the most important means are cash and cheques and for these purposes the clearing banks operate deposit facilities, comprising current accounts and deposit accounts withdrawable on demand or at short notice and maintain a stock of cash in the form of notes and coins. In Scotland the three clearing banks handle the vast majority of payments. These facilities are used by all sectors of the economy – public, personal, business and financial. Settlement of indebtedness occurs largely by way of non-cash payments through the Scottish clearing system. Current account balances transferrable by cheque form the largest proportion of such payments but credit transfers, standing orders and direct debits are also significant.

Indebtedness arising from the daily cheque clearings in Edinburgh and Glasgow between the three Scottish banks are settled by drawing on their balances at the Bank of England. A similar procedure operates for settlement with other UK banks through London.

Figures for the inward paper clearing of the three Scottish banks and TSB Scotland indicate that 202 million items were cleared in 1982 and this increased to 227 million items by 1985.[4] Almost 90 per cent of the clearings were debit items such as drafts and cheques, which are drawn on the reporting bank, and the remainder credit items such as credit transfers and standing orders, which are presented for crediting to accounts held with the reporting bank. The English clearing system by comparison handled 2871 million paper items in 1985. In recent times there has been a substantial rise in the cost of operating the payments system due to the rapid growth in the volume of paper transactions, predominantly payments by cheque, that require to be handled by the banks.[5] This has led to closer co-operation between the clearing banks both in the development of a clearing house and electronic payments systems which can help reduce the volume of paper processing.

The Royal Bank of Scotland is one of nine settlement members of the Cheque and Credit Clearing Company, which operates the high-volume paper (general debit and credit) clearings through the Clearing House in London. All three Scottish clearing banks are settlement members of Bankers Automated Clearing Services (BACS), which carries out electronic clearing of items such as direct debits, standing orders and credit transfers. They are also settlement members of the CHAPS[6] and Town Clearing Company since many of their high-value transactions pass through their City offices, particularly their inter-bank and other large money-market transactions.

The Scottish clearing banks are members of the Society for Worldwide Inter-bank Financial Telecommunications (SWIFT), which operates computer systems for the processing of international payments between the 1257 member banks at mid-1985. Bank of Scotland, along with Mellon Bank of Pittsburgh, has developed TAPS (Trans-Atlantic Payments System), a satellite-linked, computer-based international remittance system to provide a cheaper and faster means of sending personal volume payments to the United States.

Credit cards provide an attractive means of payment and a ready source of credit for personal customers of the banks. An innovation of American origin, the first UK cards were promoted by the London clearing banks in the late 1960s and early 1970s. The Access card venture (now part of the Mastercard operation) was set up by Lloyds, Midland, National Westminster and the Royal Bank Group. Both Clydesdale Bank and the Royal Bank of Scotland issue their own Access cards under the Mastercard scheme. Bank of Scotland is affiliated to the Visa scheme and issues its own Visa card. Membership of these schemes brings the advantages of centralised administration and widespread acceptance of the card by retail and service trades. At present credit cards are second only to bank loans and overdrafts as a means of credit purchases in Britain. Unfortunately there are no credit card statistics for Scotland alone. Credit cards are not a substitute for paper handling since transactions generate vouchers and cheques are used to settle accrued payments at monthly intervals. However, vouchers do not enter the clearing system and generally fewer cheque payments are made by card owners.

One of the most significant modern innovations in money transmission has been the development of automated cash dispensers which provide customers with access to current account funds outwith the banks and often on a 24-hour basis. The Scottish clearing banks have been at the forefront of this application of technology to money transmission and the Royal Bank of Scotland is credited with having successfully pioneered the electronic cash dispenser in the UK. The three Scottish clearing banks operate automated teller machine (ATM) networks throughout Scotland. At the end of 1984 the Scottish clearers had a total of 753 cash dispensers in place. Including the Royal Bank's ATM installations in England, by the end of 1985 over 1000 cash dispensers were operated by the Scottish clearers. Automated cash dispensers have also been extensively introduced by the English clearing banks although customers of the Scottish clearing banks have recorded a higher usage than those of the English banks. In 1984 average transactions per machine per month in Scotland and England were estimated at 6000 and 4200 respectively. The Royal Bank of Scotland processed 25.5 million ATM transactions out of a Scottish clearing bank total of 53.2 million in 1984 (Clydesdale 14.5 million, Bank of Scotland 13.2 million) and was among the first to provide access to deposit account funds through its machines.

The advantages to the Scottish economy of an efficient payments system are clear. The advantage to the Scottish clearing banks lies in the ability to build relationships with users from whom they obtain retail deposits and to whom they can offer a range of loans and other financial services. The banks consider retail funds (current and deposit) as a 'premium' source as they are more stable and reliable than wholesale money. Howcroft and Lavis (1986) argue that the clearing banks see payments systems only as a means to attract cheap deposits and potential borrowers and not as a product in its own right. The banks form an oligopoly in the provision of payments services but members compete strongly with each other for market share. The result of this is that the clearing banks adopt, according to Howcroft and Lavis, 'irrational' pricing policies for their payments systems. Fee income recovers only 35–40 per cent of the costs of operating the payments mechanism and notionally free current-account balances, the main mechanism for money transmission, only contribute when interest rates rise above their costs of operation. These are estimated to amount to 9 per cent in terms of equivalent interest payments on outstanding current account balances.[7]

Howcroft and Lavis argue that the clearing banks are faced with dilemmas arising from the way they perceive and provide payments systems. In order to control the rapidly rising volumes of transactions and associated costs which are not recovered by direct charges closer co-operation among the clearing banks and with other institutions is desirable. For example, the admission of new members to the clearing settlement organisations or shared cash dispenser networks. However, co-operation may also speed up the elimination of the clearing banks' oligopoly and may compromise the ability of the banks to pursue their own innovative payments systems. Payments services are seen as a way of establishing a share of the lending and financial services market. The result is that competitors have a strong incentive to provide more efficient and less costly payments facilities. To protect or increase their market position the clearing banks have to respond by further investment in new payments technologies but at the same time must maintain their existing costly and less efficient systems.

Different approaches are taken to resolve this dilemma. The Scottish clearing banks are involved in co-operative ventures such as BACS and CHAPS and credit card links with Access and Visa. The three banks continue to underprice their payments services in an attempt to maintain their market share of cheap deposits and potential borrowers and rely on co-operation to assist in the containment of overheads. Money transmission is not always viewed as a separate product in its own right and investment in new technologies is often aimed at maintaining market share under the threat of competition from the TSB, building societies and other banks. However, co-operative ventures do not always include the same companies. Clydesdale Bank is linked to a separate cash dispenser network from the Bank of Scotland and the Royal Bank, and new approaches to payments technology, as for example, Bank of Scotland's home banking service, have been adopted. The three banks, in general, seek to distinguish their payments services.

The choices the Scottish clearing banks face in developing their payments systems are complex. They will have to countenance greater external co-operation and competition and must decide how best to strike a balance between these. More rational pricing and new attitudes to money transmission may be called for. Money transmission lies at the heart of their retail banking operations and it is probable that strategies for its development will influence many areas of their banking activity.

Deposit-Taking and Lending
In this section of chapter 4 we look at both sides of the Scottish clearing banks' balance sheet and discuss their main deposit-taking and lending activities and at how they facilitate the flow of funds between the different sectors of the Scottish economy. Where appropriate comparisons are drawn between the three Scottish banks and the five London clearing banks.[8]

Table 4.1 presents the aggregate balance sheet of the three Scottish clearing banks and their subsidiaries for November 1975 and 1980, and August 1985. It shows the main assets of the banks and their deposit liabilities. At August 1985 total sterling deposits amounted to just over £10.6 billion, with sight deposits accounting for 35 per cent, and the balance consisting of interest-bearing time deposits including certificates of deposits.

Table 4.1. Balances of the three Scottish clearing banks and their subsidiaries, as at 1975, 1980 and 1985.

	1975	1980	1985
Liabilities			
Sterling deposits:			
Sight	986	1791	3753
Time (inc. CDs)	1494	3248	6862
Total	2480	5039	10615
Foreign currency deposits	369	1436	2986
Total deposits	2850	6474	13600
Notes in circulation	271	487	745
Other liabilities	587	1018	2186
Total liabilities	3708	7979	16532
Assets			
Sterling			
Notes, coins and balances with Bank of England	304	505	815
Market loans	531	941	2019
Bills	198	274	134
Special deposits with Bank of England	60	—	—
Investments	201	241	522
Advances	1621	3780	8663
Other sterling assets	409	748	1159
Foreign currencies	383	1489	3219
Total assets	3708	7979	16532

1. Figures for 1975 and 1980 are for the Banking Sector and figures for 1985 are for the Monetary Sector. This gives rise to a very small discrepancy in the series (see note 9 at end of chapter).
2. Figures for 1975 and 1980 are at November. Figures for 1985 at August.

Source: Statistical Unit, Committee of London and Scottish Bankers.

Foreign currency deposits amounted to almost £5 billion. The remaining liabilities of the banks comprise notes in circulation, and other liabilities which consist of items in suspense and transmission, that is to say payments due but not yet made or cleared, and capital and other funds. These liabilities amounted to £2.9 billion, representing 17.7 per cent of total liabilities.

The sight deposits of the Scottish clearing banks comprise non-interest bearing and interest bearing current accounts, money at call (except where there is an agreement not to withdraw before a certain date or to call at a

Domestic Banking Operations

specific number of days' notice) and money placed overnight. Sight deposits are transferable or withdrawable on demand without a penalty being imposed in the form of loss of interest.

Table 4.2 shows the division between current accounts and deposit and savings accounts by number, for both the Scottish clearing banks and the London clearing banks between 1975 and 1984. The current accounts of the Scottish banks have shown the greatest growth over the period, and are now very close to deposit and savings accounts in number.

Table 4.2. Number of accounts with London and Scottish clearing banks (thousands).

End December	1975	1979	1980	1981	1982	1983	1984
Scottish Clearing Banks							
Current accounts	1206	1725	1886	2000	2133	2224	2317
Deposit and savings accounts	1962	2286	2343	2402	2437	2507	2570
London Clearing Banks							
Current accounts	18862	21097	21769	22506	23428	23918	23755
Deposit and savings account	11341	11428	12227	12724	13143	14054	14923

Source: Statistical Unit, Committee of London and Scottish Bankers.

Figures for the relative values of current and deposit accounts are unavailable but current accounts form a smaller proportion of total sterling deposits, by value, for the Scottish clearing banks (16 per cent at August 1985) than they do for the London clearing banks (19 per cent). It is unlikely that this slightly higher endowment of non-interest bearing accounts provides a cost advantage of any great significance to the London clearers. Both the Scottish clearing banks and the London clearing banks have recently introduced interest-bearing current accounts so that the distinction between current and deposit and savings accounts is disappearing.

At August 1985 almost 68 per cent of Scottish clearing bank total sterling deposits had an outstanding maturity of less than 8 days and most of these deposits (40 per cent of the total) were sight deposits. Just over 13 per cent of the total had an outstanding maturity of 8 days to one month; and a further 10 per cent, one to three months. Very few time deposits, only 9 per cent, had an outstanding maturity exceeding 3 months.

Table 4.1 shows that between November 1975 and August 1985 the total sterling deposits of the Scottish clearing banks grew from just under £2.3 billion to £10.6 billion, equating to an average annual rate of growth of 16.0 per cent.[9] Although these figures are expressed in nominal terms this represents a real growth in sterling deposits. By comparison, the average yearly growth of the sterling deposits of the London clearing banks over the same period was 14.3 per cent. These deposits amounted to just under £104.1 billion at August 1985.

It is impossible to distinguish statistically between the retail and wholesale activities of the Scottish clearing banks. They are involved with the full spectrum of lending and compete aggressively for new opportunities to make loans with the funds that they can raise through issuing deposits. This has led the banks to state that the growth of their banking business is asset-driven. Certainly, given the existence of the wholesale money markets it is unlikely that the banks would be prevented from making a loan due to a shortage of retail bank funds. When they have a shortage of funds, they will bid for them in the wholesale market.

Borrowing in the money market by the Scottish banks from other banks is not large. They do, however, accept significant sums from their corporate customers which can be considered wholesale in nature rather than retail. These funds may in turn be placed in the market as circumstances dictate. It appears that the two Edinburgh banks make greater use of wholesale funds, including inter-bank deposits, to finance their loans than does the smaller Clydesdale Bank. As well as channelling retail and wholesale deposits into loans the three clearing banks receive a flow of loan repayments which are available for redeployment in new loans or other investments.

At August 1985 almost £3 billion of the Scottish clearing banks' funds were held in a variety of short-term assets either as balances with the Bank of England, market loans, local authority and other sterling bills or notes and coins. Banks with eligible liabilities of £10 million or more are liable to lodge with the Bank of England non-operational, non-interest-bearing deposits (cash ratio deposits) amounting to 0.5 per cent of their eligible liabilities.[10] While these funds represent liquid reserves for the banks their main function is to provide a subsidy for the Bank of England. The eligible liabilities of the three Scottish banks amounted to £8660 million at August 1985 requiring cash ratio deposits of £43m.[11] The banks are also liable for calls to lodge special deposits, which can earn interest, with the Bank of England and these deposits have been used to assist control of the supply of bank finance in the economy. However, there has been no call for these deposits since 1980. The three Scottish banks also keep small working balances with the Bank of England. The bulk of the £3 billion, however, reflects the Scottish banks' own judgement of their need for short-term or liquid assets and the majority of these assets (68 per cent) consist of market loans to members of the London discount market or other monetary sector institutions including certificates of deposit and all balances (including correspondent balances) with banks overseas. Bain (1981) points out that while these assets satisfy the need for liquidity of the individual bank which holds them, they cannot be regarded as a source of liquidity for the banking system as a whole.

Notes, coins and balances with the Bank of England is an interesting feature of the Scottish clearing banks' balance sheet. At August 1985 notes, coins and balances formed 6.1 per cent of their total sterling assets compared to 1.3 per cent for the London clearing banks. The higher figure arises because the Scottish banks still issue their own notes and these need only be 'covered' by Bank of England notes and coins after they have actually passed into circulation. The asset entry of £815 million is therefore partly matched by the oustanding notes entry of £745 million on the liabilities side of the balance sheet. The £745 million also includes a fixed amount of Scottish bank notes that do not require to be covered by Bank of England notes for historical reasons. This 'authorised' circulation of notes amounts to £2.7 million. The remainder of the asset entry for notes, coins and balances (£815 million less £742.3 million) is composed of Scottish clearing bank holdings of each others' notes, 'free' notes held to meet the requirements of depositors and balances at the Bank of England.

The principal earning assets of the three Scottish banks are their advances to customers and investments. Advances amounted to almost £8.7 billion at August 1985 (52 per cent of total assets) and include loans made to the UK public and private sectors and to overseas residents. Investments comprise British government (mainly gilt-edged) and local authority stocks, and investments in other members of the monetary sector (mainly subsidiary and associate companies). These provide interest income to the banks and because most are short-dated and marketable also provide additional liquidity. Other sterling assets consist of items in suspense and collection, assets for leasing and land, premises and equipment.

Table 4.1 shows that the sterling advances of the Scottish clearing banks and their subsidiaries increased from 65 per cent of total sterling deposits at November 1975 to a level of 75 per cent by November 1980 and 82 per cent by August 1985. The ratio for the London clearing banks over the same period stood at 56 per cent in 1975, 63 per cent in 1980 and 70 per cent in 1985. The greater proportion of advances to deposits by Scottish banks may reflect the relatively greater volume and value of London clearing banks' current accounts as a proportion of their total sterling deposits and thus a need to maintain a higher proportion of liquid assets, though it is not a complete explanation. Between 1975 and 1985 the advances of the three Scottish banks grew by a factor of 5.3 compared with 4.6 for the London banks.

The appendix to chapter 4 deals with the lending operations of the three Scottish clearing banks in greater detail than space allows here. The main concern in this section is to look at the role of the three banks in transferring funds between surplus and deficit units in the Scottish economy. The Scottish clearing banks carry out two main types of lending: short term or retail lending which includes overdrafts and bills of exchange or acceptance credits, and term or wholesale lending where loans are made for periods of between 2 to 10 years. Because the overdraft facility is very often renewed or 'rolled-over' annually some borrowers effectively have a permanent loan equivalent to the minimum overdrawn balance. Overdraft finance can be used for a variety of financing needs but most corporate customers use it for

Table 4.3. Sources and distribution of banking funds (UK residents)[1] of Scottish and London clearing banks[2] (£ billion).

	Scottish clearing banks						London clearing banks					
	Sources of funds (deposits)			Distribution of funds (lending)			Sources of funds (deposits)			Distribution of funds (lending)		
	1978	1981	1985	1978	1981	1985	1978	1981	1985	1978	1981	1985
Public sector	0.10	0.10	0.14	0.04	0.14	0.08	0.58	0.83	1.30	0.28	0.37	0.35
Other financial institutions	0.34	0.56	1.72	0.07	0.06	1.07	2.03	3.37	7.63	0.73	1.23	5.05
Industrial and commercial companies	0.77	1.27	2.25	1.02	1.89	2.76	8.18	11.94	16.85	11.59	20.37	22.72
Personal sector:												
Persons, households and individual trusts	1.40	2.39	2.93	0.43	1.09	2.38	14.49	24.08	29.68	5.00	11.11	24.24
Other[3]	0.65	0.99	1.52	0.58	1.12	1.84	5.19	8.14	11.68	2.97	7.02	12.28
Total all UK residents	3.26	5.31	8.56	2.14	4.30	8.13	30.47	48.36	67.14	20.57	40.10	64.65

1. Excluding deposits from and lending to monetary sector institutions, and lending under special schemes for exports and shipbuilding.
2. Including subsidiaries.
3. Comprises unincorporated business of sole traders and partnerships and private non-profit making bodies.

Source: Statistical Unit, Committee of London and Scottish Bankers.

working capital. Unlike the overdraft the term loan is not repayable on demand but subject to an agreed contractual repayment arrangement which can be linked to the financial benefits or cash stream accruing from the funded project.

Other types of bank lending include instalment credit, mortgage finance, leasing and factoring. The Scottish clearing banks provide a range of financing for the different sectors of the economy for a variety purposes.

The sources of the Scottish and London clearing bank sterling deposits and their distribution (lending) by sector is shown in table 4.3 at the end of 1978 and 1981 and for June 1985. These figures provide a broad indication of how the banks are involved in transferring funds from one sector of the economy to another, though transfers also occur within sectors. The figures for the personal sector are disaggregated to show separately lending to persons, households and individual trusts. The rest of the sector, or 'other' includes unincorporated business of sole traders and partnerships. Thus, some lending to industry appears under the personal sector heading.

The banks have traditionally been viewed as collecting funds from the personal sector and channelling these deposits to industrial and commercial companies. At the end of 1978, the personal sector accounted for 63 per cent of the Scottish banks' sterling deposits, but only 47 per cent of the banks' lending was returned to this sector. The respective figures for the London banks were 65 per cent and 39 per cent. In contrast, industrial and commercial companies received 48 per cent of the lending but supplied only 24 per cent of the deposits of the Scottish clearing banks (56 per cent and 27 per cent, London banks). However, clearing bank advances to the personal sector have risen consistently faster than advances to the other sectors throughout the 1980s. Thus at June 1985 the personal sector accounted for 52 per cent of the Scottish banks' sterling deposits but also received 52 per cent of the lending (62 per cent and 56 per cent, London banks) whereas the industrial and commercial companies received a smaller share of lending (34 per cent) and provided 26 per cent of deposits (35 per cent and 25 per cent, London banks). The public sector tends to hold a higher level of bank deposits than bank loans as also do other financial institutions.

The increased proportion of lending to the personal sector in recent times is, in part, due to the less regulated financial climate in which the banks have operated. There has been little official action to limit the expansion of monetary sector lending to persons. In addition the strong growth in the demand from individuals for loans for house purchase and consumer spending has coincided with more modest demands from industry as a result of the erosion of Scotland's industrial base. A more detailed look at the allocation of the Scottish clearing banks' sterling and foreign currency funds is provided in the appendix.

The terms and conditions on which Scottish clearing bank finance is made available to borrowers differs little from that of the UK monetary sector.

Table 4.4. Number of Scottish clearing bank branches, 1975–85.

End December	1975	1976	1977	1978	1979	1980	1981	1982	1983	1984	1985
No. of Branches											
Bank of Scotland											
Full	398	387	386	381	377	378	375	375	374	369	
Sub	182	181	190	193	191	191	191	183	176	176	
Mobile	10	10	9	10	10	10	9	9	9	9	
Total	590	578	585	584	578	579	575	567	559	554	551
Clydesdale Bank											
Full	331	330	330	333	337	339	342	341	343	340	
Sub	31	37	38	38	38	37	37	41	38	35	
Mobile	5										
Total	367	367	368	371	375	376	379	382	381	375	370
The Royal Bank of Scotland											
Full	486	485	485	484	481	474	470	461	448	429	
Sub	94	95	97	99	113	125	121	123	126	120	
Mobile	17	16	16	17							
Total	597	596	598	600	594	599	591	584	574	549	
Total incl. Williams & Glyn's	916	918	923	920	915	913	903	901	894	873	864
Total Branches											
Full	1215	1202	1201	1198	1195	1191	1187	1177	1165	1138	
Sub	307	313	325	330	342	353	349	347	340	331	
Mobile	32	26	25	27	10	10	9	9	9	9	
Total	1554	1541	1551	1555	1547	1554	1545	1533	1514	1478	
Total incl. Williams & Glyn's	1873	1863	1876	1875	1868	1868	1857	1850	1834	1802	1785

Source: Statistical Unit, Committee of London and Scottish Bankers.

Borrowers are normally charged interest on their overdrafts or loans at a fixed margin over the banks' base rates or some other base such as the London Inter-Bank Offered Rate (LIBOR), though this is now less influential than during the 1960s and 1970s. The margin depends upon the borrower, the purpose of the borrowing, the term of the loan, the security offered and loan vehicle used. The base rate of interest is influenced by the general structure of interest rates that prevail in the UK (see also appendix). The rates of interest that banks offer to their retail depositors will depend upon their required margins though competition ensures that they pay the going price.

Branching and Employment

Branching. The three Scottish clearing banks are distinguished from other financial institutions in Scotland by their extensive branch networks.[12] The size and location of their branch networks is an important factor contributing to the competitiveness of the banks. For most customers their main point of contact with the bank is through the branch where they hold an account. The branches of the banks collect retail deposits, arrange loans and provide advice to borrowers on their financial needs, issue cash and facilitate payment transfers within the banking system, and increasingly sell a wider range of financial services from travellers cheques and foreign currency exchange to securities purchase, insurance and general financial advice.

The branches of the Scottish clearing banks are dispersed throughout Scotland, although greater concentration occurs in major centres of population. The Royal Bank of Scotland has a large number of branches in England and Wales, which were formerly branches of Williams and Glyn's, the majority located in the North West. As table 4.4 illustrates, the total number of branches in Scotland fell from 1554 to 1478 between 1975 and 1984,[13] a net closure of 76 branches. The fall in the number of branches in Scotland accelerated towards the end of this period largely due to the two Edinburgh banks amalgamating a number of their own overlapping outlets. The Royal Bank's Williams and Glyn's branches in England and Wales remained steady in number between 1975 and 1984, the net result of some amalgamations and a programme of new openings. The total number of Clydesdale Bank branches increased slowly until 1983, a reflection of its smaller network and its historical concentration in the West and North East of Scotland. However, numbers have been reduced in the past two years. The desire to cut costs has motivated the closure of less economic branches. The dilemma facing the banks is how to rationalise their branch networks while maintaining a geographical dispersal that serves both the major urban populations and the more isolated communities. The banks are aware that their extensive and long established branch networks bring with them a certain social responsibility and that the sudden closure of a large number of less economic branches would deprive customers and communities of ready access to the banking system and result in a significant loss of goodwill. Branch closure policies are motivated by long-term considerations.

It is often observed that Scotland has more bank branches per head of population than does the rest of the United Kingdom and it is certainly true that many of Scotland's main towns and urban areas have a branch of each clearing bank and often the TSB. More significant, however, is that a number of branches of the same bank are to be found in close proximity to one another, where one large branch would appear to offer cost savings to the bank through economies of scale without a diminution in the level of service provided. Suitable larger premises, however, are not always available whilst the costs of expanding existing premises may outweigh the potential savings. The banks on occasion have instead found it feasible to down-grade the status of branches so that they provide only the more basic deposit-taking, money transmissions and lending facilities while a 'parent' branch in the locality is responsible for handling the larger accounts, dealing with complex business accounts and providing customers with the full range of the bank's financial services.

If the Scottish clearing banks could readily redistribute and rationalise their branch networks in Scotland it is likely that the country would be served by perhaps half as many branches as there are today. The strong competition from other deposit-taking institutions in Scotland, in particular the building societies and the TSB (see chapter 5), requires the three clearing banks to maintain their branch networks at some minimum acceptable level to gather retail deposits and provide other financial services including payments and lending to their customers. It is impossible, however, to determine what the 'optimum' branch density should be.[14] While changing population and urban land-use patterns in Scotland mean that some new branches require to be opened, the future branch expansion of the two Edinburgh banks will occur mainly in England. The Royal Bank of Scotland will seek to expand its network of branches in the South East and South West where they are lightly represented at present. Bank of Scotland is relying on the success of its Home and Office Banking System (HOBS) to increase its share of the retail market in the South and branches have been established to cater for the requirements of the small to medium-sized company market. Access to customers through the branch networks of other financial institutions is also a possibility.

As well as branch rationalisation in Scotland the role of the retail bank branch is being re-defined as a result of technology, competition and the search for increased productivity and reduced overheads. Greater attention is being given to the requirements of customers so that the banks have increased their branch opening hours and now open selected branches on Saturdays. Banking halls have been redesigned and refurbished to provide a more attractive place for the customer and technological developments have been implemented such as counter terminals which link with central computers to enable transactions to be recorded on-line and in real time. However, successful retail banking still depends in large measure on personal contact. In order to utilise the branch to its full potential the Scottish clearing banks are having to adopt the cross-selling of different financial products and services and move towards a consultative selling relationship where branch managers and staff perform the function of providing financial advice to a greater extent than hitherto. The development of automated-teller machines and electronic funds transfer at the point of sale and their subsequent improvement mean that money transmission facilities can be provided with fewer branches and that payments services are less demanding of branch management time.

Employment. The staff of the Scottish clearing banks represent their major resource. Staff performance and productivity is influenced not only by pay and conditions of work, but also by the training they receive, the equipment they use, the premises in which they operate and the skill of the management in producing the best performance. Successful management produces not only successful institutions but an efficient Scottish banking system.

The numbers of group staff employed in the UK by each of the Scottish clearing banks between 1975 and 1985 are provided in table 4.5. These figures show the average number of persons employed during any one year.[15] The growth in staff employed by Bank of Scotland and the Royal Bank has been similar over the period at an annual compound rate of 2.4 per cent and 2.2 per cent respectively. The number of staff employed by Clydesdale Bank has grown more rapidly at an annual compound rate of 3.7 per cent. Between 1980 and 1984 the Royal Bank shed staff but in 1985 largely as a result of increased business this did not occur. Indeed the inclusion of staff of Charterhouse, the merchant bank and development capital company acquired during that year, considerably increased the numbers employed by the Royal Bank.

The figures in table 4.5 treat part-time staff as being equivalent to full-time staff although many employees of the three banks work on a part-time basis. All three banks employ staff in England. About 7 per cent of Bank of Scotland staff and half of the Royal Bank staff are based south of the border.[16]

Staff costs form a major proportion of the annual operating costs of the Scottish clearing banks. The most recent annual accounts data for Bank of Scotland and the Royal Bank of Scotland[17] indicate that staff costs accounted for 57 per cent and 59 per cent respectively of total operating expenses, slightly lower than the corresponding figures for the big four London clearing banks.[18] Staff costs per employee in those years amounted to just over £10000 for Bank of Scotland and £11200 for the Royal Bank. The Scottish banks have usually paid lower average salaries than the London clearing banks, gaining a useful cost advantage. In 1975 the two Edinburgh banks

The Scottish Clearing Banks

Table 4.5. Scottish clearing bank groups – UK staff.[1]

	1975	1976	1977	1978	1979	1980	1981	1982	1983	1984	1985
Bank of Scotland	7851	7963	8332	8594	8791	9112	9252	9318	9538	9608	9952
Clydesdale Bank	4848	5110	5381	5718	6246	6792	6958	6947	6991	7000	7000
The Royal Bank of Scotland	13842	13934	14457	15010	15696	16354	16213	16153	16240	16000	17269
Total	26541	27007	28170	29322	30733	32258	32423	32418	32769	32608	34221

1. Average number of persons employed, including non-clerical and part-time staff, but excluding staff working completely or mainly outside the UK.

Sources: Statistical Unit, Committee of London and Scottish Bankers; Clydesdale Bank.

paid their UK employees an average salary of £2632 compared with £2884 for the big four London clearing banks. By 1985 the average salary of the UK employees of the Edinburgh banks had risen to £8688 and that of the London banks to £9266.[19]

A comparison of tables 4.4 and 4.5 reveals that the Scottish clearing banks' staff numbers have grown as the number of branches have declined. This is largely accounted for by the increased use that has been made of part-time staff in branches, increased numbers of staff employed at remaining branches and greater numbers employed at head and chief administration offices and in subsidiary companies. Within branches the structure and members of staff have been influenced by the introduction of computer technology. Electronic data processing systems have not displaced large numbers of staff, partly because the changes in back office systems and practices have been evolutionary but mostly because of the large growth in transactions in recent times.

Current account banking generates the highest volumes of retail bank transactions and associated employment. The Scottish clearing banks have a growing number of current account holders and the provision of current account services is seen as an important means of attracting new customers who may be persuaded to purchase other bank services. Deposit account holders in Scotland have often also used their accounts for payments by depositing their weekly wages in these accounts and making frequent cash withdrawals. A large number of individuals in Scotland do not have a bank account and success in the attempt to woo this group by the banks is likely to further fuel growing volumes of current account transactions although the profitability of such business may be questioned.[20] The banks may be assisted in achieving this by the 1986 Wage Act. New systems introduced to cope with rising business volumes must be implemented within the constraints imposed by existing systems and costs and since the impact on employment is not immediate it is very difficult to assess the future trend in Scottish bank branch employment. There are also considerations of how far and at what pace organised Scottish bank labour will be willing to accept further introduction and implementation of new technologies. The TUC-affiliated Banking, Insurance and Finance Union represents the majority of Scottish clearing bank employees although some employees are members of ASTMS. Negotiations are conducted on a bank-by-bank basis.

The need to make adequate provision for the training of professional bank staff has long been recognised in Scotland. The Institute of Bankers in Scotland (IOBS) was established in 1875 to provide a system of formal education and examination in addition to branch training. The Institute was the first of its kind in the world and was a national and not a local body, unlike other professional institutes of that time. Success in the Institute's examinations is generally regarded as necessary to enter the clearing bank promotion stream. The number of staff of the Royal Bank of Scotland with

The Scottish Clearing Banks

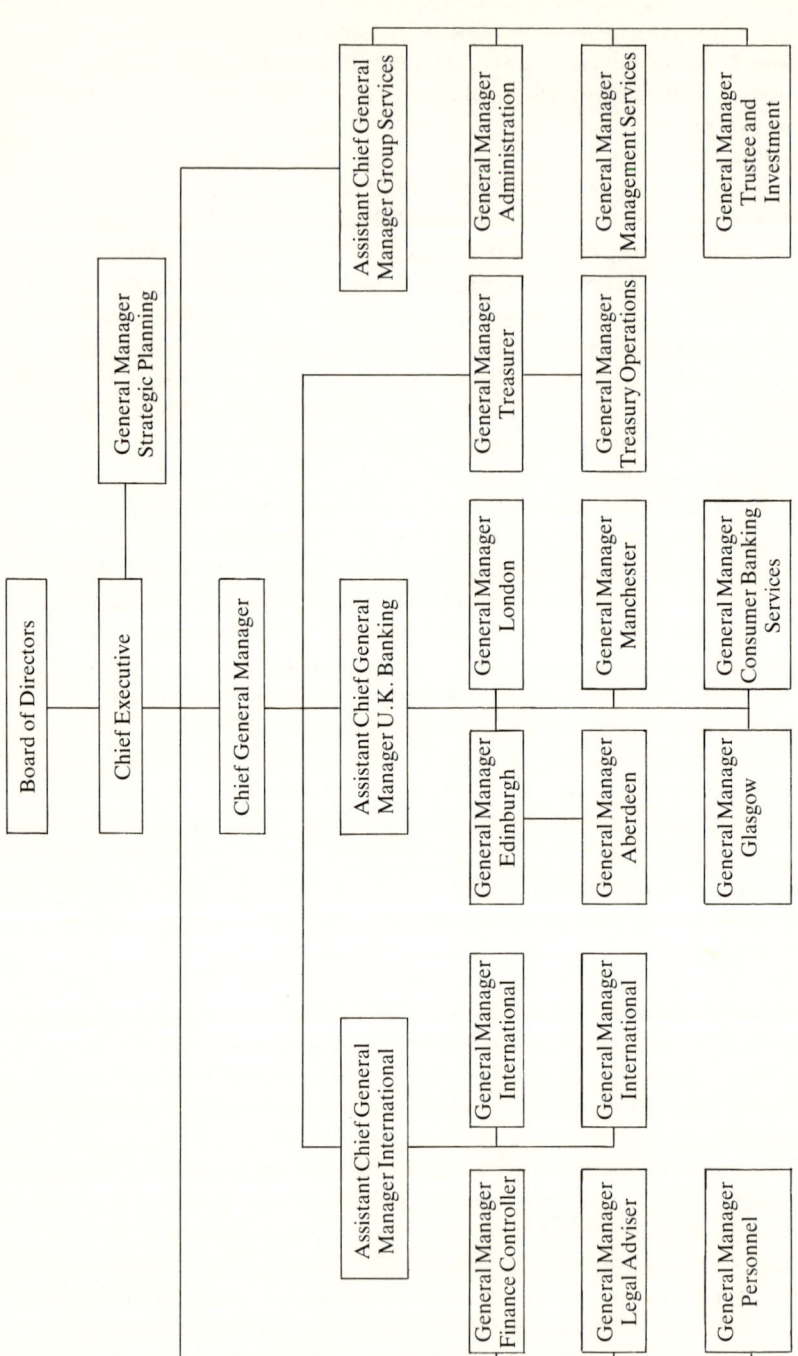

Figure 4.1. Senior management structure of the Royal Bank of Scotland plc (the clearing bank) at 1 October 1985.
Source: Annual Report and Accounts 1985.

IOBS or IOB qualifications is almost 17 per cent of total bank staff.

Further practical training on technical and administrative aspects of banking business is carried out at the staff training colleges owned by the Scottish clearing banks.[21] In 1985, courses varying from one day to three weeks at Bank of Scotland's training college involved 3200 members of staff, almost one-third of the Bank's total staff. The Scottish clearing banks were late to recognise the advantages of recruitment from the graduate market but have in recent times introduced graduate trainee schemes. The Royal Bank of Scotland, between 1980 and 1985, accepted 166 graduates onto its scheme. Bank of Scotland intake is around 10-20 graduates each year. The banks have also found it necessary to recruit trained personnel to work in specialist areas such as agriculture, oil, accounting, law, marketing, economics, property and computing. They have become more open to recruiting senior personnel in mid-career in banking and in specialist departments.

The Scottish clearing banks use internal as well as external courses provided by the Scottish higher education sector for the training of managerial staff. The markets in which banks and financial service organisations operate are expanding and changing rapidly and management must have the necessary training and flexibility to adapt and lead in this environment. Marketing skills are becoming more important for both branch and central management.

The introduction and emphasis given to professional development by the Scottish clearing banks bodes well for their future. There has been concern in the past, however, that highly qualified staff often leave Scottish banks due to lack of promotion prospects. Whether or not entirely justified such a concern points towards a need to consider existing fast promotion streams as well as appropriate financial rewards and career prospects. The banks have indicated that their turnover of trained and qualified staff is now lower than previously.

The two most important organisational entities within the Scottish clearing banks are the board of directors and the senior executive management. The non-executive directors who are the majority on the boards have traditionally been drawn from senior posts in the Scottish financial sector, industry and commerce to provide a source of business experience and breadth of knowledge. They are an important source of impartial advice on the long term strategy of the banks and help to scrutinise the performance of management. It is important for the Scottish banks that non-executive directors continue to be drawn from a wide field and are encouraged to contribute to the development of the business of the banks.

Acknowledging the need for management structures that are responsive in a highly competitive market subject to rapid change the Scottish clearing banks have made organisational changes. The merger in 1985 of the Royal Bank of Scotland with its sister company Williams and Glyn's enabled a new, streamlined management structure to be created which is illustrated in figure 4.1 and reveals the short lines of communication in the post-merger Royal Bank of Scotland. The Bank of Scotland has created a management board of executive directors to establish more effective control over the day-to-day running of the bank. As well as responsibility for the operational conduct of banking business the senior executives have a duty to initiate and choose between alternative policies and strategies which determine the longer term position of the banks in financial markets.

International Banking Operations

All three Scottish clearing banks carry out international business. International banking has grown rapidly in the last 15 years along with the rapid growth and integration of financial markets worldwide.[22] In recent times the most important influence bearing on international banking has been the technological revolution in communications and data manipulation, and the ability that this has provided to move funds around the world in search of the highest return. Large borrowers, including nations, depend upon international banking and financial markets to fund their needs and international banks continue to play an important role in the provision of finance for major capital projects, trade finance and payments services for international companies and exporters.

Before the 1970s the overseas banking activities of the Scottish clearing banks were mainly restricted to financing overseas trade for their Scottish and UK customers and business was conducted by using a network of correspondent banks. This business involved the banks in providing foreign exchange services, documentary credits and acceptances and travellers' cheques, but formed only a small part of their banking operations which were concentrated on retail banking in Scotland. At this time the London clearing banks had only small international banking operations with few branches overseas. Extensive growth in world trade and the growth of the Eurocurrency market, centred on London, coupled with the decline in sterling brought about substantial change by the early 'seventies. The Euromarkets, in particular, escaped many of the restrictions placed upon banking nationally[23] and brought large numbers of international banks to London. The response of the London clearing banks was to develop their international banking activities and overseas presence. Wider representation abroad was achieved by the purchase of large shareholdings in London-based international consortium banks and was developed further by full ownership and the establishment of international banking subsidiaries. In this way Barclays Bank and Lloyds Bank gained considerable networks throughout the developing world and National Westminster established a European network. Subsequent expansion occurred in North America and Asia by opening branch offices and by acquiring American state banks.

The expansion to the international side of the Scottish clearing banks' business came later than that of their London counterparts. The major impetus came not from the growth of the Euromarkets in London, but from the discovery and development of North Sea oil and gas 'which demanded recourse to external sources of finance'.[24] There were a number of other factors, however, which the three banks cite as having influenced the growth of their international business: the greater availability of cheap foreign currency funds (almost entirely due to Euromarket growth); the abandonment of fixed parity exchange rates and thus a more volatile and active market; increased trade within the European Community; the requirements for overseas guarantees and bonds in regard to foreign contracts; and the increased awareness of customers of the advantages to be gained by becoming more sophisticated in their international operations.

The Scottish clearing banks did not develop large overseas branch networks, although overseas purchases were made in the 1970s. Bank of Scotland undertook a joint venture with a European consortium of banks, acquiring trade investments (15 per cent) in Banque Worms et Associes (Geneva), and was involved in the formation of the International Energy Bank, a 'club' of North American and European banks which provided a vehicle for worldwide joint lending ventures. Both holdings have since been sold. The Royal Bank of Scotland acquired holdings in a Singapore merchant bank (64 per cent) and an Indonesian finance company. Clydesdale Bank's overseas activities were more limited due to the international business development including overseas purchases of its parent, the Midland Bank. Whilst continuing to rely on correspondent banking for their international payments, the three Scottish banks have, nonetheless, established a number of branches and representative offices overseas, mostly in the United States and the Far East. These are given in table 4.6.

A distinction is made between branches and offices in table 4.6, although the difference is often one of degree rather than substance and there are no hard and fast definitions. Broadly speaking, overseas representation takes three forms:[25] branch operations, which are fully integrated into the parent company's balance sheet, and whose commitments bind the bank as a whole; a subsidiary company set up under the laws of the host country and 100 per cent owned by the parent which is not, however, directly liable for its subsidiary's commitments, although it has a strong moral responsibility since its international reputation is at stake; or a representative office which looks after relations with government, banks and customers as well as facilitating business contacts and gathering information but does not run a banking book. The three Scottish banks operate through a combination of branches, representative offices and subsidiaries[26] and each bank has established an international division with the responsibility for all aspects of international business.

The needs of the major American oil companies for information about investment in Scotland was a major factor in the decision of the three banks to open representative offices in Houston. The banks' other offices and

Table 4.6. Overseas representation of the Scottish clearing banks.

Region	Bank of Scotland	Royal Bank of Scotland	Clydesdale
Western Europe			
Switzerland		The Royal Bank of Scotland AG	
Netherlands[1]	Scotland International Finance BV	Royscot International Finance BV	
Greece		Branch	
United States			
New York	Branch	Branch	Branch
California	Office	Branch, office	
Chicago	Office	Office	
Houston	Office	Office	Office
Other			
Hong Kong	Branch	Branch, 14.3% Inter Alpha Asia	
Singapore		Branch, 14.3% Inter Alpha Asia	
Moscow	Branch		
Sao Paulo		Office	
Sydney		Office	
Tokyo		Office	

1. Eurocurrency booking offices or 'shell' branches having no contact with the Dutch market. Actual banking activities take place in Edinburgh/Glasgow.

Source: Published accounts.

branches in the United States perform a similar function for other American firms, though the New York branches, which were set up as offices in the 1960s, provide an important source of dollar deposits for the Scottish banks and carry out a wide range of lending activities in the US. Branches were opened in the Far East by the two Edinburgh banks and shareholdings bought by the Royal Bank in recognition of the growth potential for international trade of the Pacific Basin. The branches in Hong Kong carry out foreign currency dealing, the acceptance of deposits and the granting of loans, and payments services.

Foreign exchange dealing is a major part of the international business of the Scottish banks and all three have dealing operations in Glasgow and London. The two Edinburgh banks have established dealing rooms in New York and Hong Kong and the Royal Bank also has dealing rooms in Singapore and Zurich. This enables the banks to trade in the foreign currency markets on a 24-hour basis. As well as carrying out currency lending, taking currency deposits and dealing in foreign exchange the Scottish clearing banks provide acceptance credits, the discounting of bills of exchange, ECGD short- and medium-term finance, currency overdrafts, Eurocheques and travellers' cheques, overseas guarantees and performance bonds, finance for exports, and international payments remittance.

North Sea oil exploration and development provided the Scottish clearing banks with new lending opportunities but on a scale that required banks to combine in consortia to provide syndicated loans, each carrying their own share of the loan on their own books. Syndicated loans for North Sea oil and other major capital projects are normally arranged in London. In 1984 Bank of Scotland was chosen by ELF UK, along with Banque Nationale de Paris and Citibank, as a lead manager for ELF's £650 million financing for the Alwyn North Field, the largest single loan yet raised for a North Sea project. In other cases the Scottish banks can carry the entire loan on their own books. Overseas companies which have established themselves in Scotland use the Scottish banks as one source of foreign currency borrowing. At August 1985 the total foreign currency lending of the Scottish clearing banks was equivalent to £1845 million divided as follows: UK private Sector £798 million, UK Public Sector £27 million, and overseas residents £1020 million. Total foreign currency lending at November 1976 was equivalent to £423 million so that by 1985 advances had grown by a factor of 4.4. The foreign currency advances of the London clearing banks grew over the same period by a factor of 3.8 to £21220 million. Whilst comparison of foreign currency lending with earlier years is distorted by fluctuating exchange rates these figures nonetheless illustrate the growth in this area of clearing bank operations.

Although considerable expansion has taken place in the international business of the Scottish clearing banks the scale of their international operations does not compare with that of the large English, American, Japanese and European banks. These banks have established branches in all the key financial centres and in many other capitals and large cities around the world and the American and Japanese banks, in particular, are major players in the Eurobond and Euronote markets. The overseas representation of the Scottish clearing banks is, by comparison, much smaller and their Euromarket business is mainly foreign exchange business. The international expansion of the Scottish clearing banks, with no significant impetus until North Sea oil, contrasts with that of some relatively small American banks.

American banks became engaged in international banking and rapidly expanded their overseas branch networks in the 'sixties largely as a consequence of the regulatory environment under which they operated in the US. A series of regulations under the Federal Government's capital program[27] ensured that large corporations had to rely on external sources of finance to fund their overseas investments. American banks had an incentive to establish networks of foreign branches to tap foreign funds and provide loans and banking services to their multinational customers which host-country banks could not provide. Regulation Q also provided an impetus by reducing the competitiveness of the banks in the domestic deposit market.[28] Many of these banks were US regional banks with little or

The Scottish Clearing Banks

no tradition of international operations. Whilst regulation had an important effect on the internationalisation of some American banks, the banks also exhibited a flexibility in adapting to new markets, an ability to innovate and a willingness to accept reduced returns on their loans at least during the initial phases of their expansion.

The international expansion of the European banks was largely a response to the international challenge which they encountered from the American banks. Many expanded in countries where they had traditional links, and participated in bank consortiums. Japanese banks tended to follow Japanese companies but they also set up foreign branches to tap additional sources of funds. Most international banks have established themselves locally in the US which has attractions as the world's largest economy and as a source of dollar deposits. Paltzer (1977) points out that banks expanded in certain locations not always because of banking opportunities in the national economy but because of the pattern of international finance. This would apply, to some extent, to London, Tokyo, New York and Switzerland, but also to Hong Kong, the Bahamas and Panama for example, where there are liberal tax and transfer conditions.

Correspondent banking still forms the backbone of the Scottish clearing banks' international operations and enables payments to be remitted abroad.[29] Credit facilities for customers with a number of banks in different countries are also provided on a reciprocal basis. This form of banking does not, however, provide any means of generating overseas loan business nor does it provide Scottish and UK customers with the continuity of service of a branch. Major advantages of an overseas branch include offering customers abroad a service facility backed by the head office's name, the gathering of foreign credit information and the facilitation of very rapid funds transfer.

It has been suggested that the acquisition of an overseas bank by a Scottish clearer would be motivated by a desire to provide shareholders with some earnings from an overseas base rather than stemming from an intention to service existing customers more efficiently, since the chances of having a branch in the right place to meet customers needs are extremely small, almost regardless of the number of overseas branches. Acquisition of an overseas branch would reflect the desire of the Edinburgh banks to diversify their banking business and provide a profitable source of overseas earnings. The alternative to acquisition of establishing an international branch network would be a costly exercise since it would involve the acquisition of premises, support from the bank's international division and recruiting scarce personnel.

However, an overseas network of branches may provide customers with a more efficient service, though not simply for settling trading accounts. The bank can provide an introduction to a range of local contacts in industry, business and government as well as provide detailed economic information and technical advice on the local market and the most appropriate financial arrangements for carrying out transactions in the market, together with direct assistance in fund raising. There are also competitive considerations for setting up overseas offices; services can be made directly available to both existing and new customers operating in foreign countries who might otherwise do business with already established international banks. Perhaps of greater significance in periods of high interest rates is that a branch network can speed transactions and payments.

Rapid advances in computer technology and telecommunications has enabled the large international banks to develop global fund transfer, information services and access to transactions processing. Some American banks, for example, have developed their own private telecommunications networks linking together all their branches and putting all their services at the disposal of overseas branch customers. Financial transactions can be monitored, up-dated and reported electronically, and up-to-date information provided in many different time zones. It is unrealistic to expect the Scottish clearing banks to develop branch networks and telecommunication systems that compete with the major international banks which carry out a much greater range of international banking activities but technology does provide them with new international banking opportunities. Bank of Scotland, for example, provides an automated funds transfer service to the DHSS to transmit retirement pensions and other benefits abroad which amount to around £180 million each year[30] and the system is available to other organisations or companies who make regular, small value payments abroad.

Further development of the international banking business of the Scottish clearing banks will depend on which operations each bank chooses to provide (although Clydesdale Bank's operations will largely be determined by Midland Bank). The ability of the banks to draw on a qualified staff with experience in foreign operations remains an important constraint. The Scottish banks have no desire to compromise their sound and solid background by embracing high additional risk which rapid expansion of international activities might bring. Moderate expansion is, however, foreseeable.

Ownership, Competition and Performance

Ownership and Integration
The most recent structural changes in the ownership of the Scottish clearing banks occurred after a period of consolidation following the merger of the Royal Bank of Scotland with the National Commercial Bank of Scotland in 1968 which reduced the number of Scottish banks to three. Of these, two were independent (Bank of Scotland, the Royal Bank of Scotland) and the third (Clydesdale Bank), 100 per cent owned by Midland Bank but with its own board fully responsible for all aspects of its business. Traditionally it was the policy of the English banks not to operate under their own names in

Scotland. Instead substantial shareholdings were held in the Scottish banks. In 1969 Barclays Bank exchanged its Scottish subsidiary, the British Linen Bank, for a 35 per cent shareholding in Bank of Scotland while Lloyds Bank retained, through earlier involvement with the National Commercial Bank, a diluted 16 per cent investment in the newly formed National and Commercial Banking Group, which had as its principal bank subsidiary in Scotland the Royal Bank of Scotland.[31] Barclays and Lloyds had common directors with Bank of Scotland and the National and Commercial Group respectively, but did not seek to intervene in their day-to-day management.

During the 1970s overtures were made by Lloyds Bank to the Royal Bank of Scotland with a view to amalgamating their businesses. However, a link with an overseas network emerged as the favoured choice of the Royal Bank and a merger was proposed with the Standard Chartered Bank in 1981. This was closely followed by a takeover bid for the Royal Bank by the Hong Kong and Shanghai Banking Corporation. Reference to the Monopolies and Mergers Commission (MMC) followed and despite assurances by the parties to the bid that the Royal Bank would retain a degree of autonomy and control from Edinburgh over the domestic operations of the newly formed bank group the Commission stated that the process of 'centralisation' was in its opinion likely to occur so that headquarters and direction would be relocated from Scotland with a resultant lessening of Scottish managerial talent and damage to entrepreneurial spirit and business leadership. Loss of control and power it was argued would damage the Scottish financial industry and the Scottish economy. Principally on these grounds both bids were found to be against the public interest and failed.

Further ownership changes did not occur until 1985 when Barclays sold its shareholding in Bank of Scotland to the Standard Life Assurance Company of Edinburgh, and Lloyds divested itself of its ownership stake in the Royal Bank of Scotland Group. The decision by the MMC is unlikely to remain as a constraint to future merger proposals but Bank of Scotland at least would now appear to be safe from the threat of takeover. The Kuwait Investment Office has been the other notable holder of Scottish bank stock with a 14.7 per cent interest in the Royal Bank of Scotland. The ownership position of the Scottish clearing banks as at February 1986 is illustrated in figure 4.2.

In 1985 the Royal Bank of Scotland Group merged the businesses of its two principal bank subsidiaries, the Royal Bank of Scotland plc and Williams & Glyn's plc into the Royal Bank of Scotland plc to become the first bank with a national branch network in the UK, the re-organisation being partly a reaction to the failure of the takeover bids.[32] These structural changes have brought about a substantial change in the domestic bank market in Scotland and the UK. Though dominant in their home market the Scottish and London banks now compete with each other in both Scotland and England and Wales. Midland Bank is the only remaining London clearing bank that is represented in Scotland by way of ownership of a

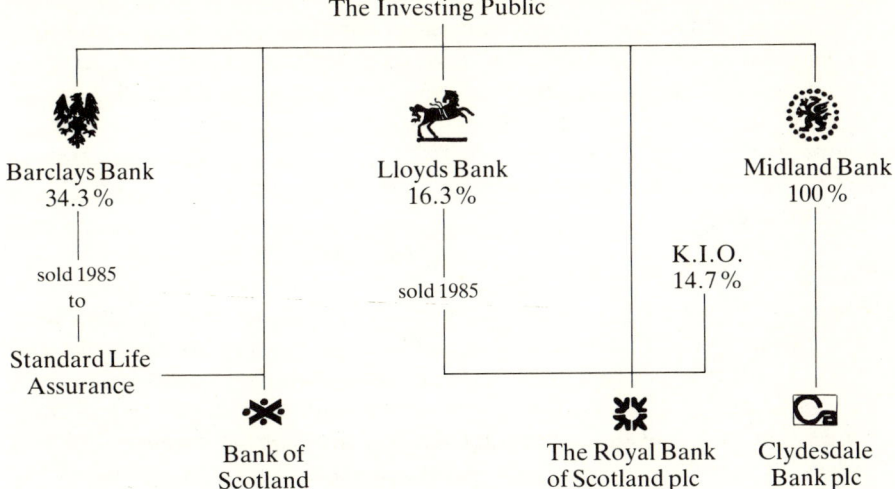

Figure 4.2. Ownership of the three Scottish clearing banks, 1986. (K.I.O. = Kuwait Investment Office.)

traditional Scottish banking company and there are signs that the activities of Clydesdale Bank will be coordinated more closely with those of its parent, though the name is likely to survive.

The two Edinburgh banks have increased the size of their branch networks in the South of England. Bank of Scotland has targeted the small to medium corporate market and in recent years has opened regional offices in Birmingham, Bristol, Leeds, Manchester, Newcastle, Norwich and Southampton. Branches have also been opened in Leicester and Carlisle which provide the full range of personal banking services. The Royal Bank has embarked on a branch expansion programme competing head-on with the big four London clearing banks. Both these moves are, in part, a reflection of the more limited growth opportunities facing the two banks in Scotland and the opportunities to be found in England.

At present the executive management of the Royal Bank of Scotland is split between Edinburgh and London. The functions based in Edinburgh are strategic planning, financial control, data processing, public relations and personnel as well as secretary, consumer banking, trustee, registrar, economics and property. Treasury operations and international operations are based in London. There are fears that if the Royal Bank is successful in increasing its share of the English domestic market (about 3 per cent) and expands its international business and investment banking business (through Charterhouse) then strategic decision making and other functions will gravitate to London with Edinburgh relegated to the administration of Scottish affairs only. There are, however, no reasons to believe such fears are justified in the foreseeable future. Advancements in telecommunications enable communication lines within the bank to remain short and London presents no obvious advantages over Edinburgh for controlling a UK-wide retail bank network. It may be more difficult in the future, despite the history and traditions of the Royal Bank to maintain a singularly Scottish identity, but from a wider and less parochial perspective, the increased competition that the bank can bring to the UK banking market by carrying out business both north and south of the border is likely to be beneficial to the industry's structure.

Competition

The retail bank markets in Scotland and England are characterised by a substantial degree of concentration and by strong competition. At the end of the 1970s retail banking was dominated by the three Scottish clearing banks and the big four London clearing banks and the regulatory authorities were concerned that further mergers among the clearing banks would lead to less effective competition. However, changes in ownership among the London and Scottish banks, liberal regulation and active deregulation has since fostered increased competition between the clearing banks and new or potential entrants to the bank market. The clearing banks have become more competitive and aggressive for business and this has brought them into competition with many other financial institutions in different segments of the banking and financial services sector.

Benston (1973) has suggested that where entry to the bank market is unrestricted a sufficient basis for competitive behaviour that benefits the public exists. This idea is not dissimilar to the theory of contestable markets[33] which states that efficiency of the market[34] will be determined by the existence of a pool of potential entrants rather than the size or number of the incumbents *per se*. The main feature of a contestable market is that new institutions may freely enter and leave it. The main deterrent to entry is the need to commit large sums of money which are not retrievable or easily transferable on exit. This barrier to entry is low in the banking and financial services markets. The main barriers to entry are regulatory ones and these have been progressively dismantled in recent years leading to greater integration of financial markets and an increase in potential competitors.

The activities of the clearing banks are only sustainable in a contestable environment if they can produce their range of products as cheaply as potential entrants to the various market segments. Technology, for example, has enabled other institutions to challenge the comparative advantage of the clearing banks in the provision of money transmission services. The clearing banks have had to respond by increasing their own competitiveness and by innovations.

In Scotland the major potential retail banking competitors to the Scottish clearing banks are the building societies and the TSB. The Royal Bank also faces strong competition from the TSB in England, and the London clearing banks. The TSB has evolved from a simple savings bank to become a financial services bank providing competition to the clearing banks in the personal market and increasingly in the small to medium company market. The TSB has a large number of deposit holders and has, in recent years, increased its share of the lending market. It has successfully targeted a number of segments in the personal banking sector with a range of products such as credit cards and insurance, and has, for example, captured a share of the youth market, realising that latent demand for a wide range of financial products lies within this group. It competes with the Scottish clearing banks in the provision of money transmission facilities in Scotland, and it poses a potential competitive threat to the corporate business of the three clearers.

Building societies have for a long time been major competitors of the Scottish and London clearing banks for personal sector deposits. New legislation is enabling the societies to compete across a much wider range of financial instruments and products, including unsecured lending. Competition between the banks and the building societies in the mortgage market is intense. The building societies are also becoming involved in money transmission. (For a full discussion of the TSB and building societies see chapter 5.)

The integration of UK bank markets has also brought the Scottish and London clearing banks into closer competition. Barclays has moved from providing international trade finance through its Scottish branches (an area of relative weakness in Scottish banking) to offering personal and UK corporate finance services. While this is competition at the margin of the bank market (Citibank provide a similar example in the UK context) the possibility of future competition across a wider spread of activities must force the Scottish banks to re-assess their own performance. Competing institutions, including those freed from regulatory constraints, have realised that parts of Scottish clearing bank business can be profitably attacked and exploited.

The Scottish banks compete with international and London merchant banks in the provision of corporate finance and related services. They compete through their subsidiaries with finance houses (often owned by other banks), corporate advisory organisations, venture funds and investment houses and in insurance markets. Marketing (discussed in the next section) has become a key part of success in these highly competitive markets.

The banking industry in Scotland and the UK has progressively increased in competitiveness over the 1970s and particularly the 1980s. The UK regulatory authorities have responded to pressure for structural change in bank markets by attempting to remove restrictions to change and to competition. Increases in statutory powers are mainly aimed at protecting the public from fraud and maintaining confidence in the system. The higher degree of competition faced by the London and Scottish clearing banks has ensured a more optimal banking structure for the public as evidenced by the wider range of financial instruments and services readily available to customers on highly competitive terms. Increased competition has focused attention on the financial performance of the Scottish clearing banks.

Performance

The presence of a strong banking sector in Scotland that can contribute positively to Scottish and UK economic growth requires a sector that is profitable. Profitability is the principal measure of management performance and important to maintain the confidence of depositors, shareholders, trading associates, other banks and financial intermediaries and supervisors, and to ensure that the banks can continue to play their part in the financing of industry and commerce. Profits also provide additions to reserves thereby contributing to the capital base and providing a source of funds to meet unexpected losses. The contribution to profits from the banks' various activities varies from year to year and differs between banks. The greater part of Scottish clearing bank profits comes from domestic operations with the balance made up of international banking and related banking activities.

Tables 4.7 and 4.8 have been put together using available published data for both the Scottish clearing banks and the London clearing banks. Table 4.8 provides a further series of statistics on profitability and capital resources drawn from the earlier tables. The profits (historic cost) of the clearing banks before the payment of tax, for the eleven years from 1975 to 1985, are given in table 4.7. The percentage rise or fall in profits over each year are shown in brackets below the profit figures. Between 1975 and 1985 the growth of clearing bank profits has fluctuated quite markedly though none of the banks have recorded a loss and profits have risen in real terms. There is no obvious difference in the profit trend between the Scottish and London clearing banks. Over the ten-year period Bank of Scotland achieved annual compound growth in profits of 20 per cent and the Royal Bank of Scotland 16 per cent. National Westminster achieved the highest compound growth per annum at 23 per cent and Barclays and Lloyds both recorded 19 per cent. Midland fared less well with profits growing at 16 per cent compound per annum, a consequence of an ill-timed expansion in the United States with the acquisition of the Crocker Bank causing a substantial drain on resources before its eventual sale.

The pre-tax return on the clearing banks' assets and shareholders' funds is given in table 4.9. The denominators of the two sets of ratios – total assets, and shareholders' funds and minority interests – are as presented in the balance sheets of the clearing banks at the end of each year. Average ratios have been calculated for the big four London clearing banks. Pre-tax return on assets is one measure of overall profitability which shows the ability of the bank to earn profits on its assets as a whole. The two Edinburgh banks have fared better in this respect than the big four London banks over the

Table 4.7. Scottish and London clearing bank profits before taxation (historic cost). Profits in £ million, with % increase in brackets.

Group profit before taxation[1]	1975	1976	1977	1978	1979	1980	1981	1982	1983	1984	1985
Bank of Scotland	13	18 (38)	28 (56)	30 (—) *	35 (17)	42 (20)	45 (7)	55 (22)	50 (—) *	59 (18)	80 (36)
Royal Bank of Scotland	37	58 (57)	64 (10)	68 (6)	97 (43)	103 (6)	108 (5)	91 (−16)	96 (5)	131 (36)	166 (27)
Clydesdale Bank	n/a	n/a	n/a	n/a	n/a	n/a	23	17 (−26)	18 (6)	24 (33)	30 (25)
Barclays	149	198 (33)	295 (49)	373 (26)	529 (42)	523 (−1)	567 (8)	495 (−13)	557 (12)	655 (18)	854 (30)
Lloyds	97	145 (49)	180 (24)	189 (5)	286 (51)	305 (7)	373 (22)	329 (−12)	419 (27)	468 (12)	561 (20)
Midland[2]	81	167 (106)	197 (18)	231 (17)	315 (36)	230 (−27)	231 (0)	251 (9)	225 (−10)	135 (−40)	351 (160)
National Westminster	104	188 (81) *	241 (—)	306 (27)	441 (44)	415 (−6)	500 (20)	449 (−10)	518 (15)	671 (30)	804 (20)

1. Financial year-end for Bank of Scotland is 28 February. Financial year-end for Royal Bank of Scotland Group is 30 September. Financial year-end for other banks is 31 December.
2. Includes Clydesdale Bank.
* Indicates a break in the series, due to bank restating published accounts at later date. Figures in brackets show year-on-year percentage increase.
Sources: Published accounts; Statistical Unit, Committee of London and Scottish Bankers.

Table 4.8. Scottish and London clearing bank accounts data for 1975, 1979–85.

	1975	1979	1980	1981	1982	1983	1984	1985
Shareholders' Funds and Minorities[5] (£ millions)								
Bank of Scotland[1]	88	182	202	238	303	339	324	404
Royal Bank of Scotland[2]	231	427	496	563	725	803	701	885
Clydesdale Bank[3]	n/a	n/a	108	115	124	144	148	163
The Big Four[3,5]	2942	5883	6722	8214	9570	10776	9700	10765
Total Assets/Liabilities[5] (£ millions)								
Bank of Scotland[1]	1251	2395	2761	3568	4357	5334	6143	7217
Royal Bank of Scotland[2]	3345	5175	6147	7763	9292	11077	13386	15031
Clydesdale Bank[3]	n/a	n/a	1626	1908	2196	2254	2516	2805
The Big Four[3,4]	51208	96819	116847	160713	195967	215966	250632	239543
Aggregate Assets/Liabilities[6] (£ billions), December[7]								
Scottish Clearing Banks	3.56	6.39	7.90	9.31	11.36	12.70	15.03	15.14
London Clearing Banks	31.50	54.32	63.45	76.91	95.17	106.98	117.75	140.90
Aggregate Deposits[6,8] (£ billions), December[7]								
Scottish Clearing Banks	2.22	3.54	4.23	4.82	5.71	6.41	7.57	8.20
London Clearing Banks	20.23	30.70	36.54	41.06	45.71	50.17	54.16	59.77

1. As at 28 February each year. 2. As at 30 September each year.
3. As at 31 December each year.
4. Barclays, Lloyds, Midland, National Westminster. Figures are aggregates.
5. London and Scottish clearing banks and their subsidiaries.
6. Balances of the six London clearing banks and the three Scottish clearing banks at 12 December.
7. 1985 figures are at 18 September.
8. Sterling deposits of UK private and public sectors only (excludes CD's and deposits from banking/monetary sector).

Sources: Bank of England; Published Accounts; Statistical Unit, Committee of London and Scottish Bankers.

Table 4.9. Annual profitability and resource data: ratios %.

	1975	1976	1977	1978	1979	1980	1981	1982	1983	1984	1985
Pre-tax profit on assets											
Bank of Scotland[1]	1.0	1.3	1.7	1.5	1.5	1.5	1.3	1.3	0.9	1.0	1.1
Royal Bank of Scotland[2]	1.1	1.6	1.7	1.5	1.9	1.7	1.4	1.0	0.9	1.0	1.1
Clydesdale Bank[3]	n/a	n/a	n/a	n/a	n/a	n/a	1.2	0.8	0.8	1.0	1.1
The Big Four[3,4]	0.8	1.2	1.3	1.4	1.6	1.3	1.0	0.8	0.8	0.8	1.1
Pre-tax profit on shareholders' funds											
Bank of Scotland[1]	14.8	16.8	24.1	20.6	19.2	20.8	18.9	18.2	14.8	18.2	19.8
Royal Bank of Scotland[2]	16.0	22.6	22.8	19.8	22.7	20.8	19.2	12.6	12.0	18.7	18.8
Clydesdale Bank[3]	n/a	n/a	n/a	n/a	n/a	n/a	20.0	13.6	12.6	16.4	18.4
The Big Four[3]	14.7	20.4	22.8	22.7	26.4	21.5	19.9	15.6	15.5	19.4	23.3
Free capital[5] to total assets/liabilities											
Bank of Scotland[1]	3.8	3.2	3.3	3.9	3.8	3.7	3.6	4.9	4.8	4.4	5.8
Royal Bank of Scotland[2]	2.8	3.5	4.4	4.6	5.8	5.2	5.0	4.3	4.5	4.2	4.9
Clydesdale Bank[3]	n/a	n/a	n/a	n/a	n/a	2.6	2.2	2.1	2.8	2.6	3.0
The Big Four[3]	2.6	3.2	3.5	4.1	4.0	4.0	3.2	3.7	4.1	3.9	5.6

1. As at 28 February each year.   2. As at 30 September each year.
3. As at 31 December each year.
4. Barclays, Lloyds, Midland, National Westminster. Figures are averages.
5. Free Capital Base is Capital Base (share capital, reserves, minorities, subordinated loan stock) less Infrastructure (property, equipment, trade investments and associates).

Sources: Published Accounts; Statistical Unit, Committee of London and Scottish Bankers; tables 5.11 and 5.12.

eleven-year period from 1975 to 1985, though the London banks' figures have been pulled down in recent years by the poor performance of Midland Bank. The Edinburgh banks have also tended to be more profitable than Clydesdale Bank, though the pre-tax return on assets has been very similar since 1982.

The pre-tax return on bank assets is, however, influenced by the composition of liabilities. Banks with a high ratio of shareholders' funds, on which no interest is payable, might be expected to earn relatively high margins overall. The Scottish banks have generally had a stronger equity base than the London banks – in 1985 their shareholders' funds and minorities to total assets ratio averaged 5.8 per cent, compared with 4.5 per cent for the big four London clearers.[35] The ratios of pre-tax profits to total assets have generally been lower in the 1980s than in the 1970s, largely due to a contraction in the banks' operating margins. The ratios for 1984 and 1985 indicate the beginning of a reversal of the earlier decline. If profitability is too low then it is not possible to retain sufficient profits to support the expansion of business.

Table 4.9 also measures profitability as the pre-tax return on shareholders' funds. The trends are very similar to those for the pre-tax return on assets, but the Scottish clearing banks' stronger equity bases have resulted in returns on shareholders' funds in recent times which have been lower than those of the London clearers.

The strength of a bank's balance sheet can be measured by considering its free capital to total assets/liabilities ratio. Free capital[36] is basically free shareholders' funds[37] plus any subordinated loan stock. Figures for the Scottish and London banks are given in table 4.9. The ratios for Bank of Scotland and the Royal Bank of Scotland have, in general, been higher than those for the other banks over the eleven-year period from 1975 to 1985. This is partly explained by their strong equity bases and, in recent years, the addition of subordinated foreign currency loan stock. A bank's ability to grow is determined by the level of capital it has available to support the subsequent size of its balance sheet. Table 4.8 shows that the Bank of Scotland and the Royal Bank increased their shareholders' funds by factors of 4.6 and 3.8 respectively between 1975 and 1985. The corresponding increase for the big four London clearing banks, in aggregate, was 3.7. Foreign currency loan capital helps to increase the proportion of total deposits that can be taken in the same foreign currency by providing support against fluctuations in interest and exchange rates.

The free capital ratios of the clearing banks are generally higher than those expressed in table 4.9 since free capital is usually measured as a proportion of deposits and other non-capital liabilities, rather than of total liabilities. Banks have been under pressure from supervisory authorities to increase these ratios as a protection against international lending of uncertain value and because of the growing fashion for 'off-balance sheet' lending where the commitment of the bank to borrowers is not always fully reflected in the balance sheet. The Scottish clearing banks are less affected by these concerns and are in a reasonably strong position to support further growth.

A further indicator of performance is the growth of the Scottish clearing banks' business. The entry in the top half of table 4.7 shows that in the five years from 1980–85 the total assets/liabilities of the Scottish clearing banks grew at a faster rate than those of the big four London clearing banks by a factor of 2.4 compared to 2.0. Of the Scottish banks, Bank of Scotland and the Royal Bank of Scotland have shown the fastest growth and Clydesale Bank the slowest. The entry in table 4.8 for aggregate assets/liabilities provides a measure of growth for the three Scottish clearing banks operating in Scotland and their six London counterparts excluding group subsidiaries.[38] The aggregate balance of liabilities for the London banks outpaced that of the Scottish banks between December 1975 and September 1985, by a factor of 4.4 compared to 4.2.[39] However, despite the more rapid expansion of the London clearing banks' balance sheet, sterling deposits have been accumulated at a faster rate by the Scottish clearing banks. Sterling deposits from the UK public and private sectors grew by a factor of 3.7 between 1975 and 1985 for the Scottish clearers and only by 3.0 for the London clearers. Over the same period the total foreign currency deposits of the Scottish clearing banks have grown by a factor of 8.1 against a growth factor of 9.7 for their London counterparts.

The composite growth of total sterling and foreign currency deposits, including banking/monetary sector deposits and certificates of deposit for the five years to mid-1985 has been similar for both the London and Scottish clearing banks, with respective growth factors of 2.3 and 2.2. However, sterling deposits have still been accumulated at a more rapid rate over this period by the Scottish clearing banks. The nominal rates of growth do, however, tend to obscure the fact that real growth in sterling deposits, whilst not eluding the clearing banks, has been low. After adjustment for inflation the growth factor between 1975 and 1984 is 1.4 for the Scottish banks and 1.1 for the London banks. On the other hand, foreign currency deposits have demonstrated consistently high growth in both nominal and real terms.

The Scottish clearing banks occupy the central place in the Scottish financial system and their activities extend to many areas throughout Scotland and the UK and also overseas. It is important that the three banks should maintain a level of profit at least consistent with the resources that they employ, and a record of profitability and controlled growth is necessary to attract and instil confidence in customers. The Scottish clearing banks have been at least as profitable as the London clearing banks over the past ten year period and very secure. This has enabled them to continue to play a full and effective role in the Scottish economy.

New Directions and New Technologies

The three Scottish clearing banks have evolved into major financial service organisations which carry out a wide and ever increasing range of financial activities. In addition to taking deposits and providing overdrafts and term loans they are involved in merchant banking, hire purchase and instalment credit, leasing, insurance, investment management and advice, computer services, credit card operations, factoring, stock exchange services, international banking, estate planning and trustee services. This list is not exhaustive but it does convey the extent to which diversification has been fostered through the need to compete with other banks and financial institutions.

The four key influences on the future development of retail banking are technology, competition, regulation, and marketing. Technology is the major influence since it is capable of bringing about major changes in the ways that the clearing banks carry out their business. Technology provides the ability to store, sort, analyse, retrieve and communicate large quantities of information at rapid speed. The banks have applied technology to mechanise clerical operations and counter services in their branches and to improve cash transfer and clearing services for the banking system as a whole. Technology has made it easier to carry out centralised credit scoring and provided the banks with instantaneous access to price and other market information such as company news, general economic statistics, forecasts and performance measurement. It has provided the banks with the opportunity to improve their decision-making. Changes in technology are affecting the structure of bank costs, including the economics of branching. Technology is also linked to competition and marketing. The application of technology offers new competitive opportunities, encouraging in turn further applications of technology. Marketing is involved in harnessing technology as part of its broader objective of increasing competitiveness and market share.

The Scottish clearing banks have been involved in a number of innovative applications of technology to the retail bank market. The Royal Bank of Scotland is credited with introducing the first widespread ATM (automated teller machine) network in the UK, though rapidly followed by other deposit institutions. The bank market in Scotland is now well covered by cash dispensers.[40] Further developments are likely to focus on refinement of ATM systems to allow more complex transactions to be carried out. Agreements on reciprocal cash withdrawal facilities have been reached between major UK banking groups allowing customers to use the ATMs of any of the subscribing banks. Clydesdale Bank was the first Scottish bank to install computer-linked electronic counter terminals operated by the teller or customer for recording transactions.

Cheque payments are likely to remain the most important form of payment in the UK in the foreseeable future, but high costs of paper processing has led the clearing banks to experiment with alternative forms of payment, most notably electronic funds transfer at point of sale (EFTPOS). Clydesdale Bank was the first UK clearing bank to experiment with EFTPOS, enabling customers to direct debit their accounts by using plastic cards at counter terminals in retail and filling stations in Aberdeen. Despite operating successfully for four years, however, the scheme has not yet been expanded. Plans are afoot to double the number of outlets to 60 by the end of 1986. The success of such schemes will depend on the extent to which the use of cheque and consequent clearing requirements can be minimised. Cost is also a major stumbling block to widespread implementation. Extensive development of EFTPOS will require the co-operation of the UK clearing banks, large building societies, retailers and customers.

Bank of Scotland has pioneered the development of customer-located banking in the UK, better known as Home and Office Banking (HOBS). The attraction of this system to the bank is that it can attract new personal and small company business, predominantly in England, without the need to develop additional branches. This interactive electronic service provides the customer with access to his personal account information and enables the transfer of funds between accounts as well as the regular payments of bills using remote terminals. The most promising application of such systems is to the professional and small firm market.[41]

All of these retail banking technologies, along with the computerisation and centralisation of a number of personal lending and deposit-taking services have important implications for the role of the Scottish banks' branches. Electronic funds transfer reduces the need for widespread branch networks and many of the functions carried out at bank branches have been, or are becoming, automated. Centralised credit card operations also pose a challenge to the payments processing and lending roles of branches. As Llewellyn (1985) has written

> There are many who use banks almost exclusively for cheque facilities. If technology undermines this banks could lose personal customers on a large scale. What emerging technology is doing is making branches of banks and building societies largely redundant. It is a fiction to believe that a bank account is held at a particular branch.

The banks may need to find new ways of attracting customers into their branches or find new uses for their branches. Automation has tended to free staff resources within branches although to some extent this has been offset by a growth in volumes. Surplus staff may be redeployed selling new personal financial products, making use of the technological benefits of information systems.

The future success of the Scottish clearing banks in the retail banks market, then, will not so much depend on technological innovation *per se*, but on the marketing of new and existing financial products and services that technology (including payments technology) has made possible through their branch networks. Successful marketing depends on the banks discovering the needs and desires of the customer and then shaping their products and delivery systems to both satisfy the customer and make a profit. Banking is potentially the most powerful segment of the financial services field because the customer-bank relationship has historically been a long term one. For this reason the Scottish and London clearing banks are better placed than most to capitalise on the growth in demand by the personal and company sectors for improved financial products. By offering the customer continuity of the banking relationship over a wide range of financial services customers may be persuaded to meet all their financial needs with the one bank. However, the willingness of large corporate customers, and increasingly personal sector customers, to be price sensitive in their banking requirements together with competition from other banks and deposit institutions extending the range of services available in Scotland, either through their Scottish branches or their subsidiaries, represents a real threat to the Scottish clearing banks.

If the three Scottish clearing banks are to share in the growing source of bank revenue represented by fee income from financial services, management must have accurate information on a range of financial products and have complementary marketing abilities. The Scottish clearing banks have built up a wealth of data on customers over the years which could be used to help identify and target customers as potential users of particular financial instruments.[42] In the past, Scottish clearing bank branch managers were often unwilling to entertain the idea of cross-selling financial services due to the fear of losing funds from their deposits or because they could not be persuaded of the potential profitability of the new products. Bankers have had to change in more recent times and the banks are aware of the need to train their staff with an understanding of the new marketing concepts. The banks have improved communications between branches and central marketing staff. The Royal Bank, for example, operates a Business Development Workshop aimed at improving the performance of the bank in cross-selling financial products. Since the strategies of the clearing banks to retail banking are broadly similar, implementation is the key to success, and this crucially depends upon the quality and motivation of staff.

The Scottish banks have a reasonable record of producing new and innovative ideas in the retail bank market. Recent examples include the development of the Money Market Cheque Account by Bank of Scotland, which combines money-market rates of interest with easy access to funds, whilst the Royal Bank has established its own insurance underwriting company, RBS Group Insurance Company Limited, to carry out motor insurance business by telephone. Innovations are easily copied by other financial institutions but effective marketing of new products and services will provide financial rewards and communicate an image of a helpful, innovative and successful financial institution alongside the still fundamental need of a bank to present an image of safety and security, such as is associated with the three Scottish banks.

The Scottish clearing banks market a comprehensive range of banking and other financial services and are considered by many to be financial conglomerates. The economies of scale that have been made possible by technology have accelerated the trend towards large diversified financial service institutions. The Scottish banks can be expected to move further down this road. Substantial competition in UK markets for deposits and lending has narrowed the margins of the clearing banks on their traditional banking business and increased the importance of fee and commission based services and credit and leasing activities. The need to support their branch structure whose role technology is changing has hastened the move of the clearing banks to offer one-stop financial service shopping. Llewellyn (1985) points out that the clearing bank groups

> have hitherto not offered this. They conduct their different activities from different premises (frequently through separate subsidiary companies). Whether this structure confers the advantage of the 'department store' is questionable. In this case the benefit to the consumer must derive from any alleged efficiency advantages to be gained from within the conglomerate. But it is likely to be small if different parts of the group are managed as separate companies.

The Scottish clearing banks will have to take a more positive step in this direction if the potential advantages to users of their financial services are to be fulfilled and if they are to maximise the benefits from their legacy of branches. With few existing conventions the TSB may be in a better position to take this altogether more radical approach to banking. The response of Clydesdale Bank will almost certainly be determined by the Midland Bank. The two Edinburgh banks express reservations about building retail financial conglomerates and may seek to continue to carry out a wide range of specialist financial service business but managed separately. There is as yet little indication that closer links will be forged between Bank of Scotland and Standard Life.

Financial conglomerates are also being created among commercial banks, merchant banks and stockbroking and jobbing firms primarily to compete in UK and international securities markets. This is largely a response to deregulation centred on the Stock Exchange and the major injections of capital required by stockbroking firms to be able to compete with foreign investment banks and securities houses. Bank of Scotland has made no attempt to become a major player in this market. The Royal Bank of Scotland has indicated a desire not to be left out of these structural changes by purchasing Charterhouse Japhet, a London merchant bank, and Tilney, a Liverpool-based stockbrokers, though it remains a small player.

A Perspective on the Scottish Clearing Banks

The three Scottish clearing banks are the most important financial institutions in Scotland. They sit right at the heart of the Scottish financial system, operating the payments mechanism and gathering a range of deposits from economic units who are in surplus. They are the principal source of finance for most borrowers in the Scottish economy and compete aggressively to make loans and provide a wide range of banking and other financial services to persons, companies and organisations. The three banks are also major employers in Scotland. Professor Gaskin (1965) writing about the Scottish banks asserted

> In a financial system as highly integrated as that of the UK one may legitimately doubt if such localisation makes much difference to the financial facilities of the region. It is certainly impossible to demonstrate that Scotland receives a clear differential benefit from her native financial system; nevertheless, one may feel persuaded, on general grounds, that some advantages must accrue . . . there is a close interconnection at the board level between the banks and the other Scottish financial institutions; and indirectly, the existence of this locally-based system of banks helps sustain the whole separate financial structure of the region.

Substantial changes in the business of the Scottish clearing banks, their operating environment and their operating structure, as well as in the structure of the banking industry in general have all occurred since Professor Gaskin's observation yet we would still agree that the existence of clearing bank headquarters in Scotland and the activities associated with such location is of major importance in sustaining a separate, regional financial centre in Scotland.

There is little criticism of the payments facilities provided by the Scottish clearing banks today. They have been successful in applying technology to money transmission services increasing the efficiency with which they can handle payments in the Scottish economy and also UK and international retail payments. They have often led the London clearing banks in the development and application of retail banking technology. However, new technology and its application by other institutions is challenging the traditional domination of the money transmission mechanism by the clearing banks. The Scottish clearers will have to continue to demonstrate willingness to meet the large investment necessary to provide competitive systems, perhaps also involving themselves in a number of different co-operative ventures. The current strong position of the Scottish banks in the payments system should provide a base from which to move forward before competing systems become widely available and acceptable.

The Scottish clearing banks are also successful mobilisers of savings in the economy, that is to say, the collection and channelling of savings from surplus to deficit units. There is very little restriction on bank lending in the UK and the Scottish clearers have been able to meet the demand for loans from all sectors of the economy while maintaining adequate standards of prudent operation. The growing share of lending to persons and the declining share to manufacturing industry has resulted from the relative demand for bank finance from these sectors. The Scottish clearing banks have encountered no difficulty in raising funds in the wholesale markets when required to support their lending activities. They have been less successful than the building societies at securing personal sector retail deposits, though in recent years greater priority has been given to collecting these deposits. Their record of attracting retail deposits has been better than that of the London clearing banks.

The performance of the Scottish clearing banks in transforming risk and maturities in the economy is more difficult to assess. Although not every request for finance will be granted, and some customers may feel that the terms on which finance is to be made available are unduly onerous, it is difficult to believe that in a highly competitive banking system the Scottish clearing banks display caution in taking risks or impose requirements on borrowers that are any more excessive or burdensome than those to be found in the UK banking system in general. Critics of the UK banking system have been able to marshal little evidence that the system performs less well than other banking systems in these respects. It has been suggested, however, that banks in the UK do not have close enough relations with their corporate customers which would allow technical and economic insight into lending proposals.[43] There are signs that the London banks are now giving a high priority to corporate relations[44] and the Scottish banks may have to adopt a similar strategy.

The three Scottish clearing banks are important supporters of a strong and expanding Scottish economy to which they have a long-term commitment. Their local presence may confer advantages for both the banks and their competitors. In some cases lending propositions may not be judged only on their banking merits but some consideration may be given to the consequences of the decision for employment and income in the local community. It is also possible that the three banks have provided funds in certain cases when it was not always financially prudent to do so in order to protect the workforce or the creditors (typically other customers of the bank) and in the hope that the customer will ultimately prosper and expand. Assuming the general desirability of such lending criteria it is an important part of any claim that a separate Scottish financial sector provides additional benefit to local industry and commerce than would otherwise be the case. Not too much significance should be attached to this, however, for it is often difficult to demonstrate that no other competing institution would have been prepared to provide the funds were the Scottish banks to withdraw support. Advice on reconstruction and the arranging of finance for these purposes can be provided to customers by the merchant banks and corporate divisions of the Scottish clearing banks, but such advice is also readily available elsewhere in the financial sector. Nevertheless, in general terms, the commitment of the three banks to the Scottish economy does mean that Scottish enterprise will receive a sympathetic ear.

The local presence of the Scottish banks also means that they are able to build up local knowledge and expertise which may give them some small advantage over competitors particularly in the small or medium sized corporate market.

The major weakness of the Scottish clearing banks has been their inability to provide large enterprises with a commercial banking service of the same scale and comprehensiveness as that of the London clearing banks and international banks. They are not major competitors in wholesale banking or in international bank markets. This has partly been due to their small size and their predominantly Scottish customer base, but until recently little attempt was made by the banks to widen their customer base in England[45] and there has been no major attempt at expansion and diversification of business overseas. It is likely that the two Edinburgh banks will seek to become involved in more bank and financial services markets. The purchase by the Royal Bank of Scotland of a London merchant bank and Liverpool-based stockbrokers suggests that the Royal Bank intends to become a more significant participant in the capital markets. It is also the most likely Scottish bank to make an overseas purchase if a suitable opportunity arises, in order to diversify and strengthen its international operations and to make itself more bid-proof. Bank of Scotland, which does not have the benefit of a branch network in the south, has targeted the small company sector in England as an area of expansion that can be served by regional branches and computerised systems. Clydesdale Bank is restricted to expanding its share of the Scottish market. Not only does closer integration of the parent Midland Bank's domestic operations mean that the development of Clydesdale's business will depend more closely on the priorities and strategies of Midland Bank but its international banking development will also be determined by Midland.

On the retail side the role of the bank branch is being re-appraised as new technology displaces many of the standard functions carried out by branches. With large branch networks that cannot easily be rationalised the Scottish clearing banks need to undertake the marketing of a wide range of financial services from many of their more major branches aimed at persons, professionals and small business. The Royal Bank of Scotland has perhaps the best opportunity to adopt a more radical approach to retail banking as it seeks to expand its small existing branch network in the South. In recent years the three banks have had to adopt a more competitive and innovative ethos, balanced by an appropriate degree of prudence and solidity. This has required an improvement in the calibre and training of senior and middle management, including the need to learn and practise marketing skills. This has not yet penetrated all layers of the organisation but should not prove insuperable.

As the Scottish clearing banks diversify further as banking and financial service institutions, new management skills capable of bringing together the many separate activities of the bank under an overall strategic plan will be called for. There will be an increased emphasis on the general business administration and marketing skills of senior management and old conventions must be discarded, where appropriate, for new. Changes in management skills will be necessary if the Scottish banks are to expand their share of markets outwith Scotland where the major growth opportunites for the banks lie. The Scottish clearing banks have a reasonable record of change and adaptation at least within a retail banking frame of reference. There is therefore reason to be optimistic about their future performance in the United Kingdom retail bank and financial service markets.

Appendix:
The Deposit-Taking and Lending Activities of the Scottish Clearing Banks

In this appendix particular features of the deposit-taking and lending activities of the three Scottish clearing banks are described in greater detail.

Deposit-Taking

The Scottish clearing banks issue a range of deposit liabilities which can be considered as either sight deposits, that is to say those deposits which are withdrawable or transferable on demand without a penalty of loss of interest and time deposits which include all other deposits. Funds collected into current accounts as part of the clearing banks' money transmission activities provide a large share of sight deposits. In table 4.10 the sterling deposits of the Scottish and London clearing banks are broken down between sight and time deposits and the amounts accounted for by current accounts and certificates of deposit (CDs) are shown. The table also shows the proportion of total deposits (excluding CDs) received from UK banks, UK residents and overseas residents.

Just under two-fifths of Scottish and London clearing bank deposits are sight deposits. However, a smaller proportion of Scottish bank sight deposits (and total deposits) are current account deposits. At November 1980 current accounts formed 69 per cent of Scottish clearing bank sight deposits but over 80 per cent of London clearing bank sight deposits. By August 1985 the difference had become much smaller with respective proportions of approximately 45 per cent and 50 per cent. These figures also show that current accounts have become a less important source of deposits relative to other types of sight deposit. This can be seen from table 4.10, where for both

Table 4.10. Scottish and London clearing banks' sterling deposits[1]: analysis by type, 1975, 1980, 1984 and 1985 (£ million).

Mid-November[2]	1975	1980	1984	1985
Scottish Clearing Banks				
Sight	986 (39.8)	1791 (35.6)	3481 (34.6)	3753 (35.0)
of which current accounts	n/a	1234 (24.5)	1741 (17.3)	1684 (15.7)
Time	1494 (60.2)	3248 (64.5)	6583 (65.4)	6962 (65.0)
of which certificates of deposit	70 (2.8)	374 (7.4)	614 (6.1)	387 (3.6)
TOTAL	2480	5038	10064	10715
received from (excluding CDS):				
UK banks	52 (2.1)	205 (4.1)	960 (9.5)	1046 (9.9)
Other UK residents	2319 (93.5)	4345 (86.2)	8126 (80.7)	8765 (82.6)
Overseas residents	40 (1.6)	115 (2.3)	363 (3.6)	416 (3.9)
London Clearing Banks				
Sight	10103 (35.7)	18198 (34.5)	33010 (34.8)	39515 (38.0)
of which current accounts	8933 (31.6)	14645 (27.7)	19964 (21.0)	19916 (19.1)
Time	18187 (64.3)	34588 (65.5)	61850 (65.2)	64572 (62.0)
of which certificates of deposit	1562 (5.5)	2293 (4.3)	6375 (6.7)	6155 (5.9)
TOTAL	28291	52777	94860	104086
received from (excluding CDS):				
UK banks	2605 (9.2)	5731 (10.9)	18120 (19.1)	20133 (19.3)
Other UK residents	22610 (79.9)	40297 (76.3)	60824 (64.1)	66261 (63.7)
Overseas residents	1514 (5.4)	4465 (8.5)	9541 (10.1)	11537 (11.1)

1. Figures include clearing bank subsidiaries.
2. Figures for 1985 are at August.
3. Figures for 1975 and 1980 are for the Banking Sector and figures for 1984 and 1985 are for the Monetary Sector. This gives rise to a very small discrepancy in the series (see note 9 at end of chapter).
4. Figures in brackets are percentage of total deposits.

Source: Statistical Unit, Committee of London and Scottish Bankers.

groups of banks sight deposits have remained a fairly steady proportion of total deposits but current account deposits have declined steadily since 1975. This is probably accounted for by the banks taking a greater proportion of wholesale overnight and call deposits and the recent introduction of high interest personal accounts which offer similar facilities to current accounts but also pay interest. The banks are therefore paying interest on a greater proportion of their deposits and this means that deposits have become relatively more expensive than in the past.

The main difference in the sterling deposit bases of the Scottish and London clearing banks is the source of deposits. At August 1985 almost 83 per cent of the Scottish banks' sterling deposits were held by UK public and private sector residents whereas only about 64 per cent of the London clearing banks' deposits were held by these sectors (table 4.10). About 10 per cent of Scottish bank sterling deposits were held by UK banks and about 4 per cent by overseas residents, compared with 19 per cent and 11 per cent

Appendix: Deposit-Taking and Lending

respectively for the London clearing banks. The share of sterling deposits emanating from UK residents has declined between 1975 and 1985 for both clearing bank groups whereas the share emanating from UK banks and overseas residents has increased fairly rapidly, though from a small base. The Scottish clearing banks have tended to be net lenders to the inter-bank market. This was also true of the London clearing banks up to the end of the 1970s, though they have become net borrowers in the inter-bank market during the 1980s.

Another source of clearing bank deposits, which are shown separately in table 4.10, is certificates of deposit (CDs).[46] The amount of CDs issued by the Scottish clearing banks has fluctuated between 1975 and 1985 but by and large this means of raising funds in the UK has never assumed any great significance, possibly because there is no lender of last resort. Up to the 1980s the Scottish banks were from time to time net lenders to the market in CDs, though more recently they have become net borrowers. The London clearing banks have mostly been net borrowers.

Table 4.11 provides a more detailed breakdown of Scottish and London clearing bank deposits from UK residents. The figures show that at June 1985 individuals held about a third of the Scottish clearing banks' total sterling deposits, firms held about two-fifths,[47] and financial institutions held another fifth, with the balance due to the public sector and other elements of the personal sector. Firms and individuals each held something like two-fifths of the London clearing banks' total sterling deposits, whilst financial institutions held about an eighth, with the remaining deposits held by the public sector and other elements of the personal sector. The personal sector deposits of the Scottish banks formed a much larger share of total sterling deposits at the end of 1978 (63 per cent) and 1981 (64 per cent) than at June 1985 (52 per cent). In contrast, the sterling deposits held by financial institutions (other than banks) has increased from about 10.5 per cent at December 1978 and 1981 to about 20 per cent at June 1985. The share of the London clearing banks' deposits held by the different sectors has fluctuated between 1978 and 1985 though financial institutions have shown a notable increase.

Table 4.12 compares the nominal growth of sterling deposits of the Scottish and London clearing banks, the building societies in Scotland, and TSB Scotland over five- and ten-year periods to 1985. The Scottish clearers have amassed sterling customer deposits at a greater rate than the London clearers, by a factor of 3.7 compared to 3.0 between 1975 and 1985, and in the last five years the Scottish growth factor of 2.2 still exceeds the corresponding English level (1.7). The building societies have fared even better than the Scottish clearing banks over the ten year period during which their deposits grew by a factor of 5.4, though growth rates have been similar over the last five years. The TSB had the slowest growth in deposits between 1980 and 1985.

The Scottish Clearing Banks

Table 4.11. Scottish and London clearing banks' sterling deposits[1] from UK residents-outstanding by sector,[2] 1978, 1981 and 1985.

End December	1978 £ million	%	1981 £ million	%	1985[3] £ million	%
Scottish Clearing Banks						
Public sector	97	3.0	94	1.8	143	1.7
Other financial institutions	340	10.4	556	10.5	1717	20.1
Industrial and commercial companies	769	23.6	1269	23.9	2250	26.3
Personal sector						
Persons, households and individual trusts	1401	43.0	2393	45.1	2925	34.2
Other	650	20.0	993	18.7	1521	17.8
Total personal sector	2051	63.0	3386	63.8	4446	52.0
Total all UK residents	3256	100.0	5306	100.0	8556	100.0
London Clearing Banks						
Public sector	579	1.9	823	1.7	1301	1.9
Other financial institutions	2028	6.7	3373	7.0	7626	11.7
Industrial and commercial companies	8181	26.8	11942	24.7	16855	25.1
Personal sector						
Persons, households and individual trusts	14485	47.5	24076	49.8	29681	44.2
Other	5195	17.1	8145	16.8	11680	17.4
Total personal sector	19680	64.6	32221	66.6	41361	61.6
Total all UK residents	30468	100.0	48359	100.0	67142	100.0

1. Including subsidiaries.
2. Excludes deposits from banking/monetary sector.   3. June 1985.
Source: Statistical Unit, Committee of London and Scottish Bankers.

Table 4.12. Deposit growth – Scottish and London clearing banks, building societies and the TSB, 1975–85.

	Deposit balances outstanding[1] (£ million)			Growth factors	
	1975	1980	1985	1975–85	1980–85
Scottish Clearing Banks	2190	3798	8201	3.7	2.2
Building Societies	1174	2958	6338	5.4	2.1
Trustee Savings Bank	n/a	1037	1366	—	1.3
London Clearing Banks[2]	19927	34911	59771	3.0	1.7

1. Figures for Scottish and London clearing banks are at September, those for the building societies at December and for the TSB at November in each year.
2. Scottish figures exclude and London figures include Williams & Glyn's. Figures are for UK Public and Private Sector sterling deposits.
Sources: Bank of England; BSA Bulletins; TSB Annual Report and Accounts.

Appendix: Deposit-Taking and Lending

The rate at which the Scottish clearing banks can increase their deposits is principally determined by two factors. Firstly, the Scottish clearers operate within a single monetary union with official monetary policy controlled by the Bank of England. Attempts to control growth of the total supply of money in the economy must inevitably put a brake on the overall expansion of the deposit market although individual institutions may be able to grow at a proportionately greater rate. This will be determined by the second factor which is the competitiveness of the institution, since all deposit-takers cannot outpace the expansion of the money supply as a whole. The three Scottish clearing banks compete with all other major deposit-taking institutions in the UK for new deposits. However, banks are now rarely restricted from lending to their customers by these constraints on lending resources. Controls on the growth of the money supply are weakly exercised and deposits could always be bid for outwith the area of UK monetary controls. Deposits are not scarce for banks with a record of prudence offering a competitive rate of return. The nature of banking has also changed in recent times. Llewellyn (1985) points out that banks have become more innovative in funding strategies and have developed and perfected new techniques of liability management (including seeking out new sources of funds) to a high degree of sophistication. Liability management was initially concentrated on the wholesale sector but in recent years a higher priority has been given to liability management in the retail sector. Banks are now asset-driven rather than deposit-driven. Through liability management they can secure deposits and reserves to fund the desired volume of assets (Llewellyn).

The consequence of this is that the growth of the Scottish clearing banks' balance sheets are largely determined by the existence of attractive loan opportunities. Although the three banks are not significant participants in the inter-bank market they can, for example, easily secure deposits in this market should these funds be required to make a loan commitment and are likely to have little difficulty in arranging to share a loan where it is merited by the risk of exposure.

Maturity Structure of Deposits and Loans
Tables 4.13 and 4.14 give the maturity breakdown of the Scottish clearing banks' deposits and advances. At August 1985 40 per cent of the Scottish clearers' sterling deposits were sight deposits, withdrawable on demand, and a further 27 per cent had a maturity of less than 8 days (table 4.13). Only 9 per cent of sterling deposits had a maturity of more than 3 months. Foreign currency deposits which tend to be wholesale in nature have longer average maturities. Only 15 per cent were sight deposits and almost 18 per cent had a maturity of between 8 days and 1 month with a further 26 per cent having a maturity of between 1 month and 3 months. Comparison of table 4.13 with table 4.14 shows that liabilities are of considerably shorter maturity than claims. Only 1.3 per cent of sterling deposits had a maturity of one

The Scottish Clearing Banks

Table 4.13. Scottish clearing bank groups' deposits[1] by outstanding maturity,[2] August 1985 (%).

	Sight	Less than 8 days	8 days to 1 month	1 month to 3 months	3 to 6 months	6 months to 1 year	1 year and over	Total	£ million
Sterling deposits	40.2	27.4	13.4	10.0	4.8	3.0	1.3	100.0	10615
Foreign currency deposits	14.7	13.4	17.7	26.0	15.8	6.8	5.6	100.0	2986

1. UK banking sector and other deposits, including CDs and promissory notes.
2. Sterling and foreign currency deposits have been analysed by residual period to earliest maturity date (which could be the first roll-over date or the shortest period of notice).

Source: Statistical Unit, Committee of London and Scottish Bankers.

Table 4.14. Scottish clearing banks groups' advances to UK residents by outstanding maturity,[1] August 1985 (%).

	Overdrafts	Less than 1 year (including sight)	1 year – less than 3 years	3 years – less than 5 years	5 years and over (including undated)	Total	£ million
Non-personal	63.5	21.5	5.2	3.2	6.6	100.0	5897
Persons	25.5	18.8	11.1	3.8	40.8	100.0	2449
Total	52.3	20.7	6.9	3.4	16.7	100.0	8346

1. Includes lending under DTI special scheme for shipbuilding.

Source: Statistical Unit, Committee of London and Scottish Bankers.

Appendix: Deposit-Taking and Lending

year or more, whereas 27 per cent of total sterling advances had a duration of over one year. Although 52 per cent of advances were overdrafts and therefore theoretically repayable on demand, many overdrafts are, in practice, fully utilised or 'rolled-over' sufficiently frequently and for successive annual periods as to make them effectively term loans of fairly long duration. Table 4.14 also shows that the maturity of sterling advances to persons differs from that for other customers. The very high proportion of loans to persons which mature after five years (41 per cent) is accounted for by mortgage advances.

The Scottish banks are able to carry out maturity transformation because while some individuals may be drawing down their deposits, others will simultaneously be adding to theirs, and the banks can rely on a considerable degree of stability in their deposit-base as a whole. This allows them to regard at least part of their deposits as available for long-term loans. Moreover, their ability to bid for large deposits in the wholesale market provides the assurance they need to make loan commitments. This is an important feature of banking practice since the ability to provide medium to long-term loans without a direct matching of claims and liabilities ensures lower costs in the transfer of funds from savers to borrowers in the economy than otherwise would be the case.

Lending

The Scottish clearing banks are the main providers of short- and medium-term finance in the Scottish economy. The most common form of short-term finance is still the traditional overdraft which is widely used by all groups in the economy to meet their working capital needs and is seen as being relatively cheap. A line of credit is agreed with the bank upon which the customer may draw and interest is charged only on the daily oustanding balance. The bank is commited to make the funds available within the limit agreed but has no control over the use of the facility which is determined by the actual borrowing of the customer. The overdraft is therefore a self-liquidating and flexible form of finance. Short-term finance is also made available by the banks through the discounting and acceptance of bills of exchange and the banks have established subsidiaries to carry out factoring of the trade debts of clients.

The introduction of medium-term loans by the Scottish clearing banks did not occur until the late 1950s and early 1960s when facilities were first provided for small and medium-sized businesses. Term loans have an initial term to maturity of more than two years. They are not repayable on demand as is the case with the overdraft (unless in default), but subject to an agreed contractual repayment arrangement which can be linked to the financial benefits or cash stream accruing from the funded project. The banks can also match their term loans, to a degree, by the purchase of term deposits in the wholesale market. Official schemes to assist the export of capital goods and shipbuilding, offering preferential interest rates, were set up during the 1960s enabling term loans to be made, backed by the guarantee of the Exports Credit Guarantee Department and often refinanceable with the Bank of England.

Further expansion of term lending at this time, however, was limited due to a series of restrictive regulatory controls on the clearing banks. The easing of regulation during the 1970s, the development of sophisticated liability management techniques and, in the particular case of the Scottish banks, rising economic activity associated with North Sea oil, led to a fairly rapid expansion in medium-term lending. The clearing banks were also keen to convert the hard-core element of their overdrafts into medium-term contractual loans on which they could charge higher rates of interest and have moved in this direction in recent years. The dominance of the overdraft as a means of securing finance in Scotland has been eroded (see below).

The Scottish clearing banks also provide medium-term finance in the form of instalment credit and leasing facilities. At February 1986 9.6 per cent (£558 million) of Bank of Scotland's advances to customers comprised leased assets and 5.5 per cent (£318 million) comprised instalment credit and other financial agreements. The amount receivable by the Royal Bank of Scotland under finance leases at September 1985 was £641 million, 6 per cent of total advances.

We now take a fairly detailed look at the Scottish clearing banks' lending to industry and persons. There are no rigid conventions which determine the pattern of bank lending between the different sectors of the economy and factors such as customer demand, profitability of the enterprise, the business cycle and the level of interest rates, are all likely to affect the availability and use of the Scottish clearers' loan facilities.[48] In order to understand the lending activities of the three banks it is necessary to focus on loan commitments as well as actual borrowings. The changing importance of each sector to the overall economy is also relevant.

Table 4.15 provides details of total sterling and foreign currency advances and acceptances committed to the main UK industrial sectors and persons, and the extent to which these borrowing arrangements have been utilised at November 1983 and 1984, and at August 1985. Not all lending commitments have been taken up. At August 1985 the Scottish clearers made available almost £14 billion in overdrafts, loans and acceptances of which 68 per cent was utilised. Lending commitments to the manufacturing sector have increased from £2149 million in November 1983 to £2539 million as at August 1985, an increase of 18 per cent. Actual lending to the manufacturing sector at November 1983 was £1053 million and at August 1985 was £1346 million, an increase of approximately 28 per cent. Thus in recent years, as the Scottish clearing banks have increased their commitments to the manufacturing sector, manufacturing firms have been expanding their use of those available facilities at a faster rate.[49]

Appendix: Deposit-Taking and Lending

Table 4.15. Scottish clearing banks and their subsidiaries – advances and acceptances: total facilities outstanding and percentage utilisation,[1] 1983–85.

Mid-November	£ million (% utilisation in brackets)		
	1983	1984	1985[2]
Total Sterling and Foreign Currency Facilities			
Agriculture, forestry and fishing	1083 (78)	1164 (79)	1245 (82)
Energy and water supply industries	408 (18)	531 (34)	552 (29)
Manufacturing industry	2149 (49)	2272 (55)	2539 (53)
Construction	411 (59)	484 (63)	537 (64)
Garages, distribution, hotels and catering	1268 (67)	1469 (68)	1499 (70)
Transport	317 (72)	337 (73)	337 (69)
Postal services and telecommunications	18 (9)	31 (6)	36 (14)
Financial	1143 (59)	1777 (67)	2606 (63)
Business and other services	1455 (66)	1826 (63)	1830 (66)
Persons	2151 (89)	2440 (89)	2777 (89)
Total	10404 (66)	12330 (68)	13956 (68)
of which			
overdraft facilities	6032 (57)	6849 (58)	7566 (60)
loan and acceptance facilities	4372 (77)	5481 (82)	6390 (78)

1. Total facilities outstanding include all loan, overdraft and acceptance facilities whether or not they have been drawn, excluding market loans and lending under special schemes for exports and shipbuilding. The percentage utilisation is the ratio of the amount drawn (i.e. advances and acceptances) to the total facility outstanding. The industry groups shown are based on the Standard Industrial Classification, 1980, which was introduced into the banking statistics in November 1983.   2. August.

Source: Statistical Unit, Committee of London and Scottish Bankers.

The figures in table 4.15 show that persons account for the largest share of total outstanding loan facilities, with the lending commitments of the three Scottish banks amounting to £2777 million at August 1985, almost 20 per cent of the total. The financial sector is the next largest with available loan facilities amounting to £2606 million, almost 19 per cent of the total, slightly more than the manufacturing sector (18 per cent). However, the service trades when grouped together (garages, distribution, hotels and catering, business and other services) have a greater amount of lending facilities available than persons, amounting to £3329 million at August 1985 or 24 per cent of total facilities. The undrawn facilities of the services sector are also greater than persons so that actual lending of the three Scottish banks to persons (£2472 million) is still higher than to any other sector of the economy.

In recent times persons have increased their share of Scottish clearing bank commitments (it was around 11 per cent in 1975) both by way of actual lending and increased facilities most likely due to the rapid expansion in bank mortgage lending during the 1980s and the rising demand for consumer credit. Lending commitments to the financial sector show a substantial rise between November 1983 and August 1985, from £1143 miilion to £2606 million. Funds drawn by the financial sector will normally be passed on to ultimate borrowers in other sectors, in particular by leasing and instalment credit companies. The other main borrowers of bank funds in the financial sector in Scotland are the investment trusts.

The total outstanding sterling and foreign currency loan facilities of the London clearing banks at August 1985 amounted to £125.3 billion. Compared to the Scottish clearing banks a higher proportion of commitments have, over the past ten years or so, been made to the manufacturing sector. These amounted to £29392 million or 24 per cent of total commitments at August 1985. The manufacturing sector's share of total commitments in Scotland fell from about 28 per cent in November 1975,[50] when it was the same as the London banks, to 18 per cent as at August 1985. It has been suggested that this has been because the private sector's manufacturing base was in the Midlands of England where many corporations were owned and managed from London; there has been no reluctance by the Scottish clearing banks to lend to manufacturing industry but demand in Scotland has not always existed at the same level as in England. The strategy of the Bank of Scotland in opening regional offices in England aimed at the small to medium company market lends some support to this view.

In recent times the take-up of the Scottish clearing banks' loan facilities have tended to be higher across all sectors of the economy than has been the take-up of the commitments of the London clearing banks. One possible reason for this is that the Scottish clearers have fewer large corporate customers with a wide choice of funding, but relatively more small and medium-sized business customers which have less choice as to their sources of finance or inclination to change sources and therefore make greater use of the facilities made available by the Scottish banks.

At the bottom of table 4.15 total sterling and foreign currency facilities are divided into overdrafts, and loans and acceptances. At August 1985 approximately 54 per cent of total facilities comprised overdrafts. This proportion has declined steadily in recent years. At November 1983 overdrafts formed 58 per cent of total facilities and in November 1975 the proportion was around 72 per cent. The decline in overdraft finance and corresponding increase in term lending, with its definite repayment commitment, occurred much earlier for the London clearing banks so that by November 1978 loans and acceptances accounted for more than half of outstanding facilities. Overdrafts formed nearly 44 per cent of London clearing banks' commitments at August 1985. Not surprisingly, since loans are likely to be associated with particular investment projects or capital purchases, a higher percentage of loan facilities have been drawn down (see

Appendix: Deposit-Taking and Lending

table 4.15). Overdraft facilities are also often held for precautionary purposes.

Table 4.16 shows actual sterling and foreign currency lending to UK residents as at August 1985 by both the Scottish and London clearing banks and by all banks in the United Kingdom. Lending to persons by the three Scottish clearing banks amounted to £2457 million and accounted for the largest share of total lending at 26.8 per cent. Of this, £1260 million, or just over half, was house purchase finance. The mortgage lending business of the Scottish clearing banks has grown markedly over the 1980s (see section on building societies in chapter 5). Virtually all lending to persons is in sterling. Lending to the services sector amounted to £2195 million, 24 per cent of total advances, and manufacturing industry received advances of £1256 million or 13.7 per cent of total advances. In recent years the trend has been for persons and the financial sector to take an increasing share of Scottish bank lending whilst the share of manufacturing has declined, though lending to the financial sector will often reflect a requirement for funds by industry and commerce channelled through other lenders.

The activities of the three Scottish clearing banks are not confined to Scotland. Table 4.16 shows the level of Scottish clearing bank advances to UK residents (about 5.6 per cent of all bank advances) and is not therefore a strict reflection of lending in the Scottish economy. However, most of their lending is made in Scotland[51] and comparisons with the advances made by all banks in the UK and with the London clearing banks in particular enables some distinction to be drawn that can be attributed to the composition of the Scottish economy. Major differences appear only in advances to the agriculture, forestry and fishing and financial sectors, and in advances to persons. The three Scottish clearing banks have traditionally been strong supporters of the agriculture industry in Scotland which is a sector of major importance to the Scottish economy. Just over 11 per cent of the Scottish clearers' advances, or £912 million, were made to this sector at August 1985, compared to under 6 per cent for the London clearing banks.

The higher proportion of the total Scottish clearing banks' lending to the financial sector is largely accounted for by a greater proportion of advances being made to investment and unit trusts, though they also lend proportionately more to insurance companies and leasing enterprises, than do the London clearing banks. This is probably due to the high concentration of investment trusts in Scotland, and the presence of large life assurance offices. About 32 per cent of the Scottish clearing banks' lending to the financial sector is in foreign currencies. A much higher percentage of the total advances made by the London clearing banks and all banks in the UK is to persons than is the case for the Scottish clearers. This may be due to high demand for personal credit in the South and also a reflection of higher average house prices in London and the South East.

Table 4.16 shows that the Scottish clearing banks' lending to manufactur-

Table 4.16. Advances to UK residents in sterling and other currencies: industrial analysis,[1] August 1985 (£ million).

UK residents	Scottish clearing banks and their subsidiaries (% of total advances)	of which in sterling (% of total)	London clearing banks and their subsidiaries (% of total advances)	of which in sterling (% of total)	All banks[3] in UK (% of UK total)
Agriculture, forestry and fishing	1016 (11.1)	1016 (12.2)	4325 (5.7)	4370 (6.2)	5860 (3.6)
Energy and water supply industries	146 (1.6)	87 (1.0)	1599 (2.1)	611 (0.9)	5435 (3.3)
Manufacturing industry	1256 (13.7)	1137 (13.6)	11238 (14.7)	9659 (13.8)	26891 (16.4)
Construction	321 (3.5)	320 (3.8)	3259 (4.3)	3151 (4.5)	4976 (3.0)
Garages, distribution, hotels and catering	996 (10.9)	972 (11.6)	9709 (12.7)	9176 (13.1)	21171 (12.9)
Transport	232 (2.5)	161 (1.9)	1678 (2.2)	1229 (1.7)	} 3734 (2.3)
Postal services and telecommunications	5 (0.0)	5 (0.1)	56 (0.1)	56 (0.1)	
Financial	1544 (16.8)	1053 (12.6)	8095 (10.6)	6263 (8.9)	34044 (20.7)
Business and other services	1199 (13.1)	1146 (13.7)	9778 (12.8)	9059 (12.9)	24018 (14.6)
Persons	2457 (26.8)	2449 (29.3)	26565 (34.8)	26542 (37.9)	38270 (23.3)
Total advances to UK residents	9170 (100.0) (5.6)[2]	8346 (100.0)	76302 (100.0) (46.4)[2]	70166 (100.0)	164397 (100.0)

1. Definitions of the industry groups are based on the 1980 SIC, with the addition of the personal sector.
2. Percentage of all banks.
3. Reporting institutions includes retail banks, accepting houses, other British banks, American banks, Japanese banks, other overseas banks, consortium banks.

Appendix: Deposit-Taking and Lending

ing industry accounts for 13.7 per cent of their total advances to UK residents. This represents a fall from around 25 per cent in 1975[52] reflecting the decline of Scotland's manufacturing base as the loss of traditional industries has not been offset by the growth of new technology industry such as electronics. Manufacturing industry took only a slightly larger share of the total advances of the London clearing banks (14.7 per cent) at August 1985 and of the total advances of all banks in the UK (16.4 per cent).

The proportions of actual lending to the various sectors of the Scottish economy will differ between each of the three Scottish clearing banks. Bank of Scotland, for example, has built up fairly substantial interests in the oil and energy sector and Clydesdale Bank has traditionally lent to heavy industry in the West of Scotland. There are, however, unlikely to be substantial differences between the sector lending of the three clearing banks. Table 4.16 illustrates that the Scottish clearing banks lend funds to all sectors of the economy; taken as a whole they show no sector preference or specialisation, so that in recent years, for example, they have increased the relative share of their lending to the personal sector in the absence of the same level of demand from other sectors.

The capacity of a business to borrow is largely determined by its profitability record and prospects, an adequate capital base in relation to the amount of borrowing since it is the task of equity to take the residual risk in a business, and an acceptable degree of liquidity to meet liabilities as they fall due. When a bank lends money it does so in the expectation that the borrower's business will be successful, will earn profits of a sufficient amount to enable the borrowing to be repaid with interest, or will grow to the extent that short term finance on a revolving basis can be justified. When making loans to persons the bank will consider the income and job security of the borrower and any other existing borrowing commitments. Banks will also be concerned with the general maturity pattern of their advances and deposits, the spread of advances so that they are not overly exposed to any one borrower, to any one group of related borrowers or to any particular sector of industry, and with their bad debts experience. Where lending to a credit worthy customer or to a particular sector is considered to be at a high enough level in relation to the overall lending portfolio and to the shareholders' funds the bank may impose a restraint on its commitments and participate in a shared or syndicated bank lending arrangement. Banks may often seek to obtain security against the loan as a safeguard against failure of the enterprise or the failure to repay the loan within an acceptable period, including the prospect for repayment in the future were further support in time of difficulty to be forthcoming.

There is very little evidence that the Scottish clearing banks have provided inadequate support for Scottish industry and commerce. Bain and Reid (1984) argue that 'the evidence would seem to suggest that by and large the Scottish clearing banks provide a satisfactory service to their industrial and commercial customers'.[53] The Scottish banks provide a wide range of lending facilities that can be suited to their customers' needs and North Sea oil exploration and development provides a good example of the banks quickly acquiring the necessary expertise and often playing a leading and innovative lending role.[54] The Scottish clearing banks have also improved their corporate financial advice in recent years enabling them to devise and arrange the financing of new or reconstructed enterprises and advice on the financing of existing customers (see chapter 6).

The ownership structure of enterprise in Scotland plays a part in determining the demand for borrowing from the Scottish clearing banks. A fairly high proportion of enterprises in Scotland are branches or subsidiaries of externally owned companies and their financial requirements for investment and liquidity will normally be met by the parent company with little recourse to local financing. These companies will instead use the Scottish banks to provide payments facilities. The large independent Scottish companies may use the Scottish banks as one source of banks funds but are likely to use also the London clearing banks or one of the many international banks based in the City of London, a few of which have established offices or branches in Scotland. The Scottish clearing banks are, however, important providers of finance to many independent small and medium-sized companies in Scotland and increasingly compete for this business in England.

Other Forms of Lending
The three Scottish clearing banks play a very small part as lenders of long-term finance or providers of equity in the financial system.[55] There are three major vehicles used by the Scottish clearers to provide longer-term finance to industry and commerce. Each of the banks has a shareholding[56] in Investors in Industry Group plc (3i), the development and venture capital company owned by the UK clearing banks and the Bank of England, and their borrowing facilities are made available to the Company. Second, the three Scottish banks each have a share of 33.3 per cent in the Scottish Agriculture Securities Corporation Limited, which provides long-term loans for farm purchase and improvement. At March 1985 the total assets of the Corporation amounted to £16.5 million of which about £14.8 million was in loans and £1.0 million in investments. Most of the Corporation's liabilities are debenture stocks (£10 million).

Direct equity participation by the three banks has traditionally been limited. A major consideration is the criticism of conflict of interest that the banks would probably receive from competing firms who were also dependent on the banks for loan finance. Actual equity involvement may on occasion occur as part of a package deal with the clearing bank holding an option to purchase under agreed and clearly defined circumstances. Most of the banks' equity holdings, however, are obtained through specialist subsidiary or associate companies (the third vehicle) which are involved in providing venture capital to mainly new and small unquoted companies both in Scotland and England.

Interest Rates

The equilibrium level of the rate of interest in the market for loanable funds is set where the level of savings in the economy and the increase in the supply of money equates with the level of investment in the economy and the increase in the demand for money.[57,58] In the short term it is monetary conditions which are the principal determinant of the interest rate for sudden and substantial changes in the demand for money often occur as a response to temporary economic and political uncertainty both in the UK and elsewhere in the world. Sharp changes in the demand for money may not be completely met by adjustments in the supply since monetary policy may be in force to act as a brake and the banks may also be unwilling to make substantial adjustments in the scale of their assets and liabilities which could increase the supply of money. In these circumstances it is interest rates which adjust. Official pressure is also exerted on the rate of interest from time to time by the operations of the Treasury in the money market as part of monetary policy or in an attempt to control or help stabilise economic variables such as the value of sterling against the other currencies. For example, if money flows rapidly out of sterling and into dollars then interest rates may be adjusted upwards to dissuade asset holders from attempting to alter further their money holdings and thus prevent a fall in the value of sterling.[59]

There is no one rate of interest in the economy but rather a structure of interest rates. The rate of interest which has probably the greatest influence on the cost of funds from the money-market is the three-month inter-bank loan rate. Significant changes in money-market rates will lead to the banks changing their own 'base' rates. The specific rates of interest charged by the banks on their loans and offered on their deposits will depend on a whole number of factors. Thus the rate of interest charged to borrowers by the Scottish clearing banks will be influenced by the general level of interest rates in force at the time of the loan, and the risk of default by the borrower and the security offered. A large 'blue-chip' company, for example, will have sufficient standing among the financial community to command a lower rate of interest on loans. The rate of interest must also include an allowance for setting up, monitoring and servicing the loan. Economies of scale are likely to be present so that the transactions costs associated with small loans are proportionately greater which is one reason why loans to the Scottish banks' retail customers bear higher rates of interest than do wholesale loans.

The rates of interest charged by the Scottish clearing banks will also include an element to cover their costs of operation and to provide a profit. We have seen that the margins on their banking business must cover the costs associated with operating the payments mechanism since this service is not priced to recover the full cost of operation. Margins will be influenced by competition. Competition among the clearing banks and other banking and deposit institutions ensures that the rates of interest offered on deposits and charges on loans are fairly similar throughout the UK. There is no evidence that the Scottish clearing banks provide support to Scottish industry on terms that are more costly or onerous than those available elsewhere.

In certain sectors of the market for loanable funds and for deposits, however, other institutions may be more competitive. In the wholesale money-markets there are many potential lenders and competition is very keen. Borrowers will shop around for the best rates and the large international banks are often willing or able to operate on finer margins and are highly competitive. The Scottish banks are not heavily involved in the money-market but do face strong competition in the retail market. In the past, competition in the retail bank market was more restrained since borrowers were often more concerned with maintaining the goodwill which arises from a long-established relationship with their banks and were reluctant to shift from one bank to another in search of slightly lower interest rates. With a wider range of financing available to potential borrowers and generally greater competition in the retail loan market as well as plentiful advice on raising loan capital many more borrowers are now willing to negotiate with different banks. It has therefore become important for the banks to attract and hold borrowers by building solid relationships and offering other financial services and innovative financing packages as well as offering competitive loans.

NOTES
1. Source: Committee of London Clearing Bankers' Statistical Unit. These figures slightly understate the relative size of the Scottish banks since Williams & Glyn's, which has been fully absorbed by the Royal Bank, is included in the London bank and not the Scottish bank figure. Figures exclude subsidiaries. Coutts & Co. (a subsidiary of National Westminster Bank) is the sixth London bank.
2. These banks are not the only participants in the clearing system. The Co-operative Bank, Girobank, the TSBs, Citibank and Standard Chartered Bank are also involved with clearing operations.
3. The lending and borrowing figures of these subsidiaries are, however, very often included in the totals for the parent bank.
4. Source: Statistical Unit, Committee of London and Scottish Bankers. Inward debit and credit clearing includes both inter-bank and inter-branch clearing.
5. Weyer (Chairman, Barclays Bank UK, 1982) has suggested that cheque processing absorbs 60 per cent of the clearing banks' operating costs and staff resources.
6. Clearing House Automated Payments System. CHAPS is an electronic switching system developed to replace Town clearing (i.e. sterling cheques drawn and paid into branches within the 'square mile' of the City of London) and the aim is to provide same-day settlement of payments.

Notes

7. The London clearing banks calculate the cost of their 'free' retail funds at 9 per cent. Gaskin (1980) gives the figure of 8 per cent for the Scottish clearing banks which was widely quoted at that time. Discussions with the Scottish banks indicate that it would be within the range of 8–10 per cent.
8. Statistical data for the Scottish and London clearing banks has in the past been collected separately for the three Scottish banks and for the five London banks of Barclays, Lloyds, Midland, National Westminster and Williams & Glyn's. Figures for Williams & Glyn's were included in the London and not the Scottish totals and similar treatment was given to Clydesdale Bank, although it is a subsidiary of Midland Bank. For official statistical purposes, following the merger of the Royal Bank of Scotland with its sister company Williams & Glyn's (September 1985), the London and Scottish clearing banks have been considered as one distinct group of banks in the UK. Most of the statistics in both this section of chapter 4 and the appendix are based on the old format but elsewhere in the chapter figures for the Royal Bank include Williams & Glyn's, or it is made explicit that they do not.
9. In November 1981 the basis of the banking and monetary aggregates was changed from the 'banking sector' to the 'monetary sector', which comprises the UK offices of institutions either recognised as banks or licensed to take deposits under the Banking Act 1979, together with the National Girobank, the TSBs, the Banking Department of the Bank of England, and those institutions (including branches of mainland banks) in the Channel Islands and the Isle of Man which have opted to participate in the new monetary control arragements introduced in August 1981. A number of institutions in the Isle of Man and Channel Islands opted out of the new monetary sector and therefore ceased to be included within the clearing banks' figures as from November 1981. Tables therefore contain a small discontinuity between the figures for 1981 and after, and earlier years.
10. Eligible liabilities comprise sterling deposit liabilities, excluding deposits with an original maturity of over two years, plus any sterling resources obtained by switching foreign currencies into sterling. Net inter-bank transactions and items in transit are also included in the calculation of the individual banks' eligible liabilities.
11. Actual adjustments to the amount of cash ratio deposits each institution is required to hold take place in November and May each year, based on average eligible liabilities in the six months to October and to April respectively.
12. The establishment and development of the Scottish bank branch network has a well documented history. For example, see Gaskin (1965), Checkland (1975) and Munn (1981).
13. A tiny number in these totals will be branches in England. Note also that branches which were formerly Williams & Glyn's are not differentiated in the 1985 statistics.
14. This assumes that the clearing bank branch networks are subject, in general, to decreasing returns to scale in Scotland, but that there is some optimal point on the cost and revenue curves below which the loss in revenue resulting from branch closure would exceed the savings in cost. It is difficult to judge whether the smaller branch networks of TSB Scotland and the large building societies are subject to decreasing, constant or inceasing returns to scale. Interviews suggest that where only one or two branches have been established by incoming London and American banks the marginal revenue of the Scottish operation considerably exceeds the marginal cost.
15. Figures include non-clerical and part-time staff, but exclude staff (of which there are few) working completely or mainly outside the UK.

16. Figures provided by the Royal Bank indicate that 8768 bank staff are employed in Scotland and 8023 in England. These figures cover bank staff only, although in relation to overall numbers the inclusion of group staff will not significantly influence the figures.
17. Year ending 28 February 1986 for Bank of Scotland and year ending 30 September 1985 for the Royal Bank of Scotland.
18. For year ending 31 December 1985 Barclays (60 per cent), Lloyds (64 per cent), Midland (58 per cent) and National Westminster (62 per cent).
19. Source: *Annual Reports* and *Accounts*; and de Zoete & Bevan *Bank Review* July 1984.
20. Current account services are not priced so as to recover the costs involved. The revenue deficit incurred in providing current account services demands a minimum return of about 8 per cent on the endowment element for the trading operation to break even. These balances would become a burden if the general level of interest rates were to fall below 8 per cent. Gaskin (1980) observes that this is one of the factors which stimulates the efforts of the clearing banks to contain the volume of work required to service these accounts and associated monetary costs.
21. TSB Scotland also has its own training college.
22. The Euromarket, the recycling of petro-dollars, rapid growth of financial markets in the Pacific Basin, and the demand for Western credit have all been important stages in the development of international banking.
23. Paltzer (1977).
24. Initial Submission of the Committee of Scottish Clearing Bankers to the Wilson Committee, Memorandum I (Part I).
25. See Paltzer (1977).
26. The Royal Bank of Scotland AG, for example, is a subsidiary set up in Switzerland by the Royal Bank, and both Edinburgh banks have established subsidiaries in the Channel Islands where banks enjoy certain taxation advantages.
27. The Federal Government's capital program consisted of the Foreign Direct Investment Program (FDIP), the Interest Equalisation Tax (IET), and the Voluntary Foreign Credit Restraint (VFCR). Under FDIP US corporations were limited in the amount of funds they could transfer to their corporate affiliates overseas and foreign affiliates themselves were constrained as to the amount of locally generated earnings they could retain for re-investment purposes. The EIT, by imposing a tax on the yields of securities of foreign origin, lowered the effective yield on such securities, making them less attractive to US residents – and thus making it more difficult for foreigners, including the foreign affiliates of US corporations, to finance their capital requirements in the US market. Under VFCR the head offices of the US banks were requested to limit their foreign lendings to ceilings that reflected their historical foreign credit levels. See Frankel, A.B., 'International Banking: The Activities of US Banks Abroad', in Havrilesky and Boorman (1980).
28. Regulation Q places a limit on the rate of interest US banks are allowed to pay on deposits received at their branches in the United States. Foreign US bank branches are not subject to these constraints.
29. The three Scottish clearing banks are also members of SWIFT – see earlier section on Money Transmission.
30. Approximately 300000 payments are made each month to beneficiaries mostly residing in the United States, Canada, Australia, the Republic of Ireland and South Africa.
31. The other principal bank subsidiary was Williams & Glyn's Bank which operated in England and was a member of the Committee of London Clearing

Notes

Bankers. The Group subsequently changed its name to the Royal Bank of Scotland Group.

32. In effect the undertakings of the Royal Bank of Scotland plc and Williams & Glyn's Bank plc were transferred into a 'new' company, the Royal Bank of Scotland plc. The Royal Bank of Scotland Group plc remains the holding company of the banking group, with three principal subsidiaries – the Royal Bank of Scotland plc, the Charterhouse Group (holding company) and the Royal Bank of Scotland Insurance Company Ltd.
33. Button (1985) provides a helpful discussion of the theory of contestable markets and its application.
34. Rather simply efficiency means no scope for consumer exploitation or profiteering.
35. This comparison is complicated by the fact that the London clearing banks obtain a slightly higher proportion of their retail deposits in the form of non-interest bearing current acounts than do the Scottish clearing banks.
36. Sometimes known as free capital base.
37. Free shareholders' funds incorporate issued share capital, reserves, general debt provisions, minority interests, less goodwill, property, equipment, trade investments and associates.
38. The balance and deposit figures cover the business of the offices of the three Scottish clearing banks, including their offices in England, and the offices of the six London clearing banks in Great Britain, the Channel islands and the Isle of Man. Williams & Glyn's figures are included in the latter totals. It must also be remembered that the London branches in particular account for a not insignificant proportion of Scottish domestic bank business and the figures do not therefore reflect a 'true' split between English and Scottish bank business.
39. It is possible that growth figures are distorted as a result of changing allocations of business between the clearing banks and their subsidiaries.
40. The Scottish clearing banks' ATM networks are discussed under Money Transmission at the beginning of chapter 4.
41. In the larger corporate market sophisticated cash management systems for corporate treasurers have been developed and introduced by the large American banks in recent years. Potential loss of corporate clients forced the UK clearing banks into providing similar systems for businesses. Bank of Scotland has recently set up a treasury service which operates by time-sharing on the Geisco Worldwide network, and the Royal Bank has established a link with National Data Corporation of Atlanta to provide such a service, also on a worldwide scale.
42. In so far as it does not fall foul of the Data Protection Act.
43. An interesting article on this is 'Banks' Relations with Industry: an International Survey', D. Vittas (1986).
44. For example, by establishing posts in which a bank officer has full responsibility for ensuring that the needs of the client company are met by the bank. These officers may be expected to build up greater knowledge of the company's business than otherwise would be the case, raising the flow of information between both parties, and may acquire some expertise in the industrial aspects of its business.
45. The ownership stakes held by the London clearing banks in the Scottish clearing banks (see Ownership section) may have prevented earlier expansion in England.
46. A certificate of deposit is a document issued by a bank certifying that a deposit has been made with the bank which is repayable to the bearer on surrender of the certificate at maturity. The existence of a secondary market in London

enables holders of CDs to sell their claims at any time at the prevailing market price. The advantage to the banks is that they can issue CDs with longer maturities than wholesale deposits in general since the depositor has the benefit of a negotiable certificate.

47. A fairly substantial part of the 'other' component of the personal sector consists of unincorporated businesses.
48. Banks in the UK are relatively free to choose the assets in which they invest within the constraints set by solvency and liquidity considerations and by the need to comply with official credit control requirements and any other guidelines which may be in force. Supervision of the banks is undertaken by the Bank of England which monitors the composition of each UK-registered bank's assets and liabilities and provisions made for bad and doubtful debts.
49. The reasons behind the changes in the level of borrowing by the manufacturing sector and other sectors of the economy from banks are complex and a discussion is outwith the scope of this book.
50. Based on the 1968 SIC.
51. Note that Williams & Glyn's is included in the figures for the London clearing banks and not those for the Scottish clearing banks.
52. See note 50.
53. See Bain and Reid (1984) for a discussion of financial provision for industry and commerce in Scotland.
54. The total loans and commitments of the three Scottish clearing banks to licencees for UK oil and gas development amounted to £411 million at August 1985, 53 per cent in foreign currencies.
55. Banks in the UK are sometimes criticised for not lending to industry for longer periods than they do. On this see Bain (1981).
56. Bank of Scotland 3.1 per cent; Clydesdale Bank 1.4 per cent; the Royal Bank of Scotland 7.6 per cent.
57. See Bain (1981, chapter 5), whom we follow here.
58. The increase in the supply of and demand for money are not wholly independent of the rate of interest. Thus the effect on the rate of interest arising from any shift in either of these two variables, savings or investment, will depend on the interest elasticity of these variables.
59. Under this analysis the demand and supply of money will alter together in the long-run and it is the flow of savings and investment which are the more important determinants of interest rates. The determination of the cost of capital in the economy is a matter of open debate. Two opposing approaches – stocks and flows – were considered and summarised in the Wilson Committee Report (chapter 11).

5

RETAIL DEPOSIT INSTITUTIONS

The previous chapter has reviewed the progress of the Scottish clearing banks in the changing environment in which they operate. This chapter turns to the two other major competing retail deposit institutions, the TSB and the building societies. With the incorporation of the TSB the distinctiveness of the organisation has been removed as it now stands on an equal footing with other commercial banks, the trustee element having been expunged. Its different background and development require it to be considered separately from the other banks but in time this will become less appropriate. The building societies, although largely headquartered outside Scotland, deserve extended treatment both because of their key role in the retail deposit market in Scotland and the potential impact of recent legislation which allows them to compete, at least partially, in the provision of banking and other services.

The Trustee Savings Bank

Recent Background
Until the early 1970s the Trustee Savings Banks (TSBS) operated as an association of independent savings banks, closely supervised by the Treasury, and had a narrow concentration on personal savings offering a high degree of security, with assets invested in safe but low earning government securities through the National Debt Commissioners. In the past ten years the TSBS have undergone considerable change and have evolved into a major banking organisation offering competitive rates of return and a comprehensive range of financial services to personal customers and, increasingly, to small businesses.

The changes to the TSBS can be traced back to 1971 when the government set up a Committee under the chairmanship of Sir Harry Page to review the National Savings Movement. The Page Committee reported in 1973 and recommended a revised role for the TSBS, free from the previous level of tight Government regulations, providing personal banking services in competition with the London and Scottish clearing banks. The Report also placed emphasis on the need to clarify, by way of legislation, the status of the TSBS, the powers to be retained by the Treasury and the rights of both trustee and depositor. The first stage of the transition occurred under the Trustee Savings Bank Act 1976 which authorised the TSBS to commence lending and provide additional banking services to the general public. The Act included provisions relating to the appointment and removal of trustees and established the TSB Central Board to control and coordinate overall management of the individual savings banks.

Following the publication of the Page Committee's Report the TSBs started to re-organise. In 1974 the number of independent savings banks fell from 73 to 19. By 1982 there were 16 TSBs, including 4 in Scotland, each nominating members to the Central Board. Further amalgamation occurred and in 1983 TSB Scotland took over the business of the Aberdeen, Tayside & Central, West of Scotland and South of Scotland TSBs. Three other TSBs were also formed – TSB England and Wales, TSB Northern Ireland and TSB Channel Islands.

Table 5.1. TSB Group principal subsidiaries 1985.[1]

Subsidiary	Activity	Country of incorporation
Central Trustee Savings Bank Ltd	Banking, clearing and investment services for TSB Group and other customers.	England (Staff 816)
TSB Trustcard Ltd	Credit card services.	England (Staff 690)
TSB Trust Company Ltd	Life assurance, unit trust management, gilt fund management, insurance broking, marketing general insurance products.	England (Holding Company) (Staff 1413)
United Dominions Trust	Instalment credit, finance for industry and commerce, vehicle leasing, rental and distribution.	England (Staff 4008)

1. Proposed reorganisation will incorporate Central TSB with banking arm of TSB England and Wales.
Source: Annual Report and Accounts.

Following the 1976 Act the TSBs developed and diversified their banking activities both through in-house initiatives and the purchase of specialist subsidiaries. Shareholdings in the subsidiary operations were purchased through a holding company vehicle. TSB Scotland was effectively a partner in a consortium, comprising the TSB Central Board and all the other TSBs, which held the entire share capital of TSB (Holdings) Limited. This is shown in figure 5.1. Table 5.1 shows the principal subsidiaries of the TSB Group, other than the regional banking arms, along with their primary business activities. The largest subsidiary is United Dominions Trust (UDT) which is one of the major finance houses in the UK. None of the financial service subsidiaries is registered or headquartered in Scotland.

Organisational developments of the TSBs have recently centred on the change in status from unincorporated societies, managed by boards of trustees, to a public limited company managed by a board of directors. The change in status was necessary because the TSB structure did not meet the First EEC Council Directive on Credit Institutions of December 1977, which required formal licensing arrangements to be set up for all deposit-taking institutions. The Banking Act of 1979 brought the supervision of banks and deposit-taking institutions into line with the requirements of the Directive. The TSBs, however, as unincorporated societies, could not be recognised under the 1979 Banking Act and exemption was granted from the Directive until 1985. Supervision was carried out by the Treasury which had powers to direct certain activities and determine liquidity requirements. The Bank of England was delegated to provide prudential guidance to the TSBs.

After consultation with the TSBs the government decided in 1982 to introduce legislation which would allow the TSBs to transform themselves into public limited companies. The attainment of full banking status brought the TSBs within the full control of the Bank of England for supervisory purposes in addition to already existing controls for monetary policy purposes. Pressure for a change to corporate status also came from the executive management of the TSBs who wished to achieve full banking status and secure the removal of Treasury restrictions which prevented the management from fully developing the TSBs as financial service organisations. The 1976 Act, for example, specified the classes of assets in which the banks could invest.

Figures 5.1 and 5.2 show the TSB structure before and after the incorporation of the TSB. Under the new structure TSB Scotland is one of several principal subsidiaries with the primary business of banking and the provision of TSB Group financial services to both corporate and personal customers. The TSB Group, incorporating the four regional banking arms and other principal subsidiaries, is the sixth largest domestic banking concern in the UK, measured by total assets.[1] TSB Scotland is now the fourth largest domestic bank in Scotland behind the Clydesdale Bank. For the year ending November 1985, the balance sheet of TSB Scotland was just under £1.6 billion with deposits of £1.37 billion. Comparable figures for the Clydesdale Bank are £2.8 billion and £2.2 billion.

The re-organisation of the TSBs into a new structure has been a more emotive issue in Scotland than elsewhere. The very long history, the strength of the TSB in Scotland and a strong commitment to the mutual principle helped to vocalise fears regarding the loss of autonomy of an important and sizeable Scottish financial institution, echoing concerns raised in 1981 with the take-over bid for the Royal Bank of Scotland. An attempt was made in the passage through Parliament of the TSB Bill to separate TSB Scotland from the rest of the Group. Lord Taylor of Gryfe argued, during the House of Lords committee stages, that 'Some of the dynamism needed to create an effective instrument operating out of Edinburgh could be

Retail Deposit Institutions

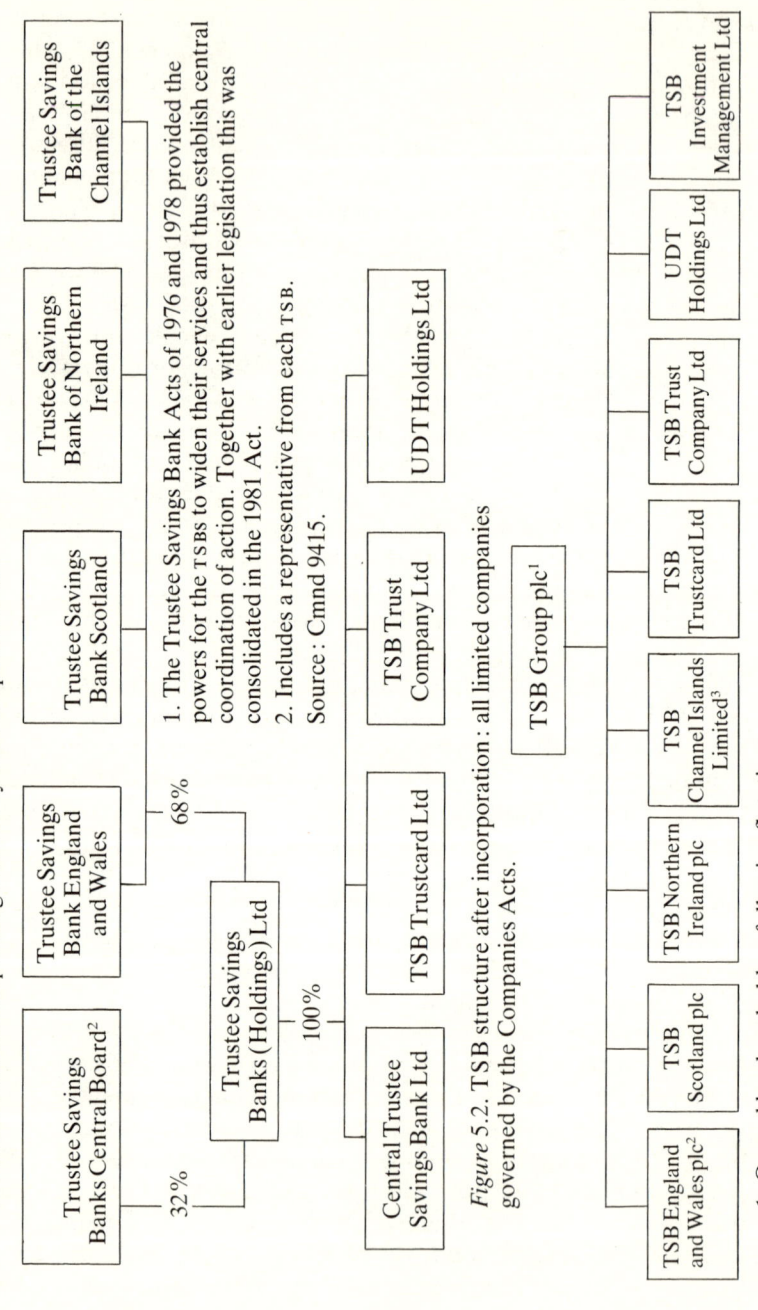

Figure 5.1. TSB structure prior to incorporation. *Top line*: Trustee Savings Banks Central Board and the four Trustee Savings Banks governed by the Trustee Savings Banks Act 1981.[1] *Middle and bottom lines*: five limited companies governed by the Companies Acts.

1. The Trustee Savings Bank Acts of 1976 and 1978 provided the powers for the TSBs to widen their services and thus establish central coordination of action. Together with earlier legislation this was consolidated in the 1981 Act.
2. Includes a representative from each TSB.

Source: Cmnd 9415.

Figure 5.2. TSB structure after incorporation: all limited companies governed by the Companies Acts.

1. Owned by shareholders following flotation.
2. Incorporating the operations of Trustee Savings Bank England and Wales and Central Trustee Savings Bank Limited.
3. 49% owned locally in the Channel Islands (other subsidiaries wholly owned by TSB Group plc).

Source: TSB Group Offer for Sale Document.

diminished by its being part of a centrally controlled institution' (Hansard). A compromise was reached with special undertakings given to Parliament so that TSB Scotland 'can, should and will continue to function as an independently managed Scottish Bank within the Group' (TSB Scotland *Annual Report*). The new TSB Group is to be registered in Edinburgh. Only time will reveal the true extent of TSB Scotland's independence.

Operations of the TSB

TSB Scotland is primarily a retail deposit bank with a large personal customer base. Apart from collecting funds from savers and making loans to individuals and small businesses the TSB is involved in the payments system in Scotland[2] and provides the full range of TSB Group personal financial products. The deposits of the TSBs are largely composed of interest-bearing accounts. Upgrading of the product range after the Page Report led to the introduction of cheque accounts and wholesale deposit facilities have also been introduced. Leslie (1983) has charted the change between 1970–81 and this can be followed from table 5.2. Savings accounts (which provided money transmission by way of standing orders and direct debits) declined in number and value from 1978 onwards, in part due to an uncompetitive level of remuneration when compared with the banks and building societies,[3] and to cheque-book holders no longer being required to hold a minimum sum in their savings account. The investment account also offered attractive higher rates of return after the abolition of the tax concession on interest earned on savings accounts. As a percentage of total funds savings accounts declined from 41 per cent in 1970 to just under 22 per cent in 1981. Investment

Table 5.2. Trustee Savings Banks' deposits and branches, 1970–85 (£ million).

End November	1970	1975	1978	1979	1980	1981	1982[4]	1983	1984	1985
TSB Group[1]										
Savings[2]	1050	1541	1768	1557	1439	1309	}6800	7393	8080	9070
Investment[3]	1474	2216	2893	3405	3752	4145				
Cheque	14	95	346	468	555	622	714	830	921	1124
Total funds	2538	3853	5007	5430	5746	6076	7514	8223	9001	10194
No. of branches	1505	1579	1660	1657	1656	1657	1610	1612	1614	1600

1. All Trustee Savings Banks.
2. Ordinary Accounts known as Savings Accounts after 1979.
3. Investment Funds include investment account, maxi-yield and term deposits.
4. Group Accounts distinguish interest bearing and non-interest bearing deposits. It is assumed the latter correspond with the cheque entry.

Sources: Leslie (1983); TSB Group Accounts; *Abstract of Banking Statistics* (Vol.3), CLSB.

accounts now form the most important source of interest-bearing retail deposits and are similar to the range of personal deposit accounts offered by the clearing banks.

Prior to 1976 each TSB had two main departments, an Ordinary Department dealing with cheque and savings accounts, and a Special Investment Department (SID) dealing with investment accounts. Ordinary savings deposits invested through the National Debt Commissioners were lodged by the National Debt Commissioners in government securities. Interest payments to the TSBs were determined by the Treasury. SID funds were invested in a wider range of public sector stock offering higher rates of return. These departments no longer exist but the investments still form part of the range of assets held against TSB liabilities. From 1979 ordinary savings investments have been repaid to the TSBs with final repayment taking place in November 1986.

The TSBs appear to have been successful in persuading customers to open cheque-book accounts. Table 5.2 illustrates the increase in the value of cheque accounts between 1970 and 1985 for all TSBs.[4] Growth in cheque account deposits have averaged 15 per cent per year over the 1980s and reflects the small initial base and intensive marketing. Non-interest bearing accounts formed 11 per cent of TSB Group total deposits at November 1985 (table 5.2) but only 6.4 per cent of TSB Scotland's total deposits (table 5.3). The reason for this difference is not clear but there appears to be a preference amongst Scottish depositors for pass-book rather than cheque-book banking. By 1984 the TSBs had some 3.5 million cheque account holders but with a personal customer base 6 million strong, as large as any bank in the UK, opportunities exist for still further expansion. TSB Scotland has 1.25 million customers, a high proportion of the available total. Many accounts will, however, be inactive. The TSBs have attempted to change their customer profile. TSB cheque accounts were, in the past, rarely held by the younger banking population or by the high-earning 30s–40s age-group.[5] A range of financial products and services may attract the latter and an intensive marketing campaign has been targeted on the teenage and student market segment.

The credit-card operations of the TSBs have also grown strongly in recent times. The total number of TSB Trustcards issued grew from 574000 at the end of 1979 to 2368000 at the end of 1985,[6] and now accounts for almost 13 per cent of the total number of cards in issue in the UK. However, Trustcard owners do not use their credit card as often as other credit card holders. In 1985 each Access card was, on average, reponsible for 21 transactions valued at £28 each. The figures for the two main Visa cards were Barclaycard 21 transactions at £27, but Trustcard only 11 transactions at £26.[7]

In order to compete in the retail bank market the TSBs have introduced automated teller machines (ATMs) and their Speedbank ATM is generally recognised as being one of the most sophisticated. By November 1985 TSB

Scotland had 177 ATMs from a Group total of 1148 ATMs. The networks of the constituent TSBs are to be combined to enable customers of the TSB to make cash withdrawals and deposits throughout the UK.

Insurance services are another major area of TSB expansion in the past decade. These include both unit-linked life assurance and general insurance products. TSB Trust Company is the seventh largest UK unit trust management group, holding 4.5 per cent of the market. It is also the second largest UK bank unit trust management company (although the Scottish fund managers Murray Johnstone provide investment management for the largest TSB unit trust). Experience of developing and marketing products in this segment of the financial services field has been accumulated over the 17-year life of the TSB Trust Company. In 1986 TSB Scotland acquired a Glasgow-based estate agency, increasing the Bank's involvement with property-related financial services.

TSB Scotland has 284 branches (1985) which compares with Clydesdale Bank's 370. The TSB Group has a total branch network of 1600, almost twice as many as the Royal Bank of Scotland (864). The number of branches has fallen from the 1978 peak of 1656 (see table 5.2) reflecting the process of branch rationalisation that has taken place in recent years. Branches have been closed where they are no longer cost effective and branches opened in new centres of population and shopping developments. This has occurred both in Scotland and in the South. Historically the TSBs attracted the small savings of the working classes and were well represented in Scotland and the North of England. Their ability to secure wider geographical spread was restricted by their 'public fund' relationship with the Treasury which limited the ability of the TSBs to use surplus funds for the expansion of the number of branches. A post-war Loan and Mutual Assistance Scheme allowed surplus interest income to be channelled into bank branch expansion but few branches were opened in the South. Flotation of the TSBs has provided the capital for branch development but expansion in Scotland, already well covered, must be considered doubtful. A branch expansion strategy in Southern England would be costly and would have to compete with the building societies and the Royal Bank of Scotland, as well as the English clearers, but nevertheless seems the most likely option.

Performance and Competition
Financial details of TSB Scotland for the six years to 1985 are set out in table 5.3. Prior to 1983 the figures are presented as the aggregate of the four regional Scottish TSBs but the discrepancy arising is likely to be small. Deposits stood at just over £1.36 billion at November 1985, forming about 13 per cent of the TSB Group total of £10.2 billion. The growth of deposits has been slow over the 1980s with an average yearly growth rate of only 5.7 per cent compared with 12 per cent for the TSB Group as a whole. The growth of TSB deposits cannot easily be compared with that for the Scottish

Table 5.3. TSB Scotland[1] six-year financial summary (£ million).

End November	1980	1981	1982	1983	1984	1985
Interest bearing accounts	n/a	n/a	1074.6	1108.0	1152.1	1278.9
Non-interest bearing accounts	n/a	n/a	58.8	71.0	81.3	87.0
Total current deposit and other accounts	1037.3	1087.8	1133.4	1179.0	1233.4	1365.9
Profit before taxation	15.8	12.5	19.0	25.7	32.6	36.5
Total reserves	80.4	89.0	93.7	114.8	132.8	155.6
Total assets	1127.6	1188.7	1254.7	1315.5	1396.6	1578.4
Advances to customers	46.4	94.2	146.6	254.1	362.5	531.5

1. The figures for 1980, 1981 and 1982 comprise the aggregated published results of the four former constituent banks. The figures for 1983 and 1984 are the consolidated published results of TSB Scotland. There is therefore a small discrepancy in the continuity of the table.
Source: Published accounts.

clearing banks as a whole since TSB deposits are predominantly retail deposits and do not include wholesale deposits or foreign currency deposits. A comparison with the growth in the personal sector deposits of the clearers, however, can be made. Between December 1980 and June 1985 the personal sector sterling deposits of the Scottish clearers grew by a factor of 1.5 and the deposits of TSB Scotland (November to November) by a factor of 1.3. The building societies' personal sector deposits grew faster than either the TSBs or the Scottish clearing banks. The large proportion of fixed loans and government securities that remain in their balance sheets has meant that the TSBs have not always been able to offer the most competitive rates of interest for deposits. Even in Scotland, where the TSBs have traditionally been strong, personal savers have been attracted to the building societies and to other investments such as National Savings.

Loans to TSB customers have grown by £485 million between 1980 and 1985 and now amount to £531.5 million (see table 5.3). This has brought about a significant change in the balance sheet of the TSB as liquid investments have been replaced by loans and overdrafts. In 1980 advances accounted for 4 per cent of total assets. By 1985 this had grown to almost 34 per cent (70 per cent for the Scottish clearers) and compared with 38 per cent for the TSB Group. Given the nature of the TSBs' balance sheets in the 1970s, with large amounts invested in government securities and other public sector debt, the development of the asset and lending portfolio of the TSBs in recent years has been impressive. By 1985 the advances to deposits ratio of TSB Scotland stood at 39 per cent (4.5 per cent in 1980) and compares with 45.6 per cent for the TSB Group and 81 per cent for the Scottish clearing banks. A significant proportion of the growth in TSB Scotland personal credit provision can be attributed to mortgage business and, by 1984, outstanding mortgage loans amounted to £183 million (£17 million in 1980). In 1984 new mortgages accounted for one-third of increased advances to customers and formed over 50 per cent of total advances at that time.

In terms of profitability TSB Scotland has performed well. The 1985 pre-tax surplus of £36.5 million exceeded that of Clydesdale Bank. The growth in pre-tax profits over the five years to 1985 is shown in table 5.3. An average annual compound growth of 18 per cent between 1980–85 has more than matched that of the Scottish and London clearing banks and the TSB Group as a whole.

There is considerable scope for growth in the fee income of TSB Scotland. In 1985 'other operating income' amounted to £8.4 million, equivalent to only 10 per cent of net interest income, well below the 33 per cent and 40 per cent for Bank of Scotland and the Royal Bank on their total operations. TSB Scotland recorded an interest expense of almost £82 million in 1985 representing an effective rate of 6.7 per cent on average interest-bearing deposit balances and 6.2 per cent on average total deposit balances. Estimated figures for the Royal Bank are 7.7 per cent and 6.3 per cent respectively. These indicate the Royal Bank's dependence on more expensive wholesale deposits and the offsetting effect of current account endowments. Comparisons cannot be extended too far, however, given the still considerable differences in their banking and financial service business. As the TSB Scotland's balance sheet stands falling interest rates assist net earning potential, given the relatively high fixed returns on its liquid asset base and comparatively low deposit base rates. On the other hand, the Scottish clearing banks suffer a reduction in the endowment effect with falling interest rates. As interest rates rise TSB net income comes under pressure. The yield on its fixed loan and gilt-edged security portfolio does not adjust as quickly as the rates that have to be paid on deposits. These differences can be expected to become less significant as TSB Scotland converts its liquid investments into bank loans.

Published accounts data allow a comparison of TSB Scotland's capital adequacy ratios with those of the Scottish clearing banks. Total reserves presented in table 5.3 can be considered equivalent to shareholders' funds. Free shareholders' funds to public liabilities[8] stood at 6.6 per cent at November 1985, which compares with 5.2 per cent for Bank of Scotland (Feb 1986) and 3.2 per cent for the Royal Bank of Scotland (Sept 1985). This emphasises the current strength of TSB Scotland's balance sheet, a view that is reinforced by the fact that the TSB has now raised subordinated loan stock which will provide further potential for balance sheet growth.

New Directions for the TSB
The TSB Group is a well diversified banking institution, carrying out the wide range of activities shown in table 5.1 as well as personal sector banking and a developing commercial banking business. The TSB in Scotland, with

its large customer base, poses a new competitive threat to the Scottish clearing banks in the retail bank market and can be expected to develop further its small corporate lending portfolio and related treasury services.

The key issue in the development of the TSBs has been incorporation. The Page Committee envisaged the creation of a new force in the UK banking system, catering for personal sector financial needs within a mutual form of organisation. In many ways the TSBs have met and surpassed the Committee's expectations yet it is not altogether clear that the preference to move to corporate status as a UK-wide banking group is well founded. The desire of the decision-takers in the TSBs to organise into a Companies Act structure has received the support of the Banking Authorities and the approval of the banking community at large. Corporate status enables the TSBs to be supervised by the Bank of England under the 1979 Banking Act and this avoids the need to adapt the supervisory regime to accommodate mutual banks.[9] From the London and Scottish clearing banks' point of view the TSBs will be regularly exposed to the same market assessment through the standard reporting requirements of the Companies Act and the Stock Exchange, enabling its performance to be compared with other banking companies.[10]

The executive management has been a powerful lobby for incorporation expressing the belief that it would provide 'an effective operational and commercial structure to meet the demanding needs of the changing financial services market' and would 'enable the Group to have access to capital at the time of flotation and in the future' (TSB *Group Report 1985*). A mutual bank would certainly have dificulty in raising capital although other forms of mutual organisations such as the large mutual assurance companies and building societies have shown themselves to be successful in the financial sector.[11] Among the main advantages seen by the TSB management are the further integration of the TSBs and the ability to develop the banking business of the TSB Group with full Banking Act status. There is some evidence that the amalgamation of the four Scottish regional TSBs provided advantages in product lines, scale economies and uniformity in management philosophy. The structure of the TSBs after incorporation (figure 5.2) may provide opportunities to achieve similar economies and benefits with a shortening of communication lines and information flows. Branch and computer facilities are areas of potential cost saving.

The new structure does hold out the prospect, however, that the local autonomy of the TSBs may be reduced. Under the new structure TSB Scotland will become a principal subsidiary of the TSB Group rather than an effective partner of the organisation as in the past (see figure 5.1). The centralisation imposed by the company structure may result in TSB Scotland losing its ability to respond to local needs and preferences, particularly if these are seen to be in conflict with the overall Group strategy or require resources earmarked for developing the business of the Group elsewhere. The TSB Group may give a higher priority to strengthening and expanding its representation in the South East of England rather than in Scotland where it is relatively well established. TSB Scotland hope that the provision of a full range of financial services will maintain the present strong depositor loyalty, attract new depositors and customer loyalty, and that such loyalty will in turn be encouraged by membership of an effective national TSB Group providing both marketing and financial economies. There are, nevertheless, fears that the pull of the central TSB organisation coupled with the natural advantage of London as a financial centre will result in some key decision-making processes and their associated jobs gravitating south away from Scotland. Under the new TSB structure the Central Trustees Savings Bank (CTSB) is to be integrated with TSB England and Wales. CTSB carries out clearing operations in London and banking operations in the sterling money-markets as well as corporate finance business and commercial leasing. This should significantly strengthen TSB England and Wales' position within the TSB Group.

The flotation of the TSBs has resulted in a large flow of funds to the TSB Group. This provides management with a substantial volume of funds to convert into earning assets.[12] The TSBs have also their listed investments and the final repayment of funds from the National Debt Commissioners to redeploy into income-generating loans to the personal or corporate market. In the short run management may find the deployment of available funds poses some difficulties. Constraints include the availability of suitable loan opportunities as well as the ability to assume and administer the higher levels of risk that unsecured lending will bring. The middle management of TSB Scotland have limited expertise and experience of unsecured lending, particularly to the corporate sector. Development of this type of business may make the TSB a riskier enterprise than hitherto and it is fair to question whether TSB Scotland should be seeking to expand into the highly competitive company market. The TSB has a strong retail deposit base with latent opportunities for the cross-selling of a range of personal financial services. It is in this market segment that it poses the greatest competitive threat to the clearing banks. The Wages Act increases the opportunity to expand further their customer base.

However, TSB Scotland has shown a willingness to recruit appropriately experienced personnel. The TSB also has a strong incentive to train more bankers as well as to develop the talents of existing staff. With few preconceived views of how banking should be conducted or attitudes enshrined in tradition the TSB could take a radical and innovative approach to banking in the retail and corporate sectors of the market and pose a serious competitive threat to the Scottish clearers in the small to medium corporate market. TSB Scotland has already demonstrated an understanding of the important and significant role marketing has to play in developing banking and other financial services.

Conclusions

The TSB is now well on the way to becoming the force in banking which the Page Committee envisaged, albeit as part of the private banking sector which that Committee saw as being neither practicable nor desirable. The transfer to corporate status has resulted in the attainment of full banking status under the 1979 Banking Act which was regarded as being necessary to produce a flexible and efficient organisation capable of meeting the needs of the fast moving financial services industry.

Success is being achieved in moving from a savings bank with a diminishing role in the community to a banking and financial services organisation providing a strong competitive threat to similar existing institutions in Scotland and the UK. The large customer deposit base of TSB Scotland, combined with effective marketing, poses a competitive threat for the Scottish clearing banks in the retail bank market. In view of the changing nature and structure of TSB business in recent years conclusions on the profitability and growth performance of the bank must be tentative. The loss of retail deposits to the building societies has not been reversed to any significant extent although the TSB is still restrained from offering highly competitive interest rates due to the composition of its balance sheet. On the other side of the balance sheet, lending including mortgages to the personal sector, has developed rapidly representing a reallocation of funds from Central Government.

There is, however, concern that the TSB lacks management experience and expertise in the corporate and unsecured loan markets. This may be overcome in the longer term if effective training programmes, capable of improving the ability of TSB management to cope with rapidly extended and diversified functions, are implemented. Concern has also been expressed that TSB Scotland will lose its present level of autonomy within the new TSB Group structure, further removing independent decision-taking at high level from Scotland.[13] There is also a fear that Group resources will be used to expand business in the South possibly at the expense of expansion in Scotland. The activities for expansion highlighted in the TSB prospectus are all headquartered outside Scotland. It is too early to evaluate these fears but it is certain that TSB Scotland has the potential to extend its role as a major player in financial markets in Scotland.

Airdrie Savings Bank

Airdrie Savings Bank is the sole survivor of the traditional Trustee Savings Bank providing savings facilities for a restricted geographical area and controlled by local trustees. It was established in 1835 under the 1819 Act for the Protection of Banks for Savings in Scotland. This Act allowed considerable discretion to the trustees with regard to investment but this was not extensively utilised until the 1970s when the range of services was extended and lending to customers was introduced. The Airdrie Savings Bank is a licensed deposit taker under the 1979 Banking Act but is nevertheless entitled to use the words Savings Bank under the Act. The bank has retained its independent status, resisting overtures to amalgamate in the 1970s, arguing that it was sufficiently strong financially to operate independently and that there was merit in doing so because of its ability to serve its local community.

The bank has seven branches with total deposits of just under £24 million in 1985 and a balance sheet total of £28 million. These totals have remained fairly static in recent years. The bank has extended the range of services offered to customers beyond the traditional savings account. As well as current accounts, cheque guarantee cards and cash cards, standing order facilities and a range of other services, about 10 per cent of the bank's deposits are now advanced to customers in overdraft and other credit arrangements. The major investment is still in British Government securities.

To cope with the bulk of its work, which is conducted through the savings account passbook, the Airdrie Savings Bank pioneered the introduction of on-line real-time computing facilities in banking in 1975 and this has enabled the bank to cope effectively with this work and extend its range of services and allowed it to accept with equanimity the prospect of increased activity.

The direction of the bank is controlled by the trustees who meet regularly to determine the bank's policies, including interest rates, subject to the interest earned on their assets and the competing rates offered by other banks and building societies.

In common with other banks the Airdrie Savings Bank is having to improve its marketing in response to changing customer needs and the economics of branch operations. Even in a locally entrenched bank customer loyalty can no longer be taken for granted and competing services require an effective response. As a small bank with a strong local identity and seeking to serve the community the bank should be well placed to respond. Branch expansion may not be a realistic option but operating banking facilities in large shopping centres offers one way of extending operations within the locality. The bank has demonstrated that it is possible to operate successfully in a limited geographical area so long as it meets the needs of the local community and can apply modern technology to overcome any disadvantage associated with small scale.

The Building Societies

Introduction
The post-war growth of the building society movement in the UK has been impressive by any standard. The past twenty years have seen the building societies develop a significant intermediation role within the financial system. There was a seven-fold growth in the real value of their assets between

Table 5.4. Buildings society flow of funds in Scotland, 1975–85 (£ million).

	1975	1976	1977	1978	1979	1980	1981	1982	1983	1984	1985
Net receipts[1]	215	161	334	222	213	221	203	360	451	582	447
Interest credited	60	69	83	98	160	210	230	231	259	287	344
Principal repaid	275	230	417	320	373	431	433	591	710	869	791
	114	130	170	210	231	272	376	464	537	604	727
Total funds available	389	360	587	530	604	703	809	1055	1247	1473	1518
Contribution to liquidity[2]	86	—	164	−18	58	128	80	153	113	98	180
Net funds available	303	360	423	548	546	575	729	902	1134	1375	1338
Lending	310	396	450	579	595	685	840	1076	1289	1686	1811
Outflow (+), Inflow (−)	−7	−35	−27	−31	−49	−110	−111	−173	−155	−311	−473

1. Of new savings.
2. A proportion of the increase in savings is generally diverted to liquid funds rather than lending. Figures assume Scotland's share of the total increase in building society liquidity is equal to its share of net receipts.

Source: BSA *Bulletin*, April 1986.

1945 and 1980 (Davies 1981), exceeding the real growth rate of the economy as a whole. This growth underlines the importance of these mutual organisations in extending home ownership [14] and their success in collecting personal savings.

Unlike most UK regions Scotland does not have a strong indigenous building society industry. The slow and rather limited development of the movement in Scotland has been attributed to the historic success of Scottish banking, life assurance and investment trust savings media, as well as the housing tenure structure with its low levels of owner occupation (40 per cent in 1984 compared to 63 per cent in England), and the successive waves of building society mergers very often with transfers of engagements to larger and more dynamic English societies. At the end of 1985 there were five building societies headquartered in Scotland with only the Dunfermline Building Society of any significant size. It is, nonetheless, useful to look in some detail at the building society industry in Scotland. The building societies are powerful competitors for personal sector savings, a major source of house purchase finance, and potential competitors to a number of financial institutions in Scotland including the clearing banks and the TSB.

Operations of Building Societies

Since 1973 building society advances in Scotland have exceeded the net funds available for lending. To meet the demand for mortgages funds have been drawn from the rest of the UK and by 1985 this flow of funds had risen to in excess of £473 million. Table 5.4 shows the flow of building society funds within Scotland as well as between Scotland and the rest of the UK. Total available funds for lending are made up of net receipts of new savings, interest credited to savings accounts and repayments of mortgage principal. Depending on the general state of the building society industry a proportion of new funds may also be diverted into the societies' liquid reserves.

In general, about 80 per cent of the funds attracted by building societies are used to make mortgage loans, with most of the remainder invested in liquid assets, particularly Government securities, cash and bank balances.[15] The liquid funds of the building societies are held to meet deposit withdrawals, mortgage commitments, taxation and interest payments and also to insulate lending from the fluctuations that occur in the inflow of net receipts. Thus liquidity may be expected to rise when net inflow of funds is high (as in 1977 and 1982) and be drawn down or accumulated less rapidly (as in 1976, 1978 and 1981) in order to finance lending when funds are being attracted less easily. Table 5.4 is presented on the assumption that Scotland's share of the total increase in building society liquidity is equal to its share of net receipts and should therefore be treated with some caution. No allowance has been made for Scotland's share of wholesale funds. This has, since 1983, become for the larger societies an increasingly important means of funding loans.

Table 5.5. Regional distribution of loans and owner occupation in 1979 and 1985.

Region	Number of loans (000s)[1] 1979	Percentage of total	Number of loans (000s)[1] 1985	Percentage of total	Owner-occupied stock as percentage of total[2]	
					End 1978	End 1984
Greater London	63	9	98	9	48	54
South West	64	9	95	9	63	69
East Anglia	28	4	42	4	57	65
South East	167	23	238	22	62	69
Northern	36	5	56	5	46	54
Yorks and Humber	69	10	104	10	54	61
North West	78	11	113	11	58	64
East Midlands	58	8	81	8	57	65
West Midlands	67	9	97	9	55	62
Wales	29	4	36	3	59	66
Scotland	47	6	90	8	35	40
Northern Ireland	11	2	25	2	48	59
United Kingdom	717	100	1075	100	54	61

1. Figures for loans are based on the monthly return which building societies make to the Department of the Environment.
2. Columns of owner-occupied housing are from DOE Housing and Construction Statistics.
Source: BSA Bulletin, April 1980, 1986.

The bottom of table 5.4 shows the amount by which advances have exceeded net funds available for lending in each year from 1975 to 1985. The difference has grown markedly over the period resulting in a consistent and substantial inflow of funds to Scotland, doubling between 1983 and 1984 and then rising sharply again to £473 million in 1985. This reflects the rapid growth in the demand for home loans in Scotland in recent times, almost certainly helped by the sale of local authority and new town dwellings to sitting tenants.

The number of building society loans granted in Scotland over a year rose from 22000 in 1969 to 90000 by 1985. Scotland now accounts for 9 per cent of total building society loans in the UK compared to less than 5 per cent in 1969. The growth in loans has been more marked over the 1980s. Between 1969 and 1979 the number of loans increased from 22000 to 47000 but thereafter rose more rapidly to peak at 95000 in 1984, before falling slightly in 1985. These figures can be explained, in part, by the high level of council house sales but also by the increased level of competition in the mortgage market that has occurred in the 1980s. This has led the building societies to issue more mortgages than might otherwise have been the case.[16] The total number of loans made in the UK has also grown rapidly over the 1980s but Scotland is the only region to have increased its share. Table 5.5 shows the

The Building Societies

Table 5.6. The housing stock and tenure pattern in Scotland 1966–84 and distribution of the housing stock by tenure in Great Britain, December 1984.

End year	No. of dwellings (000s)	Percentage of dwellings		
		Owner-occupied	Local authority rented	Private rented and other (incl. HA)
1966	1710	29.1	47.3	23.6
1968	1749	30.2	49.6	20.2
1970	1796	30.9	51.3	17.8
1972	1837	31.7	52.8	15.5
1974	1868	32.8	53.7	13.5
1976	1921	33.6	54.2	12.2
1978	1964	34.6	54.3	11.1
1980	1997	36.1	53.8	10.1
1981	1986	35.8	54.4	9.7
1982	1997	37.1	53.6	9.3
1983	2012	38.5	52.4	9.0
1984	2028	39.9	51.3	8.8
Country – 1984				
Scotland	2028	39.9	51.3	8.8
Wales	1112	65.9	24.0	10.0
England	18574	62.9	25.6	11.4
Great Britain	21715	60.9	27.9	11.1

Figures for 1981 to 1984 are estimated based on 1981 Census data and are not strictly comparable with the earlier figures which are based on the 1971 Census.

The local authority rented sector includes dwellings owned by new towns. HA = Housing Associations.

Source: BSA *Bulletin*, No. 46, April 1986.

UK regional distribution of mortgage loans and owner occupation in 1979 and 1985. The Scottish share of building society loans increased from 6 per cent to 8 per cent over the period and owner occupation has risen from 35 per cent to 40 per cent of the total housing stock.

Housing tenure in Scotland is still biased towards renting from local authorities. Only 40 per cent of housing is owner-occupied in comparison to 54 per cent in Greater London and the North, the next two lowest regions. Owner occupation is high in the South East and South West. Table 5.6 shows the change in housing stock and tenure in Scotland between 1966 and 1984 and the distribution of housing stock by tenure in Scotland, Wales and England at the end of 1984. Almost 320000 dwellings were added to the stock between 1966 and 1984. Both owner-occupied property and local authority rented dwellings now account for a greater proportion of the total stock than in 1966 but the private rented sector has declined in size from nearly a quarter of dwellings in 1966 to less than a tenth in 1984.

The proportion of owner-occupied dwellings in Scotland is much lower than in England and Wales, as can be seen from the bottom of table 5.6. Local authority stock accounts for over half of all dwellings in Scotland compared to about a quarter in England and Wales. Over 78,000 houses and flats were sold under the Tenants' Rights etc. (Scotland) Act 1980 between 1980 and the end of 1985, equivalent to 7.3 per cent of the public sector stock at the end of 1979.[17] Many of these purchases have been made by mortgage loans granted by building societies and this has had the effect of increasing the total size of the mortgage market in Scotland. In 1985, 59 per cent of borrowers in Scotland were first-time buyers, 40 per cent of whom comprised new households. Only Northern Ireland (66 per cent) and Greater London (63 per cent) had a greater proportion of loans granted to first-time buyers. About 16 per cent of the loans went to purchasers who were previously renting from the public sector, a figure higher than in any other UK region except Northern Ireland. If these trends continue and the growth of the public sector stock continues to slide (86.3 per cent of new houses completed 1945–65 falling to 45.2 per cent 1975–85) then owner-occupation may be expected to increase substantially in Scotland.

In his survey on employment in the Scottish financial sector Gaskin (1980) found that the English societies were attracted to Scotland as much by the opportunities to grant mortgage loans in a country with a low level of owner-occupation as by the ethos of Scottish thrift. Davies (1981) is more critical of the potential created by owner-occupation statistics and argues that the difference between the proportions of owner-occupation in Scotland and the UK is more an indication of need and attitudes than actual effective demand. However, the changes that are occurring in the housing tenure structure in Scotland, assisted by the greater availability of mortgage finance, would seem to suggest that there is a real demand for owner-occupation. Owner-occupation in Scotland may stabilise below the 60–70 per cent of the total housing stock to be found in Great Britain (see table 5.6) but there is some way to go before owner-occupied property in Scotland forms the greater part of the housing stock, and it should remain an attractive market for society loans.

Industry Structure and Organisation
Checkland (1975) observes that the building society movement in Scotland developed from the 1840s, although it is known that the Glasgow and West of Scotland Savings Investment and Building Society was operating as early as 1808.[18] Most of the early societies were of the terminating type, and they went out of existence once the objects of the society, which were to finance house building and purchase for members, had been achieved. By 1900 there were 140 building societies in Scotland, a number which has fallen persistently since then so that by 1985 there were only five societies with headquarters in Scotland. This decline has been part of the broader national trend for the transfer of small society engagements to other societies and

Table 5.7. Number of building societies in Scotland and Great Britain, 1900–85.

End year	No. of societies with head office in Scotland (A)	No. of societies in Great Britain (B)	A/B %
1900	140	2286	6.1
1910	132	1723	7.7
1920	104	1271	8.2
1930	76	1026	7.4
1940	57	952	6.0
1950	45	819	5.5
1960	37	726	5.1
1970	26	481	5.4
1980	14	273	5.1
1981	13	253	5.1
1982	11	227	4.8
1983	9	206	4.4
1984	6	190	3.2
1985	5	167	3.0

Source: BSA Bulletin, Nos. 36, 46.

mergers between large societies. The change in building society numbers from 1900 to 1985 for Scotland and Great Britain are shown in table 5.7.

Table 5.8. Regional concentration of building societies at end 1984 (BSA members only).

Location of head or chief administrative office	No. of societies		Total assets	
	No.	% of total	£m	% of total
Yorkshire and Humberside	11	7.1	36803	35.6
Greater London	24	15.6	34553	33.4
East Midlands	15	9.7	8518	8.2
South East (ex. GLC)	35	22.7	6683	6.5
West Midlands	15	9.7	6606	6.4
South West	14	9.1	5702	5.5
North	17	11.0	2641	2.5
North West	8	5.2	655	0.6
East Anglia	5	3.2	539	0.5
Wales	5	3.2	445	0.4
Scotland	3	1.9	280	0.3
Northern Ireland	2	1.3	74	0.1
Total	154	100.0	103499	100.0

Source: Individual societies balance sheets as published in the *Building Societies Year Book 1985*. The figures reflect the aggregate position for end of societies' financial years ending between 1 February 1984 and 31 January 1985.

Retail Deposit Institutions

Table 5.9. *Building society representation in Scotland, 1984–85.*

Society:[2] year end 31/12/84 (unless otherwise indicated)[3]	Total assets £ million	Total membership Shareholders and depositors	Borrowers	No. of branches[1] UK	Scotland
1. Halifax[a]	20492	7881930	1305728	685	51 (regional office: Edinburgh)
2. Abbey National	16988	8100805	968154	678	54
3. Nationwide	8738	3315754	501898	520	33
4. Leeds Permanent[b]	5904	2516256	375296	471	44 (regional office: Dunfermline)
5. Woolwich Equitable[b]	5723	2526402	341651	395	25
6. Anglia[c]	4449	1922637	283382	393	11 (regional office: Edinburgh)
7. National & Provincial	4449	1390743	295491	335	30
8. Bradford & Bingley	3267	1542808	201592	240	21
*9. Alliance	3220	935098	183447	207	31 (chief office: Edinburgh)
*10. Leicester	2950	1155929	192577	245	32
11. Britannia	2847	1048517	174324	241	5 (regional office: Hamilton)
12. Cheltenham & Gloucester	2639	657957	133957	148	5
13. Bristol & West	1912	676388	89454	162	11
14. Yorkshire	1522	584610	102124	157	18
15. Gateway	1366	443881	80920	145	8 (regional office: Edinburgh)
16. Northern Rock	1317	502972	88329	123	11 (regional office: Edinburgh)
18. Midshires	801	414405	58198	99	1
23. Leeds & Holbeck	508	207752	34328	69	2
25. Skipton	471	151690	34848	54	2
26. Leamington Spa	457	110643	20717	58	1
31. Newcastle	351	94997	22854	51	8
37. Dunfermline	244	83255	16400	37	34 (head office: Dunfermline)
44. Cumberland	168	67726	12231	23	4
55. North of England	114	61056	9006	21	6
76. Universal	58.7	21135	4837	11	1
93. Scottish[a]	35.3	12883	2576	6	5 (head office: Edinburgh)
—. Century	6.2	1488	1336	0	0 (head office: Edinburgh)
†154. Huntly[d]	1.2	—	—	0	0 (head office: Edinburgh)
—. Wishaw Inv.	0.3	100	27	0	0 (head office: Wishaw)
—. Leith Property Inv.	—	—	—	0	0 (head office: Leith)
Total					454

1. Only units listed as branches in the *Building Societies Year Book 1985* are included, units listed as regional, chief or head offices have not been counted.

2. Number before society name indicates position in UK league of BSA members.

3. Year end: (a) 31/1/85, (b) 30/9/84, (c) 4/4/85, (d) 8/5/85.

The Building Societies

At the end of 1984 the total assets of building societies based in Scotland amounted to just over £287 million. The Dunfermline Building Society accounted for £244 million of this but had only 1 per cent of the assets of the largest UK building society, the Halifax. Not surprisingly, the downward trend in building society numbers has been matched by an increased concentration of the share of total building society assets held by the large UK building societies. Over 55 per cent of total industry assets, which amount to £102.7 billion (end-1984), were concentrated in the hands of the top five building societies. Table 5.8 provides regional figures showing the control of building society assets by head office location. Most assets are controlled by societies based in Yorkshire and Humberside, although the South East has more building societies. Very little control over building society assets is exercised from Scotland.

Building society representation in Scotland in 1984/85 is shown in table 5.9. The large English societies are well represented, the top ten having 332 branches in Scotland, or 73 per cent of all building society branches in Scotland. The Halifax and Abbey National have over 50 branches each. In total 26 societies were represented through 454 branches and numerous agencies. At least a further 11 societies operate solely through agents who channel deposits to them, or make applications for mortgage loans on behalf of clients. As well as the national building societies, a number of medium-sized societies from the north of England have branches in Scotland. Transfers of engagements have been widely used as a means of gaining wider geographical coverage.

The Dunfermline Building Society had, at the beginning of 1985, 37 branches, virtually all in Scotland. The society had 83300 shareholders and depositors and 16400 borrowers. From table 5.9 it is apparent that Scotland's five other societies in 1984 (one of which transferred its engagements during 1985) are very much smaller. The Scottish Building Society had assets amounting to £35.3 million, 12900 shareholders and depositors, and 2576 borrowers. The society operates from six branches.

The rapid growth of building society branches in Great Britain was a feature of the 1970s. In table 5.10 the growth of building society branches in Scotland is compared with that of the Scottish clearing banks over the past ten years. The figures show that the rapid growth in society branches has slowed down. In contrast, clearing bank branches are declining in number. Building society branches now account for nearly one-quarter of the total. Building society branches in Scotland have a higher population/branch ratio than in most other UK regions, a result of the spatial dispersal of population and the greater number of small local societies in the English regions.

Davies (1981) points out that for the building society movement as a whole, 'branch expansion has taken place to some considerable degree as an alternative to price competition'. In the past building societies did not

Table 5.10. *Building society and bank branching in Scotland,*[1] *1975–84. Branches of Williams & Glyn's are not included.*

End year	No. of branches	% increase over previous year	No. of Scottish clearing bank branches	Increase/decrease over previous year	Building society branches as % of total
1975	196	12.0	1554	+7	11.2
1976	226	15.3	1541	−13	12.7
1977	256	13.3	1551	+10	14.2
1978	313	22.3	1555	+4	16.8
1979	332	6.1	1547	−8	17.7
1980	375	13.0	1554	+7	19.4
1981	423	12.8	1545	−9	21.5
1982	433	2.4	1533	−12	22.0
1983	441	1.8	1514	−19	22.6
1984	452	2.5	1478	−36	23.4

1. A very small proportion of the Scottish clearing bank branches are in England.
Source: BSA *Bulletin,* No. 42.

compete with one another in setting interest rate charges but followed recommended rates and were protected from outside competition, particularly from the banks which were subject to monetary controls. Instead the building societies competed for deposits and mortgage borrowers by expanding their branch networks.[19] The concentration of assets in a few large societies, alongside the reduction in the smaller local societies which often maintained interest rate differentials, helped to sustain non-price competition. In more recent years competition from banks, and among building societies themselves, has reduced interest rate margins. The combination of lower margins and rising staff and branch office costs has meant that the profitability of existing and new branches is being examined more closely.

A large part of the growth of employment, which took place between 1971 and 1981, in 'other financial institutions' in Scotland (see chapter 2) was due to building society expansion. Gaskin (1981) observed that rapid growth in building society branch offices was a striking feature of the 1970s and argued that with minor exceptions employment in building societies in Scotland is branch office employment. There is little evidence to suggest that the picture has changed in the interim.

The number of full-time equivalent staff employed per branch in the UK stood at 6.0 for the year-end 1983 (BSA). On this basis total building society staff, including part-time staff in the 452 branches in Scotland (end 1984) is 2700. Adding numbers employed at the head offices of Scottish societies and the regional offices of English societies suggests that total building society employment in Scotland is around 3000. Building society employment in the UK has grown more slowly in the 1980s than in the 1970s. There appears to be a fairly close relationship between growth of staff and growth of branches. The slower level of new branch development in Scotland in recent times suggests, therefore, that building society employment is rising more slowly in the 1980s than in earlier years. Large numbers of staff are employed part-time. Building Society Association figures indicate that in 1983, over 25 per cent of branch staff in the UK were part-time.

Competition and Performance
The flow of personal savings into building societies in Scotland has grown impressively in recent times. Table 5.11 compares the growth of building society shares (the main form of saving with building societies) and deposits in Scotland and the UK with growth in the personal sector deposits of the Scottish banks over the late 1970s and early 1980s. Between 1975 and 1984 savings with building societies in Scotland increased by a factor of 4.7, higher than the four-fold increase for the UK as a whole and equating to an average yearly increase in shares and deposits of 18.8 per cent. The personal sector deposits[20] of the Scottish clearing banks grew at only 13 per cent per annum between 1978 and 1984. The interest-bearing accounts of TSB Scotland, which are predominantly personal savings, increased by 7 per cent between 1982 and 1984. At the end of 1984 the total outstanding personal sector sterling deposits of the Scottish clearing banks stood at £4265 million compared to £5547 million for the building societies in Scotland.

Table 5.12 shows changes in the shares of personal sector liquid assets between 1966 and 1985. Despite a number of changes to the composition of the various sectors the figures indicate that the building societies have been highly successful in attracting an increasing proportion of personal savings. At the end of 1985 deposits with the building societies amounted to £103.4 billion, just over 52 per cent of the total. The share of National Savings has shown the largest decline and the percentage of deposits with the monetary sector has remained much the same, showing a substantial relative loss of ground to the building societies. A strong growth in personal savings was recorded in the 1970s in both nominal and real terms (see table 5.12).

The absence of effective competition for the funds of small savers up to the end of the 1970s favoured the building societies. Both the National Savings Bank and the Trustee Savings Banks failed to offer competitive rates of interest to the personal investor with small savings. The ordinary savings accounts of these banks were intended to provide a simple and safe haven for funds and the money deposited in these accounts was statutorily controlled by the National Debt Commissioners. The rate of interest received by the saver was either fixed or varied at low rates.[21] The investment accounts of the TSBs and the NSB did not offer much competition to building society accounts. The clearing banks were slow to recognise the growth in the personal savings market. The banks had passively amassed the savings of individuals and up to the late 'seventies had maintained a remoteness from

Table 5.11. Building society and bank personal savings and house purchase loans, 1975–84 (£ million).

Year end	1975	1976	1977	1978	1979	1980	1981	1982	1983	1984
Building society shares and deposits[1]										
Scotland[2,3]	1174	1404	1821	2141	2523	2958	3420	4012	4678	5547
UK	22696	26101	32200	37022	42791	49950	57146	67661	78225	91442
Scottish clearing banks personal sector sterling deposits[1]										
TSB Scotland interest-bearing accounts[1]	n/a	n/a	n/a	2051	2499	2972	3386	3692	3950	4265
	n/a	n/a	n/a	n/a	n/a	n/a	n/a	1075	1108	1152
Building society advances on mortgages[1]										
Scotland[2,3]	1105	1235	1515	1884	2242	2655	3117	3732	4487	5569
UK	18882	22500	26600	31715	36986	42708	49039	57186	68114	82686
Scottish clearing banks lending for house purchase[4]	67	84	95	118	165	203	374	713	1038	1141

1. Balances at year end.
2. The figures for Scotland are based on the activities of 25 societies and relate to the inflow of funds through Scottish branches and agencies.
3. The figures for Scotland relate to societies' financial years ending between 1 February and 31 January while the figures for the UK relate to calendar years. In practice there would be little difference between calendar year and financial year figures.
4. Amounts outstanding mid-November.

Sources: BSA Bulletin; Abstract of Banking Statistics, Vol. 2, Statistical Unit CLCB.

Table 5.12. Personal sector liquid assets: market share (%).

End years	1966	1970	1974	1978	1980	1982	1984	1985
Deposits with building societies	26.3	34.6	38.0	47.5	46.2	47.6	49.1	52.2
Deposits with monetary sector[1]	33.9	34.6	40.0	31.7	34.8	36.7	35.0	32.2
National Savings[2,3]	31.6	22.6	15.7	14.6	11.3	15.4	15.6	15.4
Deposits with savings banks	5.4	6.1	5.4	5.8	7.1	—	—	—
Local authority temporary debt	1.5	1.1	0.7	0.3	0.3	0.2	0.2	0.1
Other liquid assets[4]	1.1	1.0	0.2	0.1	0.3	0.1	0.1	0.1
Total liquid assets	100.0	100.0	100.0	100.0	100.0	100.0	100.0	100.0
£ billions	22.0	29.1	48.2	77.1	107.4	140.7	177.7	198.0
At 1974 prices	41.7	44.9	48.2	44.2	45.5	50.5	57.9	61.1

1. The monetary sector includes from the first quarter of 1982, the former banking sector, the trustee savings banks and some small previously non-reporting institutions.
2. National Savings include Trustee Savings Banks' ordinary department up to 30 September 1979.
3. From the first quarter of 1981 deposits with the NSB investment account are included in National Savings. They were formerly included in deposits with savings banks.
4. Other liquid assets include deposits with other financial institutions. From the first quarter of 1982 tax instruments only are included.
Source: Financial Statistics.

the small saver, accounting in some measure for the strength of the TSBs among the working classes in Scotland. At various times over the period government measures designed to restrain money supply and credit growth had also restricted the banks' competitiveness in the savings market. Public attitudes were shaped by the ease and informality of building society branch transactions whilst the mutual rather than profit orientated status of the societies and a desire to become a society member in the hope of eventually securing mortgage finance were undoubtedly also important. Building societies pay a composite rate of income tax on behalf of their investors, representing the average marginal liability to basic rate and lower band tax rate of investors.[22] Until 1985 this privilege was denied to the banks and provided a fiscal incentive to save with a building society.

The number of persons holding share investments with building societies grew from 10.3 million in 1970 to 39.4 million in 1984. Although these figures, inevitably, contain an element of double counting they underline the involvement of the population in the building society movement. A UK regional survey carried out for the BSA by the British Market Research Bureau in March 1983 indicated that 34 per cent of adults in Scotland held a building society account in comparison to 57 per cent for the rest of Great Britain. The corresponding figures for bank deposit/savings accounts were 50 per cent and 32 per cent. Other sampling exercises also indicate that the proportion of building society accounts held in Scotland is less than at the national level, possibly because of the stronger and more effective competition provided by the Scottish clearing banks and the TSB for personal sector deposit liabilities.

In the 1980s the building societies have faced stronger competition both from National Savings and the banks, including the TSBs. These institutions have increased the range of products on offer to the personal saver, segmenting the market and attempting to raise the average balances held by the small investor. The banks have launched a range of higher interest cheque book accounts and made access to savings accounts easier through their automated cash withdrawal networks. The banks also realised that personal customers were a potentially large market for other financial services such as credit, insurance services, mortgages and investments. The building societies have had to respond to the increased competition by widening their range of products to include higher interest accounts with more flexible terms of withdrawal as well as by cheque books and cash dispenser facilities. The success of the clearing banks and the TSBs in attracting personal savings will be measured by whether they can arrest or reverse the trend for building societies to take a larger share of increased personal sector savings.

In the mortgage market outstanding building society mortgage advances in Scotland grew by a factor of 5.0 between 1975 and 1984 compared to 4.4 for the UK (lower section of table 5.11). Between 1980 and 1984 the Scottish clearing banks increased their mortgage lending by a factor of 5.6, an average of 54 per cent per annum. The clearing banks have always provided bridging finance for house purchase but until 1980 were not large-scale lenders in the residential mortgage market. Bridging finance is a very small part of the total amounts outstanding for 1982 to 1984 (table 5.11). The rapid growth in mortgage finance provided by the clearing banks reflects the changes that have occurred in the UK mortgage market in recent years. Building societies no longer have a monopoly over the provision of mortgage finance to house buyers. Whereas in the past the building societies had followed a recommended interest rate system which was largely responsible for fluctuations in the availability of mortgage funds,[23] there is now price competition with banks and other financial institutions, and among the societies themselves. Mortgages are readily available for most house buyers and there is intense competition for a share of the mortgage market. The building societies have turned to the wholesale money markets to help fund their mortgage commitments. At the end of 1984 building society advances in Scotland had reached £5569 million, about 4.5 times the amount advanced by the Scottish clearing banks. The growth in bank lending for house purchase has more than offset the decline in local authority mortgage provision.

The Building Societies

New Directions and Future Competition

The Building Societies Act 1986 provides for a major change to the regulations governing the building society movement. Strong competition from the clearing banks and other financial institutions in the mortgage and personal savings market has led to a range of new products being offered to customers and savers by the building societies. Borrowing in the wholesale money markets to fund mortgage advances has become popular whilst a number of societies are indirectly involved in land ownership by sponsorship and lending support to housing associations. Large sums are being spent on advertising and the large UK building societies have moved away from any simple 'social' purpose of channelling savings into mortgage loans. The desire to provide a broader range of personal financial services is underpinned by the realisation that neither savings nor mortgage demand may be expected to grow as rapidly in future years as it had done throughout the 1970s and in the early 1980s.

Regulation of the building societies was previously confined to 'prudential' controls only, concerned with protecting the members of the societies.[24] A desire by government to regulate the changes that were occurring found expression in the 1984 Green Paper,[25] and subsequently the passing of the 1986 Building Societies Act. The new regulations envisage that the principal purpose of the building societies will remain as specialists in the provision of housing finance, directed towards extending home ownership, coupled with the provision of a safe and attractive home for savings. Beyond this it is intended that the societies should be able to engage in a range of related activities but subject to quantifiable limits depending on the class of assets or type of liability. Restrictions have also been imposed on holdings of liquid and unsecured commercial assets.[26] The new activities which the societies can engage in include money transmission, the provision of cheque guarantee cards, foreign exchange services for individuals, house buying services (including conveyancing but not for their own borrowers), agency and insurance broking of any description, ownership, development and management of residential land, unsecured lending, the selling of stocks and shares and unit trusts, establishment and management of PEPs and lending in the European Community, most of which are seen as extensions of present building society activities.

Although the Act extends the permissible activities of building societies, the government still insists that the provision of housing finance is different so that there are continuing limitations on the activities building societies may engage in and in their freedom to determine the extent of their involvement. Some restrictions may be alleviated by becoming incorporated and several societies may avail themselves of the opportunity when it becomes possible at the beginning of 1988.

The societies' ability to own property provides them with the opportunity of offering shared ownership arrangements whereby the equity interest in a house can be split between the building society and a customer, with arrangements to vary the equity interest as the customers' financial circumstances change. This will represent an attractive option to first time buyers with limited capital and also to those whose capital is tied up in the house which they own.

Despite continuing restrictions the building societies under the new legislation will represent formidable competitors in the financial sector and in other activities relating to the housing market. Through their extensive branch network in Scotland they can provide attractive personal banking services including cheque guarantee cards and overdraft facilities. The extension of their insurance activities will offer attractive packages in competition with other insurance brokers and the possibility of 'own brand' insurance policies must be attractive. In Scotland, where the housing market is still dominated by solicitors, the ability to provide conveyancing services, although restricted, in association with other financial products must represent a threat to that domination, especially if associated with estate agency services. Agreement in principle has already been reached for the purchase by one of the leading societies of a major estate agency business in Scotland, whilst the Dunfermline Building Society and Forward Trust propose a joint venture to provide unsecured consumer credit to members of the Society.

Conclusions
Building societies are the main providers of mortgages for house purchase in Scotland and in recent times there has been a net inflow of building society funds to Scotland from the rest of the UK to fund mortgage advances. Scotland still has a low level of owner-occupation (40 per cent) but council house sales and changing needs and attitudes have combined to make rising levels of home ownership a real prospect. The mortgage market in Scotland is therefore an attractive one and, as elsewhere in the UK, it is now highly competitive. The building societies, the Scottish clearing banks, the TSB and other financial institutions also compete for personal sector savings. Despite the traditional strength of the TSB in Scotland and the Scottish clearing banks' deposit account the societies have had considerable success in persuading savers to invest their funds in building society accounts.

There are few indigenous Scottish building societies and only one, the Dunfermline Building Society, has a developed branch network. Most societies operating in Scotland are medium to large English societies. Some of these have regional headquarters in Edinburgh. Recent legislation enables the building societies to carry out a wider range of financial services alongside the provision of housing finance. Despite continuing restrictions the large building societies can be expected to sell a range of personal financial products through their branch network in competition with the Scottish clearing banks, TSB Scotland, insurance brokers and solicitors.

NOTES

1. The top five are the four London clearing banks followed by the Royal Bank of Scotland.
2. Clearing is discussed in chapter 4.
3. Leslie notes that the return on the savings account was fixed at 4 per cent between 1972 and time of writing (1982). It must be assumed that this rate was set by the Treasury. Given that during periods of high inflation savers can be expected to have greater sensitivity to interest rates it is perhaps surprising that the savings accounts did not decline at a faster rate or from an earlier date. It is possible that many savings accounts are inactive.
4. It is assumed that from 1982 onwards TSB figures for non-interest bearing accounts correspond to the cheque book account.
5. There has also been an attempt to raise the socio-economic profile of customers. In the mid-1970s the two lower socio-economic bands formed over one-third of the savings base.
6. The TSBS are affiliated to the Visa card scheme. The use of credit cards is considered in chapter 4.
7. TSB branches earn commission on the sale of insurance and credit cards providing an incentive to sell products of TSB non-banking subsidiaries. Branches have targets for the volume of introductions that they provide to salesmen. This appears to have been a successful sales approach that has not been emulated by the Scottish clearing banks. The incentive to provide many customers with credit cards may explain why usage is low.
8. For a definition of FSF and public liabilities see note 37 to chapter 4.
9. The UK supervisory authorities appear to have made no provision in the banking legislation for supervision of banks with mutual status. Other EEC members who have extensive mutual savings bank networks have not been so inflexible.
10. If adequate performance was not forthcoming the TSB Group would be exposed to the possibility of a takeover bid, something that was not possible with unincorporated status. TSB management hold the view that the TSB Group should not be exposed to takeover in the early years following re-organisation. In the first five years after flotation no one may own more than 5 per cent of the ordinary shares and after the five year period there is to be a limit on ownership of 15 per cent of the shares. This view seems unduly restrictive and too protective of the management. However there are grounds for protection in the immediate period following flotation based on the competitive benefits that an independent UK bank can bring to the concentrated domestic banking structure. It is unlikely that the authorities would give longer term guarantees to the independence of the TSB Group. The customer base and branch network provides an attractive proposition for an overseas bank or a bid similar to that made for the Royal Bank of Scotland.
11. Benefits and disadvantages of mutualisation are looked at in chapter 7 (Insurance).
12. Shareholders will have a claim to the earnings from the existing business and the earnings that will flow from the investment of the 'new' money that has been raised. On flotation shares ought to have been priced in relation to the value of these earnings taking into account any discount to net asset value that could be expected based on similar discounts in other UK bank shares.
13. The Chairman and Chief Executive of TSB Scotland will at all times be members of the TSB Group Board (*Annual Report 1985*).

Retail Deposit Institutions

14. Owner occupation increased from 29 per cent in 1951 to 57 per cent by 1983. 24 per cent of owner occupiers in 1983 owned their property outright and 33 per cent by way of mortgage (source: *Social Trends 1985*). Among outright owners are those who purchased by way of a mortgage which has since been discharged.
15. The percentage of total assets accounted for by liquid assets is usually known as the liquidity ratio. Over the past 10–15 years the liquidity ratio has varied between 17–21 per cent. An article on liquidity appears in *BSA Bulletin* No.37, January 1984.
16. The competitive performance of the building societies in Scotland and in the UK is examined below.
17. Source of all figures in this paragraph: *BSA Bulletin* April 1986.
18. *BSA Bulletin* No.46 April 1986.
19. Barnes and Dodds (1983) could find no correlation between the growth rates and operating expenses (of which branch costs are a major part) of building societies and concluded that branch expansion policies do not result in greater growth.
20. Personal sector deposits includes persons, households and individual trusts, and unincorporated businesses.
21. From 1861 to 1971 the interest rate received on NSB ordinary accounts remained at 2.5 per cent, the maximum rate payable having been stated in legislation. Interest rates were allowed to vary thereafter. For TSBs see note 3.
22. As many investors are not liable to tax the composite rate is in general substantially lower than the basic rate. If the basic rate of tax is 30 per cent, the composite rate of tax 21 per cent, and the share rate 8 per cent, building societies are, effectively, attracting money at a gross rate of 11.43 per cent, yet this money costs them only 10.13 per cent, giving a competitive advantage of 1.3 per cent. However, building societies only enjoy a competitive advantage if the additional savings attracted from taxpayers because of the gross equivalent yield being higher than the cost of funds to the societies is not offset by reduced receipts of savings from those not liable to tax, whose gross yield from societies is considerably lower than the cost to societies of paying the interest.
23. From 1939 the Building Societies Association (BSA) had recommended to member societies the rates of interest that they should pay on investments and charge on mortgages. Prior to the large scale entry of the banks into the mortgage market at the start of the 1980s the building societies held a virtual monopoly over the supply of mortgage finance and by acting in concert to maintain the mortgage rate at a lower level than that required to equate demand and supply effectively rationed the supply of mortgage finance. (The stickiness of the recommended rate, which was changed less frequently than market rates, also meant variations in the inflow of funds into building societies which fed through into the funds available for on-lending.) Governments of different shades considered this politically expedient because of the sensitivities of many households' costs to mortgage interest. Exemption from 1976 restrictive trade practices legisation was granted, ostensibly to allow interest rate agreements to act as a control on lending in line with BSA and Government guidelines. Pressure for a more competitive environment came from various quarters including the Wilson Committee, the 1979 Stow Report (BSA Working Party), the National Consumers Council and by 1984 Government objections were outlined in the Green Paper on building societies. In 1983 the BSA announced that recommended rates were to be replaced by advised rates for investments. By 1985 the larger societies had broken ranks, effectively dissolving the cartel arrangements.

Notes

24. Prudential supervision of the building societies is the responsibility of the Chief Registrar of Friendly Societies. It was recognised that the statutory powers and resources of this office were limited in relation to the scale of the movement and proposed diversification of building society services. It is proposed to vest the task of supervision in a new body, the Building Societies Commission having a wider range of powers.
25. *Building Societies: A New Framework,* Cmnd 9316.
26. At least 90 per cent of a society's commercial assets will have to consist of first mortgage loans to owner occupiers (Class 1 Assets) and no more than 5 per cent of commercial assets, within the 10 per cent of non-Class 1 Assets, are to be in the form of unsecured lending, ownership of land or property, and equity investment (Class 3 Assets). Class 2 Assets which could account for up to 10 per cent of the non-Class 1 Assets would consist of wholly secured lending other than first mortgage loans. (Ceilings on Class 2 and 3 assets can be raised at a later stage by statutory instrument.) Only large societies with commercial assets in excess of £100 million will be able to lend unsecured. These regulations appear unduly restrictive if the building societies are to be allowed to compete in the market for financial loans in the same way that other institutions are being encouraged to enter the mortgage market. It presupposes building societies will be open to greater risk as diversified financial service institutions and that such additional risk cannot be absorbed.

6

OTHER BANKING AND DEPOSIT INSTITUTIONS

This chapter examines the diverse group of financial institutions operating in Scotland that can be broadly classified as 'specialist banking and deposit institutions'. Their limited involvement in the payments system, with one or two exceptions, distinguishes these financial intermediaries from the clearing banks. Their financial claims are issued primarily to the corporate sector or to specialist market segments. The activities of these institutions, as well as the clearing banks and building societies overlap to varying degrees. We can, however, usefully identify five main sub-groupings: the merchant banks; international banks; specialist retail banks; the finance houses; and the National Savings Bank. We examine these in turn.

Merchant Banks

The Role of Merchant Banks

The term 'merchant bank' has, traditionally, conjured up a strong association with wholesale banking and specialist financial skills offered to a corporate clientele and located firmly within the City of London. It is certainly true that merchant banking business covers a wide and varied range of financial services which embrace, amongst others, commercial banking, corporate advice, investment fund management, money-market operations, capital issues and foreign exchange dealings. Their financial intermediation role is greatly assisted by their ready access to the main UK domestic financial markets, as well as to the international capital markets. The merchant banks have played an important part in the development of many of these markets as the wholesale money and Eurocurrency markets clearly illustrate. No two merchant banks offer the same mix of business and the differing traditions of the more prominent banks are demonstrated by their individual approach to specialist fields. Merchant banks not only offer financial advice but also enable clients to purchase financial instruments that match their specific requirements. In this way intermediation provides a valuable financing service to industry and commerce.

Indigenous Scottish merchant banking business was slow to develop despite the existence of a corporate sector that could benefit from a local independent merchant bank with connections in the London capital markets. The need to establish credibility and the perceived need for a presence in London were possible forces that stifled earlier Scottish initiatives.

A premium is still placed on the reputation of the most prominent merchant banks that are based in the City of London. These are the houses whose history and stature have ensured preferential contacts and who have a network of personal links both throughout the City and with other international financial centres. They are all members of the Accepting Houses Committee (AHC) and bills of exchange accepted by them are discountable at the Bank of England at the finest rates of interest, although the acceptance of bills is now only a relatively small part of London Accepting House business and membership of the AHC is of historical rather than practical significance.[1] The advantage gained by the older London merchant bank groups is not exclusive. Japanese and US investment banks have succeeded in capturing new business and the merchant bank subsidiaries of Lloyds Bank and National Westminster have been among the fastest growing. It is not so much the lack of a credible reputation that distinguishes the Scottish merchant banks but rather their comparatively small size.

It is useful to summarise the financial activities carried out by the merchant banks in order to understand the role of merchant banking in a financial system and to provide a backcloth for discussing Scottish experience. Merchant banks are concerned with the efficient allocation of financial resources in three main ways:[2]

1. As bankers, providing a full banking service, with the emphasis on corporate borrowers;

2. As corporate financial advisers advising clients on and arranging the procurement of other funds from the capital markets, as well as advising on financial structure and strategy, including mergers and acquisitions;

3. As investment managers, advising on the disposition of new funds generated largely by the institutionalised savings media such as pension funds.

Unlike the clearing banks the banking business of the merchant banks does not include retail banking but is restricted to wholesale banking. Large deposits attracting the market rate of interest are collected and intermediated on a short- and medium-term basis to the corporate sector. For the Accepting Houses as a whole, at the end of 1985 sterling sight deposits formed around one-quarter of total sterling deposits[3] and foreign currency assets and liabilities, just under a half of the balance sheet totals. Total loans and advances by the Accepting Houses made through the market stood at 15 per cent of the corresponding UK retail bank figure. Market loans form a higher proportion of assets than do advances because the merchant banks are active in placing the funds of large corporations and institutions such as insurance companies on the money-markets. Sterling deposits are received mainly from the UK private sector, foreign currency deposits mainly from overseas although the UK monetary sector is also an important source.

The direct provision of funds is a somewhat misleading measure of the banking business of merchant banks since it ignores the distinction between

Other Banking and Deposit Institutions

the procurement and provision of finance. Procurement of finance is concerned with mobilising funds (sterling or foreign currency) collected by other banking institutions through the vehicle of syndication. Expertise and experience enable merchant banks to act as lead manager and to construct complex project finance packages which meet the needs of industry. These merchant bank activities depend on skill, connections and flexibility and fulfil an important function in a financial system. The construction of often sophisticated deals involving large sums assists the efficient allocation of resources to ultimate users, although the merchant banks may not themselves be large providers of funds.

The merchant banks' role as corporate financial advisers encompasses the organisation and underwriting of capital issues both in the UK domestic market and in the international capital market, the arrangement of takeovers and mergers, and advice on future financial strategies from which fees or commission are earned. Most merchant banks are members of the Issuing Houses Association. Membership of the Association requires either the sponsoring of capital issues, the sale of securities to the public generally, or the representation of parties interested in making offers for the capital of a company. There are three Scottish members: The British Linen Bank, James Finlay Corporation, and Noble Grossart. From involvement in capital issues it is only a small step for the merchant bank to secure a role as corporate financial adviser. Here the aim is to establish and retain a close relationship with the client so as to be able to give advice on the raising of capital from a position of knowledge as well as providing general financial counselling and technical advice on a wide range of corporate decisions.

The merchant banks have enjoyed a considerable degree of success in capturing a slice of investment management business in the UK. In the past twenty years the development of the fund management industry in the UK has followed the rapid insitutionalisation of UK portfolio investment, born out of the success and growth of pension fund and life assurance business. The merchant banks have moved from managing predominantly private client and charitable investments to offering fund management services to pension funds, insurance companies, quoted investment trust companies, unit trusts and corporate clients. This is an activity where location in the City of London is of less significance and comparisons with the Scottish life offices and fund management groups are more appropriate than with the merchant banking sector in Scotland (see chapter 8).

Changes to the regulations governing the operation of, and participation in, London capital markets has led the merchant banks to expand their activities into investment banking, that is to say the buying and selling of securities. Most merchant banks have joined forces with stockbroking and jobbing firms in an attempt to set up dealing organisations that can compete with the financial muscle of the large American investment banks and Japanese security houses. The merchant banking sector in Scotland is so small that the merits or otherwise of this debate do not really arise north of the border.

Merchant Banking in Scotland
The roots of Scottish-based merchant banking were put down only recently and the sector is still a small, although growing, part of the financial system in Scotland. Checkland (1975) notes that the formation of Glasgow Industrial Finance (Development) Ltd in 1946 was an early attempt to develop Scottish merchant banking.[4] It provided a financial service for Scottish businessmen, including issuing house facilities, but was eventually taken over in 1964 by the Industrial and Commercial Finance Corporation (now 3i). An interesting move occurred in 1963 when Alexander Stone took the British Bank of Commerce (founded 1938) from London to Glasgow. Between 1963 and 1969 it was linked with the London accepting house Samuel Montagu and Company but failed to survive the secondary banking crisis.[5] The largest independent Scottish merchant bank, Noble Grossart, was formed in Edinburgh in 1969 with the support of four Scottish investment trusts. This was an interesting example of collaboration within the Scottish financial community. The aim was to provide specialised and well-defined services with a high profit margin without taking on high-volume, low-margin banking. Regarding these initiatives, Checkland (1975) observes that

> there were certain initial difficulties, including the need to project the very idea of Scottish merchant banking, for it was not easy to persuade clients that it was possible to operate as efficiently and with as good quality of staff as in London and that it was not necessary to be on the City network of information.

The provincial tag has not been an easy one to shake off.

The development of merchant bank subsidiary operations by the Scottish clearing banks followed the path taken by the English clearing banks, although a lag occurred in much the same way as it did for international banking and foreign currency business (see chapter 4). In the 1960s official controls on liquidity prevented the clearing banks from operating in the rapidly expanding London money markets. In order to compete for large-scale term deposits, against which could be held assets with an average earning power considerably above that of other clearing bank assets, 'bidding subsidiaries' were established. Subsequent to the Competition and Credit Control measures of 1971 and the freeing of restrictions on the parent banks the special bidding subsidiaries largely became redundant. However, as part of the clearing bank move into a wider range of financial activities the subsidiaries were retained for sterling wholesale business and developed as merchant banks. The Midland Bank, however, eschewed in-house merchant bank development and purchased a stake in the accepting house Samuel Montagu & Co. The needs of the Clydesdale Bank's corporate customers could therefore largely be met from elsewhere within the group. Clydesdale has, however, set up a corporate division and brings in Samuel Montagu when scale or complexity necessitates.

The two Edinburgh clearing banks did not act until the 1970s, by which time it was clear that there were opportunities for merchant bank initiatives in Scotland. Both the business community and investors were facing an increasingly sophisticated financial environment and often had little alternative but to turn to the London institutions to meet their needs. Improvements to communications also reduced some of the disadvantages of remoteness from the London capital markets. The Bank of Scotland in 1969 set up Bank of Scotland Finance Company Limited to operate in the sterling wholesale money markets and to carry out long-term lending. Bank of Scotland Finance Company operated independently from its parent and it became the forerunner of a merchant bank. In 1969 the Bank acquired the British Linen Bank from Barclays Bank in exchange for the 35 per cent shareholding in Bank of Scotland that was eventually sold to Standard Life. The British Linen Bank name was retained and in 1977 became the merchant bank arm of the Bank of Scotland.

The British Linen Bank carries out a range of commercial banking and corporate advisory services as well as investment management (including pensions business), securities dealing, leasing finance for capital projects, and venture capital, often through subsidiary companies. Both the banking book and the client base of the British Linen Bank are separate and distinct from that of the Bank of Scotland. Clients of the Bank of Scotland requiring merchant banking services would be referred to the British Linen Bank. Close co-operation between the two banks arises where full exposure by the merchant bank would exceed the limits of prudence or those set by the Bank of England. The small size of the corporate market in Scotland, and the limited growth in new enterprise, has forced the Scottish merchant banks to seek business in the South. The majority of British Linen's corporate lending is to English-based clients and a large amount of banking business is transacted through the London branch. The Bank also has branch offices in Glasgow and Manchester.

The investment banking and fund management activities of the British Linen Bank are conducted through two main subsidiary vehicles, British Linen Securities Limited and British Linen Fund Managers. The former was set up to allow the British Linen Bank to aquire equity stakes in companies for its own account. British Linen Fund Managers act as Managers to five funds investing in private companies. The largest of these is Melville Street Investments (Edinburgh) Limited, an investment company that provides equity capital for larger private companies in Scotland and England.[6] Scottish Ventures Fund has been created to allow the pension funds of the Scottish Local Authorities to invest in emerging companies in Scotland. British Linen Fund Managers was one of the first companies in the country to capitalise on the new regulations for Business Start-up Schemes and has created three companies to enable the public to make investments under the auspices of this Scheme.

British Linen Fund Managers is responsible for the management of Bank of Scotland's £400 million pension fund. Pension fund management has been one area of the financial sector that has grown rapidly in recent years and the London merchant banks have had considerable success in attracting this type of business (see chapter 8). The British Linen Bank has captured the business of a number of pension funds although no attempt has yet been made to market their fund management services to the international pensions market. Melville Street Assets (Edinburgh) Limited deals in UK-listed securities and participates in the sub-underwriting of share issues.

The Royal Bank of Scotland provides a range of banking and other corporate financial services through National Commercial & Glyn's, which began as National Commercial & Schroder in 1964 under the National Commercial Bank. (National Commercial merged with the Royal Bank in 1969.) Business had initially consisted of money market operations but was expanded into the provision of long-term lending and equity participation, as well as leasing and hire purchase. The Royal Bank's bid to compete with the London clearing banks as a major UK banking group required a larger merchant banking operation than provided by National Commercial & Glyn's. In 1985 the Royal Bank acquired the Charterhouse Group and subsidiaries, including the London merchant bank Charterhouse Japhet and its associated development capital companies. National Commercial & Glyn's has been integrated with Charterhouse Development Holdings Limited to form the Edinburgh end of operations specialising in the provision of loan and equity capital to developing companies, including management buy-outs and buy-ins.

British Linen Bank and National Commercial & Glyn's were developed by the two main Scottish banks to widen their operations in the field of corporate finance. Noble Grossart provides an interesting example of independent initiative in the Scottish financial sector. The bank aims to exploit a gap in the financial system in which neither the Scottish clearing banks nor the London merchant banks had taken a head start. The bank's merchant business is concentrated on high-quality clients and involves the controlled expansion of its activities from corporate advisory status to a more rounded merchant banking organisation. The development of the business could be considered to have been conservative and it is possibly true that growth has been held in check by the discounting of high risk/return opportunities. Nevertheless, Noble Grossart has been successful in establishing a reputation for excellence. The profit margin on merchant bank activities carried out on a small scale employing specialist skills is typically high, unlike the margins on wholesale banking business in the money markets or large-scale underwriting. Noble Grossart offers deposit banking business, project financing and lending, leasing, underwriting and share placements, as well as corporate financial advice. A 46.9 per cent shareholding is held in Noble Grossart Investments Limited, which is an equity capital fund providing risk capital backing for unquoted companies. The operations of the bank are not confined to Scotland. Joint ventures have been undertaken in London, the United States, Canada and Australia.

Table 6.1. Scottish Merchant Banks[1] (£ million).

Latest balance sheet date[2]	British Linen Bank	National Commercial & Glyn's	Charterhouse Japhet	Noble Grossart	James Finlay Corporation
Profit before taxation	4.1	9.6	n/a[3]	2.2	n/a
Total assets	590.4	493.3	1123.5	45.1	24.7
Shareholders' funds	24.9	37.4	77.7[4]	7.2	3.5
Total deposits	410.4	295.6	915.0	34.5	17.4
Advances to customers	261.7	281.0	341.8	9.8	10.3

1. Charterhouse Japhet is included for purposes of comparison.
2. For British Linen Bank and Noble Grossart as at 31 January 1985. For National Commercial & Glyn's as at 30 September 1984. For Charterhouse Japhet and James Finlay Corporation as at 31 December 1984. Allowances for differing accounting practices must be made in comparisons.
3. Not disclosed in accounts.   4. Excludes inner reserves.
Source: Companies' Reports and Accounts, *Bankers' Almanac*.

Before the restructuring of the Royal Bank the Scottish financial sector could be considered to have four companies recognised as merchant banks; British Linen Bank, National Commercial & Glyn's, Noble Grossart and James Finlay Corporation. Published accounts data for the four banks, along with Charterhouse Japhet, are given in table 6.1. Measured by total assets under ownership both British Linen Bank and National Commercial & Glyn's are substantially larger than Noble Grossart and James Finlay Corporation, but less than half the size of Charterhouse Japhet. (The size of the banks is also reflected in the measure of shareholders' funds.) Charterhouse Japhet is among the smaller of the London merchant banks but is, nevertheless, active in the large company market. In 1985 the bank handled nine rights issues valued at £221 million and two flotations totalling £55 million.[7]

It can be seen from table 6.1 that there is a marked difference in the ratios of total deposits to customer advances between the banks. Although accounting practices differ it is reasonable to assume that the figures indicate the relative importance of commercial banking business between the groups. Just over 24 per cent of British Linen Bank's advances can be attributed to corporate leasing (rentals receivable). This figure rises to 72 per cent for National Commercial & Glyn's, which would indicate that commercial banking is less significant to its balance sheet. The ratio of deposits to advances is lower for the two Scottish-based clearing bank subsidiaries (1.6 British Linen Bank, 1.0 National Commercial & Glyn's) and for James Finlay Corporation (1.7) than for Charterhouse Japhet (2.7) or Noble Grossart (3.5). If the advances of the latter two banks are adjusted by adding in other loans to 'local authorities and banks' and to 'banks and financial institutions' respectively (distinguished from short notice loans), the ratios fall to 1.8 and 2.7 respectively. Assuming that similar lending figures are included under the one entry in the balance sheets of the other three banks, these figures probably provide a more accurate comparison. Taken together with its other balance sheet entries it would appear that Charterhouse Japhet is more involved in the short-term money markets. Noble Grossart also holds a large slice of assets in a liquid form which suggests that banking business is used to support the range of transactions carried out rather than being a major activity itself. The ratio of shareholders' funds to customer advances would also point to this as the figure is substantially higher for Noble Grossart than for the other two Edinburgh merchant banks.

There is a small number of other independent Scottish institutions which carry out merchant banking business or offer corporate advisory services. While small they have been able to capture a share of the market by meeting the needs of small and medium-sized companies that often cannot attract the larger London and Scottish merchant banks, or cannot meet the costs of doing so. Quayle Munro was formed in 1983 as a specialist investment management and issuing house, with one of its founding members a former director of the British Linen Bank. The company concentrates on investment in unlisted companies and the provision of corporate advice on financial structure and capital procurement. McNeill Pearson, which operated a small banking service and corporate advisory arm, was acquired in March 1985 by Quayle Munro to provide it with access to commercial deposit-taking and lending. The intention is to provide specialist lending packages and venture capital. The company is already involved in medium-sized unlisted company financing. Noble & Company, also based in Edinburgh, offers banking services alongside investment management and corporate advisory functions. There are two principal factors which perhaps prevent these institutions from being considered as Scottish merchant banks in the widest sense of the term. First, the higher degrees of specialisation in the range of business conducted, and, secondly, the small scale of operations, particularly their banking business.

The need to specialise has largely been governed by small resources and by the gaps that have been found in the provision of corporate financial services in Scotland. At the same time success in a market where there are large players often depends on the ability to offer a high quality specialised product. Market opportunities have arisen in recent years as the perceptions of the corporate sector towards receiving advice from Scottish institutions has changed. The increasing complexity of financial markets and the sophistication of corporate treasurers has also been responsible for stimulating a higher level of demand for corporate advisory services. The corporate sector in Scotland no longer beats a path straight to the City for its advisory or financing needs and the small and intermediate size Scottish company now has a greater range of merchant bank and corporate advisory institutions to choose from. There is, however, a correlation between the size of the corporate sector in the Scotland and the amount of merchant banking business that can be sustained. Both the British Linen Bank and Noble Grossart have found it necessary and benefical to broaden their horizons south, away from the small Scottish corporate market and both are represented in the City of London.

It is not possible to contemplate a merchant bank based in Scotland which would be equivalent in scale to the larger London merchant banks. While this means it is unlikely that a major contested take-over bid or a large new share issue could be underwritten by a Scottish merchant bank alone this does not prevent involvement as a supporting party to these activities. Mergers and takeovers have recently provided a very profitable field of enterprise for UK merchant banks.[8] Large sums of commissions have been earned from their advisory and underwriting services but such takeovers have been relatively rare in Scotland and there can be little point in building up resources to enter a game that may only be played at infrequent intervals. A substantial balance sheet is not necessary for the development of an efficient and dynamic merchant bank. A high premium, however, must be put on goodwill by the Scottish merchant banks and discussions indicate a strong awareness of the need to build up and extend contacts over time. This is especially important if business is to be acquired in England and if opportunities to participate in medium-sized or large issues or bids are to be forthcoming. British Linen Bank and Noble Grossart have both recently been involved along with large London merchant banks in a very large take-over battle involving a major Scottish company. This helps to raise the profile of the two banks and enables them to increase their experience of large-scale corporate takeover battles.

If financial resources are insufficient to underwrite the equity issues of medium to large Scottish companies, the pooling of resources among Scottish institutions including investment trusts and insurance companies is an alternative that might be explored. Venture capital deals to provide funds for new enterprise is also an area where the Scottish investment banks have been active, as have the Scottish portfolio management institutions, often on behalf of venture capital syndicates. Part of the attraction for the merchant banks is the prospect of establishing longer corporate advisory and banking relationships. Many of the UK's largest public companies were advised and supported by the top London merchant banks whilst small private companies, and have retained their client relationship with the bank to this day.

English Merchant Banks
At the end of the 1960s and beginning of the 1970s certain of the London-based merchant banks saw merit in opening Scottish offices. Singer and Friedlander was among the first and started its Glasgow office in 1969. Interviews suggest that the exploration and extraction of North Sea oil provided one impetus. Both the scale and international nature of project financing required the syndication of bank loans, providing opportunities for the mixture of risk/return and management skills appropriate to the operations of the major merchant banks. However, it was entirely feasible that such arrangements could be made from London and other leading merchant banks did not extend their operations to Scotland at that time. Subsequent expansion by other London-based merchant banks in the 1970s was based on wider criteria than simply oil business.

There are now five London merchant banks operating in Scotland: County Bank, Hill Samuel, Kleinwort Benson, Morgan Grenfell, and Singer and Friedlander. A sixth City representative is the Union Discount Company, a London discount house which has a shareholding in Aitken Campbell, the Glasgow stockjobbing firm. Hill Samuel and Singer and Friedlander are located in Glasgow; the other four have Edinburgh offices. The merchant bank activities carried out at these provincial offices varies from one bank to the other but Scottish representation has the common characteristic of acting as a repository for local business information and offering an executive level link, when Scottish clients require it, to the merchant bank's banking and advisory services in London. When the bank is involved in a large Scottish deal such as a takeover bid the office in Scotland can act as a base for operations, strengthened by personnel from London. Undoubtedly part of the reason for maintaining a Scottish office is to have what could best be described as a 'ground presence' albeit with a low profile. The intention is to attract business to London that would otherwise be lost. At least one of the London merchant banks is primarily concerned with running a banking book from its Edinburgh office with the funds of the life assurance companies providing an important source of short-term deposits.

Discussions with the banks indicate that they have little difficulty in attracting new clients and that dealing with existing client relationships established through London form an important part of their activities in Scotland. The London merchant banks also have long-established and firmly cemented relationships with large blue-chip Scottish companies. Corporate clients will normally be firms that are listed on the Stock Exchange with pre-tax profits in excess of £500000. New clients are often those who need assistance with the raising of finance or capital restructuring.

Investors in Industry (3i)
The major venture and development capital player in Scotland outside the public sector is Investors in Industry (3i). The company also offers hire purchase and leasing facilities and through subsidiaries a wide range of fee earning services. The company is owned by the English and Scottish clearing banks and the Bank of England and has some 40 years' experience in the area. Although it operates largely independently of its shareholders, given its ownership structure and the results it has achieved it enjoys the highest credit rating so that the availablility of funds has never been a restraint on its operations.

The company is regionally organised and considerable discretion with regard to investment resides with the regional executives. The Scottish region has investments in approximately 600 companies with about half of these of an equity nature. In Scotland, due to the competitive stance of the Scottish banks in the loan market, equity holdings are a more prominent element in the portfolio than in many regions. Investments in Scotland for the year to 31 March 1986 amounted to £17.4 million, representing 5.5 per cent of 3i's investment for the year. The amount outstanding in Scotland at that date amounted to £84.2 million. Development finance accounts for about 60 per cent of the capital advanced, with start-up, management buy-outs and share purchase schemes accounting for the remainder. Management buy-outs have been the growth point in the last five years and offer one successful way of offsetting the continuing pressure through mergers and takeovers for key decision-making activities to move to London and the South East. In common with other venture capital providers 3i has not found Scotland to be as productive a source of new business as some other regions and much effort is expended in marketing the company's services directly to potential customers and through other financial advisers. The portfolio is widely distributed outside the agricultural and property sectors. The company employs 17 executives in Scotland in three offices in Aberdeen, Edinburgh and Glasgow, with supporting secretarial staff.

The company has established offices overseas and as well as developing local business hopes to generate a flow of business involving its clients in all the countries in which it is located.

Conclusions
The level of competition in the Scottish merchant banking sector has intensified in the 1980s after the slow build-up throughout the 1970s. The Scottish company, especially the smaller firm, has now a wider choice of merchant bank services available without the need to turn to the City.[9] The market for corporate advice and underwriting is currently growing in Scotland with company restructuring and small firm take-overs and mergers particularly lucrative. The provision of these services by the Scottish merchant banks

and small corporate advisory organisations can be informed by intimate knowledge of local and regional economic conditions alongside established and growing national contacts and thus ease of access to the London and international financial markets. Relationships with Scottish institutions are likely to be stronger because of past connections and interlocking interests. The growth of the small corporate advisory and merchant banking sector is a positive sign for the Scottish financial system.

It is, nevertheless, pertinent to ask how the sector can develop. One approach would be to aim to provide a full range of banking service and advice to Scottish companies of all sizes. It is questionable, however, whether this market is strong enough to support a variety of growing merchant bank initiatives since the Scottish economy has failed to generate many new companies. The British Linen Bank and Noble Grossart have found it desirable and rewarding to expand their horizons beyond Scotland and the Royal Bank's Charterhouse Development operates nationally from its Edinburgh office. Neither is it entirely feasible to attack that part of the corporate market that is dominated by English and foreign banks. Here success does not always depend upon price since all the institutions offer very similar terms (although the large established merchant and foreign banks can command the finest rates in the market which does gives some advantage), but rather on contacts, reputation and the ability to innovate. Relationships and reputation must be cultivated over time and the Scottish merchant bank sector is still in its infancy. The largest Scottish merchant bank, the British Linen Bank, has achieved growing recognition in financial circles and appears well placed to compete for business from the small and medium-sized company in the UK. Noble Grossart has chosen to promote itself by providing high quality, independent merchant banking services.

The major growth in the UK corporate sector is to be found in the South of England. It is not always certain that these growing companies will seek advice and financial assistance from Scotland when their needs can be met in London or throughout the South East. The Scottish merchant banks and corporate advisory organisations must therefore seek to provide either a higher degree of specialisation and innovative financial services that are not available elsewhere, or develop the Scottish corporate market by generating local use of more sophisticated financial products. The availability of new financial instruments and financial packages appropriate for assisting enterprise may in turn contribute to the stimulation of economic activity.

International Banks

The great majority of overseas banks represented in Scotland are concerned solely with international banking. These banks have global branch networks and are capable of handling the most complex of international financial transactions. Some had been present in the City of London for a number of years before opening offices in Scotland. International banking consists of wholesale sterling and Eurocurrency borrowing and lending as well as foreign exchange dealing, Eurobond underwriting, syndicated credits, export services and finance, bullion services, leasing, financial futures, corporate advice (often in association with their own merchant banks), mergers and acquisitions where they are especially well placed to assist with international deals, portfolio and trust management, and international cash transference and management. The banks are engaged in these activities to varying degrees and although the individual banks offer different levels of service at their Scottish branches or offices, arrangements can swiftly be made for access to all the banks resources and facilities in London.

The Bank of Nova Scotia was the first of the overseas banks to set up in business in Scotland, opening its Glasgow branch in 1964, followed five years later by a second branch in Edinburgh. The first European bank to commence trading in Scotland was Credit Lyonnais, opening in Glasgow in 1972 (although now in Edinburgh) and heralding the start of the 1970s influx. Among the international banks now trading in Scotland the American and French banks are particularly well represented. The Standard Chartered Bank, which is principally a British international bank, is also present. There are, however, no German or Japanese banks.

The international banks have given a number of reasons for opening Scottish regional offices and branches. The political situation with regard to Scotland in the 1970s was one reason. The prospect of some form of devolution created uncertainty as to the freedom of entry that might be permitted in Scotland as well as the extent of possible future regulatory obstacles and barriers to international bank entry. Some of the international banks were thus repeating the patterns and experience of their earlier world-wide branching policies. Scotland also had attractions both as a source of corporate and institutional wholesale deposits, and as a source of demand for loans and other international banking services. One way to overcome the sometimes very real reluctance of Scottish firms to deal with London was to establish a local presence. Scotland was seen as a distinct market by the banks that had opened UK offices in London. The American banks were attracted to Scotland, at least in part, to service the subsidiaries of American companies with whom the bank already had a relationship in the United States, a traditional feature of American overseas banking. The development of North Sea oil and gas appears to have played a limited role in attracting the international banks to Scotland. As Gaskin (1980) has already commented the major financial transactions involved in North Sea developments are normally concluded in London.

Certain of the international banks run a banking book from their Scottish office although most act as a conduit for the deposits and loans for their main UK branch in London, where their treasury and commercial banking facilities are based. Several of the banks mentioned that the Scottish life assurance offices provided a substantial, but by no means the only, source of deposits. The business of the banks tends to be divided between the Scottish financial institutions, large corporations and to a much smaller extent the Scottish banks. Apart from the insurance companies the Scottish investment management houses and pension funds are also a target for loans and deposits and foreign exchange services, whilst at least one American bank provides securities custodianship in the United States. Many Scottish investment trusts have had long involvement in the purchase of US securities and the American banks offer convenient facilities to assist the flow of investment funds. Since correspondent banking rather than overseas branch banking, is the primary means by which the Scottish clearing banks take part in international bank markets, the international banks in Scotland often had long-standing relationships with the clearing banks. Closer liaison can now take place with respect to international banking transactions between the banks.

The international banks have targeted three main market segments in Scotland. These are large Scottish companies with overseas export markets, international companies operating in Scotland where the American banks have attempted to establish banking relationships with the subsidiaries of American companies and the Scottish financial institutions.[10] Large companies are the main targets and some of the banks interviewed have indicated that they would not be interested in making loans of less than £500000 although banking services may be made available to smaller companies if the bank is already dealing with its multinational parent. At least one bank had decided to target the top twenty-five major companies with interests in Scotland. It would appear that both loans and deposits are predominantly short term and while negotiated in Scotland are most often matched in London. Bank of America has its own dealing room in Edinburgh enabling the branch office to be actively involved in the London foreign exchange and short-term money markets holding a separate position from the Bank's London office. Few of the international banks offer retail banking services and where personal banking is provided it tends to receive neither emphasis nor promotion and caters mainly for home nationals (usually tourists) and the provision of travellers' cheques and currency although some branches do take small deposits.

One obvious advantage that the international banks offer large companies with overseas interests is access to the world-wide branch and office networks of the banks.[11] These inter-connected branch networks can provide an information-gathering and dissemination service to customers. Thus Scottish branches are electronically linked to the world-wide offices of the bank enabling the expeditious transfer of funds and information. The banks have the capacity to transact international payments at speed and at low cost.[12] The ability of the banks to raise finance in different currencies and often at more competitive rates than the Scottish banks, allows them to deal on finer margins and offer finance at very competitive rates. The international banks also offer a wider range of specialised financial instruments to large companies in Scotland. The American banks, for example, have been among the most active in promoting swaps, options, and forward deals, often provided in conjunction with their merchant bank subsidiaries. Discussions with international banks would suggest that there have been few credit syndications arranged in Scotland and any such participation in longer term funding has been selective. On the other hand, both French and American banks indicated that corporations and institutions in Scotland are increasingly willing to raise money in the Eurobond market. These banks are well placed to take advantage of this growth.

Giddy (1983) usefully draws a distinction between international banking that is either 'arm's length' or 'host-country' in nature. Banks engaged in arm's length banking limit their international activities to holding correspondent account balances in foreign banks and accepting deposits from, and granting loans to, foreigners.[13] Host-country banking, on the other hand, requires foreign banks to enter domestic markets to do local business through offices, branches or subsidiaries. The advantages that the incoming banks offer to institutions and corporations in the host-country depends on their familiarity with multinational firms and in the application of their loan marketing skills. Both these features have been present in the success of the international banks in Scotland. The banks do not typically become the sole bankers to these large corporations and institutions. The companies they serve usually maintain a close relationship with a domestic clearing bank to meet UK banking needs. There is little desire to disrupt this relationship.

Few of the international banks see themselves in direct competition with the Scottish clearing banks but they accept that the large corporations and institutions will be approached by their international competitors. This is met by the aggressive marketing of the banks' products, and the protection of existing contacts and relationships, a prime role of a representative office. Nevertheless, while the international banks have filled a gap in the Scottish financial system by providing a previously unavailable banking service, they have also attempted to cream off the most profitable business in Scotland.

Giddy suggests that an important factor determining the success of foreign banks is the impact that they have on the host-country banking structure. This proves advantageous to both the incoming banks and their customers because it involves competing in an oligopolistic market and may bring about the dissolution of a concentrated market structure. Corporate and institutional customers benefit from increased supply and lower cost as well as having a wider range of international banking opportunities. The incoming banks gain from a share of the previously excessive profits. The evidence suggests that the international banks had such an impact on the Scottish bank market. The early aggression of the American banks, operating on considerably lower margins than the Scottish banks, enabled them to acquire business from the large Scottish corporations and institutions.[14] The low margins of the incoming banks resulted in a reduction in the rates offered to corporate borrowers by the Scottish banks.

The success of the international banks in capturing business in Scotland is demonstrated by the fact that most of those that set up in the 1970s remain here today. If their branches and offices were not cost-effective it is unlikely that they would retain a presence. Several of the banks have, however, rationalised their UK branch business in recent years and this has often meant a reduction in personnel in Scotland. Few of the international banks maintain more than one branch or office in Scotland. There is some suggestion that the volumes of business expected in the 1970s did not materialise. Improvements in telecommunications to London has allowed staffing overheads to be kept to a minimum. Employment in the institutions varies from 2 to 20 although at least one employs up to 36. There does not appear to be a typical figure. This is a mobile sector of the banking world. Although continuity of relationships with clients is important senior executives will expect to move on elsewhere at some later stage. These are international bankers who will work in different regions of the world and it is clear that sales acumen and the ability to cope with new financial products is as important as the more traditional banking skills.

Conclusions

The international banking sector in Scotland brings together a surprisingly varied and interesting collection of banking institutions and, indeed, forms an important element in the composition of the financial superstructure. Most of these banks arrived in Scotland during the 1970s bringing techniques of international banking to the doorstep of businessmen and offering Scottish companies access to international financiers. The overseas banks have made a valuable contribution to the level of competition and efficiency in the Scottish bank market.

The prospect for the future growth of international bank business in Scotland depends on the longer term prospects for the Scottish economy. The Scottish financial sector is now well provided with wholesale and international banking services. The established international banks may be expected to offer a wider diversity of services in the future with credit syndication, Euromoney deals, and specialised financial instruments such as currency and interest rate swaps and options as potential areas of expansion. As international trade becomes increasingly important the international banks are well placed to meet the requirements of customers.

Specialist Retail Banks

There are a few banks in Scotland that carry out retail banking in competition with the Scottish clearing banks. While their business is substantially smaller than that of the clearers they do business with personal customers and some corporate customers who would otherwise use the clearing banks.

Ethnic Banks
Of all the overseas banks to enter the Scottish bank market the Irish banks are the closest in approach to the Scottish clearing banks, offering the same range of banking and fee-related services from within their banking Groups. Allied Irish Bank opened its Glasgow office in 1973, and was followed seven years later by the Bank of Ireland. These are the two largest Irish banks and both have small branch networks extending throughout the UK which enables them to participate in the UK clearing system.[15] Expansion into Scotland arose from the lack of new opportunities for rapid growth in their own domestic market, in much the same way as the two Edinburgh clearing banks have sought to expand south of the border. The large Irish community in the West of Scotland provided a natural customer base upon which to build. Both banks are competing directly with the Scottish clearers for personal sector customers and offer a range of services encompassing current and deposit account banking, overdrafts and mortgages, credit cards, and the like. Instalment finance is also sold through the banks' branches. Bank of Ireland owns British Credit Trust, a UK finance house with a regional office in Edinburgh, and Allied Irish Bank owns Allied Irish Finance.

There are other overseas banks, mostly located in Glasgow and serving the Asian communities, which carry out some retail banking. The full scope of their activities is not known but it is likely that they facilitate the transfer of funds to and from their home country and provide a range of personal banking services including loans to small businesses.

Specialist Personal Sector Banks
Adam & Company was formed in Edinburgh in 1983 and is licensed by the Bank of England to take deposits under the terms of the 1979 Banking Act.[16] It has the distinction of being the first new Scottish retail 'bank' of this century. The formation of the company was an attempt to bring the American idea of personal and non-standardised banking packages, offered to high income individuals and entrepreneurs, to Scotland. Distinctive banking packages have also been offered in the UK for a number of years by small London-based companies, such as C. Hoare & Co. and Close Brothers. These banking companies trade, at least in part, on the willingness of the client to pay more for a service of higher quality or for a service not available elsewhere. This often means offering the client a more personal service and attention from senior executives.

The banking services offered by Adam & Company include deposit and loan facilities (cheque clearing arrangements are with the Royal Bank of Scotland), financial management, and advisory services such as personal financial planning, investment advice and introductions. A cash-dispensing agreement allows customers to use the Royal Bank's ATM network and this adds the all-important ingredient of flexibility to the bank account where there is no branch network. Product differentiation is an important ingredient of the Adam & Company approach. Current account statements, for example, provide full narrative details of each entry whilst a variety of methods of paying for bank charges are offered together with the provision of a cheque guarantee card to the value of £250. Interest is paid on current accounts with large balances (over £1000).

The total assets of the company, at the end of June 1985, amounted to £14 million of which approximately £6.8 million comprised short-term loans to banks and other financial institutions. A large proportion of assets were therefore held in highly liquid money-market instruments. Advances, including accrued interest, amounted to just over £4 million with mortgages for house purchase making up a large part of these loans. Deposits with the company amounted to £8.5 million. Over 1000 accounts were opened during the year to June 1985. Most of Adam & Company's clients are individuals, although some corporate customers have been attracted.

Balance sheet growth is likely to be circumscribed by the prudential demands placed on a new entrant to the banking market both by the requirements of the supervisory authority and by the need to appear secure to potential banking business. Adam & Company has indicated a conservative and cautious approach to the build-up of its assets and liabilities with the objective of securing a standing in the financial community and gaining the confidence of a selected clientele. It faces an inevitable conflict between the desire for prudence to reassure customers and the need for profits to find growth and expansion. A profit of £50000 was earned in the first full trading year to June 1985.

Specialist banks are frequently attempting to fill gaps or perceived shortcomings in the provision of financial services by either targeting a specific market segment or by introducing an innovative or distinctive product. With Adam & Company and similar UK banks competition focuses more on the product than on price. Perhaps the most interesting question posed by the formation of Adam & Company, however, is whether there is scope for further similar specialist banks in Scotland. The market in Scotland is small and the longer term growth and success of such ventures is likely to depend on attracting customers from elsewhere. About one third of Adam & Company's private clients live in the South and the Company has recently acquired Continental Trust, a small London-based bank.

The innovative drive and foresight which brought Adam & Company into existence, and the energies, skill and experience necessary to consolidate its position in the market must also be present in Scotland if other similar initiatives are to be taken. It is interesting to note that those who originated the company gained their banking experience with American international banks in London and New York. Despite the success and reputation of Scottish clearing bank managers in the domestic retail scene there is little evidence of the three banks providing a well-spring for entrepreneurial talent in the financial services field in Scotland. It is notable that Scottish merchant bank and corporate advisory initiatives have closer personnel links with the investment management sector in Scotland or with those who have gained experience outwith the Scottish financial sector.

National Girobank

The National Girobank was launched by the Post Office in 1968. The role of the giro system is to provide a cheap and secure money transmission service for the majority of the population who do not have a bank account, making use of the convenient branch network provided by post offices. A centralised accounting system assists with the rapid transfer of funds. After the Girobank had sustained losses in its early years it was decided to change direction by concentrating on the provision of a payments service for business customers and the bank achieved profitability by 1975. The system caters for persons having to meet periodic bills such as gas, electricity or local authority rents. A wide range of services has, however, been introduced including deposit accounts, personal loans and limited overdraft facilities, cheque guarantee cards and recently house purchase mortgages. The Department of Health and Social security is one of the largest deposit holders and uses the system to remit payments to individuals. The National Girobank also takes part in the clearing system and has, since February 1983, been an operational member of the Bankers' Clearing House. The Wilson Committee found that the competition provided by the Girobank (along with the TSBs and Co-operative Bank) had contributed to reducing charges and improving services to bank customers generally, and that it helps maintain the commercial viability of the network of sub-post offices. Thus the success of the Girobank, or its privatisation, as with the National Savings Bank has repercussions for Scottish post office staff. The Girobank also competes directly with the Scottish clearing banks, attracting members of the unbanked population who may otherwise be persuaded to open a bank account.

Finance Houses

Most of the finance houses carrying out business in Scotland are English in origin although there are a few small Scottish finance companies. The major UK and foreign-owned finance houses are well represented with branches or regional chief offices in the main centres of population. The bulk of their business is conducted by offering credit facilities at the point-of-sale, with the retailer or dealer having a standing relationship with one or more finance houses for the provision of credit to his customers. Finance houses are primarily involved in the provision of medium-term instalment finance to both individuals and businesses. Credit of this nature takes various forms and perhaps the best known are the hire-purchase agreement and the credit sale. The larger houses have diversified their business beyond instalment credit instruments and many are active in the corporate leasing market or engage in factoring and receivables financing, usually through subsidiaries and associated companies. A number of finance houses have also developed their banking services and now offer current and deposit account facilities as well as personal and commercial loans including mortgages. Certain of these houses have been listed as banks by the Bank of England under the 1979 Banking Act.[17]

There are 44 members of the Finance Houses Association (FHA), accounting for over 90 per cent of all business transacted by finance houses in the UK.[18] At the end of 1985 outstanding credit (excluding unearned finance charges) stood at £20.6 billion, 38 per cent of which was attributable to leasing, 35 per cent to consumers and the remaining 27 per cent to business customers (other than leasing). The total figure outstanding has risen by approximately £12.5 billion since 1980. In recent years by far the greatest proportion of the new credit extended has been to consumers (43 per cent in 1985) most of which continues to be provided for new and used car purchase, usually arranged in the form of hire-purchase agreements through motor traders and garages. Car finance accounted for 40 per cent of all new consumer credit in 1985. Mortgage finance for house purchase (8 per cent) is, however, growing rapidly, as is finance for household and personal goods (22 per cent). Credit that is extended to business is also mainly used to acquire vehicles, whereas leasing is used to finance a range of vehicles, industrial plant and heavy equipment and, increasingly, computer hardware.

Wholesale borrowing in the money markets, primarily from banks, accounts for the majority of finance house liabilities. Despite operating through branch networks deposits from the personal sector are very small and those deposits that they do secure mostly come from banks and commercial and industrial companies. It would appear that the maturities of assets and liabilities are not closely matched, or at least not to any significant extent. Assets are predominantly loans and advances to consumers and business customers although a proportion of real assets are held for leasing agreements. Interest rate charges to customers depend on the credit risk and the type of commodity for which the loan is advanced. The Finance House Base Rate is the rate of interest used as a basis for calculating charges to businesss customers for variable-rate transactions.[19]

Most of the large finance houses are owned by banks and other financial institutions, although some are subsidiaries of manufacturing companies primarily engaged in offering credit finance for the purchase of the parent's products. One such example is the Ford Motor Credit Company. Sometimes retailers find it practical to finance the transactions themselves and can realise the funds tied up in debts by selling a block of existing instalment credit agreements to a finance house at a discount in much the same fashion as receivables financing.

Other Banking and Deposit Institutions

Finance companies have been present in the Scottish financial system for nearly sixty years, with United Dominions Trust opening its first Scottish office in 1927 (Checkland 1975). Expansion in the sector has, for the most part, been due to the establishment of branches by incoming English and American houses although there have been a small number of Scottish initiatives such as the Scottish Discount Company, which started in 1954, but has not moved beyond its Glasgow location. Perhaps the best known Scottish initiative in the field of finance companies was the earliest example of a bank acquisition of a hire-purchase finance house, with the Commercial Bank of Scotland buying the Edinburgh-based Scottish and Midland Guarantee Trust in 1954, some four years before a whole series of similar bank ventures.[20]

Both the Scottish clearing banks and their London counterparts became active in purchasing shareholdings in finance houses during the instalment credit boom of the late 1950s and early 1960s. Most of the houses in which shareholdings were held have been fully assimilated into the clearing bank groups. Today the big four London clearing banks each own a major finance house through which credit facilities and other services such as leasing are offered. Bank of Scotland owns North West Securities (NWS), a house that is registered in England and has its head office in Chester. It has a branch network that extends throughout the UK. The outstanding balances of NWS (at the end of 1983) amounted to £673 million, which placed it, as the fifth largest UK finance house, behind the finance house subsidiaries of the London clearing banks and the TSB. NWS is involved in instalment finance, commercial and car leasing and, increasingly, in the personal sector credit market by providing financial services for retail organisations, British Rail and the Automobile Association. These mainly take the form of credit and charge-card operations.

The Royal Bank of Scotland has recently divested itself of its 39 per cent holding in Lloyds and Scottish finance house to its partner Lloyds Bank. The main consumer instalment credit and leasing arms of the Royal Bank of Scotland are now St Margarets Trust, formerly a subsidiary of Williams & Glyn's, and Charterhouse Japhet Credit. The outstanding balances of these two companies amounted to, respectively, £79.7 million and £45.9 million.[21] The Charterhouse Company also offers credit finance and leasing to the business sector, often at point-of-sale. Clydesdale Bank offers an instalment credit service in Scotland as part of the activities of the Clydesdale Bank Finance Corporation (total resources £8.1 million, September 1984)[22] and its parent Midland Bank owns Forward Trust, one of the largest UK finance houses (outstanding balances £2377 million). The Scottish clearing banks also have a share of Scottish and UK leasing activities. Leasing services are provided for industrial and commercial concerns either through subsidiaries set up by their finance house arms or separate specialist subsidiaries.

The largest finance house employer in Scotland is the Lloyds Bowmaker Finance Group, which was formed in 1984 following the merger of Lloyds and Scottish Finance Limited with Bowmaker Limited. Lloyds and Scottish were previously based in Edinburgh and while the registered office of the new Group is now in London the Group's Dealer Finance Division is headquartered in Edinburgh. The Dealer Finance Division provides financial packages to the motor trade and home improvement market and has its own 38-branch network divided into five regions throughout the UK. The Division provides motor dealers with finance to purchase cars as well as finance and insurance to the car-buying public. In effect Lloyds Bowmaker owns the stock of cars in its dealers' showrooms. Lloyds Bowmaker also has joint venture arrangements with five major overseas car manufacturers to provide point of sale finance to their UK dealerships. The major competitors of the Division are the other bank-owned finance houses and motor company finance houses. Most of these finance houses will offer similar prices and in order to win new business and retain existing dealer clients competition largely centres on the service provided to the dealer.

Technology, marketing and the training of dealer staff in techniques for selling finance are therefore important. As well as on-line computer links between branches and the Division in Edinburgh, large dealerships are also linked into the network providing a fast response to proposals and enquiries and the facility to produce local documentation. The Dealer Finance Division employs about 750 staff in Scotland with just under 700 located at the head office in Edinburgh of whom about half are involved in computer operations. Technology has had a significant impact on the Dealer Finance branch network enabling a reduction in branches from about 100 to the present 38. This has meant a reduction in employment, mainly clerical, including staff in Edinburgh. Lloyds Bowmaker is, nevertheless, an important financial sector employer in Edinburgh and the Dealer Finance Division is run from Edinburgh with a degree of autonomy within the Group.

Conclusions

It is unfortunate that only Lloyds Bowmaker has its headquarters in Scotland. A large proportion of finance house business is conducted through the head office leading to a concentration of employment there. Investment in computer technology has enabled the finance houses to centralise their credit records and carry out credit scoring from their main offices. Branches provide some employment dealing with local administration and acting as field locations for sales and marketing staff and some of the large houses have regional branch offices in Scotland. Much of the marketing is aimed at point-of-sale outlets. Point-of-sale finance does not, however, encourage any kind of loyalty by the borrower to a particular lender and this has limited the ability of the finance houses to cross-sell a wider range of financial services from their branches.

The National Savings Bank

The purpose of National Savings in Britain has long been to provide secure savings opportunities for the small individual saver and to channel these surplus funds into the public sector. In the immediate post-war period National Savings represented the most important form of personal savings but increasing competition from other deposit institutions, especially the building societies but also life assurance and pension funds, led to a sustained decline. At the end of the 1970s National Savings received new-found recognition as an important source of revenue and competitive savings medium. For the first time the Government set a target (financial year ending March 1981) for the net contribution of National Savings to the Public Sector Borrowing Requirement (PSBR).

It was the intention of the Government to tap directly the large volume of UK personal sector savings in an effort to reduce its call on the gilt-edged market. The theory was that upward pressure on long-term interest rates would then subside encouraging the revival of the corporate debt market as an alternative to bank finance. There is little evidence to suggest that these aims were realised but National Savings have remained important to the funding of the PSBR. From the financial year 1982–83 to the current year ending in March 1986 the target contribution has been £3 billion measured by the excess of deposits and interest accrued over withdrawals within the year. Actual savings transactions account for half of this figure, accrued interest for the rest.

The resurgence of National Savings over the 1980s has been engineered by improving the terms on which existing financial instruments have been offered and the introduction of new savings instruments. In 1979–80 the National Savings inflow amounted to £1.13 billion. The first target for net contribution to the PSBR was set at £2.0 billion in 1980–81 and was exceeded by a total net inflow which amounted to £2.27 billion. Each successive target has also been met. In 1984–85 a total net inflow of £3.10 billion was recorded. The Department for National Savings operates a monthly monitoring exercise on target inflows which allows a more immediate response than in the past to competitive initiatives from other sectors and, in particular, to interest rate changes. The decision to alter rates of remuneration on savings instruments rests with the Treasury, who prefer not to be market leaders.

Responsibility for the administration of the national savings function is vested in the Department for National Savings. The Department comprises a Headquarter Office in London and three decentralised divisions. These are the Savings Certificate and SAYE Office located in Durham, the Bonds and Stock Office in St Annes and Marton near Blackpool, and the National Savings Bank in Glasgow. The National Savings Bank (NSB) was moved to the south side of Glasgow in 1966 as an act of regional policy. The movement of civil service functions and hence employment opportunities out of London was seen as one means of assisting the correction of regional economic imbalances. The initial connections of the NSB with Scotland, therefore, were of a political kind. It is important, nonetheless, to look at the operations of the NSB since these determine the numbers of staff employed.

The NSB handles two forms of savings account, the Ordinary Account and the Investment Account. The former offers depositors day-to-day access to their savings and the latter access at one month's notice compensated by a more competitive rate of interest. These two accounts generate by far the greatest volume of National Savings transactions, measured at over 42 million in 1984–85, or 73 per cent of the total. Passbook banking through the postal system is used to make deposits and withdrawals. Savers can use the system to make direct application to the NSB or, alternatively, the UK Post Office network provides a counter service. With more than 20000 post office branches covering the UK the NSB is within reach of a higher proportion of the saving population than any other deposit-taking institution. The most obvious advantage to the bank of this arrangement is that it has no branch overheads. The cost to the Department for National Savings of maintaining the network takes the form of agency payments to the Post Office. In 1984–85 these agency costs amounted to £53.8 million, of which £34 million was attributed to the administration of Ordinary Accounts.[23] A further advantage of the Post Office collection and distribution network is the familiarity of customer with the use of Post Office services. Disadvantages to the NSB include the lack of direct contact with the saving public and no direct management control of front-line operations. A settlement system is operated by the NSB and the Post Office. The NSB is strictly a savings insitution having no role within the clearing system.

The future of the NSB in Glasgow depends not only upon the longer term Government policy towards National Savings[24] but also on the contribution and status of its savings instruments. Table 6.2 brings together balance sheet and financial flow data for Ordinary and Investment Accounts and for Deposit Bonds which are also handled at Glasgow. Figures for Savings Certificates and Income Bonds are included for comparison. The Ordinary Account has shown little growth in the total amount invested over the past five years. In 1984–85 it provided a negative contribution to Government funding, i.e. there was a reduction in Government liabilities. The Ordinary Account is the only National Savings instrument whose funds are passed to the National Debt Commissioners for investment in public stock. In a similar fashion to the Savings Accounts of the trustee savings bank movement (see chapter 5) it has lacked the necessary competitiveness in an interest-rate sensitive era. In contrast the Investment Account has continued to attract funds and its growth rate over the past five years is similar to that for Savings Certificates, providing a positive inflow toward the PSBR target. National Savings schemes are now the only form of savings in the UK

Other Banking and Deposit Institutions

Table 6.2. National Savings Bank statistics, financial year 1984–85 (£million).

	Receipts	Accrued interest	Repayments excluding interest	Accrued interest repaid	Total net contribution to funding	Balance outstanding				
						1984–85	1983–84	1982–83	1981–82	1980–81
Ordinary account[1]	664.4	80.6	754.3	—	−9.3	1756.1	1765.4	1734.1	1702.0	1740.1
Investment account[1]	1215.6	510.9	1330.0	—	396.5	5148.4	4751.9	3951.3	2995.1	2320.3
Deposit bonds[1]	133.5	21.7	17.7	—	137.6	247.3	109.7	—	—	—
Savings Certificates										
Fixed-interest issues	2132.5	1036.7	844.1	327.6	1997.5	12114.7	10117.7	8514.8	7187.7	5690.4
Income bonds	1075.8	—	245.3	—	830.5	2787.5	1957.0	891.3	—	—

1. National Savings Bank products.

Source: Annual Report, Department for National Savings.

The National Savings Bank

which pay income gross of tax. Non-taxpaying savers should therefore have an incentive to invest in National Savings products. There is little evidence, however, that the banks and building societies have lost many non-taxpayers' accounts to National Savings.

National Savings data for 1984–85 indicates that there are 15 million Ordinary Accounts and 3 million Investment Accounts. The average value of transactions in the year were, respectively, £33 and £213. Although both the Ordinary Account and the Investment Account are operated by use of the passbook system the former is responsible for 75 per cent of the workload at Glasgow when measured by employee resources. The 36 million transactions involved is five times the volume created by the Investment Account. Both these Ordinary Account figures, however, continue to decline whereas the corresponding figures for the Investment Account and Deposit Bond are on an upward trend. The declining importance of the Ordinary Account as a source of National Savings has been offset by the success of new financial products. The future existence of the NSB must depend, in part, on the administration of such instruments. Product development decisions, as well as marketing and interest-rate decisions, are taken in London (and not Glasgow) notwithstanding the input of the three divisions of the bank where opportunities for new instruments are perceived. Three innovations have been introduced since 1982–83: the Income Bond, the Deposit Bond and the Yearly Plan. Each division has been given the responsibility for the administration of one of these products with the NSB receiving the Deposit Bond. It is not altogether clear whether this reflects a continuing commitment to tripartite regional decentralisation by the Department for National Savings. The figures in table 6.2 indicate that both the Deposit and Income Bond have provided a useful contribution to National Savings.

Between 5 and 6 per cent of all NSB transactions occur in Scotland, which is below the ratio expected in terms of UK population distribution. These lower figures are probably accounted for by the traditional strength of the trustees savings bank movement in Scotland. Greater publicity in Scotland aimed at expanding the transactions ratio is not seen, at least at present, as a cost effective exercise. The profile of the NSB's customers differ from other retail deposit-taking institutions operating in Scotland. Ordinary Account savers are concentrated in two age bands of young children and teenagers, and older persons over fifty, some of whom may have used the National Savings medium before. The loss of male savers in the 20–50s age bracket is more marked than for women, which may reflect the number of women who continue to hold a small separate account after marriage.

The significant contribution made by the NSB to the Scottish economy is its employment impact and the associated multiplier effects. After relocation in 1966, total employment at the Bank was built up to a peak of 5300 in 1976. The introduction of electronic processing systems to what was largely a mechanical and labour-intensive operation, and reduced ordinary account activity, have mostly been responsible for the subsequent decline. At the start of the 1985–86 financial year the NSB employed a total of 3047 personnel, a net fall of 120 over the previous year's figure. Employment needs for the Ordinary Account fell by twice this figure and were partly offset by the creation of new jobs on the Investment Account and Deposit Bond. Redistribution of employment from servicing the Ordinary Account has been a feature of the 1980s.

By its very nature Post Office counter, or postal passbook banking, requires a labour intensive, assembly-line type of operation and this includes visual display unit operators. Future job loss due to the further application of electronic data processing, such as the conversion of customer records to an on-line basis, cannot be accurately assessed but must be expected. It should also be noted that National Savings account for approximately 7 per cent of all Post Office business in the UK and this too has employment repercussions. For example, the attempt by the NSB to decrease the volume of Ordinary Account transactions and to increase the value of each transaction has implications for Post Office staff needs as well as any more obvious impact in Glasgow.

The NSB is a Civil Service operation and staff are graded accordingly. Senior management comprises three classes of executive officers and a group of controllers totalling over 400. The remainder of the employees are on clerical grades. Staff are predominantly women drawn from the south side of Glasgow. All staff training is internal. Like any major local employer the economic benefit is mainly confined to the vicinity. An NSB wage bill of £20 million for example, provides income to spend in the local economy. The NSB has also assisted in providing computer terminal skills to a local labour force which has proved attractive to other employers seeking similarly skilled personnel.

Conclusion
It must be made clear that the NSB, despite its location in Glasgow, is part of a central government operation. It is not directly involved in the Scottish financial system and the two have very little inter-relationship. The future of the NSB, which continues to be an important service sector employer in Glasgow, is closely bound to the Ordinary Account and to the introduction of new products. Unfortunately, there is no direct Scottish control over any decisions that may be taken on these matters.

NOTES
1. The London Accepting Houses carry out the full range of merchant bank activities and are properly considered as merchant banks.
2. See First Stage Evidence of the Accepting Houses Committee to the Committee to Review the Functioning of Financial Institutions, HMSO, 1977.
3. Bank of England *Quarterly Bulletin*.

Notes

4. The following paragraph on initial merchant bank development in Scotland is largely based on Checkland (1975).
5. Checkland suggests that the link provided valuable insights into the working of a merchant bank but is not clear whether this had significance for Scottish merchant banking in general.
6. British Linen Bank has a 20 per cent shareholding in the company. 80 per cent is held in varying proportions by a number of UK institutions. By the end of 1985 over £17 million had been invested by the company.
7. This was down from six flotations valued at £136 million in 1984. In comparison Morgan Grenfell headed the 1985 Leagues with 10 flotations (£2063 million), 12 rights issues (£675 million) and 93 takeovers and mergers (£6794 million). (Source: *Financial Times*.)
8. Takeovers and merger deals concluded in 1984 amounted to £5.2 billion compared to £2.3 billion in 1983 and £2.2 billion in 1982. (Source: *Financial Times*.)
9. The financial and advisory assistance that the merchant banking sector provides to indigenous Scottish industry and commerce is perhaps more important than the levels of employment in the sector. British Linen Bank, for example, employs 150 people, 120 of which are based in Scotland. Employment in the sector is non-labour intensive and an estimate of the total, based on scant evidence, is 300–400.
10. Indications are that the Japanese companies which have set up in Scotland receive finance from their own group bank located in London.
11. A number of the banks are represented in more than 50 countries with a spread of branches and representative offices.
12. A major weakness of the Scottish clearing banks is possibly their inability to meet the foreign trade needs of their corporate clients other than through their established correspondent networks. They are susceptible to losing their existing business in this area to the international banks, the London clearing banks and merchant banks, and British international banks such as Standard Chartered. The latter has branches in Glasgow, Edinburgh and Dundee and has traditionally been concerned with the provision of import and export services and finance, both short and medium-term as well as foreign currency borrowing, to large and medium-sized UK companies.
13. Correspondent account balances will be held for the purpose of clearing international payments, the extent of which depends upon the bank's specialisation in gathering information concerning domestic customers with international trade and investment activities. Deposit and loan activities offer the chance of portfolio diversification or higher returns and the extent of the bank's activities will be determined here by the transferability of its risk and currency transformation skills. Arm's-length banking is still important to the Scottish clearing banks (see chapter 4).
14. Giddy observes that a well-developed domestic inter-bank money market considerably assists a foreign bank in entering a host-country banking market. Where no organised market for deposits exists the bank has to create an internal market, in effect through a branch network, and faces formidable barriers in comparison to local banks with an established network. (The disadvantage is not so apparent with lending because the larger size and smaller number of borrowers makes the costs of participating lower.) A well-organised money market, however, allows the incomer to borrow funds on the market to finance its loans and a local loan business can subsequently be developed by offering unbundled services or simply lowering interest rates. Since the international banks in Scotland are represented in London where their banking book is

matched, local loan business and a range of international banking services could be provided without the need for Scottish deposits to match advances. As already pointed out interest rates were also lower because the international banks had access to a wide variety of financial instruments to raise funds at cheaper rates and because they were dealing in large amounts could operate on fine margins. This is not to deny, of course, that Scottish deposits are important to the branch and representative office location decision.

15. Bank of Ireland carries out clearing in Scotland by way of an arrangement with the Royal Bank of Scotland.
16. The Banking Act 1979 distinguishes between recognised banks and licensed deposit-takers (LDTS). Adam & Company is not yet entitled to include the word 'bank' in its name. The granting of recognised bank status under the Act depends on the range of banking service offered and reputation and standing in the financial community. The banking authorities have proposed to abolish the present two-tier system and LDTS with paid up equity of more than £5 million will then be entitled to use the word 'bank' in their titles. Adam & Company has authorised share capital amounting to £10 million, of which almost £5.6 million is paid-up.
17. Most finance houses are licensed deposit-takers. See note 15.
18. Source for this and following figures: Finance Houses Association (FHA).
19. At the end of each month the FHA calculates the average rate of interest over the previous 8 weeks on money deposits for three months in the sterling inter-bank market and rounds this figure to the 0.5 per cent above.
20. After the merger of the Commercial Bank with the National Bank of Scotland in 1958 the hire-purchase interests of the two banks and National's parent Lloyds were re-organised to form Lloyds and Scottish Finance. Ensuing clearing bank mergers and share deals resulted in the Royal Bank of Scotland and Lloyds becoming the principal shareholders in the company.
21. For Charterhouse Japhet Credit outstanding balances are at end-December 1984 and comprise customer balances less provisions. For St Margaret's Trust outstanding balances are at end-September 1984 and comprise balances on HP and instalment credit (before unearned charges) plus assets on lease or hire plus loans and other advances. Source: Extel.
22. Source: *Bankers' Almanac and Year Book* (1986).
23. These costs are determined under an Agency Service Agreement with the Post Office which is renegotiated at four-yearly intervals.
24. If the Post Office were to be privatised post office branches would form a formidable distribution network with the sale of financial services an obvious target. These would not necessarily be limited to National Savings and if privatisation occurred it is likely that the Government would have to legislate to ensure a continued outlet for National Savings instruments.

7

INSURANCE FUNDS AND INSURANCE BROKING

Earlier chapters having examined the Scottish deposit institutions we now turn to Scotland's investing institutions, starting with the insurance sector. The life assurance offices based in Edinburgh and Glasgow are among Scotland's largest and most notable financial institutions and together with Scotland's one significant general insurance company, the General Accident Fire and Life Assurance Corporation, whose head office is in Perth, they form the second major centre for insurance enterprise in the United Kingdom, behind the City of London. The market for insurance has, however, long been both national and international in scope. For this reason the Scottish insurance offices operate extensively throughout the UK with the large offices also operating overseas. The Scottish market accounts for no more than 10–15 per cent of the business of the Scottish insurance offices and for this reason it is important to review the size and importance of the British insurance industry as a whole before considering in greater detail the Scottish insurance offices, their performance, share of the insurance market, and place in the Scottish financial sector.

The first part of chapter 7 sets out a brief overview of the British insurance industry. The second section takes a more detailed look at general insurance, with particular reference to General Accident, whilst the third part is devoted to life assurance. Pension funds, excluding those managed in-house or by independent fund managers (chapter 8), are included in the discussion of life assurance since pensions business may be viewed as a special type of life assurance and it forms a substantial part of the ordinary long-term business of the Scottish life offices. Finally, the chapter briefly examines other Scottish intermediaries, primarily insurance brokers, who operate in the insurance sector.

The British Insurance and Pensions Industry

Many individuals face situations where economic loss may be unpredictable both as to amount and time. Risk-averse individuals and firms will be willing to pay a premium to transfer the risk of loss to insurers thus protecting their resources. There are two main classes of insurance business in the United Kingdom: 'long-term insurance' and 'general insurance'.

Revell (1971) has suggested that insurance consists of spreading risks in two directions: (a) over time, and (b) between persons and organisations.

Insurance Funds and Insurance Broking

Both long-term insurance companies[1] and general insurance companies are concerned with the spreading of risks in both directions, though long-term business has an emphasis on the spreading of risks over time, whereas general insurance is mainly concerned with spreading risks between persons and organisations. There are important distinctions between the two classes of business.

General insurance business is concerned with providing financial protection to policyholders against economic loss incurred over the period of the insurance contract. Most general business contracts are short term, usually of twelve months' duration, with both parties renewing the policy at the end of this period if terms can be agreed. Insurance companies vary their premium charges in the light of their claims experience. Claims are unpredictable both in their timing and amount. General insurance business covers six different classes of risk. These are: liability; marine, aviation and transport; motor vehicle; pecuniary loss; personal accident; and property. General insurance companies also transact 're-insurance' business where they accept in part or in whole the risks other insurance companies have entered into in their direct insurance business. All insurance companies will re-insure some of their business in order to spread large and risky liabilities.

Long-term insurance business includes all types of life assurance and annuity business, group pensions business and permanent health insurance.[2] It not only provides financial protection, primarily to dependents on the death of the insured, but also represents long-term savings with the balance between life-cover and savings depending on the type of policy chosen by the insured. Premiums are payable yearly but do not normally vary over the period of the insurance contract. With this in mind premiums are fixed by the insurer taking into account mortality experience, expenses and interest rates at the time of issuing the policy. Life insurance business is divided, by statute, into industrial insurance and ordinary long-term insurance with the principal difference being that premiums for industrial policies are collected at regular intervals throughout the year at the home of the policyholder by agents of the insurance company. Long-term business also distinguishes between individual and group insurance business. Individual business is made up of life assurances, whether ordinary branch or industrial branch, annuities and personal pensions. Group business includes group pensions and life schemes as well as permanent health insurances which may be written either on a group or individual basis.

Most of the major companies in the UK are composite offices, transacting both long-term and general insurance business. The statutory distinction between the two classes of insurance necessitates their long-term funds being kept separate from their other funds and held against long-term liabilities. The Scottish life offices are specialist insurance companies concerned only with long-term business. Insurance companies may be organised on either a proprietary basis, with public or private status, or on a mutual basis where the policyholders are the owners of the company and have a claim on the profits from the business. Most mutual offices are to be found in the life assurance sector although there are at least two notable English composite offices that operate on the mutual principle. There are 23 mutual companies writing one-third of all long-term business in the UK, and of these eight are based in Scotland.

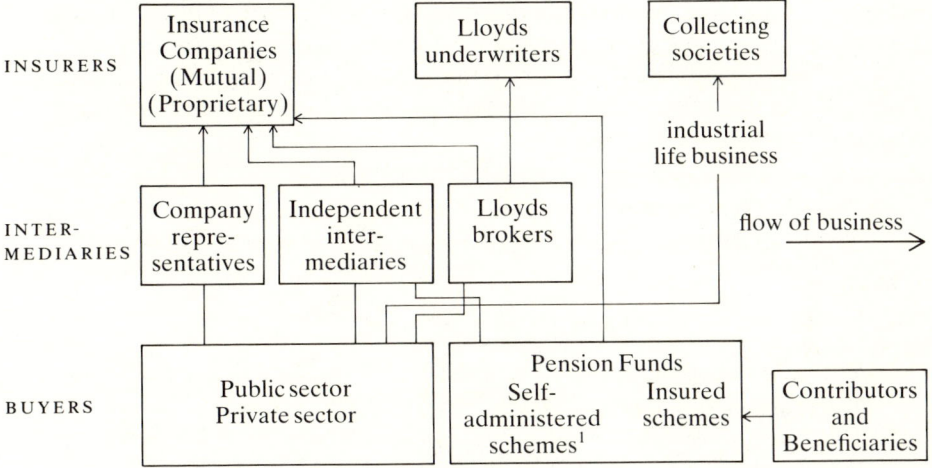

Figure 7.1. The British insurance and pensions market, showing the flow of direct insurance business only.

1. Some self-administered funds have part of their benefits placed in life office pension and insurance schemes.

Source: based on a diagram in R. L. Carter *Economics and Insurance*, 2nd ed.

Figure 7.1 provides a simple picture of how the insurance and pensions market is organised in the United Kingdom. The British insurance industry comprises British-controlled companies, foreign-controlled UK companies and the branches of overseas insurance companies. At the beginning of 1983 there were a total of 849 insurance companies authorised to transact business in the UK. Not all of these units are in direct competition nor are they all independent. Removing inactive offices, special-class underwriters and bringing together subsidiary companies within the same insurance group effectively reduces the total number of offices to 446 independent firms. Out of this total there were 304 carrying on general business, 95 carrying on long-term business and 47 composite offices carrying on both types of business. The composite insurance offices dominate the British insurance industry. By the end of 1983 the top ten offices, all of which were composites, accounted for 75 per cent of world-wide general premium income and 38 per cent of world-wide long-term premiums.

Insurance Funds and Insurance Broking

The size and growth of the British insurance industry is often measured by premium income. The total world-wide net premium income of British insurance companies amounted to over £30 billion in 1984, divided almost equally between the general and life insurance sides of the industry. This figure was equivalent to 10.8 per cent of Gross National Product (GNP), having risen from 8 per cent in 1979, indicating that premium income had grown faster than the economy as a whole. In 1984 UK domestic premiums amounted to 7 per cent of GNP. Table 7.1 shows British insurance company net worldwide premium income for 1984. By far the major part of long-term business is under the ordinary life branch whilst fire and accident and motor together dominate the general insurance account. In recent years long-term business has expanded at a faster rate than general business. Life insurance is predominantly written in the UK although exposure to insurance markets overseas has risen in recent years.

Table 7.1. Worldwide net premium income of British insurance companies in 1984 (£ million).*

Fire and Accident (non-motor)†	8659
Motor	4537
Marine, Aviation and Transport	1119
Total General Business	14315
Ordinary Long-Term	13037
Industrial Long-Term	1175
Total Long-Term Business	14212
Total	28527

* excludes premium income of Lloyd's.
† includes premiums for accident and health, property damage, general liability and pecuniary loss insurance specialist offices.
Source: Association of British Insurers.

The transfer and spreading of risks is only one function of the insurance industry. Insurance companies are active in the market for both savings and investment. In the life assurance sector the provision of a range of savings contracts for individuals and pensions schemes is almost certainly as important as the provision of life insurance cover. The premiums accumulated by the life offices are placed in a fund from which claims are met in future years and this fund is available for investment in the capital markets. In most cases, due to the long-term nature of life-insurance and pensions contracts, and continuing increases in the volume of new premiums, claims can be met from annual premium income received. This has resulted in a very large build-up of life funds available for long-term investment.

The British Insurance and Pensions Industry

The general insurance companies have also been able to accumulate surplus funds despite the short-term nature of their business. The companies receive a regular flow of premium income and as long as premium income plus investment income exceeds underwriting losses and expenses in any one year, additions can be made to the pool of funds available for investment.

General Insurance

The function of general insurance is to facilitate economic activity through the bearing of risks. Carter (1968) distinguishes pure risks, the occurrence of which can only result in loss, from speculative risks which also offer the prospect of a profit. Losses arising on the occurrence of pure risks may take the form of destruction of wealth, loss of capital, injury and death and the loss of production, all of which can have serious economic implications. Carter also points out that 'society suffers indirect losses resulting from the psychologically repellent effect of risks which deter investment in risky forms of production and so deprive consumers of commodities which would otherwise be produced'. General insurance [3] provides a means of handling some of these risks, offering protection against direct and indirect losses. It does this in two fundamental and inter-related ways: by risk-transfer where the insurance company provides a (monetary) guarantee against the risk of loss in return for a known premium payment;[4] and by combining like risks in order to reduce the inherent uncertainty.

The probability of insurance losses occurring can be statistically measured from past experience. Premiums are set by the insurance company to yield a profit taking into account the likely value of future claims and administrative expenses. Although the occurrence of the risks insured against can be statistically measured individual losses cannot be predicted. Neither is there complete certainty as to the absolute value and precise timing of the total losses that do occur. Risk exposure may also be affected by risk-prevention measures which may embrace protective measures against loss, and salvaging. Insurance does not remove all the costs associated with uncertainty. The premium imposes a cost on the individual, although one substantially less than the potential financial loss, and the consumption of resources in the provision of insurance services is a cost borne by society at large. Insurers have no claim to any special privileges or status in risk-handling. In an efficient financial system the cheapest form of managing risk is preferred, whether it is insurance or some other alternative method.

Scotland has only one significant general insurance company, General Accident Fire and Life Assurance Corporation, whose Head Office is in Perth. Unlike the Scottish life offices, General Accident is a publicly quoted company. It is the fifth largest composite insurance company in the UK, and in terms of worldwide general premium income, it is the third largest composite in the UK. In 1985, total general business premium income

Table 7.2. Geographical analysis of General Accident's general business premium income and underwriting results 1984 and 1985.

General business (before internal reinsurance)	1985				1984			
	Premium income (PI) £m	% of total	Underwriting result £m	% of PI	Premium income £m	% of total	Underwriting result £m	% of PI
UK	582.0	34.4	(79.6)	13.7	505.0	29.9	(72.4)	14.3
USA	677.4	40.0	(96.6)	14.3	752.6	44.6	(136.1)	18.1
EEC other than UK	102.8	6.1	(15.1)	14.7	92.1	5.4	(16.3)	17.7
Canada	144.7	8.6	(32.1)	22.2	157.9	9.3	(33.8)	21.4
Australia	34.1	2.0	(5.4)	15.8	43.2	2.6	(1.5)	3.5
Others including reinsurance	91.0	5.4	(8.7)	9.6	87.8	5.2	(5.4)	6.2
Marine and aviation	59.3	3.5	(0.5)	0.8	50.4	3.0	(2.8)	5.6
Total	1691.3	100.0	(238.0)	14.0	1689.0	100.0	(268.3)	15.9

Source: Annual Report and Accounts.

reached almost £1.7 billion, but only about £528 million (34 per cent) came from the UK, and less than 10 per cent of this from Scotland. The United States contributed the greatest share of general income, £677 million (40 per cent), in 1985 (see table 7.2). Nearly half of the company's worldwide general insurance business is in vehicle insurance. As a composite insurance company its investment income (£256.7 million in 1985) is a much smaller proportion of its premium income (£1691 million plus £205 million long-term premium income) than for the life companies.

Worldwide assets at the end of 1985 amounted to over £4 billion, including general fund investments of £2.3 billion and long-term fund investments of more than £1.1 billion. Measured by total assets, General Accident is one of Scotland's largest financial institutions. Because of the need to match assets to liabilities in the country of origin, assets held in respect of overseas business are invested in the country or currency concerned. Most overseas territories have their funds managed locally, sometimes in-house and sometimes by independent professionals. However, the main board has responsibility for all investment matters so that most funds are closely under the control of the investment team at Perth. Due to the nature of its liabilities the company maintains a significant proportion of its assets invested in short-term securities.

With over 65 per cent of General Accident's non-life premium business derived from markets outwith the UK the company is similar to other large UK general insurers but unusual among Scottish financial institutions which tend to compete mainly in Scottish or UK domestic markets. Of General Accident's 17000 worldwide employees, almost 8500 live in the UK and of these about 2000 are based in Scotland. The head office at Perth employs over 1000 and there are large offices in Glasgow and Edinburgh which handle both premiums and claims. The Scottish Boiler and General Insurance Company, a subsidiary company based in Glasgow, employs around 300 people and carries out its own underwriting activities in the engineering field.

General Accident transacts general insurance business of all major classes in the UK although motor and property damage insurance account for over 80 per cent of its business. In 1983, the company's UK net general insurance premium income was £520.3 million, almost 7 per cent of the total UK market.[5] General Accident dominates the UK private motor insurance market with over one eighth of the total and is well represented (about 8–9 per cent) in each of the property damage, liability, and pecuniary loss insurance markets. However, the company does not, in comparison with most of the major composites, have a large long-term business account. Premium income in 1985 was £205 million and the long-term fund amounted to £1.1 billion.

Comparisons of company performance are not always helpful and distortions can easily arise. When comparing growth in general insurance business

Insurance Funds and Insurance Broking

Table 7.3. Intercompany comparisons of general insurance business, 3-year averages, 1978–85.

	% increase in written premiums (3-year average growth rates)				Underwriting results as % of written premiums (3-year averages)				
	1979–81	1980–82	1981–83	1982–84	1983–85	1979–81	1980–82	1981–83	1982–84	1983–85
Royal	6.9	11.5	15.4	15.0	17.8	−3.83	−6.64	−9.22	−12.02	−12.92
Commercial Union	11.2	16.3	17.2	12.6	−0.0	−5.15	−9.54	−13.47	−17.35	−18.54
General Accident	11.7	14.8	16.8	17.6	11.1	−3.47	−6.88	−9.44	−13.04	−13.56
Guardian Royal Exchange	11.6	13.5	12.8	12.8	10.0	−3.06	−4.65	−6.19	−7.30	−10.07
Sun Alliance	10.6	13.1	13.9	[1]	[1]	−4.38	−5.76	−7.27	−9.66[1]	−10.35[1]

1. Accounts figures from 1984 onwards include the figures of the Phoenix Insurance Co.

The 3-year averages are calculated as follows:
(1) Premium growth rate is a compound annual growth rate.
(2) Underwriting results are averages of the annual percentages.

Sources: Carter & Godden; Annual Report and Accounts.

Table 7.4. Overall trading profit of worldwide general insurance, 1979–84.

	1979	1980	1981	1982	1983	1984
Net premiums written	7509	8147	9654	11053	12199	14315
Underwriting profit/loss for 1 year account basis						
Motor	−103	−164	−214	−301	−347	−565
Fire and accident	−106	−138	−351	−691	−694	−1219
Transfer to profit and loss account for other business	−7	−38	−46	−254	−323	−407
Total	−216	−340	−611	−1246	−1364	−2191
Investment income	981	1131	1436	1734	1913	2142
Overall trading profit	765	791	825	488	549	−49
Profit as a percentage of premiums	10.2	9.7	8.5	4.4	4.5	−0.3
Underwriting loss as a percentage of investment income	22	30	43	72	71	102

Table is compiled from worldwide figures provided by insurance companies having head offices in the United Kingdom, and UK premiums for those companies with head offices outside the UK.

Source: Insurance Facts and Figures.

considerable difficulties are created by the differences in geographical and class mix of the companies' operations. Exchange rate movements and exposure to different competitive conditions in insurance markets cause obvious problems. It is, nonetheless, of interest to look at the performance of General Accident in recent years and this is best achieved by making broad comparisons of the general insurance business growth and underwriting performance of the top five general insurers which dominate the market. General Accident's premium income grew on average, between 1976 and 1985, at a rate close to 12 per cent per year, higher than for the other four companies. Table 7.3 presents three-year average premium growth rates for the companies between 1978 and 1985. This is a more useful measure of premium growth performance since it allows changes in the general trend to be identified. General Accident has performed consistently well ranking either first or second over the seven-year period although growth trends have faltered towards the end of the period. Only the Royal managed to improve its performance.

A second, and widely used means of measuring the performance of general insurance companies is a comparison of their non-life underwriting results. The recent underwriting result of the top five, relative to written premiums, and given as three-year averages, are presented in the right-hand side of table 7.3. The results for all five companies over the period have shown growing losses. Guardian Royal Exchange leads the rankings with the poorest performances coming from Commercial Union and General Accident.

Underwriting difficulties have not been confined to the five largest general insurers in the UK but are a feature of the general insurance industry at large. This is clearly illustrated in table 7.4, which shows that healthy growth in net premiums written by the UK insurance industry worldwide has been more than matched by the growth of underwriting losses. Despite rising investment income general insurance trading profit has continued to decline. This has been attributed to fierce competition and price cutting in all sectors of the insurance market. The growing levels of insurance claims in most lines of business, but especially in the major US and UK markets, have made matters worse.

Sustained losses of this nature pose interesting questions about the use of shareholders' funds. The top five companies have made underwriting losses each year, virtually without exception for at least the past ten years. Table 7.5 presents the trading results of the top three companies, Royal, Commercial Union and General Accident, for selected years from 1976 to 1985.[6] Investment income [7] has been used to offset underwriting losses (except in 1984 when it proved insufficient). However, in recent years underwriting losses have risen faster than combined investment income and long-term insurance profit so that the levels of pre-tax profits shown in table 7.5 for 1984 and 1985, for all three companies, are below the 1976 profit figures.

Table 7.5. Trading results of top three companies writing general insurance business, 1976, 1981, 1984–85 (£ million).

Company	Year	Premiums non-life	Underwriting result	Investment income[1]	Long-term business profit[2]	Other income	Profits before tax	After tax
Royal	1985	2779.5	−347.1	354.5	25.3	8.7	41.4	29.1
	1984	2268.4	−347.4	324.6	20.7	13.3	11.2	−6.4
	1981	1489.9	−102.9	201.3	12.1	7.0	117.5	72.6
	1976	1091.8	−17.8	92.4	2.2	1.8	78.6	50.6
Commercial Union	1985	1753.2	−325.7	236.7	80.3	8.9	0.2	−30.8
	1984	2159.5	−439.4	275.9	77.9	12.8	−72.8	−87.6
	1981	1514.5	−131.9	186.4	30.4	4.6	89.5	68.3
	1976	1148.9	−59.8	95.0	12.1[3]	—	47.3	33.3
General Accident	1985	1691.3	−237.0	254.7	8.8	—	26.5	36.5
	1984	1689.0	−268.3	264.5	7.7	—	3.9	12.0
	1981	1039.7	−52.9	156.9	4.2	—	104.9	73.2
	1976	620.3	−17.6	58.3	1.9	—	42.6	30.7

Revenue Account:

Premiums written
less
increase in
unearned premiums
= Earned Premiums

Earned Premiums
less
claims, commission,
expenses
= Underwriting Result

1. Before tax and after deduction of interest paid.
2. Shareholders' proportion of long-term business profit.
3. Indicates net of tax.

Source: Carter & Godden, Annual Report and Accounts.

Given the continuing underwriting losses the dissolution of the company and distribution of its assets to its shareholders might appear to be a more attractive proposition than its continued existence in highly competitive areas of the insurance market, offering little or even negative returns. The companies continue to write general insurance business on the expectation that underwriting experiences will improve. For shareholders the question must be whether there is a realistic prospect of this happening. However, dissolving a company is not a costless exercise so that the benefits to shareholders are uncertain. There is some evidence that insurance companies have been passing up insurance business where desired premium levels cannot be obtained and reducing exposure to some unprofitable lines of business. The decline in Commercial Union's premium income is largely due to such steps being taken with regard to North American business. General Accident has also cut its US and Canadian exposure (table 7.2) although underwriting losses continue to be made in both these and other world markets. In the UK motor market General Accident has taken the lead in pushing up premium rates. The willingness of companies to take such steps is often constrained by the fear of loss of market share and the penalty has been increased underwriting losses as claims have risen. In recent years General Accident has performed better than the Royal or Commercial Union when measured by after-tax profits (see table 7.5).

The costs incurred by insurance underwriters comprise claim settlements, commission payments to brokers, and mangement and other administrative expenses. It is the combination of rising claims and claim settlement costs that have contributed to growing losses on underwriting. The operating ratios of General Accident are shown in table 7.6, alongside premiums written.

Expenses, as a proportion of premium income, have remained fairly constant over recent years and compare favourably with other top insurance companies.[8] Claims experience has been less satisfactory. Nonetheless expenses play an important part in determining how efficiently and competitively insurance business can be transacted and the large insurance companies have spent large sums on computerisation and branch and head office reorganisation. General Accident has benefited from the location of its world headquarters in Perth where accommodation and staff costs are below those in the South East or London. Staff levels in the large insurance companies have been falling over the 1980s as part of the effort to cut costs. The yearly number of General Accident's UK employees has fallen from 10887 in 1981 to 8709 in 1985.

There are other ways in which the insurance companies can decrease reliance on loss-making general premium business, most obviously by developing their long-term business. General Accident receives relatively less of its profits from life assurance than other top composites (see table 7.5) and this is one area of operations where the company may wish to expand.

Table 7.6. Worldwide underwriting: General Accident's premium income and operating ratios for one-year insurance business (including funded business), 1980-85.

Year	Premiums written (£m)	C (%)	E (%)	T (%)
1980	856.0	71.3	30.3	101.6
1981	1039.7	73.4	30.9	104.3
1982	1233.0	80.6	31.3	111.9
1983	1395.0	79.2	31.1	110.3
1984	1689.0	84.2	31.3	115.5
1985	1691.3	82.6	30.7	113.3

C claims incurred as percentage of earned premiums. E commission and management expenses as percentage of written premiums. T total of C and E.
Source: Carter & Godden, annual report and accounts.

The large composites can be expected to move towards becoming broader based financial service organisations. Both Prudential and General Accident have recently acquired estate-agent chains which can be used to sell investment and insurance related products to the house buyer.

Conclusions

It is important for the Scottish financial sector that General Accident should be a profitable and successful company. The presence of an institution with a large share of UK general insurance markets and significant international insurance business brings a level of decision making and related employment to Scotland that would not readily be replaced.

In general the upward trend in claims in most classes of insurance business, whether social, technological or legislative in origin, poses interesting questions for underwriters of risks. Insurance companies may have to become more involved with risk-prevention or make greater efforts to control the cost of claims. General Accident and Guardian Royal Exchange, for example, are involved directly in the car repair business. Responsibilities of insurers to provide continuing insurance protection to policyholders at reasonable or acceptable cost could conflict with the interests of shareholders, managers and employees, who may be better served by the elimination of underwriting losses. Large rises in premiums and more selective underwriting, however, may lead to an increase in the amount of risk carried without insurance cover where potential policyholders are unable or unwilling to purchase insurance.

Life Insurance

Introduction
There are nine Scottish life assurance offices, eight of which are mutual companies.[9] The one proprietary company, the Life Association of Scotland, is the UK life subsidiary of a Dutch insurance group but has considerable autonomy and may be considered a Scottish company. The life insurance business of General Accident is administered from England and is not considered here. All nine offices have branch networks extending throughout the UK and by far the greater part of their insurance business is conducted south of the border, at least 80 per cent and, for certain individual offices, over 90 per cent. Two of the largest offices, Standard Life and Scottish Amicable, carry out life assurance business overseas in Canada and Australia respectively. Scottish Provident also has overseas life interests.[10] The large life offices are major UK as well as Scottish companies. As a group the nine offices form an important part of the Scottish financial sector providing employment for 6000 people.

Operations of the Scottish Life Offices
Products and Operation. There are many different types of life assurance contract available, most of which combine the provision of protection and security with the opportunity to accumulate savings. These contracts are long-term in nature enabling the life office to spread the risk of a claim, arising on the death of a policyholder, over time. The policyholder pays a series of regular and equal payments over the period of the contract. The size of the payments depends upon the level of cover desired and on the life expectancy of the policyholder which is assessed from mortality tables. The regular stream of premium income is used by the life office to create a fund which can earn interest and out of which payment is made in the event of the death of the insured or on the maturity of the policy at a chosen date. Life cover forms only a small part of long-term insurance business with the major part being the provision of a vehicle for long-term contractual savings. The predominant role of the life office is to protect the value of these savings.

The life assurance companies have developed a wide range of life assurance products aimed at meeting the needs of different groups of consumers. The majority of these product variants are derived from four basic types of life assurance policy[11] – term, whole life, endowment and annuities. Policies are offered on a with or without profits basis, with profit policyholders paying higher premiums to the life office in return for an entitlement to a share in the profits of the office in the form of bonuses.

Term assurance was the earliest and simplest type of life assurance policy and provides payment only if the insured dies within a fixed period determined at the outset of the contract. This type of policy is issued without profits and there is no savings element present. Term assurance provides the life cover element in most other types of policy, including insured pension schemes. Whole life policies may be with or without profits and provide a lump sum payable only on the death of the insured. Premiums are paid over the life-time of the policyholder, although arrangements may be made for payment to be in the form of an initial single premium. Endowment assurance combines term assurance with a savings plan and policies may be written with or without profits. Payment of the sum assured is made either on the maturity of the policy, after a predetermined term of years, or on death, should this occur earlier. Annuities provide guaranteed regular income to the insured, usually in return for an initial single premium, although a series of annual premiums may be paid. Annuities may either be immediate or deferred until the policyholder reaches a certain age. Payment will include the investment income which the premiums are able to earn over the lifetime of the policyholder.

All the basic types of life assurance policy mentioned above could be either linked or non-linked. With linked-life assurance the majority of the premium is invested in a portfolio of assets which are divided into units. The benefits received by the policyholder on the maturity of the unit-linked policy will be determined by reference to the value of the underlying units but there will not generally be a guarantee as to the eventual value of these assets. The policyholder therefore takes on the investment risk.[12] A small part of the premium is used to provide life insurance cover over the period of the policy. These policies are linked specifically to equities, gilts, unit trusts or the life office's managed fund, which is composed of units in the office's equity, property and fixed-interest linked funds. Linked policies are usually without profits but some are written on a with profits basis.

The basic life assurance products which we have just outlined are flexible instruments and can be combined in various ways. One example of this is the pension plans offered by the life assurance companies. Pension schemes are similar to a deferred annuity and pension plans will usually combine an annuity policy with term or endowment assurance. An endowment or unit-linked life policy might be bought by the investor and this is converted to an immediate annuity on maturity, providing the investor with a guaranteed income on retirement. Pension plans have also been devised for the self-employed and those not in pensionable employment. Contributions to the pensions scheme (managed fund contracts both segregated and pooled) are placed in a fund run by the life office on a unitised basis similar to linked-life assurance. This has been a growing area of business for the Scottish and UK life offices.

The major source of life office funds are the premium payments on the policies in force. These comprise continuing premium payments under existing policies and premium payments on new policies, some of which will be single premium policies whilst others will produce a flow of premium receipts over the life of the policy. Premiums are normally fixed at the outset of the policy (the level premium system) by the actuary on the basis of calculations of expected mortality and an average rate of interest expected to be earned over the duration of the policy. Under the level premium system only a small amount of premium is required to provide death cover in the early years of the policy and the greater part can go into the life fund. Towards the end of the contract the position is reversed as claims on the contract require more provision for death so that less premium can enter the fund. When the policy matures the combination of premium income and interest earned on the fund should be sufficient to pay off the claims at maturity. However, since the life offices continue to write new policies with, in the early years, a greater part of premiums being invested in the fund than is required to meet current claims in those years, there is a sustained build-up of the fund and those who do survive benefit from the contributions of others (see Dodds 1979).

When setting the fixed premium on policies the actuary makes assumptions about future earnings, mortality rates and operating expenses. However, adverse changes in these assumptions could lead to the risk of insolvency of the fund and the actuary must make due allowance for this in his valuation. In writing the policies actuaries have usually made conservative assumptions about future mortality experience and expenses and have left a margin between the expected value of investment return and the return that they have built into the policy (Dodds 1979). This provides a margin for solvency purposes enabling the office to absorb unfavourable movements in the valuation assumptions and will ensure that the reasonable expectations of policyholders as regards future bonuses are fulfilled. The internal actuarial investigations compare assets with liabilities, where both are valued on a consistent basis. The basis of valuation is unlikely to be directly related to either market or book values because the actuarial valuation must make allowance for the fact that payments will be made some time in the future.[13]

The margins built into the actuarial investigations will normally lead to an excess of income over outgoings, leaving the life fund with a 'revenue' surplus. Table 7.7 shows a simplified revenue account of a life office, which summarises the total income and outgoings for the year. The fund during the year is built up from revenue items – adding premiums, investment income etc., and subtracting claims, expenses etc. Thus the value of the fund (VF) at the end of the year (VF_1) equals VF_0 plus (income less outgoings). The new funds will be available for investment to back the sums assured (and future bonuses) and the annuities which the life office will have to meet in future years.

The revenue account shows that the fund is increased or decreased by virtue of a transfer from or to investment reserves. The transfer is chosen by the actuary to ensure that the fund is sufficient to provide enough surplus to declare the bonus. 'A life fund has a surplus if the value of the fund as built up from the excess of income over outgoings is greater than the present

Table 7.7. The revenue account of a life assurance company.

Funds at beginning of year	VF_0
Add Income	
Premiums	P
Investment Income	r
Change in value of linked investments	l
Transfer from Investment Reserve	T
Total	X
Less Expenditure	
Payments to Policyholders	CS^*
Commission	C
Expenses of Management	E
Taxation	t
Total	Y
Funds at end of year	VF_1

* claims by death and maturity, cash payments, surrenders, and annuities.

value of future liabilities as determined by the actuarial valuation' (Revell 1971). As well as this revenue surplus which can benefit policyholders by being used to pay out bonuses[14] a 'capital' surplus may arise where the asset valuation in the balance sheet is below the realisation price on the market. Before looking at the way in which these bonuses are presented it is useful to illustrate the link between the revenue account and balance sheet of a life office.

Table 7.8. The balance sheet of a mutual life assurance company.

Long Term Insurance Funds represented by:	VF_1
Investments	I
Current Assets	CA
Total Assets	TA
less	
Current and Other Liabilities	CL
Investment Reserve	IR
	VF_1

Table 7.8 shows a simplified balance sheet of a mutual life office which presents the liabilities and assets of the fund. The majority of assets comprise the investments of the life office (I) which back the liabilities. The investment reserve (IR) is the balancing item in the published accounts. The link between the balance sheet and the revenue account is through the

increase in the value of life funds during the year which represent an increase in the provision for claims.

The mutual principle implies that the policyholders 'own' the company and the with-profits policyholders are entitled to a share in the surplus earned by the life office after meeting management expenses and allowing for solvency requirements. This surplus is normally distributed in the form of bonuses to give policyholders further benefits and is part of the total return which will be of concern to the long term saver.[15] In proprietary companies part of the surplus is available for distribution to shareholders. There are two main types of bonus distribution – the simple reversionary bonus which is calculated on the original sum assured and is distributed as an addition to the value of the policy, and the compound reversionary bonus, calculated on the sum assured plus the sum of any bonuses already declared. Reversionary bonuses once declared and distributed must be paid and represent an addition to the net liabilities of the life office.

Until the 1950s it was not common practice for life funds to be invested in equities. Surplus arose from the bonus loadings in with-profit premiums (the excess over corresponding non-profit premiums) and from margins in interest earnings, expense loadings and mortality bases over those assumed when the premium rate was established. This surplus – properly described as revenue surplus – emerged steadily over the years and led to distribution in the form of uniform reversionary bonuses which (as interest rates rose) grew steadily over the years. From the mid-1950s onwards the growing practice of investment in equities with low yields but significant capital appreciation led to the realisation that policyholders were entitled to have their revenue surplus enhanced in some way so as to reflect the fact that their low running yields were being compensated by capital growth. Hence the terminal bonus was introduced to be paid when policies mature or become claims. Today the process is more sophisticated and many actuaries calculate the equitable 'asset share' of each class and generation of policyholder. Thus many of today's terminal bonuses will be the result of topping-up the reversionary bonus, earned from revenue surplus, to the policyholder's true 'asset share'.[16]

Franklin and Woodhead (1980) suggest that the terminal bonus was developed in response to competition from linked-life assurance as an attempt to pay other policyholders a sum which more truly reflected the value of the assets underlying their policies.[17] Actuaries were often conservative about declaring reversionary bonuses because they take the form of a liability to the office. Under unit-linked policies the entire investment risk is passed to the policyholder with the life risk alone remaining with the office. Thus the liability of the life office depends upon the market value of the assets in the linked fund and where investment markets have risen policyholders have benefited to the full extent of the rise less expenses.

The terminal bonus approach is similar to that for unit-linked policies to the extent that they both share in the capital appreciation. The main difference is that the unit-policyholder buys a precise stake in a portfolio and receives that stake less expenses back on maturity, whereas the bonus-policyholder's share is allocated at the discretion of the actuary, with the method of calculation also at the company's discretion.

The growth of life assurance business in the UK has been encouraged by a tax regime favouring, for the individual, the accumulation of savings through life assurance policies and pensions schemes. Tax relief was previously available to policyholders on annual premiums paid under qualifying life assurance policies[18] and policyholders do not have to pay either income tax or capital gains tax on the payout they receive from the life office. The purchase of owner-occupied housing has been encouraged by tax relief on mortgage interest payments and this is the major market for endowment policies. A substantial part of the business of the Scottish life offices, and for certain offices the greater part, is mortgage-related. However, in recent times a growing proportion of their business has been pensions related.

The Scottish life offices have long been involved in the provision of group pension and life insurance schemes. These schemes are set up by employers for the benefit of employees and are of two main types: insured schemes, which include a life cover element and pool contributions together with other sums assured; and pensions managed fund contracts, where the contributions are either placed in a fund run by the life office on a unitised basis (pooled managed funds) or are administered on a segregated basis. Growth of group pensions business has tailed off in recent years and companies have switched from insured schemes either in favour of managed funds, or self-administered schemes where the management of funds may be in-house or by specialist institutions including the life offices. The threat of the loss of insured pensions business and the success of managed funds contracts elsewhere has resulted in all the Scottish life offices establishing their own managed funds. Among the most successful is Scottish Amicable's SCAMPI Fund whose premium revenue increased almost six-fold between 1980–84, an impressive growth rate by any standard. At the end of 1984 SCAMPI accounted for two-fifths of Scottish Amicable's total premium revenue.

Managed fund schemes have attracted new pensions business as well as forestalling the loss of existing insured business. Two Scottish life offices, Scottish Amicable and Standard Life, have also moved into the segregated pensions field, managing funds for self-administered schemes.[19] This step, at least at the outset, was aimed at retaining the business of major corporate employers who wished to withdraw from the managed pension fund, although both offices have also attracted new clients. Scottish Amicable now manages segregated funds on behalf of 22 clients. It is difficult to assess the extent to which segregated pensions business is new business since the gain to one life office is very often a loss to a competing institution, as self-administered funds switch between portfolio managers.

The fastest growing sector of the pensions market is individual pensions business. This includes personal pension provision for the self-employed or for those not in pensionable employment, and pension plans for directors, executives and other key employees. Life office statistics[20] show that the number of personal pension policies in force in the UK exceeded 3.5 million at the end of 1984, having more than doubled since 1979. All the Scottish offices provide individual pensions products and a growing proportion of their premium income is being attracted from this market. The pensions business of companies such as Scottish Equitable and Scottish Mutual is almost entirely individual business and both estimate their share of the UK market at between 3–4 per cent.

There are, at present, three main factors influencing the relative growth of the individual and company pension scheme sectors. Firstly, the level of economic activity in the UK remains low with the result that there are relatively few companies setting up occupational pension schemes for their employees. Secondly, for those companies who have decided against making pension arrangements for their employees there have been no new inducements from government to establish schemes. The pensions policy of the present Conservative government has, however, been one that has accepted the need for greater flexibility in personal pensions provision, encouraged by the growing numbers of self-employed and by a desire to increase the responsibility of individuals for planning their own pensions. This has heightened awareness among those who are outwith group schemes of the need to make some form of adequate financial provision for their future. These changes have been matched by a wider array of individual pensions products from the life offices. Finally, the government is proposing to introduce legislation aimed at reducing the role of the state in providing pensions and increasing that of the private sector while making it easier and more attractive for the individual to arrange their own pensions provision.[21] This has led to a rising demand for life office personal pension products. It is also intended that other financial institutions such as banks, building societies and unit trust management groups should be able to offer pension plans to individuals providing a new source of competition for the life offices. The early response of the Scottish life offices, which has enabled them to build up expertise in this type of business, means that they are well placed to maintain or increase their existing share of the market.

One area of business which the Scottish life offices were slow to develop was unit-linked business. During the late 1960s and early 1970s a number of new life offices sprang up in England, predominantly offering unit-linked contracts, and experienced a rapid growth in their funds. The outstanding examples are Abbey Life and Hambro Life. At the end of 1983 Hambro Life had the seventh largest life fund in the UK exceeded by only two Scottish offices, Standard Life and Scottish Widows. Some of the Scottish offices became involved with linked-life policies in the 1960s[22] but made little attempt to market and expand their unit business until the 1980s, mirroring the failure of Scotland's investment management houses to set up unit trusts (see chapter 8). Part of the reason for the popularity of unit-linked contracts, bearing in mind that assets are normally directly matched to liabilities, has been the growth in value of the units as the underlying assets have benefited from rising stock markets. Moreover, with the lack of guarantees, unit-linked products bear a closer resemblance to straightforward investment plans than conventional life assurance. The investor is able to receive the full value of income and capital return after allowing for charges, whereas the return on a traditional with-profits life policy is decided by the insurer.

There are a number of reasons why the Scottish life offices and other traditional life offices were late entrants to the unit-linked market. The existence of the old ASLO/LOA[23] commission agreement enabled those new offices which were outside the agreement to pay higher commission rates to intermediaries than member offices. Thus the traditional offices were effectively prevented from competing since the new offices were not party to and therefore not subject to the restrictions of the agreement and were able to carve out a niche in the intermediary market for the sale of their unit-linked policies.[24] The other principal reasons for the success of the newer offices were the introduction of the 'direct selling' method of marketing using tied agents and the discovery that Life Assurance Premium Relief (LAPR) was available for annual premium unit-linked policies. The new life offices seeking fast growth from the start realised that even with their commission advantage in the intermediary market they needed another distribution system to produce additional business. The success of the unit-linked offices was therefore substantially due to the existence of the commissions agreement and the introduction of the direct sales delivery mechanism. It is interesting to note that both Abbey Life and Hambro Life joined the LOA after they had become well established.

Nonetheless, the unit-linked offices showed an ability to seize and develop an opportunity in the life insurance market and in that sense were innovative in taking the risks of introducing a new form of life contract. The Scottish life offices and the long-established English offices did not enter the unit-linked market but chose instead to continue to develop traditional policies in such areas as house purchase mortgages. Despite the phenomenal success of the unit-linked contract supported by the self-imposed handicap of the commissions agreement,[25] the Scottish life offices and their English counterparts made little or no attempt to respond for some years.

The Scottish life offices did not enter the unit-linked market in any major way until the ASLO/LOA agreement was abandoned. By 1985 almost all the Scottish offices offered linked products. These have been very successful in attracting new premium business often raising record amounts on launch, providing some indication of earlier missed opportunities. The unit-linked contract, having lost LAPR, has now to concentrate on the single premium bond format; the profit margins are smaller and while the Scottish offices have made real inroads into the market during the 1980s critics argue that the Scottish offices have waited until the excess profits have gone before entering the market!

Marketing. Before the mid-seventies the marketing strategy of the life assurance industry was generally confined to directing sales efforts to segments of the market that were thought to fit the product. One disadvantage of this approach is that products are frequently inflexible and cannot be readily adapted to suit the particular needs of existing or potential customers. The major innovation in the marketing strategy of the life assurance companies was to take the basic properties of life products and combine these to create products to suit consumers needs. This process has been made possible by the application of information technology.

Product differentiation is probably the most common form of innovation carried out by the life companies. Product variation, however, is not by itself sufficient to increase the market share of the life company. The advantages of purchasing the product require to be commmunicated to the consumer in a way that can be understood, and this is normally achieved through advertising and by using the services of intermediaries such as brokers.

Promotional activities are aimed at different segments of the market with the identification of a target group of consumers whose needs can be addressed in the design of the products. Life companies have traditionally identified market segments by looking at demographic influences, such as age, sex, and income level, or socio-economic groupings, and these continue to be used. The market has also been segmented in other ways, most obviously between life protection, mortgage business, investment savings plans, individual and group pensions business, and tax planning services. The life companies provide a whole range of products for these markets to ensure that almost every requirement and contingency can be met.

The Scottish life assurance companies have marketing divisions and attach varying degrees of importance to market research, product development and promotion. The product differentiation of the Scottish offices may be largely defensive to meet competing products but by widening the choice and flexibility of products available to existing and potential policyholders product differentiation and market segmentation may be expected to increase the aggregate demand for life assurance products. In many industries product differentiation is a key way of obtaining a proportionately greater market share and the continued development of new and differentiated products is likely to be an important part of the future success of the Scottish life offices.

Promotional efforts and distribution systems are also likely to play a key role. Promotion is normally used to accomplish two main purposes: to persuade the customer and insurance intermediary that the product is either the best or only one available in the market suited to the prospective policyholders needs; and to engage in product branding, where the aim is to raise the general awareness of the company name with the intention that it becomes synonymous with a higher quality product, which is then reflected in higher sales. The cost of purchasing the policy and prospective policy performance are also key elements which must be taken into account in the promotional process.

The use of advertising as a form of sales promotion varies between the individual Scottish life offices and not all have been convinced of its effectiveness. Television advertising is normally used to create or strengthen a corporate image, rather than to promote an individual insurance product. Only four Scottish life offices have carried out a television campaign on the national network: Life Association of Scotland, Scottish Amicable, Scottish Widows and Standard Life. In 1984 Standard Life's expenditure on combined press and television advertising was the seventh highest in the UK insurance industry, behind four composite offices and two other long-term offices. The involvement of Scottish Amicable and Scottish Widows in television promotion is as recent as 1985 and 1986.

Table 7.9. Expenditure on media advertising by selected insurance companies in 1985.

Company	£000	TV (%)	Press (%)
Life Association of Scotland	55.7	98	2
Scottish Amicable	1998.8	55	45
Scottish Mutual	67.7	–	100
Scottish Provident	85.1	–	100
Scottish Widows	382.1	58	42
Standard Life	1851.1	100	–
Abbey Life	1058.5	–	100
Lloyds Life	4301.7	2	98
Legal and General*	2986.0	96	2
General Accident*	2979.1	72	28
Total UK	49111.0	33	67

* denotes composite office.

Source: *Quarterly Digest of Advertising Expenditure.*

Table 7.9 shows expenditure on media advertising by Scottish life assurance offices and other selected insurance companies for 1985. On the pure life side both Scottish Amicable and Standard Life were amongst the highest spenders with budgets of close to £2 million. Standard Life concentrated solely on television whereas Scottish Amicable's slightly larger budget was more evenly divided between television and the press. The total advertising expenditure of the Scottish life offices amounted to £4.4 million, 9 per cent of the UK insurance industry total. General Accident spent a further £3 million. In contrast, the English company Lloyds Life spent £4.3 million on advertising, almost as much as the combined Scottish life offices, with television being largely ignored in favour of the popular and quality press.

In the face of continuing high advertising expenditure by the large UK insurance companies aimed at promoting greater name awareness the larger Scottish life offices have had to abandon their faith in the unassailability of their reputations and respond in similar fashion. The insurance companies appear to be locked into large advertising budgets for defensive reasons.

The promotional aspect of the life assurance marketing mix is not confined solely to press and television advertising. An important part involves the provision of promotional material and product information to insurance intermediaries who must be persuaded to sell the life assurance company's policies to the prospective customer. The Scottish life offices do not have any direct sales agents and virtually all life policy and pensions sales are conducted through intermediaries such as building societies (mainly mortgage business), accountants, estate agents and solicitors, and through brokers who provide the greater part of new business.[26] The branch offices of the Scottish life assurance companies, unlike those of deposit institutions, are used to provide a service to brokers and other local intemediaries rather than to ultimate consumers. Standard Life, for example has 40 branches spread throughout the UK, facilitating contact with intermediaries in all the major centres of population. Many of these intermediaries, such as the building societies and the larger broking firms, have regional or national branch networks, enabling the life company to be represented countrywide.

Carter (1968) notes that the broker plays an important part in relation to product differentiation, drawing the client's attention to aspects of policy cover which otherwise would not be appreciated. The standard of service provided by the insurance company, general or life, to the customer, will also influence the broker's advice. This includes efficiency in generating quotations, speed of acceptance and policy preparation and the settlement of claims arising from the contract. This is a crucial part of any insurance company's marketing operation and has been helped by the development of computer and communications technology. The delivery mechanisms of the Scottish life offices are considered in greater detail later in the chapter.

Overseas business. Only two Scottish life offices, Scottish Amicable and Standard Life, carry out a significant proportion of their total business overseas. In 1985 Scottish Amicable received £34.8 million of premium income from policyholders in Australia, amounting to 6.5 per cent of total premiums. Standard Life received a larger share of total premium income from its overseas business: Canadian premiums were valued at £202 million or 18 per cent of the total in 1985 and the Republic of Ireland accounted for £163 million or 15 per cent. Scottish Provident also writes a small amount of business in Ireland. A recent change (1985) in the status of the Irish subsidiary of Life Association of Scotland has resulted in its exclusion from Group business, although LAS continues to carry on a small proportion of business in the Republic on its own account.

Scottish Amicable and Standard Life's link with the Commonwealth is an historical one, although the establishment of life assurance funds in the Dominions almost certainly brought taxation advantages at the time. Administration of both Australian and Canadian life business takes place within the two countries including the investment function since liabilities must be covered by assets held in the country of origin though overall control of investment decisions resides in Scotland. The legal requirement to maintain assets overseas as security for policyholders also has the effect of obviating the dangers of a mismatch of assets to liabilities where each are expressed in different currencies that are prone to fluctuations. It is for these reasons that most British life assurance companies operating overseas do so through subsidiaries registered abroad.

Few of the Scottish life offices have expressed a desire to enter new overseas markets. High initial costs may be involved in establishing a sales network placing restriction on the ability of the business to grow rapidly in the initial years. Operation under a different regulatory system also brings the added cost of purchasing legal expertise. These barriers are not, however, insurmountable and overseas acquisition is one route to achieving greater diversification of business and a presence in a potentially profitable market. The mutual Scottish life offices may have less incentive to carry out business abroad than proprietary companies since the benefits to existing policyholders is not always clear whereas shareholders may enjoy the benefits brought by earnings from an overseas as well as a domestic base. It is difficult, however, to measure precisely the interests of current and future generations of policyholders. There may be economies of scale in operating over wider markets which would benefit all policyholders. Harmonisation of insurance markets within the European Community should eventually lead to the elimination or reduction of legal and other technical barriers to carrying out business in this market and it is reasonable to ask whether the larger Scottish life offices should not be gaining experience of these markets at present.

Investment. The majority of policyholders are purchasing the investment expertise of the life office. The investment behaviour of the Scottish life offices is little different from that of other life assurance companies although the precise nature of the objectives and constraints faced by the different fund managers varies according to the mix of business written and the investment philosophy of the particular office. The investment behaviour of life assurance companies has received wide coverage in the literature[27] but it is useful, nonetheless, to consider some of the main determinants of their investment behaviour and the types of asset that they select for their portfolios.

The funds collected by the life assurance companies are primarily of a long-term nature. Liabilities frequently do not mature for some considerable time after they have been incurred and assuming premiums continue to be paid the life offices have a source of funds to invest over a long time horizon. For the individual, a life insurance contract means a period of net savings followed on surrender by net dis-saving. The value of the benefits received over the future term is equivalent to earlier premium contributions plus an appropriate share for qualifying policies of the profits less the expenses of the insurance company. However, the continuing cash flow received by the life offices from investment income, new business and renewal premiums has usually been more than sufficient to meet immediate payments of expenses and benefit claims (including surrenders), providing a growing source of funds[28] that can be invested in assets which have an average maturity longer than that of liabilities.[29] Net premium income and net investment income together provide only one source of funds for investment allocation. Turnover of the existing portfolio, due either to maturing assets or a deliberately active trading policy will also provide fund managers with funds to invest in financial and property markets.

Clearly there is a close relationship between the investment and actuarial functions of a life office. Investments must be selected in order to ensure that the value of the life fund exceeds the value placed upon the long-term liabilities. Policyholders must also be provided with a competitive return on their savings. For participating policyholders it is highly desirable that the value of profits earned and distributed in the form of bonuses equals (and preferably exceeds) the value of the additional premium paid (bonus loading). The ability to meet or better these expectations will have a crucial bearing on the competitiveness of the life office. This is well demonstrated by the recent difficulties of UK Provident where injudicious investments led to the prospect of bonus cuts and loss of business. Portfolio management can therefore be seen as an essential and integral part of a life office's operations.

The Insurance Company Associations, in their First Stage evidence to the Wilson Committee stated that

> It is the investment function to find the best available assets to meet the needs of the fund in the light of the precise nature of its liabilities and to provide the maximum overall return on the assets, bearing in mind the degree of risk which is acceptable.[30,31]

From this it can be seen that there are two principal constraints on the major objective of maximising overall return. First, the fund manager must seek to ensure that the flow of income from asset investments will be sufficient to meet the flow of liabilities net of premium income. The inter-relationship between the two flows would suggest that assets should be closely matched with liabilities. However, since a growing fund has a positive net cash flow managers can choose to invest for a longer average term than otherwise in

Table 7.10. Market value of long-term business investments*
at end 1984 and 1985 (£ millions).

	Securities			Mortgages and loans	Land and property	Deposits and cash	Other	Total
	Fixed interest	Ordinaries	Total					
1984								
All Scottish life offices	7546.7	9656.9	17203.6	1086.5	2534.7	1028.5	1.6	21854.9
%	34.5	44.2	78.7	5.0	11.6	4.7	0.0	100.0
Total Investments ABI†			85385	6460	20520	–	5612	117977
%			72.3	5.5	17.4	–	4.8	100.0
1985								
All Scottish life offices	8114.2	12747.6	20861.8	1138.2	2922.8	599.9	1.5	25524.2
%	31.7	49.9	81.7	4.5	11.5	2.3	0.0	100.0

* Does not include investments other than in respect of life business.
† Includes industrial business.

Sources: Scottish figures from annual reports and accounts.
ABI members from *Insurance Facts and Figures 1984*.

search of a higher return on the investment and hence improved bonus payments.[32] It is for this reason that life funds have been invested in assets such as ordinary shares and property as well as gilt-edged securities with known maturity dates and income streams.

This introduces the second principal constraint on investment policy. Whilst equity assets have traditionally been seen as providing higher rates of return there is also higher risk attached as measured by the variability of returns.[33] Fund managers must therefore take account of these risks when selecting equity investments for the portfolio, bearing in mind the need to avoid the risk of insolvency of the life fund.

To sum up, the main objective of the life office's investment policy is to secure the highest overall yield on the fund. Fund managers are constrained in reaching this objective by the need for the fund to meet its liabilities to its policyholders at all times, and by the need to minimise the risk that the overall yield deviates substantially from the expected return, thereby ensuring continued solvency. Additional factors which determine the investment policy and behaviour of the life offices include the regulations imposed on the valuation of assets[34] by the Department of Trade and Industry, where certain assets may be held to be inadmissable for solvency purposes, and the marketability of the assets, which will be important where the fund manager wishes to adjust the portfolio by switching between assets.[35]

The Scottish life offices have experienced substantial growth in funds available for investment and at the end of 1985 they were responsible for the day-to-day management of total assets valued at over £22 billion[36] and controlled assets valued at about £25 billion. This is close to twice the volume of funds under management by independent Scottish portfolio management institutions (see chapter 8) and plays an important part in distinguishing Scotland as a centre of financial skills. Some 150 professional fund managers are employed by the Scottish life offices. All dealings in the main financial markets are carried out from Glasgow and Edinburgh.

In table 7.10 the composition of the Scottish life offices long-term business investments is given for both 1984 and 1985, together with the breakdown for ABI members in 1984. Ordinary securities make up the largest part of Scottish life office investments, accounting for 44 per cent of the total in 1984 and 50 per cent in 1985. Fixed-interest securities, most of which are gilts, accounted for 34 per cent and 32 per cent in the same two years. The higher proportion of ordinary stocks and shares reflects, in part, the strength of equity markets over the 'eighties. The main difference between the portfolio holdings of the Scottish offices and the industry as a whole is the lower percentage of property held, and the correspondingly higher percentage of securities held by the former.

These figures represent snapshots taken at one given point in time. In order to detect major changes in asset holdings, figures for the past twenty years and more would be required. The global presentation of figures also hides the significant variations in portfolio composition between individual Scottish life offices. This reflects different investment philosophies, which will encompass differing expectations about future returns as well as the more clearly defined constraints imposed by a different balance of life liabilities. A life insurance company predominantly writing unit-linked contracts, for example, could be expected to hold a much higher proportion of unit trust and ordinary share investments, and a lower proportion of fixed-interest securities than an office mainly writing endowment mortgage business. Most of the Scottish life offices will set, from year to year, some broad target of how net income available for investment is to be divided between fixed-interest securities, ordinary shares, property and between UK and overseas investments.

It is clear that the investment policies of the life assurance companies have important implications for the competitiveness of individual offices as well as for the efficient allocation of funds by the financial system in general. A discussion or statistical review of these issues is outwith the scope of this chapter. The prospect of Scottish life office investment fund managers consistently earning higher (risk adjusted) returns from their portfolio selections than competing life companies is an issue which is addressed in chapter 8.

Employment. There is no comprehensive source of employment statistics for the nine Scottish life offices similar to that for the Scottish clearing banks. However, figures are available in their annual reports and accounts and during 1985 the average total weekly number of staff employed in the UK by the Scottish offices was 9068, an increase of 544, or 6.4 per cent over 1984. Some two-thirds of the total are employed in Scotland, a significant proportion as part-time staff. The average remuneration of the Scottish life offices' staff was £11,911 in 1985, significantly higher than the £8688 of the Scottish clearing banks.

Life assurance companies were among the first financial institutions to apply computer technology to processing their policies and over the 1960s and 1970s this enabled the life offices to cope with strong growth in business volumes while containing their staff costs. Computerisation also led to the re-organisation of staffing structures, so that the life offices contributed to the trend observed in the wider insurance industry in Scotland over the 1970s of less male employment but greater female part-time employment. The strong growth in the life assurance market has continued into the 1980s[37] and the main impact of computer technology has been to slow down the rate of employment growth, rather than to cause employment cuts. The introduction and development of on-line and decentralised computer systems which allow the input, processing and retrieval of information from remote locations may enable future staff savings in the life industry.[wu] This will also depend on the growth of the market and staff technology agreements. It is difficult to determine whether the headquarters staff of the

Scottish life offices (the vast majority of their Scottish staff) are any less vulnerable to this potential threat than branch staff.

Table 7.11. Staff of Scottish Amicable Life Assurance Society as at 1 June 1986.

Staff	Number	Average age	Average service
Managerial	32	45	22
Titled clerical	109	40	16
Other clerical	798	25	5
Sales managers	77	42	14
Broker sales force	253	32	5
Data processing	65	28	6
Technical specialists	37	26	2
Others	52	48	6

Source: Scottish Amicable.

Table 7.11 provides an interesting breakdown of the staff of Scottish Amicable as at June 1986. The lower clerical grade accounts for 56 per cent of total staff and the brokers sale force a further 18 per cent. Managerial and titled clerical staff together account for about 105 of total staff and have the longest average service at 22 years and 16 years respectively. It is likely that future management will be drawn from titled clerical staff (mostly actuaries).

The Scottish life offices' senior management posts are predominantly held by actuaries and actuaries have dominated the decision-making process in the past. Critics allege that this domination is not necessarily beneficial.[39] This is not to call into question the undoubted professional qualities and intellectual capabilities of actuaries. On the other hand, if the executive management have similar background and training it may limit the scope for a cross-fertilisation of ideas. The use of conservative assumptions in actuarial assessments by actuaries where enshrined as company practice may instil more general conservative attitudes leading to a narrow view of business development, particularly under the mutual structure where there is little outside pressure on management, although the importance of commercial pressure must not be overlooked. Senior personnel are not generally recruited from competing offices or elsewhere in the financial sector and the life offices have tended to rely on the eventual elevation of three or four actuarial trainees to top decision-taking posts. This may generate internal problems with dissatisfied non-actuarial staff who are passed over, as has been alleged on the investment management side. These features are also found in English life offices.

It is perhaps not surprising that actuaries have monopolised senior posts since they make up by far the greatest proportion of professionally qualified life office staff. The Scottish life offices recruit and train more actuaries than they need and suggest that they retain the brightest and best. Non-actuarial staff found in executive management positions include accountants, lawyers and marketing experts. The top decision posts, however, with few exceptions continue to be held by actuaries. Like bankers, actuaries have had to change in recent times to become more marketing orientated and better trained with general management skills. Plymen and Pullan, in a paper to the Chartered Insurance Institute Conference in 1968 (quoted in Clayton 1971), observed 'Up till now it has been traditional to regard insurance as being quite different from other classes of business'. Clayton suggests that 'Their basic point is that it is time that the industry applied modern techniques of scientific management and ceased to treat it as arcane mystery which only insurance men can understand' and 'The whole business of administering and selling insurance is permeated with mystique. Insurance know-how is too often a cover for an inability to cut free from a self-created web of routines and complications' (the *Economist,* quoted by Clayton). There still exists a perception that life assurance business can only be understood and managed by actuaries. It has also been suggested that a good manager with actuarial skills is usually a better manager than the good manager with no actuarial skills and that this is demonstrated by the English and Scottish offices managed by actuaries with growing market share and offering best value for money.[40]

The Scottish life offices have traditionally recruited their trainee staff from among university graduates with degrees in mathematics, economics and computer science, a very high proportion of which will be Scottish students. Actuarial trainees sit the examinations of the Faculty of Actuaries in Scotland. The Scottish life offices are undoubtedly staffed by intelligent and technically well-qualified people, but this of itself does not guarantee that the necessary leadership qualities will emerge.

Ownership, Competition and Performance
Ownership Structure. The Scottish Life offices, with one exception, are mutual firms. Under the mutual constitution the ownership of the life office lies with the policyholders and the profits of the assurance business belong to the with-profits policyholders. Surpluses which emerge do not require to be split between policyholder and shareholder, as in a proprietary company. In a mutual office the risk of carrying out insurance business[41] must rest ultimately with the residual claimants who are effectively contributing equity capital through the bonus loadings in their premiums.[42] In proprietary life companies the division of surpluses between policyholders and shareholders is usually either set down in the office's articles of association or is established by precedent. A figure of 5–10 per cent is often quoted for the share of the surpluses distributed as dividends to shareholders. The shareholders can be viewed as holding the minority equity interest in the company bearing the risk of meeting guarantees only after the substantial

capital contributed by the with-profits policyholders has been exhausted. In effect these companies have a 'mutual' element equivalent to the policyholders' allocation of profits.

Both the mutual and proprietary offices have similarities in the way the risk of the insurance business is borne and since they compete in the same market and operate in very similar ways, formal ownership differences are of little importance. The management of the two types of office both share the same incentive to meet guarantees and to attract new business. Nevertheless while the management of a mutual company must seek to meet the reasonable expectations of policyholders it does not come under the scrutiny of a separate group of shareholders nor of the stock market. In a proprietary company the surplus available for shareholders will either be paid as dividends or retained to underwrite the expansion of business.[43] The ability of management to generate surpluses in which shareholders have a stake is reflected in the firm's share price. In addition, large shareholders are able to bring their influence to bear by the exercise of their voting rights. Management must give consideration to the rights of shareholders as well as policyholders and this may lead to a more aggressive approach to life assurance business. Part of the additional equity contributed by the shareholders, for example, may be used to underwrite the risks of devising and introducing new types of policy which might contribute to the future growth and profitability of the office.

While the policyholders of a mutual office own the business they have little effective say in the way that it is run. Without the external influence of the market management may be more inward looking and less responsive to change, concerned only with ensuring that guarantees on existing life assurance business are met. The mutual life offices are free from the threat of an unwanted takeover bid and there is no other obvious mechanism that would bring the management of an inefficient company into more competent hands. On the other hand, it has been suggested that mutual protection allows management to take a longer term view of business development without the pressures of share-price scrutiny which may lead to a drive for short-term surplus earnings which is not in the best long-term interests of the policyholders whose funds have built up the offices. For example, the value of the shareholders' equity rises and the value of the policyholders' claims is reduced if the firm substitutes high-risk for low-risk assets.[44] It is difficult to prove, however, that the time horizons of mutual and proprietary offices in the UK differ much from one another or that the mutual offices have made more efficient and profitable use of assets over the longer run.

It is also true that mutual companies cannot offer top management incentives through share options. However, the management of a mutual office may equally well be motivated to maximise their market share and increase the overall size of life business through improving existing products, introducing new products and taking an aggressive stance in the market since this enables their salaries and status to increase. As in a proprietary company the senior executive is required to report to a board of directors which exercises a custodial role on the behalf of the policyholders, by whom they are elected. In practice boards may be self-perpetuating and have little real influence over the decisions of management, though this is also the case with proprietary companies. Nevertheless the board of directors does provide a form of check and balance to management, imperfect though it may be, and this may be of greater importance in the mutual office where there is no market rating.

Critics of the Scottish life offices have suggested that their mutual ownership has meant, at least until recently, a more conservative approach to new markets and new ideas than would otherwise have been the case if management had to contend with large shareholders and a share rating in the market. There are, however, recent studies which have suggested that mutual life assurance companies are potentially more efficient than, and have relative advantages over, proprietary offices.[45] Mayers and Smith (1986) argue that there are incentive conflicts between assurance company residual claimants and managers, and between policyholders and residual claimants and that the relative costs of controlling these incentive conflicts lead to a preference for proprietary or mutual ownership structures.

According to Mayers and Smith stockholders have an incentive to increase the value of the stock at the policyholders' expense after the policies are issued. Policyholders cannot easily maintain discipline over the stockholders. By changing to a mutual company the costs of this conflict can be reduced since mutual ownership eliminates the stockholders with their separate and disparate interests.[46] This is the major benefit of the mutual form of organisation. However, when insurance companies are organised as mutuals the market for corporate control is less effective, giving less control over the decisions of management and the costs they can impose on owners (the policyholders).[47]

> Therefore, if mutuals are efficient, the more severe incentive problems between residual claimants and managers of the firm and the loss in risk-bearing efficiency must be offset by the advantages of a mutual in controlling the incentive contracting problems between policyholders and stockholders.

Mayers and Smith (1986) carried out tests on a sample of 30 American life assurance companies and concluded 'that for this sample of firms changing from a stock to a mutual-ownership structure is on average efficiency-enhancing'. They also found evidence to support the hypothesis that the market for corporate control disciplines more effectively when firms are organised as stock companies as compared with mutuals.

The mutual ownership structure of the Scottish life offices has almost certainly been responsible for their continued presence in Scotland. Predatory insurance companies, most often the large composite offices, and other financial service groups cannot acquire a mutual life assurance company since the absence of shareholdings makes takeover impossible. It is conceivable that the policyholders, who own the mutual company, could agree to restructure their ownership interests in a manner that would enable a merger to proceed, most obviously by introducing share capital. However, as the with-profits policyholders own the entire profits from the life office enterprise they have no obvious incentive to take the proprietary route and where their interests are best served by a merger the preferred alternative may be to reach agreement with another mutual life office, as happened between Friends' Provident and the troubled UK Provident Institution (UKPI).

Acquisition and merger activity in the UK insurance industry has led to the loss of all but one of Scotland's proprietary insurance companies both long-term and general. The one notable exception is the General Accident Fire and Life Assurance Corporation, which includes among its subsidiaries former independent Scotttish general insurance companies. Under the protection of their mutual constitution the Scottish life offices have been able to remain strongly independent[48] and this has undoubtedly brought benefits to the Scottish financial sector. The concentration of life office headquarters in Edinburgh and Glasgow provides an important contribution to total insurance sector employment in Scotland. Although the loss of head office control to the south would not necessarily result in a substantial loss of jobs, the experience of Scottish insurance companies which were taken over in the mid-sixties suggests that the proportion of professionally qualified to total staff could drop considerably. The contribution made by these highly qualified professionals to the Scottish financial scene is impossible to quantify and it must be kept in mind that the Scottish offices are UK financial institutions orientated towards wider markets. Nevertheless, this concentration of professionaly qualified staff affects the way in which Scotland is perceived as an important insurance and financial centre and thus as a location for other financial or professional activity.

Mutual life offices are unable to raise long-term capital on the equity market in order to finance the expansion of their business and instead must rely solely on internal resources. The growth of life assurance business in general depends upon the attraction of new premium business, particularly annual premium business which provides a stream of income into the future. In the first year or two the premiums received are often insufficient to cover the value of the new liabilities incurred as well as meeting the expenses involved in acquiring the business. Should expansion of new regular life assurance business be rapid and extended over a period of years it might cut into the surplus available for distribution leading eventually to a slow-down. If the life office in these circumstances maintains its bonus distribution it runs the risk of becoming insolvent. The English mutual life office UKPI faced similar difficulties before merging its administration with Friends'

Provident in April 1986. The company had experienced a large expansion in new business over a short period depending upon highly competitive bonus rates which could not be maintained when the value of its investments subsequently fell. The UKPI did not become insolvent but could no longer expect to attract new business following a reduction in bonus which would have been made in isolation from the market generally.

Not all of the surplus emerging on the valuation of the life fund and the liabilities will be distributed to policyholders in a mutual office, nor will shareholders receive the full share of profits ascribed to their account in a proprietary company. Part of the surplus will be retained in the form of a capital reserve to underwrite the controlled expansion of operations. The Scottish life offices have built up a pool of reserves which can be used to finance their growth. A proprietary company, on the other hand, can also support the growth of its life business by using fresh capital from share issues. Very few of the UK proprietary life assurance companies have in fact made capital issues, relying instead on retained profits to finance expansion. Franklin and Woodhead (1980) point out that only two pure life companies made capital issues over the period 1963 to 1976, Sun Life in 1963 and Hambro Life in 1976.

As well as protecting the Scottish life offices from takeover and denying them access to independent sources of capital the mutual structure has also denied them access to the conventional take-over mechanism whereby the purchase of a company is funded in part or in whole by the share paper of the acquiring firm. The outright purchase of an existing competitor, paid in cash, is an option open to only the larger insurance companies with sufficient cash flow. Despite these difficulties mutual offices could expand their business by way of merger with other life assurance companies. It is not inconceivable that a mutual office could merge with a proprietary office and buy out the shareholders, although its ability to do so is constrained by its cash flow and the possibility that such action could be detrimental to the present generation of with-profits policyholders.

The Scottish life offices have not sought to increase their market position through a policy of active acquisition or merger, unlike the clearing banks for example. The most common reason advanced is that merger would bring few benefits to the existing policyholders of the mutual company although the value attached by management to its own independence is likely to be another major factor. Possible advantages from a merger or acquisition include the achievement of economies of scale and the accretion of new premium business enabling constraints on growth, determined by actuarial considerations to be overcome. Of course, potential economies remain just that until actually realised and while there is evidence that larger companies enjoy economies of scale in their operations researchers have not yet quantified the advantages. Nor has it been shown that faster growing life companies are the most profitable.

Competition. Casual observation suggests that the life assurance industry is dominated by a small number of large companies who wield significant market power and are capable of influencing prices and the levels of service through monopolistic or collusive practices. A number of studies have investigated the degree of concentration in the UK ordinary life assurance industry.[49] Table 7.12 provides more recent data for 1983 and shows the group concentration ratios on the basis of total worldwide ordinary long-term (OLT) premium income. The figures have been obtained from statistics tabulated by Carter and Godden (1984) showing the returns submitted to the Department of Trade and Industry. The figures exclude industrial life business. Three Scottish life offices are included in the table. Standard Life is ranked third, Scottish Amicable fifth and Scottish Widows ninth.

Table 7.12. Concentration ratios of leading groups' worldwide OLT premium income 1983.

Rank	Group name	Worldwide premium income (£m)	Share of total (%)	Cumulative share of total (%)
1	Prudential*	942.2	9.2	9.2
2	Legal and General*	669.7	6.6	15.8
3	Standard Life	659.7	6.5	22.3
4	Norwich Union	578.1	5.7	28.0
5	Scottish Amicable	454.1	4.4	32.4
6	Hambro Life†	451.9	4.4	36.8
7	Sun Life	390.0	3.8	40.6
8	Abbey Life	304.3	3.0	43.6
9	Scottish Widows	302.1	2.9	46.5
10	Eagle Star	281.3	2.8	49.3
	UK Companies' Total worldwide premium income	10210		100.0

* excludes business of re-insurance subsidiaries.
† Now Allied Dunbar Assurance.
Source: Carter and Godden (1984).

The concentration ratio of 49.3 per cent for the top ten groups writing ordinary long-term insurance is below that reported in earlier studies. Franklin and Woodhead (1980) estimated the ratio at 54.8 per cent in 1975 indicating that the industry has since experienced a fall in market concentration. If total worldwide revenue premium (as reported in group annual accounts) is used the concentration ratio falls to only 47.1 per cent with the largest three groups enjoying an increased market share of 24 per cent.[50] An alternative assessment of concentration can be made by examining ordinary long-term life funds. Using figures from Carter and Godden the concentration ratio at the end of 1983 was 56.7 per cent, below Franklin and Woodhead's estimate of 57.2 per cent for 1975 and the earlier 1968 estimate of

Table 7.13. Mobility among life insurance companies measured by size of OLT funds 1929, 1968 and 1983.

Rank	1929 Name of Group	1968 Name of Group	1983 Name of Group
1	Prudential	Prudential	Prudential
2	Pearl	Legal and General*	Legal and General
3	Norwich Union	Standard Life*	Standard Life
4	Refuge	Norwich Union	Norwich Union
5	Sun Life	Guardian Royal Exch.*	Commercial Union*
6	Scottish Widows	Commercial Union*	Scottish Widows*
7	Commercial Union	Sun Life	Guardian Royal Exch.
8	North British	Eagle Star*	Hambro Life*
9	Royal	Scottish Widows	Eagle Star
10	Legal and General	Royal	Sun Life

* denotes groups which have improved relative position since previous period shown.
Sources: 1929 Clayton (1971); 1968 Richards and Colenutt (1975); 1983 Carter and Godden (1984).

62.0 per cent made by Richards and Colenutt (1975).

A further insight into market concentration may be gained by looking at the mobility of the life insurance companies. Table 7.13 compares the ranking of the leading ten groups by size of life fund for 1929, 1968 and 1983. Although there has been movement within the group over the period, the group as a whole has exhibited a high degree of stability. One or two of the 1929 offices were acquired by other offices in the same column. Scottish Widows fell from sixth to ninth place between 1929 and 1968 and has since climbed to seventh. Standard Life rose from fifteenth place in 1929 to third by 1968.

Low mobility and high concentration might suggest that the large firms are well placed to reduce or eliminate competition and thus earn monopolistic profits at the expense of customers and smaller companies. Franklin and Woodhead (1980) observe that

> Economic theory is silent on the exact value of concentration which is synonymous with 'dominance': only if the industry is wholly monopolised is there any assumption of market control. In situations which are neither perfectly monopolistic nor perfectly competitive – such as the life assurance industry – large firms may have market power but this may be offset by new entry, product innovation and technical innovation.[51]

The life assurance market is highly competitive with no one company or group of companies able to influence the competitive position of other firms in the industry. The level of concentration has also fallen in recent years, because the smaller companies have expanded faster than the large offices.

A further aspect of market structure, which has implications for the level of competition and the business conduct of the Scottish life offices and their competitors in the UK life assurance industry, is the ease or difficulty with which new rival firms can enter the market. New firms affect the number and size distribution of companies and thereby the degree of concentration in the market, as well as influencing the competitive forces at work in the market through price and/or product rivalry. If the threat posed by potential entrants is a strong one, existing firms may adopt a pricing policy or pricing agreement which undercuts newcomers and act as a discouragement to entry. It may also act as a spur to product innovation. Profit expectations have an important influence on the number of potential competitors attracted to the market and are often the major determinant of the decision to enter. Obstacles to entry are of greater or lesser significance to different types of entrant. The barriers may include the absolute cost advantages of established insurers, economies of scale, product differentiation and legal barriers.[52] Product differentiation deserves further consideration.

Potential new entrants to any market have to overcome the accumulated preferences of consumers for the products of established firms. The new entrant faces limited demand for its products and is forced into conducting an extensive sales promotion campaign in order to achieve a greater market share. Such an exercise requires the investment of sufficient funds to compete with the promotional activities of established firms with low costs per unit of output.

It is difficult to assess the importance of customer loyalty in the life assurance market, although there is reason to believe that it does exist. Life assurance and pensions contracts are long-term in nature where the purchase price is paid at the beginning of the contract for future benefits the precise nature of which may not be specified at that time. Customers cannot therefore be entirely sure of what they are buying nor can they easily compare the contracts of different firms. Life assurance may not be purchased more than once during an individual's life time, particularly in the pensions field, and low surrender value deters changing between insurance companies. These factors favour established firms of long-standing reputation who can offer security and the prospect of providing future benefits of similar value to those in the past.

On the other hand, life assurance is not always purchased directly from the insurance company but often through an independent broker who may be expected to have no brand loyalties. Nonetheless security and performance are important considerations in the broker's mind when acting on behalf of a client, leaving new entrants at a disadvantage.

Of course product differentiation of a highly innovative nature may enable a potential entrant to attract new policyholders and raise the overall level of demand for life assurance products. The introduction and marketing of unit-linked life assurance which became very popular during the 1960s and 1970s is a good example, and new entrants such as Abbey Life, which pioneered the product, and Hambro Life were able to grow rapidly as a result.

If new innovators run into financial difficulties or meet with failure then the standing of established firms may be bolstered. The Scottish life offices have long relied upon their reputation for security and money management expertise to attract new business, and while of itself this is neither sufficient to maintain nor increase their market share the historical linkage with a continued presence in Scotland may prove a useful marketing tool.

The long-term insurance industry in Scotland appears to have been remarkably stable throughout most of the twentieth century with only one new Scottish-based office being set up in recent times. This may suggest that Scotland's record in generating life assurance enterprise has in recent times been a poor one. On the other hand, there were only 18 new entrants to the UK life assurance industry over the 25-year period to 1977[53] so that new entrants have not been a major source of new competition in the industry. When entry by firms which were subsidiaries of other financial companies not writing insurance business such as unit trusts, investment companies, banks and insurance brokers is considered, however, the Scottish record in establishing new insurance firms is poor. Scottish financial institutions do not appear to have been attracted to this market, unlike a number of English institutions.

Generally the Scottish and English life offices have faced increased competition from many other financial institutions. Since a subsantial part of life assurance is a savings contract and only a fairly small part death cover the life offices compete in the market for personal savings including pensions business. Rising equity markets since the mid-1970s have encouraged savers to invest in unit trusts and investment trusts or directly in the stock market through private client funds which are managed by stockbrokers or fund management groups. The life offices have also faced competition in the provision of mortgage finance to house buyers. The greater part of endowment business is mortgage related and the mortgage market has become intensely competitive in recent years as the clearing banks, merchant banks and overseas banks have become major participants.

Performance. One way of measuring the performance of the Scottish life offices is to look at their premium income. Premium income comprises payments made under existing policies and payments received on the generation of new business, part of which will be single-premium policies and part new regular premium policies. It is estimated that in 1983 the Scottish life offices accounted for 18.7 per cent (£664 million) of new single premium business in the British life industry, 12.9 per cent (£292 million) of new regular premium business and 15.2 per cent (£1862 million) of all premiums (revenue premiums) received that year.[54]

These figures give some measure of the size of Scottish life office business but say little about performance. Table 7.14 shows how the market share of the Scottish offices compares between 1971–84. Over the period premium income of ordinary life assurance business in the UK and overseas increased by a factor of 8.6 whilst that of the nine Scottish life offices grew by a factor of 10.6 so that their share of UK worldwide premium income stood at 17.2 per cent. At the same time the Scottish offices increased their market share of UK premium income from 13 per cent to almost 17 per cent. Table 7.12 also shows the net assets of the Scottish and UK offices at market values for the period 1976 to 1984. The Scottish offices have improved their share of the net assets of UK long-term funds by about 3 per cent over the period.

Table 7.14. Ordinary insurance business of the Scottish and UK life insurance offices 1971-84 (£ million).

	1971	1976	1981	1984
Premium Income				
UK and overseas:				
Scottish offices	237	506	1272	2514
UK offices	1694	3642	8393	14589
Scottish %	13.2	13.9	15.2	17.2
UK only:				
Scottish offices	192	416	1057	2052
UK offices	1478	2982	7143	12109
Scottish %	13.0	14.0	14.8	16.9
Net Assets (market values)				
Scottish offices	2549	3892	9851	21218*
UK offices†	n.a.	24487	61102	112851
Scottish %	n.a.	15.9	16.1	18.8*

* estimate.   † includes industrial funds.
Sources: Bain and Reid 1971-81. 1984 figures updated from Scottish life offices' annual reports and accounts; *Life Insurance in the United Kingdom*; *Financial Statistics*.

There have been variations in the growth rates of premium income and net assets of the individual Scottish life offices over the time period shown in table 7.12. However, because of the varying emphasis between companies on different life products sold direct comparisons between individual companies are fraught with difficulties.

A non-scientific but nonetheless widely used measure of performance is to consider how the Scottish offices have served their policyholders. An annual survey of the performance of around 45 life offices is carried out each year by the *Economist*[55] and a league table is published in order to illustrate how a policyholder paying £100 premium for a with-profits policy would have fared. Five of the eight Scottish life offices quoting proceeds for a whole life policy in force 40 years to 1985 were above the median, as were six of the eight quoting proceeds at maturity of a 25-year endowment policy.

Six out of nine were above the median payout occuring on the death of a policyholder after 10 years of a 15-year endowment policy. In each category four Scottish offices could be found in the top ten. These figures would suggest that the Scottish life offices have served their policyholders well.

Past performance, however, does not always provide a reliable guide to future performance. Performance measurements of this type can be misleading. They do not, for example, take account of risk. (The problems of performance measurement are discussed in some detail in chapter 8.) The expenses of the life office may in fact be more important than its investment performance in determining its overall performance.

Before premium and existing investment income can be used to generate profits the office has to meet expenses. These comprise management costs such as salaries, pension and national insurance contributions, and commission charges and can be expressed as a percentage of premium payments from policyholders. It is in the interest of the policyholder that management expenses are minimised and kept below the level built into the actuarial calculations when setting premiums, since this will afford the opportunity for increased profit. Compared with a national expense ratio of 21.7 per cent in 1984 the ratio for the Scottish life offices was 15.8 per cent.[56] The average Scottish expense ratio, however, tends to hide a wide variation between individual offices with three of the larger offices well below the national figure and two of the smallest well above.

There are problems with using the expenses ratio as a measure of competitiveness. First, new business expenses significantly outweigh the continuing renewal expenses of regular premium policies. Hence comparisons between offices should allow for rate of new business expansion. Second, certain types of business are much less expensive to write than others.[57] Group pensions business, for example, is significantly less expensive than ordinary individual business. Third, some offices carry out business in markets which may involve heavier costs. An office which encourages mortgage endowments by shouldering the burden of lenders' enquiries will incur more expense, though this service may bring a return in the form of a steady source of business. Information required to overcome these difficulties is not readily available. Thus while the cross-sectional expenses ratios calculated for 1983 and 1984 for the nine Scottish life offices consistently decline as output, measured by premium income, rises there are severe limitations on the conclusions that can be drawn on efficiency.

New Directions
Although the life assurance market continues to grow many of its sectors are sensitive to taxation and regulatory changes which seek to influence personal savings and pensions provision. In recent times the government has shown a desire to reduce the tax advantages attached to life assurance products as a means of accumulating savings. The removal of Life Assurance

Premium Relief (LAPR), for example, reduced the attraction of regular premium unit-linked business benefiting other savings plan vehicles such as unit trusts.[58] Pension schemes for the individual have also received a boost in recent times due in part to regulatory changes and proposals in this field. Ordinary life assurance lost ground to the newer types of business up until 1982 when the introduction of Mortgage Interest-Relief At Source (MIRAS) resulted in a tremendous growth in ordinary with-profits business.

The Scottish life offices have traditionally been strong in mature product lines, though in recent times they have increased their involvement in the provision of straightforward investment contracts in the individual pensions field and with unit trusts. Several companies have established their own unit trusts held separate from their life funds. Because of sensitivity to fiscal and regulatory changes it is difficult to predict the future growth areas of long-term business and it is sensible to hold a balanced portfolio of products. There has been little attempt by life assurance companies to diversify their business into other areas of the financial services market. Opportunities exist to market their investment expertise and this has occurred with segregated pensions business.

Greater emphasis is likely to be given to the development of product delivery systems by the Scottish life offices. At present they have limited control over the distribution of their products which is mostly through brokers and other intermediaries.[59] They have few company representatives dealing directly with the public.

The sale of life assurance products by an intermediary requires the payment of commission. The life assurance offices have attempted in the past to reach agreement on scales of commission that can be applied across the industry. The logic behind such an arrangement is that commission will then play no part in the placing of insurance business by the independent intermediary, and only the merits of the insurance company's product will be relevant. Implicit in this view is the belief that the insurance company can compromise the impartiality of the intermediary by offering to pay higher levels of commission than competitors. In the absence of a commission agreement the larger life assurance companies may seek to persuade brokers to sell their policies by increasing commissions (which must ultimately be borne by the policyholder), and the smaller life office which has difficulty in competing may be faced with a reduction in new business and the prospect of changing to direct selling. The establishment of a direct sales team may be too costly an exercise for many offices and unlikely to achieve as widespread a representation as is provided by the intermediary network. It is not clear, however, whether a commission war would persist for any length of time nor whether the intermediary would be receptive to tactics of this nature.

As well as commission agreements, disclosure of commission has come under the recent scrutiny of legislators. There is no existing obligation to disclose commission and under the Financial Services Act the new regime will not require commission disclosure from those life offices which join the voluntary commissions agreement to be established under the auspices of the relevant self-regulatory organisation for the marketing of investments, although the information must be provided if requested.

Critics have argued that there should be full disclosure of commission to purchasers of policies as for other financial products. The suggestion of full disclosure has been resisted by the life assurance companies on the grounds that customers will be less willing to purchase policies when faced with the knowledge that commission payments account for a substantial proportion of the first year's premium. The experience of unit trust commission disclosure does not provide evidence to sustain this view.[60] Neither is potential loss of business a sufficient reason to restrict disclosure of commission – investors have a claim to knowledge of the costs that they are required to meet when they purchase a policy. If independent intermediaries are required to disclose commissions there is no persuasive argument why company representatives should not also have to make full disclosure, although where such representatives are salaried employees, practical difficulties might intervene.

The size of the commissions paid by a selection of insurance companies on their life business in 1985 is shown in table 7.15, and is also given as a percentage of new premium business for that year. Although the figures for commissions include payments on policy renewals most charges relate to new business, where payment is up-front. The figures show the variations in costs between the individual life offices during 1985.[61] Unlike the Scottish offices both Abbey Life and Allied Dunbar have large direct sales forces.

Major change in the charging structure of the life assurance industry could be expected to alter the balance of bargaining power between the life office, the intermediary and the consumer. In so far as the shift is away from the insurance company new forms of distribution and types of delivery system will be introduced with the life office exercising greater control over the sale of its products. New distribution channels will also provide the opportunity to devise new methods of charging customers, removing the high front-end commissions on the first premium, or spreading the remuneration to the intermediary over a longer term.

Computers have brought enormous flexibility to the writing of life assurance policies and have been used to assist the selling of life products. Many large intermediaries are linked by computer lines and screens to a large number of life offices to facilitate the comparison of policy quotations, the rapid preparation of policy documents and the provision of information about alternative policies. New applications of existing technology will lead to the establishment of new distribution networks. This may favour those insurance companies which are part of a wider financial service group. The TSB Trust Company, for example, is able to operate from trustee savings

Table 7.15. A sample of selected UK insurance companies' commission expenditure as a proportion of their new premium income (NPI, long-term business) for 1985.

Company	New premium income* (£m)	Commissions (£m)	Commissions as % of NPI
FS Assurance	14.2	1.9	13.4
Scottish Equitable	247.2	21.6	8.7
Scottish Mutual	171.5	18.6	10.8
Standard Life	656.2	67.1	10.2
Abbey Life†	189.3	46.4	24.5
Allied Dunbar Assurance†‡	395.0	55.2	14.0
Commercial Union	220.5	26.0	11.8
Equity and Law	165.3	29.6	17.9

* Annual and single premiums for all types of ordinary long-term business.
† New initial commissions.
‡ Includes unit trust sales.
Source: Annual reports and accounts.

bank branches throughout the United Kingdom. Standard Life purchased a 34 per cent shareholding in Bank of Scotland in January 1985, but it remains to be seen whether the bank will form a primary sales distribution channel for Standard's products. The branch network appears to have limited potential since no more than 15 per cent of Standard's UK business is carried out in Scotland. Nonetheless the electronic home banking service being pioneered by Bank of Scotland may offer new opportunities for the sale of insurance packages direct to the consumer.

There has been speculation that the larger life assurance companies will establish closer relationships with building societies following the removal of restrictions on the range of financial services that societies can offer (see chapter 6). The logic behind the bank or building society distribution network is that the arrangement of a large proportion of personal insurance business is closely related to other financial transactions. The buying of a house brings with it the arrangement of a mortgage, household insurance, life assurance and the need for insurance against inability to maintain mortgage payments. Similar considerations may apply to high-value bank loans. These reasons lie behind the current fashion of purchasing estate agencies. General Accident is the only Scottish insurance company to acquire such a distribution network, though Scottish Life, a large part of whose business is endowment mortgages, has purchased minority stakes.

The insurance companies are in competition with banks, building societies and other financial institutions for the savings of the personal sector. Most of the products provided by a life assurance company could be sold by competing institutions, since the assurance element of the contract, which the life office alone is authorised to provide, can be bought in. These institutions have well-established networks and do not need to rely on the intermediary network. Changes are occurring in the way that life assurance products are sold with direct selling to consumers, assisted by technological developments, likely to increase in the future. The Scottish life offices depending almost entirely upon the independent intermediary must therefore develop new and additional systems of delivery.

Conclusions
The nine Scottish life offices have a large share of the life assurance and pensions market in the UK. Much of their business is in mature product lines such as house purchase-related endowments, though some of the offices have significant amounts of business in the growing individual pensions market and in managed pension funds. They were, however, slow to respond to the success of linked life assurance but more recently have diversified into unit trusts.

The Scottish life offices were among the first to apply computers to the preparation of policies and to improving statistical information. They have continued to develop their systems to allow rapid response to enquiries and the production of quotations and policy documents. This has helped them to contain their costs and has had a positive influence on their performance. The new technologies enable them to provide a wide range of products which can rapidly be launched onto the market. New product development and product differentiation have become key elements in successful operation and are part of a more marketing-orientated approach to life assurance. There are signs that the Scottish life offices are more market-led than in the past.

Pressure for change has come from growing competition in the savings market with many financial institutions offering savings products. There is some concern, however, that the mutual structure of the Scottish life offices does not facilitate rapid response. There may be opportunities to apply their investment expertise outwith the area of traditional life assurance. The Scottish life offices do not have an international outlook and, apart from two offices with business in Australia and Canada, virtually all their business is written in the UK. There appears no urgency to transact business in the European Community or to gain experience in Europe where future harmonisation of the different markets would provide a potentially large market.

The mutual form of ownership has helped to maintain the independence of the Scottish life offices and their continued presence in Scotland. The life offices view a Scottish location as having cost advantages over London and modern communications ensures that distance from markets provides no disadvantages. There is also a belief that a Scottish location enables a more detached and considered view to be taken, but it is not clear how this is reflected in performance. In the past few years a number of London-based insurance companies have decentralised their decision and administrative operations and enjoy similar advantages. However, the Scottish life offices, as a distinct group of assurance companies, have historically had a reputation for protecting and bringing benefits to their policyholders and this provides a useful marketing tool.

The products of the nine Scottish life offices are sold through independent intermediaries. The offices do not have full control over their existing delivery systems and this is perhaps where they are most vulnerable. Financial services legislation dealing with the sale of investments may have a major effect on the role of intermediaries in life assurance markets and uncertainty regarding the outcome of the process of change means that the Scottish life offices and their English counterparts may have to devise new delivery systems. There may be a need to increase the public understanding of the essential nature and attractions of life products and remove the mystique that still surrounds life assurance, even though this may make the public more critical consumers. The Scottish life offices could give a lead in this area to their benefit.

Insurance Broking

Insurance broking firms operating in Scotland include major international houses with large offices in Glasgow, Edinburgh and Aberdeen, medium-sized Scottish firms with head offices in the main centres and a small number of branch offices, and small proprietary companies operating locally. The business of the international insurance brokers covers all forms of general insurance, including re-insurance (small in Scotland), life assurance and pensions and maintaining large commercial accounts. Most other brokers will handle an equally wide range of insurance business but not on the same scale. There are also specialists to be found among the small firms, one Edinburgh firm, for example, specialising in the insurance of fishing boats. A number deal only with motor insurance.

A high proportion of general insurance and a significant part of life assurance is placed through insurance brokers. They play an important part in ensuring access to insurance and re-insurance markets. Brokers are the agent of the insured. They do not issue their own liabilities but are paid a commission out of the premiums that they generate on the sale of policies, although fee arrangements are now becoming more common. The size of the insurance broking industry can be measured by the levels of broking income earned or by the size of premium income handled. Up-do-date statistical information on the industry is, however, unavailable, and as is so often the case earlier figures provide no guide to the amount or proportion of UK business handled in Scotland.

In 1985 the British Insurance Brokers Association (BIBA) had over 150 member firms either based or represented in Scotland. Included among these were 7 of the 20 biggest brokers in the world, all of whom are members of Lloyd's. Lloyd's insurance brokers have the exclusive right to place insurance and re-insurance business in the Lloyd's market. This means that if provincial brokers or other non-members wish to arrange for risk to be underwritten on the Lloyd's market (as opposed to direct placement with an insurance company), they have to channel the business through a member firm. Lloyd's brokers can place business in the market themselves or with an insurance company. It is unlikely that much of this business is arranged in Scotland. The insurance requirements of the large oil companies based in Aberdeen are usually arranged by their head offices outwith Scotland, although oil-related insurance business has most certainly been the major reason behind the attraction of UK and international brokers to Aberdeen. The large US brokers have gained entry to Lloyd's either through shareholding links or by the acquisition of Lloyd's brokers. The attraction is access to Lloyd's underwriting capacity including profitable re-insurance business, the saving of commissions and the use of the extensive international networks of Lloyd's brokers. For their part Lloyd's brokers have been keen to establish connections in the US market, the largest insurance market in the world.

Virtually all of the international broking firms with offices in Scotland belong to large US broking groups and their presence in Glasgow has much to do with its emergence as Scotland's insurance broking centre, perhaps unsurprisingly, given the concentration of Scotland's industry and population in the West. Glasgow has historic connections with insurance broking. Hugh Stenhouse built up the broking business started by his father Alexander Stenhouse in Glasgow in 1904, creating one of Scotland's largest international companies, Stenhouse Holdings. Taken over by its Canadian affiliate, Reed Stenhouse, the combined group became one of the world's largest broking firms.[62] In turn Reed Stenhouse has recently become part of the American company, Alexander and Alexander, the second largest insurance broker in the world. There have been other more recent examples of American takeovers of independent Scottish brokers although one house has regained its independence after a successful management buy-out.

Alexander Stenhouse is the largest broker in Scotland. Based at its Glasgow office is the company's national computer system and national accounts system, the major Scottish branch of its broking business, Alexander Stenhouse UK Limited, and the headquarters of the company's financial services arm, Alexander Stenhouse Financial Services Limited. The brokerage business is concerned with servicing client accounts in Scotland and carries out business in all major general insurance sectors. Most of this business is commercial though the company also undertakes personal insurance and some life assurance. The headquarters of the company (then Reed Stenhouse) moved to London many years ago largely to overcome communications disadvantages. Alexander Stenhouse Financial Services was formed in January 1986 to coordinate the company's employee benefits, personal financial planning and investment services. Most of the business is UK based, though the employee benefit service is international in its scope. Alexander Stenhouse is a major pensions consultant in Scotland. Investment advice to individuals has been a growing area of business, though personal and pensions fund management is based in London.

In common with most of the other financial markets insurance broking is undergoing rapid change at all levels and for a variety of reasons. As a result of the large underwriting losses that have been made in American and UK markets resulting from sharp rises in the incidence of claims and excessive price competition (see General Insurance section), brokers have had difficulty in placing new business, especially re-insurance, with underwriters.[63] The large international brokers have attempted to diversify across world insurance markets, and to increase their market shares by takeovers and mergers. This has concentrated business in fewer hands, a trend that appears likely to continue. In Scotland it is probable that few large industrial and commercial insurance accounts are not already in the hands of the large international and UK brokers. Slow economic growth and the erosion of Scotland's industrial base with the continued decline of traditional industries has meant that the large brokers have to seek out business from the smaller company market.[64] This has increased competition for the independent Scottish local and regional brokers.

The smaller Scottish broker is also vulnerable to competition in the retail broking market from the clearing banks and building societies. The banks have carried out personal sector insurance broking through subsidiary companies since the early 1970s. The threat posed by the banks is a change to more innovative techniques of attracting insurance business using their branch networks, technological expertise and marketing skills. The Royal Bank was the first to move into direct selling of its own car insurance over the telephone, cutting out the intermediary. The building societies potentially offer a greater threat. A number of societies have expressed a desire to extend their provision of insurance broking services following the passage of the Building Societies Bill. Brokers have lobbied the legislators to ensure that any new or existing insurance activities of the building societies are undertaken only through insurance broker subsidiaries that are obliged to comply with the Insurance Brokers (Registration) Act 1977.[65] Whatever the regulatory requirements imposed it seems certain that insurance broking houses will face greater competition for brokerage business in both general insurance and life assurance markets. Opportunities may exist for brokers to provide a wider range of financial and investment services to customers. Some of the larger broking houses in Scotland already offer financial consultancy services including investment, pensions and tax advice, often through a separate financial planning subsidiary. The prospect for a rationalisation of the broking community in Scotland appears to be high. There will be mergers or casualties as competitive pressures increase.

Insurance brokers are also having to respond to the significant changes in the regulatory framework introduced by the government's legislation on investor protection. Under the new regime intermediaries marketing any form of life assurance or investment business will require to be registered with the appropriate regulatory body. This requirement should pose no difficulties for existing insurance brokers and it appears that intermediaries will be polarised between those that are independent (mainly brokers) and insurance company representatives selling only one company's products. This could persuade existing independent intermediaries who are not already registered as brokers to do so. A movement towards greater commissions disclosure seems inevitable. The aim is to ensure that the intermediary is not influenced in the decision to recommend policies by the level of remuneration gained.[66] Arguments that full disclosure would be of little value are not convincing. Whatever the merits of the debate on commissions it is perhaps surprising that brokers have not made greater movement towards discretionary fee options. This approach could be expected where a long-term client relationship is formed. Since the insurance companies largely control commission structures they also exercise an element of control over the broking distribution channel which would not be present if brokers operated on a client-fee basis. In the general insurance field brokers holding large commercial accounts are often remunerated by fee payment. This has become more common because commission has failed to reflect adequately the rising costs of administering accounts as the volume of insurance claims over recent years has risen. Fee arrangements have also become more common in the employee benefits field.

Investor protection legislation also has important implications for the way brokers carry out their business. In order to give informed and unbiased advice, the financial intermediary must have knowledge of the range of competitive products within a given market segment. Brokers will require to invest in the appropriate technology that can access information on products, costs and performance in real time. A competitive advantage may be secured by those who can develop existing systems to suit their own needs.

Conclusions
The Scottish insurance broking industry is an important part of the financial sector. Brokers provide a valuable economic service by bringing participants in insurance markets together and are able to offer clients independent and impartial advice and administrative assistance with all aspects of insurance contracts. The broking industry is under pressure from excess capacity in insurance markets and from increased competition. The large international brokers in Scotland are reasonably well placed – they hold the large commercial accounts, and also offer a range of financial consultancy services. Together with the larger Scottish broking firms they are likely to increase

their market shares. A period of sector rationalisation is forseen. The market does, however, have room for both international players and provincial firms as shown by a successful Scottish management buy-out. Small insurance brokers operating further afield in small regional centres of population should be recognised as having an important role to play in bringing personal sector insurance services to these communities. For them competition may come mainly from the independent insurance intermediaries who are not registered as brokers and from direct access telephone links.

The smaller Scottish broker operating in the main urban centres would appear to be in a less secure position. Slow expansion of the Scottish economy has meant little growth in new industrial business and with few commercial companies without brokers the large houses are competing for business that may not previously have appealed to them. Intensification of competition will mean that the quality of service provided will become increasingly important to survival. There is some evidence, however, that small to medium-sized brokers offering a more personal service have been successful in attracting new business.

NOTES
1. Long-term insurance companies are also known as life assurance companies or offices.
2. All life insurance is considered to be long-term even if the contract transferring risk or loss from the policyholder to the insurer is only for one year.
3. The principles underlying life assurance are similar to those underlying general insurance.
4. Insurance compensates only for losses that can be expressed in monetary terms. There are some risks such as human suffering that cannot be compensated. Carter observes that insurance may also raise actual losses by reducing the need to exercise risk-avoidance, prevention, and a reasonable standard of care in general.
5. UK market, including Lloyd's, estimated at £7750 million. Source: Carter & Godden (1984).
6. To derive the underwriting result any increase in unearned premiums is first subtracted from written premiums to arrive at earned premiums; insurance claims, expenses and commissions are then subtracted from earned premiums to give the underwriting balance. Negative balances indicate a loss. Other sources of income are added to give profits (losses) before tax. Unearned premiums represent the proportions of the premiums written which relate to periods of insurance subsequent to the balance sheet date.
7. Insurance companies hold 'technical reserves' which are provisions to meet estimated liabilities to policyholders. These comprise provisions for unearned premiums and provisions for outstanding claims, including claims incurred but not reported. These funds are invested in assets and have been built up over a period of years from premiums which have not had to be paid out to meet claims. The assets are much more liquid in nature than the long-term fund investments of life assurance companies, although a proportion of general insurance company reserves represent shareholders' funds to meet statutory and prudential requirements for a solvency margin and these are usually invested in longer term assets. A proportion of technical reserves will also be

held in equity type investments in order to hedge against inflation. Because of the underwriting losses that have been made in recent years companies have had to rely on capital appreciation and the investment income attributable to the investment of their technical reserves to increase those reserves in step with the growth in their underwriting business. Investment income is offset against underwriting losses with the balance making a contribution to company profits. Retained profits are then used to finance the growth in general insurance business. General Accident's technical reserves (£2.2 billion in 1985) have varied from 116 per cent to 130 per cent of premium income.

8. If premium rates are increased to cover a rise in the average cost (but not frequency) of claims but administration costs remain unaffected, then the expense ratio could be expected to fall giving a misleading impression of increased efficiency.
9. In addition there are two small collecting friendly societies who have their head offices in Scotland, although one of these is registered in England. If a friendly collecting society registers in Scotland it must also register in England. If registration occurs only in England the society is considered to be registered for the purposes of transacting life assurance in Scotland. The Scottish figures in chapter 7 do not include these two offices. None of the mutual offices based in Scotland nor the one composite office carry out industrial life business.
10. Standard Life and Life Association of Scotland also carry out business in Ireland.
11. For a more detailed discussion of the main types of life assurance policies see Franklin and Woodhead (1980).
12. The degree of risk sharing between the life office and the investor will vary with the type of insurance contract in force. For example, a without-profits endowment policy provides a guaranteed nominal rate of return so that the life office absorbs the risk of failure to achieve this minimum return, but collects any gain from achieving a rate of return above that guaranteed. In a with-profits endowment policy the guaranteed return may be lower but the policyholder will receive a share in any additional income generated from the investment of premiums.
13. Under the 1974 Insurance Companies Act every company carrying on long-term business is required to appoint an actuary to carry out a valuation of liabilities at least every three years. In practice valuations are carried out annually.
14. Bonuses are determined as a result of a quite separate actuarial investigation from that which determines the surplus.
15. The declaration of bonus rates is one means by which the life offices can attract new premium business. Insurance companies are reluctant to unilaterally reduce existing bonus rates and may withhold part of the capital and revenue surpluses to maintain bonus rates in future years. The total return to the policyholder will also depend on the value of the premiums paid.
16. We are grateful to Mr William M. Morrison, General Manager of the Scottish Life Assurance Company, for providing the information in this paragraph.
17. The Scottish offices have suggested that Franklin and Woodhead are wrong. Terminal bonuses performed a competitive function but it was not cause and effect.
18. Income tax relief on life assurance premiums was removed from all new qualifying policies effected after March 1984, but continues in force for the full term of qualifying policies started before that date. Life Assurance Premium Relief (LAPR), as it was known, will normally be credited to the policyholder by the insurance company in the form of a 15 per cent reduction in premium

Notes

relief with the company claiming relief in bulk from the Inland Revenue. The administration of the relief should not be confused with entitlement to relief and the actual level of relief has no connection with the individual's tax position.
19. With segregated business the life office is selling only its investment management expertise. Therefore the assets of the pension scheme are held separately from other life office assets.
20. *Life Insurance in the UK,* Association of British Insurers.
21. Benefits paid under the State Earnings-Related Pension Scheme (SERPS) are to be reduced. One likely effect is that employees relying on the State scheme will either contract out or supplement their future benefits through a private pension plan. Employees in occupational schemes are to be given the opportunity to opt out and make their own pension arrangements.
22. Scottish actuaries were among the first to carry out research into unit-linking. In the early 1950s a paper to the Faculty of Actuaries described some developments by a pensions organisation in the United States. This led to a considerable amount of research in Scotland and a few years later to a definitive paper on the subject.
23. Association of Scottish Life Offices; Life Offices Association.
24. It has been suggested to us that the growth of direct sales led to a decline in the ethics of UK life assurance salesmen and that established offices with prior experience of this type of situation in North America and Australia were reluctant to develop along these lines in the UK. This seems to imply that established offices could not have afforded to exercise ethical control themselves over any direct sales force that was set up.
25. The merits of commission agreements are discussed later.
26. The proportions vary between the individual Scottish life offices but discussions would indicate that over 70 per cent of all their business is placed by brokers.
27. See, for example, Clayton and Osborn (1965), Carter (1979), Dodds (1979) and Franklin and Woodhead (1980).
28. If an office were to cease to write long-term business the eventual cash flow would be negative and claims would be met by the realisation of assets.
29. It is for this reason that the life offices can hold equity investments which have no maturity dates. These assets could of course be realised through sale in secondary markets but there is no guarantee as to value.
30. Insurance Company Associations, First Stage Evidence to the Committee to Review the Functioning of Financial Institutions (1977), Appendix D, para.2.
31. The actuarial literature on life office objectives has also argued that the main principle of investment should be the maximisation of expected yield, subject to the life office being in a position to meet its contractual obligations. See Dodds (1979, chapter 3).
32. The purpose of a matching policy is to minimise the risk of the life office becoming insolvent. The liabilities of a life office can take a life time to mature and when policies are issued (apart from single premium policies and immediate annuities) the office receives a stream of future premiums to be invested as well as accruing interest payments and maturing or realised assets to be reinvested. Income from investments may be variable or there is always the risk of default and under most ordinary life policies the life office has guaranteed to accept future premiums at a predetermined rate regardless of the terms on which they can be invested (presently unknown) and regardless of the extent to which inflation may affect the costs of administration. The life office is concerned to ensure that it can earn the rate of interest assumed in its policies and can overcome the uncertainty by investing its funds in such a way as to make itself immune from future changes in investment conditions, or more precisely by

investing the assets so that they can be expected to match the net liabilities both in timing and amount. Dodds (1979) notes that 'this form of matching can be referred to as absolute matching and the constraints on such a policy in terms of the availability of stock as well as the difficulty of matching a growing fund are partly taken account of in a policy of immunisation which involves the life office in matching the mean term of its liabilities with the mean term of its assets.' Matching or immunisation, however, limits the freedom of the investment manager to actively seek for mispriced securities and in general reduces the manoeuvrability in the market. However, no office will seek to achieve complete immunisation of their business. 'For with-profit business the concept of immunisation has less significance because the proportion of the liabilities representing the policyholders' reasonable expectations of future bonuses is not fixed, so a company has greater freedom to invest in ordinary shares and property without endangering its solvency' and 'To the extent that the insurer is justified in expecting the flow of new business to continue, and has sufficient surplus assets to support this, he may invest the net cash flow for a somewhat longer average term if by doing so (e.g. during a period of falling interest rates) he expects to improve the return on the investment and hence the bonus expectations of the policyholders' (Insurance Company Associations, First Stage Evidence to the Wilson Committee, Appendix C, paras 13 and 14.)

33. See Copeland and Weston (1983) for a discussion of asset risk.
34. See also Dodds (1979).
35. See the Insurance Company Associations, First Stage Evidence to the Wilson Committee, para.65, and Appendix D, paras 6 and 11.
36. Authors' estimates. Annual reports and accounts have been used. These do not, however, provide accurate figures since assets held and managed from day-to-day overseas are not distinguished. Some estimate must also be made of funds under management but not held against liabilities. This is a relatively insignificant proportion of the total but could be expected to grow in the future.
37. See introductory section to chapter 7, the British Insurance and Pensions Industry.
38. See the Technical Change Centres 1984 Case Study.
39. These suggestions together with others put forward in this section have been made in interviews with actuaries and others involved in the insurance industry and although strongly refuted by Scottish life office spokesmen have been echoed sufficiently often by different observers to warrant consideration.
40. There are problems with measuring life office performance – see later in chapter.
41. Here risk is taken to mean the failure of the office to meet its guarantees in respect of sums assured on maturity or earlier death, including declared bonuses of the with-profits policyholders.
42. Part of the premium of the with-profits policyholders takes the form of a loading that the life office can use to invest in assets which offer the prospect of earning returns in excess of the contractual sum assured. In crude terms the result of this is a contribution to surplus which is distributed as reversionary or terminal bonuses. Premiums with bonus loadings also provide a contribution to the solvency of the life fund since future bonuses are non-contractual and the amount of the surplus declared is at the discretion of the actuary (see section on investment). In practice the value of UK life office liabilities has been exceeded by the value of the fund and the concern of the actuary has been with the amount of the surplus that he considers desirable for allocation as bonuses to policy-holders. The level of bonuses actually made available for distribution will partly be influenced by competitive pressures in the life industry.

Notes

43. There is a large body of financial literature which supports the hypothesis that dividend policy is irrelevant to the value of the firm (see Copeland and Weston 1983). Shareholders will be indifferent between receiving some or all of their share of the surplus in the form of a dividend payout.
44. See Mayers and Smith (1986).
45. See Mayers and Smith (1986). Earlier studies suggest mutuals are less efficient than proprietary companies.
46. Policyholders recognise the incentives faced by stockholders and rationally priced insurance contracts reflect unbiased estimates of the company's expected investment, dividend and financing policies (which influence the relative values of the claims). However, life policies are long-term and policyholders face potential costs arising from the choice of the firm's investment, dividend and financing decisions over the life of the policies. Their option to cancel the policy or perhaps to take out a policy loan are imperfect disciplining mechanisms over stockholders' actions – early surrender can impose significant costs and policy loans allow the withdrawal of the savings component of the policy from the control of the firm, but leave the term component. Note that the costs are reduced but not eliminated by mutualisation since investment and financing decisions are still controlled by management, though shareholders' interests need no longer be considered.
47. Mayers and Smith also suggest that the merging of customer and owner roles in the mutual firm imposes an additional cost since this facilitates less efficient risk bearing than in a proprietary company.
48. Life Association of Scotland is the only non-mutual life office based in Scotland. It is a wholly owned subsidiary of Nationale Nederlanden Company. The Scottish Life Assurance Company mutualised in 1968 primarily to protect itself from the real threat of takeover.
49. Johnston and Murphy (1957), Clayton (1971), Richards and Colenutt (1975), Franklin and Woodhead (1980), Sawyer and Aaronovitch (1982).
50. There are also changes in the top ten groups with Commercial Union entering above, and Guardian Royal Exchange below, Sun Life.
51. The independent intermediary may also help to offset market power.
52. See, for example, chapter 3 of *The UK Life Assurance Industry,* Franklin and Woodhead (1980) and *Economics and Insurance,* R. L. Carter (1979).
53. Franklin and Woodhead (1980).
54. Source: Carter and Godden.
55. See the *Economist,* 22 June 1985.
56. Sources: Scottish life offices *Annual Reports*; *Life Insurance in the UK 1980-84.*
57. Premium income, as a measure of output, reflects the number of policies and their price and will therefore vary between offices according to the emphasis on different types of product and pricing structures. Equal amounts of premium income received by two firms could conceal the fact that one was selling more products (and thus have higher expenses) at a lower price.
58. Investors have generally faced higher charges for unit-linked contracts than for unit trusts due to the high commissions paid by the life offices to intermediaries, which are then recovered out of premiums. Part of the premium is also diverted into paying for life cover, leaving a smaller amount with which to purchase units. The offsetting effects of tax relief have been lost with the abolition of LAPR, removing the incentive for some savers to make annual payments into a life office unit-linked scheme.
59. Under the Financial Services Act, which came into effect in 1987, life assurance intermediaries are divided into independent intermediaries and company representatives. Brokers are among the independent intermediaries along with

accountants, solicitors, estate agents, banks and building societies. Company representatives may be either employees of the life office or agents: whichever is the case they may sell only the contracts of one life office.

60. This refers to single and not annual premiums.
61. It has been put to us that the table is misleading because of the varying proportions of annual and single premium business and initial and renewal commission.
62. Stenhouse merged with the Canadian company Reed Shaw Ostler in 1973, providing it with entry to the US insurance market. The two companies operated as Reed Shaw Stenhouse in North America, and Stenhouse Reed Shaw in the UK.
63. The downside of poor underwriting experience is a contraction of insurance markets and therefore a reduction in broking activity. The upside is the resultant rise in insurance premium leading to higher brokerage commissions on available business.
64. Traditional industries also produced large premium business unlike newer industries such as electronics. Marine hull business is an example of this decline with the demise of the shipping industry in the West of Scotland. Oil-related business in Aberdeen will be affected by the present cut-back in North Sea activity.
65. The Insurance Brokers (Registration) Act is likely to be amended materially by the new Financial Services Legislation.
66. Under the Insurance Broking Registration Council Code of Conduct insurance brokers are required to disclose to the client on request the amount of commission earned.

8

INVESTMENT MANAGEMENT

This chapter examines the importance of Scottish investment fund managers in the Scottish financial sector. A number of issues of particular concern are discussed including the significance of overseas investment and the measurement of investment performance. The role played by Scottish fund managers in the unit trust, investment trust and pensions markets is also considered.

The Role of Investment Managers

Traditionally investment management has been regarded as the provision of two services to investors, diversification and management. The diversification is provided by large portfolios encompassing a wide range of assets. The management is supplied by the investment manager's information and knowledge which enable him to alter the composition of his portfolios in response to changing needs and requirements.[1] The two services are provided through a wide range of investment vehicles of which investment and unit trusts have in the past been most important although private client and charity portfolios have always provided a substantial element of some managers' workload. Managers may specialise in one type of investment vehicle but increasingly they operate across the whole spectrum of investment instruments. A growing part of management activity is concerned with the marketing of a portfolio of investments. The marketing of unit trusts has been a notable feature of the investment scene for many years, but increasingly investment managers have taken to marketing their other portfolio vehicles both by advertising and presentations to possible customers, and by tailoring and packaging portfolios to satisfy particular niches in the investment market. The aim is to parcel assets so that the manager's investment stable appeals to as wide a cross section of investors as possible. One major area of expansion has been the increasing size of pension funds and this has brought additional business to the sector. Pension funds may be managed in-house by the company, assured through assurance companies (more properly regarded as insurance business since the risk is shouldered by the insurance company and no separate investment fund exists) or the management may be delegated to specialist institutions who will provide all the necessary ingredients for pension fund management ranging from actuarial advice, through administration to investment management. Many pension

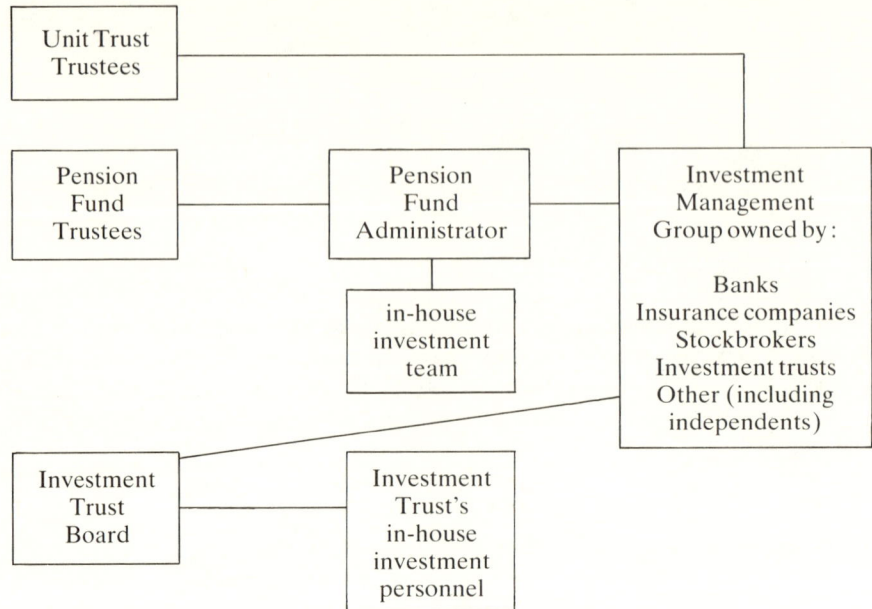

Figure 8.1. Relationship of investment fund managers to investment vehicles.

funds have taken this route, particularly smaller funds[2] (£200 million or less), and become an important source of business to investment managers. The business has been spread across a range of institutions including banks and acceptance houses, insurance companies, unit and investment trust managers and stockbrokers. Unit and investment trust managers may in turn be owned by other institutions, particularly insurance companies, banks and accepting houses, or may operate entirely on their own as independent fund managers. Figure 8.1 indicates the links between those responsible for the overall control of a pension fund, unit trust or investment trust and the investment fund managers. It ignores the administrative function which may be provided 'in-house' or bought-in and concentrates on the investment function. In practical terms the important distinction is between those institutions that provide their own investment expertise and management and those that buy in fund management from investment fund managers. Large pension funds will typically carry out their own investment fund management although they may also apportion part of their funds to outside investment managers. Investment trusts are now, with very few exceptions, part of a management group that provides investment management services to more than one trust or to other investment vehicles.

Official statistics for the total value of pension fund business managed by type of institution are not available but one estimate[3] suggests that 36 per

Table 8.1. Assets of UK investment institutions (£ million).

end of:	1969	1974	1979	1984
Unit trusts (MV* plus cost of buying securities, initial charge, etc.)	1398	1310	3937	15099
Investment trusts (MV of holdings)	4902	3739	5752	15251
Superannuation funds				
Public sector (MV of funded schemes)	1699	2517	12302	35480
Local Authority† (MV holdings)	1246	1644	5361	17649
Private (MV holdings)	4468	5108	16711	77162
Total Superannuation	7413	9269	34374	130291
Insurance companies (book values)	14201	24357	52797	134135
of which:				
General	1460	20718	10486	19974
Long-term	12741	3639	42311	114161

* Market value.

† 1969-79 figures relate to 31st March of the following year. Frequent changes in sample coverage and methods of compilation imply that the figures are only suggestive.

Source: CSO *Financial Statistics*. Insurance company statistics embrace their investment portfolios only.

cent of funds are internally managed with merchant banks (29 per cent), stockbrokers (10 per cent), life companies (10 per cent), clearing banks (8 per cent) and independent managers (7 per cent) providing the remainder. The pension fund business as a whole dwarfs the other parts of the fund management industry with a total value of £130.4 billion. In contrast unit and investment trusts managed £30.4 billion (end 1984). Table 8.1 provides a picture of funds under management by investment institutions in the UK including for comparative purposes the investment portfolios of insurance companies. The remarkable growth in pension funds, particularly the funded schemes in the public sector, and the rapid growth in unit trusts contrast sharply with the slow growth in investment trusts assets. Investment trusts have been, in relative terms, the declining sector of the market.

Official statistics of Scottish involvement in fund management are provided by a Bank of England survey of fund management (1984). The survey concentrated on the management of portfolios for clients who have given the manager discretionary powers to alter the composition of the portfolio. It excludes the management of the manager's own proprietary portfolios and pension funds since they are not fully part of the competitive market.[4] The survey was aimed at large fund managers and covered about 75 per cent of investment trust, unit trust, stockbroker and insurance business (as defined above) and about 90 per cent of merchant and clearing bank business. Table 8.2 provides details of the Scottish share of the funds managed for UK and overseas residents.

Table 8.2. Funds under management at end 1984 (£ million).

Funds managed for:	UK residents		Overseas residents	
	All managers in UK	Scottish managers	All managers in UK	Scottish managers
Analysis by client				
Government and public sector	3800	42	11600	—
Private clients	8400	399	2500	34
Pension Schemes	63800	6762	6600	248
Unit and investment trusts	23200	2824	1700	39
Insurance companies	2600	—	3200	30
Industrial and commercial companies	2000	72	1500	—
Other	3900	206	1400	20
Total	107700	10306	28500	370

Total assets managed in:	UK	Scotland
	136200	10676

Source: Bank of England.

Scotland has a 9.6 per cent share of the fund management business for UK residents but a much smaller proportion of overseas resident business reduces its total share to 7.9 per cent. The estimates should be treated with caution given the partial nature of the sample and response. The figure of £10676 million is not an estimate of the absolute amount of funds under management in Scotland. At the end of 1984 unit and investment trust funds managed in Scotland amounted to £5036 million, more than double the estimate provided by the Bank figures. The figure is even greater at £6370 million if independent investment trusts, excluded from the Bank's sample, are included. The survey indicates that the banks, particularly merchant banks, play a dominant role in the fund management process. The lack of large merchant banks based in Scotland affects the Scottish share of the fund management market. The major independent Scottish fund management groups have no ownership links with merchant banks or other non-portfolio financial institutions. They are frequently partnerships, private limited companies or even public limited companies that originally provided management expertise to investment trusts and have diversified over the years to provide investment advice to individuals, charities, pension funds and unit trusts. More recently the Scottish assurance companies have established fund management arms aimed at particular segments of the market such as unit trusts or pension funds. Table 8.3 provides a summary of the main activities of Scottish fund management groups. There have been substantial changes in the independent fund management groups in recent years reflecting both the setting up of new management groups in response to competi-

Table 8.3. Scottish fund management activity, based on information at end 1984.

Management of	Number
Independent investment trusts	5
Investment and unit trusts	5
Other investment trusts	8
Unit trusts alone	3
Insurance and unit trusts	9
Pension funds only	2

The majority of investment trust managers (excluding independents) also manage pension fund portfolios.

Insurance relates to the main activity of the company. Most unit trust groups, and increasingly investment groups, are able to offer insurance-linked investments.

tive pressures and defensive moves by a number of previously independent investment trusts to group together with a view to securing economies of scale and to present increased barriers to predators.

Comprehensive figures on the relative size of fund management houses that allow for all the different sources of funds under management are unavailable. At the end of 1984 four of the top ten investment trust managers were in Scotland although the largest was only half the size of Touche Remnant. Two of the Scottish managers were also in the top twenty pension fund managers. However, in total UK terms the £1900 million of funds managed in 1984 by Ivory & Sime or a similar amount for Murray Johnstone pale into insignificance beside the £11955 million of Flemings or £9039 million of Morgan Grenfell.

The setting up of new management teams and fund management groups is of considerable interest. Ivory & Sime, in particular, have played an important and interesting role as a breeding ground for new fund management firms. Reasons for establishing one's own business are many and varied but the training scheme operated by Ivory & Sime has undoubtedly been a contributory factor. Apart from those established by former employees and partners of Ivory & Sime few new firms have been established although several groups have merged or significantly altered their structure. It is of some concern that so few new firms have been established. The considerable concentration (and death) of companies that remain, particularly independent investment trusts, reveal the need for new entrants if the sector is to prosper.

The main difficulty in estimating Scotland's share of the total market for fund management in the UK relates to pension fund business. The lack of comprehensive reporting requirements on pension fund investment makes accurate assessment impossible and indeed official UK figures are based in part on a 1978 sample grossed up to reflect the national position.[5] Investment advisers (merchant and clearing banks and independent fund management houses) in Scotland manage pension fund assets of around £3600–4000 million (end 1984).[6] Insurance companies manage more than £3400 million of pooled (commingled) and segregated pension fund assets in addition to assured funds. A total pension fund business in excess of £7000 million compares unfavourably with UK superannuation funds of £130 billion, a total that ignores the insurance element. Total fund management activity (1984) in Scotland excluding insurance companies and in-house managed funds is estimated at £10000–10500 million and including the pension fund element of insurance companies provides an estimate in the region of £14000–15000 million. Non-pension insurance company investment greatly boosts this total (see chapter 7).

Table 8.2 reveals that the Scottish share of fund management for overseas residents has been very small partly as a result of the absence of offices of foreign managers in Scotland. The often quoted avalanche of American funds had not materialised in Scotland at least by the end of 1984. Funds under management for overseas pension funds were only £250 million and compared unfavourably with the total for the UK of £6600 million of which £3800 was managed by UK-owned fund management groups.

Table 8.4 provides a breakdown by assets of the funds managed in Scotland. Of particular interest is the extent of foreign investment by Scottish fund managers. 33 per cent of Scottish portfolios for UK residents are invested overseas, primarily in equities. The comparable figure for the UK as a whole is 22 per cent. Rather less is invested in UK equities, 43 per cent against a national figure of 49 per cent. A similar bias towards overseas investments is demonstrated in the management of overseas residents' funds although the small size of the funds involved make comparisons hazardous.

The major market for Scottish fund managers is the domestic UK market. Attempts are being made to export fund management talents by managing overseas, particularly American, funds but the bulk of the business is generated in the British Isles. Without a comprehensive analysis of share and unit registers it is impossible to know the residence of most share and unit holders. However, some estimates of indigenous Scottish pension fund business are possible and confirm the belief that the decline in manufacturing business has reduced the potential for marketing to local commercial and industrial concerns. The total market value of Scottish pension funds is in excess of £4880 million[7] with annual contributions and investment income running at an annual rate of more than £328 million and £246 million respectively, providing a substantial and growing surplus over current pension payments for reinvestment. The Scottish funds are dominated by the Strathclyde Regional Council pension fund with a market value of £1082

Table 8.4. Composition of funds under management at end 1984 (£ million).

Funds managed for:	UK residents		Overseas residents	
	All managers in UK	Scottish managers	All managers in UK	Scottish managers
Analysis by assets				
Cash and money market instruments (sterling and foreign currency)	4900	566	3300	38
Equities of UK companies	52200	4402	3100	47
Fixed-interest securities of UK companies	2800	77	300	1
UK and other public sector securities	15200	1500	1600	8
Equities of foreign companies	23800	3162	8800	211
Bonds issued by foreign companies	600	28	4700	—
Securities issued by foreign governments and international institutions	1100	211	6300	2
Other investments (UK and overseas) including property	6200	369	100	63
Total	106800	10317	28200	370

Source: Bank of England.

million (end March 1985) and corresponding large annual contributions and investment income. Despite its dominant position in Scotland it is outside the top twenty UK pension funds by size. Few other Scottish pension funds have a market value in excess of £200 million[8] and indeed the number in excess of £100 million is not large (approximately 14). The majority of pension funds are small with a median value of £11 million and annual contribution of under £1 million.

Partial information on the investment advisers of the larger Scottish pension funds (excluding those of financial institutions) suggests that much of the investment advice is supplied by London-based institutions. In the absence of a detailed breakdown, however, it is impossible to value the volume of business accruing to local institutions. Some concern has been expressed about local authorities in particular, employing London advisers, but there is little quantitative evidence to evaluate the importance of this practice. An informal postal survey of the major Scottish pension funds (excluding the banks) suggested that some £2900 million of assets (1985 but varying year-end dates) involved fourteen (non-property) investment advisers of whom four were Scottish. There was little in-house management (only DCL, now part of Guinness, and Coats Patons). In any event the market for fund management is a national one and trustees have a right, indeed duty, to secure the services of the most appropriate advisers. Such advisers may not always be Scottish although it is not always easy to identify areas in which Scottish fund managers are deficient in skills.

Investment Performance

In analysing success and growth in the investment industry it is difficult to escape from the part played by the investment selection skills of the fund managers. For this reason it is necessary to address the performance issue directly and endeavour to assess the possibility of securing and measuring superior investment performance. Two separate but inter-related issues must be addressed; the possibility of selecting investments that provide above average returns, and the cost to the investor of the investment process.

The efficient market hypothesis predicts that on average investors will secure the return for the risk they take on. The evidence is such that Fama (1970) states 'the evidence in support of the efficient markets model is extensive, and (somewhat uniquely in economics) contradictory evidence is sparse'. Despite a great number of studies since Fama's survey was written the hypothesis has remained largely intact suggesting that it is improbable that investment managers have techniques that can consistently select only successful investments.[9]

Given the difficulty of consistently securing successful investments it follows that portfolio performance is unlikely to provide returns above those required for the risk assumed. Indeed simple mathematics suggests that it is impossible for all institutional investors to secure above average performance. The dominance of the stock market by institutional investors implies that above average gains may only be obtained at the expense of other professional investors. Scottish investment managers as a group can only out-perform other managers if their techniques of investment are superior to those employed elsewhere. Qualitative evidence suggests that Scottish managers invest for longer time horizons, trade less and are generally more cautious than their counterparts elsewhere but these qualities are not necessarily synonymous with superior investment performance although they may contribute to the minimisation of costs.

In the absence of either superior investment techniques or an ability to process information more rapidly, efficiently and profitably than others, investment managers should concentrate on minimising the cost of the investment process. The existence of costs consequent on investing imply an asymmetry in investment performance. The efficient market hypothesis indicates that it is difficult for the managers to secure above average performance for the risk assumed. If, however, the managers then levy heavy charges it is possible for investors to suffer below average performance. Paying high charges for management expertise is almost certainly doomed to failure. At best, managers will purchase additional information the return on which will just compensate them for its purchase. At worst, they will provide a service based on promises of investment expertise that cannot be achieved.

Two major elements of portfolio management cost to the investor may be distinguished. The first is the annual management charge levied on the investor. This is normally calculated as a percentage of assets and with few exceptions is payable irrespective of the performance of the portfolio.[10] The second major element of cost is the transaction charge arising from changes in the composition of the portfolio. Stockbroking commission, the jobbers (market makers) turn and stamp duty result from changes in the portfolio and reduce the profitability (or increase the loss) of portfolio re-adjustment.[11] It is necessary to adjust a portfolio to changes in the investment environment such as taxes but extensive turnover is unlikely to be in the best interests of the investor. Low turnover and hence stockbroking commission and small annual and initial charges minimise costs to the investor and remove the possibility of poor investment performance as a consequence of heavy or excessive charges.

The classic study of investment performance is that by Jensen (1968, 1969). His investigation of the performance of American Mutual funds (similar in construction to UK unit trusts) concluded that the funds

> were on average not able to predict security prices well enough to outperform a buy-the-market-and-hold policy, but also that there is very little evidence that any individual fund was able to do significantly better than that which we expected from mere random chance. . . .
> Thus on average the funds apparently were not quite successful enough in their trading activities to recoup even their brokerage activities.

More recent studies have supported these conclusions. Shawky (1982) concludes that mutual funds have been doing better but it remains true that most funds do not out-perform the unmanaged portfolio. This suggests that their management expertise is not worth buying! The UK evidence on unit trusts is not as comprehensive as the American research but provides few grounds for believing in superior investment management. The performance of 97 investment trusts over the 'seventies was carefully measured by Lyall (1983) who concluded that 'very few investment trusts succeeded in achieving returns greater than the appropriate market return' and that 'less than half the investment trusts achieved positive risk premiums'.

The conclusion, that above average performance is difficult to achieve, is not popular and frequently condemned by the investment community. Two views predominate. The first argues that the tests of investment performance are not powerful enough and in particular the risk adjustment process is unsatisfactory. Clearly it is an object of research to increase the power of the tests and increase their reliability. However, many of the studies of performance provide confirmatory evidence using a number of alternative measures of risk. More powerful tests may enable improved discrimination between the performance of portfolios but are unlikely to radically change the general conclusions.

The second criticism of performance measurement is generally based on a variety of misconceptions of the management process. The role of risk, for example, provides many misguided statements. The view of the investment process expressed here is based on the premise of risk adjusted returns. It is not too difficult to perform well if no allowance is made for the impact of risk in measuring performance. High risk is accompanied by high returns so that high returns *per se*, without adjustment for the risk of an investment, provide limited guidance as to its success. The measurement of risk is not without controversy and studies of risk adjustment procedures have suggested problems with some popular techniques. Measurement problems also affect non-risk adjusted performance measures. The advantages of comparing performance to a geometric index such as the Financial Times Ordinary Share index in preference to an arithmetic index such as the Financial Times Actuaries index are well known but almost any comparison involves a compromise. The universe of securities from which a sample is chosen for an index rarely corresponds to the universe of securities from which portfolios are drawn. An obvious example is the inclusion of fixed interest or foreign securities in a portfolio and its comparison with the Financial Times Actuaries All Share index which includes only UK equities. An additional problem with indices is the weighting scheme used in their construction. This rarely corresponds with the possibilities open to portfolio investors.[12]

It is also important to emphasise consistency in investment performance. The efficient market hypothesis does not claim that investors will never do better than secure the return for the risk taken on. It emphasises that just by chance some investors will do well. It denies, however, the possibility that investors will consistently secure above average performance for the risk assumed. This is not to say that any individual investment will not stay top of the unit or investment trust league for period after period. That is possible, although unlikely, since league tables typically ignore risk with the result that high risk portfolios may appear to out-perform all others. The test is whether they can provide above average returns for the risk assumed. The evidence is not favourable.[13]

This view of the investment process has some important implications for the financial sector. The desirability of low management costs has already been mentioned but also important is the change in role of the investment manager. If exceptional performance is outside the managers control, the manager interested in growth must look to other methods of increasing the size of funds under management. Organic growth at a rate greater than the growth rate of the market becomes a matter of chance. Long term above average growth is achieved only by raising new funds thus elevating the marketing of investment instruments into the primary activity of investment management groups. This marketing involves both the promotion of existing financial instruments and innovation to establish new instruments with suitable qualities to tap new sources of funds and to compete with other financial products.[14]

Table 8.5. Joint ventures marketing investment expertise internationally.

Manager	Link	Purpose
Baillie, Gifford & Co.	Republic Bank of Dallas (informal)	Overseas investment advisers
Dunedin Fund Managers	Key Bank (Albany) (informal)	Investment overseas of US Fund money
Edinburgh Fund Managers	Sydney Fund Man. (26.65% equity)	Overseas adviser for Australian investors
	Edinburgh-Wilmington (50% equity)	Overseas adviser for American investors
	Jade Fund	Far East adviser for the Netherlands
Ivory & Sime	I. & S. (Int.) (50% equity)	Overseas adviser for American pension funds
	I. & S. (Jap.) (50% equity)	Overseas adviser for Japanese investors
Murray Johnstone	Kemper-Murray (50% equity)	Int. fixed income and equity management

Sources: Interviews, Company Accounts and publications.
I. & S. previously had links with American Express.
Walter Scott and Partners had links with First Interstate of California. The company is now a wholly owned subsidiary of Walter Scott.
Martin Currie have a small joint venture in Luxembourg.
A number of companies, including Martin Currie and Stewart Ivory & Co. Fund Managers, have wholly owned subsidiaries seeking business overseas.

On this view of the investment process it is necessary to appraise the performance of the institutions on at least two major criteria – their investment performance and their marketing and innovatory capacity. Viewed as a whole the investment performance of Scottish fund managers has been satisfactory and it is difficult to believe that it has in any way affected their ability to survive and grow. Many managers have appeared at or near the top of portfolio league tables although in common with all other managers it is rare that they have consistently stayed at the top. It is not clear that Scottish fund managers have been so successful with respect to innovation. The managers have displayed little skill in the past in attracting new funds through innovations such as unit trusts and were slow to move into the overseas fund management market although more recently, several managers have forged overseas links (table 8.5) and there is some prospect of increased business from this source. Innovation plays a crucial role in the health and vitality of the fund management industry. There is little sign that Scottish fund managers have been outstandingly innovatory in isolating new markets and instruments.

The origin of Scottish fund management expertise arose from innovation and the acceptance of unusual risks. Investment trusts invested heavily overseas at a time when information was poor and other UK investors were concerned primarily with the UK market. Their lack of success in recent years reflects, in part, the inability of Scottish fund managers to develop new areas of expertise and risk taking. The advantages of communication and economies of scale lie with London. It can also pay higher salaries and draw talent south. Scottish fund managers will find it easier to compete if they specialise in areas in which the advantages of London are not so apparent.

Unit Trusts

Unit trust management has not in the past been a well-developed activity in Scotland. At the end of 1984 Scottish management groups managed £483 million excluding the Murray Johnstone fund managed for the TSB (£220 million). This compared with the £15.16 billion funds under management in the UK (excluding offshore and non-authorised unit trusts).[15] Murray Johnstone, Edinburgh Fund Managers and Standard Life are the major unit trust managers, several of the larger independent fund managers having zero or minimal representation in the unit trust market. The position at the end of 1984 showed definite signs of improvement over the situation in 1980, mainly as a result of the entry of the Scottish life assurance societies into the field. At the end of 1979 funds managed for Scottish unit trusts amounted to £47 million in addition to the £31.1 million managed by Murray Johnstone for the TSB. Total funds managed in the industry amounted to £3879 million. This very poor situation had not always been the case. In the earlier years of the industry Ivory & Sime managed a considerable number of unit trusts so that at the end of 1974 Scottish management operated £136.3 million (Ivory & Sime £117 million) out of an industry total of £1290 million but changes in the ownership of Save and Prosper in the 'seventies resulted in Ivory & Sime giving up the management of unit trusts in 1976.[16]

Unit trusts have been particularly notable for the marketing innovations they have introduced greatly increasing their popularity and sales. So important has been the role of marketing that Burton and Corner (1968) are moved to say that unit trust management companies

> combine the attributes of an advertising agency in attempts to secure the requisite share of new savings, and those of portfolio advisers. . . .
> The success or failure of a unit trust management company depends on its ability to achieve the right balance between advertising and portfolio management.

Probably the most important innovation was the linkage of unit trusts to life assurance, which enabled the unit trust industry to benefit from the tax relief on life premiums. With its withdrawal in 1984 independent unit trust groups are endeavouring to concentrate sales in non-life savings schemes. The total number of unit trust groups was stable over the period 1974–79 at around 90, although this total figure camouflages substantial changes in the ownership of management groups. The increase in charges permitted in 1979 has resulted in an increase in the number of groups with a current total of nearly 130. Until 1979 charges were strictly controlled by the Board of Trade and its successors at 13¼ per cent over the twenty-year life of a trust. With the lifting of restrictions annual charges have doubled although the initial charge has not increased to the same extent. In 1975 the majority of units charged an initial fee of 5 per cent and ⅜ per cent per annum thereafter. A few charged lower initial fees and annual fees of ½ per cent. By 1985, although there was less uniformity in charging, the majority still charged an initial fee of 5 per cent but the annual fee had climbed to ¾ per cent. Few charged less than this and several considerably more. Initial fees ranged from 3¼ to 6 per cent and annual fees from ¼ per cent up to 2 per cent. Scottish managers do not charge more than the industry as a whole.

The justification for higher charges was to enable the better-managed trusts which secured superior performance to compensate their managers accordingly. Leaving aside the difficulty of securing superior performance it is difficult to see how if all trusts charge more performance of the average trust can be improved unless the improvement is at the expense of other investment vehicles. A non-scientific, but interesting demonstration of the difficulties, is provided by considering the annual performance rankings of the trusts.

Table 8.6. Unit trust performance.

Unit trust	1984	1979	1974
General			
M & G Midland	1	74	49
Allied Asset	3	57	23
Framlington Capital	4	18	75
Growth			
Key Equity	2	52	48
Vanguard Special Situation	3	59	64
Equity			
Barrington High Yield	3	52	32 (1976)
Prolific High Income	3	1	29 (1975)

Source: Unit Trust Yearbooks 1975, 1980, 1985.

Of the trusts included in table 8.6 only Prolific High Income managed to stay near the top over a five-year period. This may be good management but more likely it reflects a failure to adjust for the high risk involved in some high-income strategies. Taking some of the worst performers of 1984 and looking back at their performance provides equally spectacular changes. Overall, it is difficult to detect superior management performance.

As our earlier comments on performance have made clear, the level of charges is important to the investor. The increase in charges is a matter of considerable concern particularly since there are suggestions that further increases are on their way. Commissions in life assurance are traditionally much higher than on unit trusts and with the switch of emphasis into unit trust selling there is pressure to increase the charges to underwrite the marketing costs involved in competing effectively with life assurance and particularly to compete with the commission levels traditionally offered to insurance salesmen. If a higher level of charges can be established throughout the industry there will be fewer problems relating to disclosure of commission to customers under the new Financial Services Act since the Act requires disclosure if commission above the industry standard is being received by advisers. Competition in the industry is based on advertising and sales networks and performance. Competition has not held charges down but rather stimulated increased marketing in the pressure for sales.

Although regulation of the unit trust industry has been relaxed with the removal of controls over charges, the Department of Trade and Industry (DTI) retains, at present, a watching brief over the unit trust movement and exercises control over unit trust deeds although discussions are under way to relax many of the controls on unit trusts. Trust deeds set out the aims and objectives of the unit trust and govern in large part the investments that a trust may make.[17] To reduce conflicts of interest the DTI restricts unit trust management groups to one unit trust for each objective. Within a group unit trusts must have different objectives and the department requires assurances that unit holders will not be adversely affected when objectives overlap to some degree, or when mergers of management groups result in groups acquiring more than one trust with any particular objective. Groups with a full stable of unit trusts can only grow by an increase in size of existing trusts. New entrants however, are able to grow by introducing a range of trusts marketed specifically at the areas considered to be growing most rapidly. How important a marketing advantage this is, is difficult to evaluate. There is a suggestion that smaller newer trusts are more appealing to new investors but there is little quantitative evidence to support this view. The established clientele of the larger, older, established trusts with well-known names is likely to provide a substantial repeat business. In truth, there is probably room in the market for both approaches. A recent estimate suggested that there were 800000 unit holders in the UK[18] and the industry estimate there to be 2.5 million separate unit accounts. Unit holders represent a small proportion of the UK population and there is considerable scope for further growth. The move towards privatisation has breathed new life into the equity markets and attracted smaller investors back into the markets. Direct investment by small investors is unlikely to grow at a rapid rate but there is considerable scope for unit trusts which remove some of the risks, particularly unique (non-systematic) risk in the language of the Capital Asset Pricing Model, faced by investors. They also provide an easy way of securing representation in specialised, particularly overseas, sectors of the market.

An interesting aspect of the drive for new business has been a change in the way units are sold. For many years selling was largely through block offers, extensively advertised in the press. More recently the industry has shifted its sales efforts and now uses intermediaries to a much greater extent so that 70 per cent of sales are now through this avenue. This change in the method of selling unit trusts poses particular problems for the independent fund managers. Sales of units now require a distribution network and sales force. Fund managers geared to selling their services to companies and institutions do not have a suitable sales distribution network. This represents a substantial barrier to entry although prospects in the unit market are such that most fund managers may be expected to endeavour to leap such barriers. Joint ventures with retail organisations may be one method. The use of credit cards, store or bank, for investment in units or the setting up of a network of intermediaries represent other possibilities although low rates of commission to unit trust intermediaries are claimed to hamper their ability to compete with life assurance sales. The maximum commission agreed by the Unit Trust Association to licensed dealers, stockbrokers and National Association of Security Dealer and Investment Managers (NAS-DIM) members is 3 per cent but banks, accountants and other financial advisers receive somewhat less.

The relationship to the life assurance market is an interesting one. Life policies represent a major alternative saving medium to unit trusts and are a natural competitor. Life policies are an established investment medium sold by very large, well-known companies with developed sales networks and offering attractive commission to salesmen. These factors, together with the benefit of past tax advantages, have placed them in a dominant position in the market place. However, the loss of their tax advantage, the greater flexibility of unit trusts and increased awareness of unit trusts by the public, in part a reflection of the joint selling of insurance and units to take advantage of tax benefits, pose a major competitive threat to the life market. The life companies are responding by diversifying their activities into unit trusts with spectacular initial success. Most Scottish life offices now have unit trust subsidiaries and their previous absence from the market can be turned to advantage. The groups are able to offer a range of unit trusts tailored specifically to allow investors maximum flexibility including free or low cost switching between different investment objectives. The schemes on offer provide investors with much greater flexibility than has hitherto been common and aim to appeal both to existing unit investors and to widen the market by attracting new unit holders who might previously have been deterred by the relative inflexibility of many unit schemes. It is certain that the Scottish share of the unit trust market will grow rapidly in the next few years, although in part this may be at the expense of growth in the life assurance sector.

The small involvement of Scottish fund management firms, particularly the life offices, until recently raises many interesting questions. Three major factors have been suggested. Firstly the small size of Scottish independent fund managers meant that the financing of a unit trust sales organisation was beyond their means. This argument is difficult to accept given the success of several small groups in becoming large unit trust organisations. The block offer system is ideally suited to small operations with limited sales manpower. Secondly it has been suggested that unit trust operations are relatively unprofitable and hence unattractive. The argument is clouded by the nature of unit trust charges. DTI regulations set a maximum and minimum price, based on the costs of construction and liquidation of a portfolio, within which units may be traded. Managers rarely use the full allowable spread and price within the spread according to the demand for the units. Units that are redeemed and then re-sold are particularly profitable since the managers pocket the difference between the buying and selling price.[19] However, even if this aspect of unit trust income is ignored and consideration restricted to investment fee income the argument is unappealing given the typically lower management fees of investment trusts. The unit trust market is a competitive one but we have been assured by several small unit groups that provided costs are tightly controlled, even small unit trusts are profitable. Thirdly, it has been suggested that, for many investment trusts that control investment, managers have felt it inappropriate that they should be managing a competing investment vehicle. Such views are hard to support since refusal to embrace unit trust management simply deprives the trust's shareholders of the profits to be made in this area.

On balance it is difficult to escape the view that Scottish investment managers, both independent and insurance based, have been over cautious and either failed to innovate or turned their innovatory talents elsewhere. The failure by Scottish fund managers to play a major part in the unit trust market must represent one of the clearest examples of missed opportunities, poor marketing and lack of innovation in recent Scottish financial history.

Investment Trusts

The importance of Scotland in the management of investment trusts has long been recognised. From the early successful beginnings of the Scottish American Investment Trust founded by Robert Fleming in Dundee and registered as a company in 1879, the investment trust movement in Scotland has grown to 52 trusts with an asset value of £5790 million and a market value of £4488 million (end 1985) representing almost 35 per cent of the UK industry (asset value £16.16 billion, market value £12.94 billion).[20] Despite this growth recent years have not been easy for the trusts. The mid-1960s saw the environment faced by the trusts become noticeably more hostile largely as a result of fiscal changes, increasing inflation and intensified competition for savings. Despite recent improvements with the abolition of exchange control (1979) and favourable changes in the tax system, the trusts continue to face difficult operating conditions. The tax advantages of group pension schemes and the prohibition on promotion of their shares and of paying commission to intermediaries on share sales because of the Prevention of Fraud (Investments) Act put them at a competitive disadvantage *vis-à-vis* the other major portfolio investment vehicles. The relatively slow rate of growth of assets of the investment trusts compared to unit trusts, their most direct competitor, is graphically illustrated by data from The Association of Investment Trust Companies – the market value of its members at the end of 1974 was £1510 million, representing 8.7 per cent of UK-registered equities. By end 1984 the total market value was £10991 million representing 5.4 per cent of UK equities. The absolute growth in assets has also masked a steady decline in the number of trusts, the decline being most marked amongst the independent investment trusts (table 8.7).

Table 8.7. Growth in the investment trust market (assets in £ million).

	1975[1]		1978[2]		1984[3]		1985[4]	
	Scot.	Other	Scot.	Other	Scot.	Other	Scot.	Other
Net Assets	1797	3789	2016	4142	5568	9529	5790	10373
Mean Value	35	22	44	28	118	89	111	77
No. of Trusts	51	174	46	150	47	107	52	110
No. independent	13	30	12	19	5	5	5	n/a
Scot. Trusts as % total assets	32		33		37		36	

1. Figures from Arnaud (1977) for end of year.
2. Figures from first Investment Trust Yearbook (1978). Trust details as of accounting year end.
3. Figures from Investment Trust Yearbook (1985) 31 December 1984.
4. Figures from Wood Mackenzie.

Takeovers from both within and outside the sector, liquidations and unitisations have exacted a remorseless toll on the English trusts, although with the continued existence of the discount it is of considerable interest as to why the reduction has not been greater.[21] The decline in the number of Scottish trusts has been small[22] reflecting their larger size, the fewer independents, the success of some managers particularly Ivory & Sime in starting new trusts and the relative unwillingness of managers to liquidate or unitise.

In turn, this unwillingness has its roots in the characteristics of the trust's shareholdings and the influence management can wield on shareholders. The small size and independence of some of the management groups and the greater risks they consequently face may have made them less willing to innovate or diversify.

The relationship of the management groups to the trusts is a complex one. The management group negotiate a management contract with each trust outlining the services the managers will provide and the basis on which they will charge. Contracts provide for termination with frequently three or even five years' notice required. This long termination period, in sharp contrast to the immediate termination common to investment management contracts for pension funds, emphasises the close relationship that normally exists between the management groups and their trusts. Members of the management group may be members of the investment trust board,[23] whilst investment trusts may be substantial shareholders in the management group.[24] These close inter-relationships may provide an explanation for the caution and conservatism that has been exhibited by some Scottish management groups. They may also provide an explanation for the continued existence of many trusts despite the existence of a discount which makes it worthwhile to liquidate or unitise the trusts.

The charges of the management groups are typically modest by unit trust standards possibly reflecting their greater average size and more conservative investment policies with lower turnover and longer holding periods. The inability of shareholders to redeem their holdings directly, in contrast to unit trusts, enables investment trusts to invest over a longer time horizon and gives much greater flexibility in investment policy although consistently poor performance may result in a takeover or demands for new management. The increase in unit trust charges of recent years has however, filtered through to Scottish investment trusts. Expenses (per cent of assets managed) for Scottish trusts averaged 0.35 per cent in 1977 but 0.52 per cent by the end of 1984. Comparable figures for Other UK trusts were 0.49 per cent in both periods.[25] The increase in management expenses was not spread amongst all trusts. The trusts, typically large, with the lowest management expenses registered no increase. The increases were concentrated amongst the smaller, more specialised trusts with one, specialising in special situations, apparently levying 2.4 per cent.[26] The increase in costs of the more specialised trusts stems in part from the general increase in fees that has marked all sections of the investment industry induced by a greater awareness of the market and the demand for investment services. The growth in pension fund business has offered an opportunity for all investment managers and led them to demand high fees and rewards. Some Scottish investment managers faced with finite management resources have concentrated their activities on the most profitable sectors of the market. A faltering of the growth of pension fund business may well lead to a reversal of these increases although the much higher level of fees that prevails in the US is likely to deter US competitors and provide new markets for UK fund managers. The other important cause of increased fees arises from a pressure on costs induced by the much greater emphasis on specialisation, particularly venture capital and specialised overseas investment, which has marked the investment trust scene in recent years and demands greater expertise from the managers than formerly. With institutions owning a substantial part of the equity of investment trusts there has been a demand for trusts to manage investments which the institutions find difficult to manage themselves. Potential institutional holders of investment trusts, such as insurance companies and pension funds do not require non-specialised portfolio investment that they can do for themselves. To hold a trust they either require a large discount so that the investment trust's management costs are absorbed, or demand specialised investment expertise that they lack themselves. One way in which many trusts have responded has been to increase their overseas investments. Aided by the removal of exchange control, the trusts, many of whom have traditionally been substantial investors overseas, have increased their foreign holdings. AITC statistics for all trusts reveal the changes. In 1960 UK investments represented 71 per cent of their assets and the USA 19 per cent. By 1970 the figures were 62 per cent and 26 per cent, and by 1980 60 per cent and 22 per cent. In 1984 UK assets were 46 per cent and USA 30 per cent.[27] Scotland has traditionally invested rather more heavily overseas, as table 8.8 reveals. It is particularly interesting that in 1979 investment in Japan by all trusts was 3 per cent. By 1984 it had risen to 15 per cent. Investment in Europe in the same period fell from 2.4 per cent to 1 per cent. The greater orientation of Scottish managers to the US is apparent although the same does not appear true of investment in Japan.

Table 8.8. Geographical spread of trust assets.

		1978	1984	1985[1]
Scottish trusts invested in securities of	UK	57	44	47
	USA	30	33	31
	Japan	n/a	n/a	13
Other trusts invested in securities of	UK	66	52	52
	USA	20	26	26
	Japan	n/a	n/a	15

1. Wood Mackenzie. US figures include Canada.
Sources: AITC and Wood Mackenzie.

The difficulties of measuring investment performance have already been explored. The AITC Yearbook provides interesting performance figures for the sector as a whole, revealing the success of investment trusts (table 8.9).

Table 8.9. Investment trust performance.

1 January	1946	1960	1970	1980	1985
Investment Trust Price Index	100	608	1128	1365	4085
de Zoete Equity Price Index	100	271	358	443	1135
Trusts relative to Equity Index	100	224	315	308	360

Source: de Zoete and Bevan.

Unfortunately, attractive as such comparisons are, they do not allow for risk (particularly relevant given the ability of the trusts to gear themselves up) and nor do the indices adequately reflect the investment possibilities open to the trusts. Neither Lyall's (1983) careful study, noted earlier, for the period 1971–80 nor Guy (1978) for an earlier period, could find evidence indicating that the trusts secured superior risk-adjusted performance. In the absence of any evidence, and given the conclusions of the efficient market hypothesis, it must be assumed that the trusts do no better than might be expected by chance although it is possible that investment trusts, as a result of the discount, gearing and lower management costs outperform unit trusts. A discount of twenty per cent implies that an investor has twenty-five per cent more assets invested on his behalf for every one pound of his capital in the trust. Even if the discount is permanent, the extra capital will secure higher income than would otherwise be possible and in the long run this must be to the advantage of the trusts' shareholders.

The long-run future of the trusts is unlikely to depend on the performance of the trusts unless it removes the discount. Removal of the discount is at the heart of the problems of the industry since it makes it unattractive to issue new trusts or raise new capital and makes it profitable to liquidate existing ones.[28] Rationalisation and restructuring is one possibility; extensive marketing and sales innovations another. Some steps have been taken in the direction of improved marketing with the trusts linking themselves to other financial services. Three types of scheme are currently on offer: life assurance, personal pension plans and savings and dividend reinvestment schemes. The life assurance schemes offer investors the opportunity to invest in a fund of investment trusts. The schemes are analogous to the unit linked schemes common in the unit trust sector and are now being offered by at least six insurance companies. The personal pension schemes are similar in many ways and involve an assurance society investing part of the premiums in one or more investment trusts. Again a variety of schemes are now on offer, all of very recent vintage, and suggesting a possible growth market for investment trust shares. Dividend reinvestment facilities have been offered by the two Alliance trusts since 1969 and by the London Trust since 1970. However, in 1984, Foreign and Colonial (F & C) and Globe and in 1985 the Fleming Trusts introduced schemes which allow shareholders (and non-shareholders of the F & C and Fleming Trusts) to make regular monthly purchases of their shares as well as offering reinvestment and other savings facilities. Other trusts are planning to offer such facilities. It is too early to judge the effectiveness of such provisions but in so far as they make investment by the small saver easier it must encourage the purchase of investment trust shares. The introduction of the Personal Equity Plan will also help investment trusts in the small saver market although the restrictions on holdings of investment trusts will reduce the potential impact on the sector.

Unless dramatic improvements in marketing are achieved, the outlook for the trusts is not good. To be successful they must endeavour to tap the same market as the unit trusts. Asset Pricing theory suggests that investors will not pay for something they can do themselves. Institutional investors can easily and cheaply secure diversification and can have no interest in buying this service except at a heavily discounted price. It is only in the personal sector that a profitable market can exist for such a service. Specialist management will always have a market among the institutions but the number of specialist opportunities that large institutions cannot exploit themselves is small. The future for most trusts cannot lie in this direction.

Innovative marketing does not imply an aping of unit trust advertising techniques. Unit trusts cater, in large part, for the unsophisticated private investor. Investment trusts could cater for the better off, more sophisticated private investor. The low management costs of many of the larger investment trusts together with their ability to gear and their wide investment powers, confer on them advantages which could be usefully exploited. The problem is to convince investors that they have a product worth buying. It requires the managers to move from a defensive to an aggressive posture and to convince the potential investor that they have his best interests at heart. Investment trusts to survive must market themselves to the personal sector at the same time as they take action to reduce the discount by any suitable measure such as shorter management contracts and the introduction of annual winding-up provisions so as to reduce the profitability of institutional raids and increase the trust's ability to expand and issue new capital. Discounts may always arise but it is essential that they are sufficiently small that there is no incentive to break up a trust. Investment trusts provide a service to investors that includes all that an authorised unit trust can do and more besides. There is no inherent reason why they should decline in importance. They do, however, have to accept that survival is much more than a matter of good performance. The aim has to be to make themselves more appealing to the personal sector. The importance of Scottish fund managers in investment trust management suggests that the future prospects of the Scottish fund management industry depend on how well fund managers take this lesson to heart.[29]

Pension Funds

Pension funds are financial institutions which accrue funds to meet future pension liabilities. They are normally established by an organisation, commercial, industrial or government, for its employees and hold assets, accumulated from employee contributions, independently of the business of the employer. Funded, occupational schemes, the predominant pension arrangement in the private, nationalised industry and local authority sectors are of two types. Self-administered schemes where the funds are invested directly by the fund, and insured schemes where the actuarial risk is borne by a life assurance office. Under an insured arrangement, a company or institution wishing to pay its employees a pension delegates the entire process to an insurance company. Its pension fund payments become part of the common investment pool of the insurance company which accepts an obligation to provide a pension according to the contractual terms agreed on.

Self-administered schemes frequently, wholly or partly, sub-contract the fund management to other financial institutions. Two types of contract are common. The funds may be merged within a larger investment portfolio as part of a 'pooled' pension fund arrangement in which the fund receives units in one of three investment vehicles; an exempt unit trust, a property unit trust which invests in real property or a managed fund which operates under a special form of unit linked insurance pension policy. Alternatively, the funds may be managed as an entirely separate entity in a 'segregated fund'. The choice of pension fund arrangement depends in large part on the size of the pension fund flows. Very small pension funds normally choose the insurance route, very large the segregated fund path.[30]

Fund management of self-administered schemes is split between both life assurance (see chapter 7) and other financial institutions such as clearing banks, merchant banks, stockbrokers and independent fund managers. A recent survey[31] of the top twenty-four pension fund managers included two firms from Scotland; Murray Johnstone managing £1172 million and Ivory & Sime managing £1027 million, 21st and 23rd in the list respectively. Total pension fund assets managed by the two represented 3 per cent of the £68.2 billion managed by the top twenty-four firms. The poor Scottish performance reflected the dominance of the merchant banks and stockbrokers in this area of investment management in which only five firms, two of them Scottish, could be described as independent fund managers. Other Scottish fund managers are involved in the pension fund market but most are poorly represented, as table 8.10 reveals. Figures on the UK/Overseas distribution of assets are also provided for 1984, although the divergence between the fund managers makes generalisations impossible.

Growth for many managers has been rapid, reflecting in part their small base and more importantly the size of the pension fund market. The acquisi-

Table 8.10. Pension fund management in Scotland.

	1985 Total £m	1984 Total £m	1984 Equities UK %	1984 Overseas %
Independent Fund Managers				
Baillie Gifford	353	224	55	24
British Linen	490	300	50	27
Martin Currie	103	31	65	11
Edinburgh Fund Managers	163	87	11	77
Hodgson Martin	6	4	30	35
Ivory & Sime	1200	919		
Murray Johnstone	1200	940	65	13
Royal Bank	680	737	58	18
W. Scott	530	450		
Stewart Ivory & Co.	270	23	24	69
Capital Portfolio Managers	—	30		
Insurance Companies – Segregated Portfolios				
Scottish Amicable (SCAMPI)	381	212	46	16
Scottish Mutual	—	18	49	11
Scottish Widows	—	180	44	15
Standard Life	472	201	51	15

Figures are end 1984 and end 1985 where available. In most cases figures include overseas pension funds.

Sources: Pensions Fund Managers Survey May 1985, May 1986, interviews and correspondence.

Insurance Company figures included for comparative purposes.

tion of the management contract on part of a large pension fund can greatly expand the manager's business as the experience of Martin Currie in securing part of the British Rail Pension Fund illustrates. Martin Currie expect an increase in funds under management estimated at £250 million. The acquisition of clients is predominantly through pension fund actuaries and consultants who are approached by their pension fund clients to recommend investment managers. The adviser constructs a short list of potential investment managers who are then invited to make a presentation to the pension fund managers. The process is frequently likened to a 'beauty parade' with the pension fund managers attempting to assess the quality and suitability of the investment managers. This selection process places two hurdles in the path of investment managers aspiring to manage pension fund assets. The first is to be short listed by the pension fund consultants. By its nature the criteria for selection will depend on both the requirements of the client and the views of the consultants in addition to the talents of the investment managers as demonstrated typically by their past investment performance.

Investment Management

The predominantly London location of the actuarial and consulting firms does not appear to be a significant hindrance to Scottish investment managers. The major investment management firms view the whole of the UK as their market, a circumstance forced on them by the small size of the Scottish pension fund market documented earlier.

The second hurdle to be overcome is selection by the pension fund managers. There can never be any guarantee that a presentation will be successful but success is more likely if the investment managers market themselves and their philosophy. Past performance is of some interest, as indeed is specialist knowledge of particular investment markets, but more important is the underlying investment philosophy of the fund managers – long or short time horizons, general or specialist portfolios, predominantly overseas or UK investment. The extent to which this accords with the views of the trustees of the pension fund will, in large part, determine the success or failure of investment managers in acquiring pension fund business.

The role that investment management charges play in the choice of investment managers is unclear. Pension fund managers do not emphasise them as important although they must have some impact at the margin. As a result of specialisation, charges have risen in recent years but for the majority of managers they are low in comparison with other investment vehicles. However, the low administrative costs and growing size of many funds suggest that investment managers find the business very profitable. The requirement of pension funds to invest their surplus – income from contributions plus interest and dividends on existing assets less pension payments and any administration costs borne by the fund – has meant an attractive and substantial built-in growth from acquiring pension fund clients. So long as inflation and growth in GDP continue this situation is likely to persist.

Not all investment managers charge directly for their services (see table 8.11 for the range of charges). Stockbrokers have in the past relied on their commission charges, a practice that may change with reductions in commission scales. Merchant banks, it has been suggested, may also offer preferential rates, since spare cash may be kept on deposit with the bank. Many of the independent fund managers perceive these zero or preferential charges as working against their interests.[32] Changes in commission scales as a result of the ending of the Stock Exchange minimum commission rule are seen as an important marketing opportunity that should allow the independent fund managers to compete more effectively. However, pension managers have been at pains to stress to us the long-term relationship which they build up with their investment managers. Commission charges may loosen pension managers' relationships with some investment managers but there is unlikely to be any wholesale dramatic change.

Charges and performance, as noted elsewhere, cannot be divorced from each other since high charges, whether direct or indirect (for example,

Table 8.11. Fund management charges.

	Minimum Investment	Annual Charge
Baillie Gifford	£40000	To £10m 0.4%, next £10m 0.25%, over £20m by negotiation
British Linen	none	To £1m 0.5%, £1m-£13m 0.3%, over £3m. negotiable
Martin Currie	£15000	By negotiation
Edinburgh Fund Managers	£10000	£10000 on first £2m, £2m-£5m 0.4%, £5m-£10m 0.3%, excess 0.1%
Hodgson Martin		Flexible
Ivory & Sime	£30000	To £6m 0.5%, £6m-£15m 0.25%, over £15m negotiable
Murray Johnstone	£10000	To £2m 0.35%, next £3m 0.25%, next £5m 0.2%, next £10m 0.125%, next £30m 0.1%, next £50m 0.075%, next £100m 0.05%
Royal Bank	—	To £0.25m 0.65%, next £0.75m 0.23%, next £9m 0.18%, over £10m negotiable.
Stewart Ivory & Co.	£10000	To £10m 0.5%, £10m-£20m 0.375%, £20m 0.25%
Insurance Company – Segregated Portfolios		
Scottish Amicable (SCAMPI)	—	To £4m 0.3%, £4m-£100m 0.1%, 0.05% on excess
Scottish Mutual	Negotiable	To £5m 0.3%, next £5m 0.2%, over £10m 0.1%
Scottish Widows	—	To £10m 0.5%, next £10m 0.25%, over £20m 0.1%
Standard Life	—	£10000+ to £5m 0.3%, next £5m 0.2%, next £30m 0.1%, excess over £40m 0.05%

Sources: Pensions Fund Management Survey May 1985, May 1986. Insurance Company figures included for comparative purposes.

extracted by means of excessive turnover) will reduce performance. It is commonly claimed by investment fund managers (and equally commonly refuted by many pension managers) that pension funds emphasise short-term performance. Fund management firms are typically on short-term contracts and the consequences of failure to perform are held as a goad. Evidence for such a view beyond hearsay is difficult to acquire. Many pension funds appear prepared to consider performance over a three, five or even eight year cycle. Indeed it has been represented to us that the vast majority of pension funds find performance of little interest and largely ignore it. Certainly given the difficulty of measuring and securing above-average performance it would be alarming if this view of short-term performance was correct. The investment performance of the pension fund does of course benefit the contributing firm or its pensioners or both. Depending on the arrangements of the particular scheme, firms as major contributors must often meet the balance of any costs required to provide the benefits promised and in more favourable circumstances may be allowed to reduce their contributions to the scheme. Good performance is clearly to their benefit.

The market opportunities provided by changes in the City, whilst welcome, are not unlimited. Stronger groupings in the City, formed by alliances of stockbrokers, merchant banks and others will provide strong, well endowed competitors. Independent fund managers may have the advantage of a change in commission structure forcing the imposition of fees on clients, but they will not have the marketing and financial muscle of the bigger groups. Financial groups that can service every aspect of an industrial company's requirements must have substantial competitive advantages over the small independent fund managers. Despite this, changes in the City's structure must create new opportunities and it is possible that the difficulty will not be lack of opportunity but constraints on the growth of existing fund managers. The constraints arise from their own shortage of fund management resources. The response will almost certainly be a concentration on the larger, more profitable pension areas.

Constraints on managerial resources are not necessarily easily remedied. They arise from at least two causes. A lack of suitable trained manpower, made worse by the persistent leakage of talent to London and overseas, and the needs of the fund management business for continuity of managers and personal service. It is difficult to combine these requirements and attract staff particularly in competition with large financial organisations. The diversity of activities the larger institutions can provide offer a range of opportunities to their staff that the smaller independent Scottish fund managers cannot hope to offer.

A second market opportunity that has been much discussed, but as yet little acted upon, is offered by overseas pension funds. Both America and Japan have enacted regulations requiring funds to diversify internationally. The increasing internationalisation of financial markets suggests that such trends will continue. The advantages are material. Dimson, Hodges and Marsh (1980) demonstrated that international diversification enabled risk (variability of return) on a portfolio to fall from the level of 29 per cent for a UK portfolio to 13 per cent for a world portfolio. Both W. Scott and Ivory & Sime have attracted significant amounts of foreign funds ($140 million and £250 million respectively at end 1985) through joint ventures with overseas banks and institutions, and several other fund managers have been active, on a similar basis, in this area. The total however, whilst growing, is small as a percentage of funds from overseas available for investment through UK fund managers. Scottish fund managers have been slow to capitalise on their international investment expertise as the Bank of England survey indicates, and may well have missed the period of easiest growth. Competition for funds has been intensifying as American and Japanese fund managers endeavour to share in the business. UK fund managers are helped by the low level of fees they charge compared with the US but against that the conclusions of Dimson *et al.* should be considered.

> ... many fund managers are frightened off by the fact that they 'know' far less about American, German or Japanese stocks than they do about their UK counterparts. This should not be a deterrent. As long as investors in each national market have the information they need to assess domestic companies' prospects, then their trading activity will ensure that stock prices reflect all relevant information. Foreign investors can then safely buy the stocks, even if they do not know about the companies. They can rely on the domestic investors to keep the prices fair.

Putting it bluntly, it must be expected that as buying foreign equities is simplified, there will be less need to use overseas specialists.

Ancillary Activities

Despite their low representation in unit trust investment management Scottish firms or operations have picked up useful business related to the unit trust sector. Save and Prosper provide accounting services to their own trusts (based in London) in addition to a number of other major unit trusts through their Edinburgh office whilst the Scottish banks play a significant role as unit trust trustees (table 8.12).

Table 8.12. Unit trust trusteeship.

Trustees	1974		1979		1984	
	No.	£m.	No.	£m.	No.	£m.
Bank of Scotland	30	79	45	509	63	1378
Clydesdale	8	5	7	61	22	302
General Accident	2	26	4	139	19	775
Royal Bank	59	169	72	571	132	2233
Total Scottish	99	279	128	1279	236	4687
Williams & Glyn	17	54	27	165	74	1525
Total UK	377	1272	450	3858	748	15081
Scottish %		22		33		31

Sources: Unit Trust Year Books 1975, 1980, 1985.

The function of trustees is to safeguard the assets of the trust on the behalf of unitholders. Assets are held in the trustee's name and the trustee settles all investment transactions. The trustee has to ensure that the trust is managed within the terms of the trust deeds and as part of the work they vet adverts to check that they do not mislead investors.

Trustee's fees are based on the value of funds under management with a loading added if any of the fund is invested overseas. The actual fee is subject to negotiation but normally averages around 1/20 per cent per annum on a fund of £10 million. There has been a high degree of competition for business and the Scottish institutions have been noticeably successful in retaining and increasing their share.

The AITC yearbook provides some useful information on the firms offering services to investment trusts. Fifty-six firms have accounts with Scottish banks (including their London branches but excluding Williams & Glyn, now absorbed into the Royal Bank, and recognising that trusts frequently have more than one banker) whilst 38 use Scottish registrars. Scottish auditors or Scottish branches of UK firms (46) and solicitors (40) are also well represented. Scottish stockbrokers (17), reflecting their private client orientation, were rather less successful whilst no trusts employed a Scottish merchant bank. As a comparative guide the English domiciled trusts almost always used London-based merchant banks, solicitors, registrars and stockbrokers although banking facilities were also provided by a number of foreign banks. Such statistics provide no guide to the size of business transacted but they do provide a good qualitative assessment, confirmed by interviews, of the strengths (and weaknesses) of the Scottish financial infrastructure. Scottish domiciled investment trusts generate business throughout the financial community so that the health of the Scottish investment trust sector is of consequence for the financial infrastructure used by all financial institutions.

Pension funds are also important users of services besides fund management. Performance measurement for funds throughout the UK is provided by WM Company from its Edinburgh office. WM Company had its origins in the services offered by Wood Mackenzie to its clients. On the acquisition of Wood Mackenzie by Hill Samuel the partners floated the computer services into a separate company. WM Company provide performance evaluation, valuation and investment accounting services. Some 30 per cent of its business is overseas. It employs 350 people, two-thirds of whom are graduates. The high degree of capital intensity required in the business has probably restrained its expansion although growth has been rapid despite the competition from well-funded competitors such as Merrill Lynch, Extel and Datastream. With the exception of WM Company the majority of financial services in Scotland are provided by London-based firms. Reed Stenhouse, based in Glasgow, provide consultancy services but there are no other major pension consultants or actuaries based in Scotland although many of the large English actuarial and consulting firms have offices in Scotland. The other Scottish firms are small. Total Scottish employment in such ancillary services is difficult to ascertain but almost certainly rivals the numbers employed by the independent fund managers in Scotland. Such a comparison emphasises that the contribution of fund management to the Scottish economy comes not only from its direct employment, which can scarcely be more than four hundred people, but from other indirect effects. Salaries, bonuses and profits in the sector are very high and make an important contribution to regional spending. There may also be financing advantages particularly due to local knowledge to Scottish companies, especially new and small ones, although the fund managers report a lack of profitable opportunities to invest in Scotland.

Conclusions

The traditional dependence of Scottish fund managers on the investment trust industry is changing. Dynamic new firms together with some of the more forward-looking established firms and assurance companies interested in diversifying are taking the fund management industry into growing areas notably pension funds, overseas asset management and unit trusts. Changes in the City present new opportunities for the acquisition of funds as well as increased competition. The record of some fund managers in the past has been poor. They failed to innovate and recognise the importance of new markets, but changes in the market for fund management caused particularly by investment trust takeovers, have led to new, larger, strengthened groups. The Scottish presence in the fund management market is still small. Total employment is low although reduced stockbroking commission may encourage management groups to conduct their own research with beneficial effects on employment. There is no reason why the Scottish share of the fund management market should not grow so long as fund managers accept that the market has changed. Marketing and innovation are of more consequence than performance. Fund management is only half the battle. Selling the product is the other half and it is here that sustained improvement and expenditure is required. Fund management does not require a London presence although unit trust sales may require a UK distribution network. The greatest increase in business, at least in the short run, is probably to be obtained from pension fund management and it is here that managers should be concentrating their efforts.

NOTES
1. This definition excludes stockbrokers and others who provide advice but do not have discretion to act. Strictly funds run to mimic an index would be excluded but managers generally retain some degree of discretion in these cases. In truth the dividing line between discretion and advice is often a fine one! The extent of diversification may also be limited particularly as funds specialise in particular areas of the international economy. Even here it is rare for the portfolios not to be reasonably diversified since most assets are highly correlated and relatively few holdings are sufficient to provide substantial diversification. (See for example Draper 1986.)

2. Opinions vary on the appropriate size for in-house management. Some would suggest £60 million and significant growth as being the minimum, others as being perhaps £100 million. A small operation of a fund manager, analyst and supporting staff implies that £100 million might not be an unreasonable size given the level of fees recorded in table 8.10.
3. Wood Mackenzie figures quoted in *The Times*, 9 October 1985.
4. The definition excludes investment trusts that are independent. The result is to bias the figures for investment trusts against Scotland. It also excludes the assured pension fund business of the assurance companies. Whilst it may be argued that this is not easily transferable business and should not therefore be included it must be remembered that there is considerable competition for this business. Exclusion of their own pension schemes also understates the capacity of the institutions to undertake investment management.

   The response rate of the survey was in excess of three-quarters and included all the largest fund managers. Some estimate of excluded business is provided by comparing the £23200 million of the UK sample managed for unit and investment trusts with the £30400 million estimated by the industry. Part of the difference arises from the sample definition adopted.
5. Pension fund investment is divided in official statistics between the superannuation fund and insurance tables. The insurance statistics include 'the pension schemes operated on behalf of other companies' whilst the superannuation details comprise 'the self-administered funded schemes of local authorities, the rest of the public sector and the private sector.'
6. Estimates derived from interviews, Pensions Fund Managers Survey May 1985, Pension Funds and their Advisers 1985, Crawford's Directory of City Connections 1986 and NAPF Year Book 1985.
7. Estimates derived from Pension Funds and their Advisers 1985 and NAPF Year Book 1985. The estimates are only suggestive since neither yearbook is comprehensive in its coverage. The former covers companies with over 500 employees and some smaller schemes where assets exceed £2 million. The information is the latest available for a scheme and is not available for one point in time. For some funds no information as to market value and contributions is available or the information may relate to book values. The NAPF yearbook covers members of the National Association of Pension Funds. Information is the latest available for a scheme although in some cases relevant information is missing. Despite these caveats the yearbooks provide good coverage of larger pension schemes and the estimates can be regarded as reasonably accurate.
8. DCL & Associated Companies (now Guinness), SSEB, Lothian Regional Council, Bank of Scotland, Royal Bank of Scotland, General Accident, Coats Patons.
9. It would be wrong to suggest that there has been no evidence questioning the efficient market hypothesis. The 1978 issue of the *Journal of Financial Economics* was entirely devoted to examining the anomalies in the empirical evidence on the hypothesis whilst a paper by Banz (1981) on the effects of size on returns has led to extensive empirical analysis, but as yet, no comprehensive explanation of its cause. Papers by Shiller (1981) on the volatility of stock prices also pose interesting questions for efficient market theory. Despite these studies, however, the vast majority of recent empirical evidence provides results that support the concept of an efficient market.

   It is also necessary to qualify the assertion that it is unlikely that investment managers have techniques that can consistently select successful investments. Studies such as those of Banz suggest that the Capital Asset Pricing model may not be an adequate model of the pricing of small companies since investors

Notes

appear to be compensated with extra return. Investors who invest in such companies can secure above average risk adjusted returns. The suspicion remains, however, that the extra return is not something for nothing. Small companies probably involve extra risk which has not as yet been adequately modelled. Other techniques for securing extra return (risk adjusted) include improved techniques for forecasting beta (Rosenberg 1976) and for portfolio selection (Treynor and Black 1972). We have also assumed away the possibility of fund managers securing information more rapidly than the rest of the market and using this to their advantage. In so far as managers specialise in particular areas such as venture capital there may be considerable scope for securing such information. There can be little prospect of such ability for general investment.

10. Unit trust managers make an initial charge to cover the selling and other expenses on initial purchase of a portfolio. This charge immediately reduces the investor's wealth and hence his investment portfolio. Purchase of shares by an individual through a stockbroker results in transaction costs with a similar effect.

11. Purchase of stockbroking services is often tied to the acquisition of the products of stockbroking research, the benefits of which may reduce the costs associated with stock turnover although the costs are unlikely to be reduced to zero. Davies and Canes (1978) provide evidence of the value of brokers' research in the US but other studies provide a less favourable picture.

12. For a non-technical discussion of the problems of performance measurement see the Wood Mackenzie & Co. 1985 *Investment Trust Annual*.

    However, a difference in approach is worth noting. WM believe that good performance exists but it is difficult to measure. The emphasis in this chapter is that good performance happens by chance. The fund manager's role is to see that performance is not diluted by high and excessive management charges. Not all would subscribe to this viewpoint. A number of techniques have been considered in the literature proposing methods of improving investment selection skills. Accepting their theoretical validity the problem concerns the trade-off between the size of the gains and the cost of implementing the techniques. We believe the gains to be small and have yet to see any reliable, consistent empirical evidence showing otherwise.

13. Some investment managers such as Murray Johnstone have supplied us with performance comparisons which indicate the consistent growth of their portfolios over a number of recent years. Their pension fund performance, for example, has consistently beaten the industry average in each of the past seven years. It is impossible to rule out the possibility that this arises from superior management. However, by chance some managers may be expected to perform well over a number of years. Our empirical tests are unable to distinguish between the two possibilities. Accurate comparisons require long series of data and the analysis of such data does not indicate that managers, in general, have superior management abilities.

14. The competition is not necessarily portfolio investments. Building societies and national savings provide other competing investment media.

15. Offshore unit trusts are excluded although managers such as Murray Johnstone do offer investors such vehicles. Offshore trusts are normally companies not unit trusts. They are run from tax havens and are not subject to UK tax or regulation. They are consequently able to offer a wider range of securities although their non-resident status does not offer investors comprehensive protection. To qualify as offshore funds the management must not take place in the UK although in many cases this is a polite fiction maintained by overseas offices that do not in practice exercise discretion.

16. Save and Prosper were jointly owned by a number of large shareholders including Ivory & Sime, Baring Brothers, Robert Fleming and the Bank of Scotland through the British Linen Bank's pension scheme. In the late 1970s ownership changed so that Save and Prosper in effect became a subsidiary of Fleming's. Investment management was taken in-house with the secondment of Fleming personnel and concentrated in London. The Edinburgh office was left as an administrative and marketing organisation.
17. A study of the usefulness of UK unit trust objectives (Draper 1986) found that objectives relating to domestic equities provided little useful information to the investor.
18. *The Times,* 23 November 1985.
19. The accounts of Edinburgh Fund Managers (January 1985), for example, show fund management fees to be £3.079 million and the profit from unit trust trading as £1.451 million. For 1986 the respective figures were £3.332 million and £1.613 million.
20. Figures from Wood Mackenzie. AITC figures for end 1984 were 47 trusts with an asset value of £5568 million, representing 37% of the UK industry by assets. Since the discount on Scottish trusts is slightly larger than on English trusts the percentage by market value is slightly lower.
21. The causes of the discount and hence its cure generate a great deal of controversy. The common suggestion that there is an oversupply of investment trust equity provides little explanation of why this should be so particularly given the growth of unit trusts, a portfolio vehicle with similar aims. Recently there have been suggestions that investment trusts represent an inefficiency but there is no clear analysis of what this means. The evidence does not support the contention that the investment trust market is inefficient in the conventional use of the term.

    In a perfect market trusts would be priced according to the value of their assets. Allowing for transaction costs and taxes there would be a band around this value reflecting the costs associated with creating and breaking trusts up. As soon as prices went below the lower bound liquidation would follow. The evidence suggests that trust prices frequently violate this condition but liquidation does not follow because of institutional rigidities. The structure of trust groups is such as to make liquidation difficult despite substantial potential profits, a reality that is reflected in large and sustained discounts. This suggests that a removal or reduction of market imperfections would reduce the level of the discount. In particular, action to make liquidation easier would go some way to meeting the problem. Any reduction in the discount will have implications for the shareholdings of the trusts. At present, many trusts are held by institutions that do not require the services offered by the trusts. They are held because they offer the appropriate risk adjusted reward. In effect the management costs have been discounted by the discount. A reduction in the discount would make it sensible for institutions to sell and invest directly. The purchasers must be investors who require, and are willing to pay for, the services offered by the trusts. Trusts must market themselves to the personal sector.

    For a discussion of these issues see Draper and Stevens (1984) and Draper, Gibson and Stevens (1985).
22. Since 1980 eight Scottish trusts have disappeared whilst Scottish United merged with the Edinburgh Investment Trust. Twenty-five trusts outside Scotland lost their existence. Fifteen new trusts were started in Scotland compared to nine in the rest of the UK.
23. The AITC *Yearbook* indicates that every Scottish management group had at least one director on the board of an investment trust within its stable.

Notes

24. Major shareholdings in Stanecastle, Murray Johnstone, Edinburgh Fund Managers and Dunedin are all held by associated trusts. Ownership details are not known of all the fund management groups.
25. Calculated from the AITC *Yearbook* giving each trust an equal weighting. An average weighted by the trust's size would greatly reduce the mean cost.
26. The AITC *Yearbook* records the Edinburgh Financial Trust as having management expenses of 2.4% of assets. However, their management contract stipulates a quarterly management fee of ¼ per cent and must cast doubt on this figure.
27. The figures are only suggestive. Fluctuations in the market value of assets make comparisons such as these hazardous.
28. New trusts have been floated but generally embody significant modifications in their construction from the older investment trusts.
29. Wood, Mackenzie & Co. *Investment Trust Review of 1985* provide an interesting review of the possibilities open to investment trusts and note several areas where improvements could be made. Two suggestions of particular interest are the possibility of investment trusts linking up with a Building Society in order to provide a retail network for sales, and constructive investment by supplying venture capital and management skills. They cite the example of Govett trusts' bidding for control of Macarthy's Pharmaceuticals and suggest that the trusts could have a new role as catalysts of corporate change in industry.
30. For a discussion of the advantages of pooled versus segregated funds see Wolanski (1980).
31. *Financial Times* Pension Fund Investment Survey 1986. The figures differ from those of Pensions *Fund Managers Survey* May 1986. The Pensions *Fund Managers Survey* for 1985 suggested that Murray Johnstone, managing £940 million, Ivory & Sime £770 million and the Royal Bank £737 million were all in the top twenty pension fund investment managers.
32. This suggests that the cost of fund management is an important factor in selection.

9

PUBLIC VENTURE CAPITAL

This chapter considers the role of public venture capital within the Scottish economy. In contrast to chapter 6, which outlined the shape of merchant banking in Scotland and its role in mobilising capital, the concerns of this chapter are to chronicle the provision of development capital from public sources, as well as examine some aspects of the public-private sector interface and assess the impact of the ensuing provision. Following some introductory comments on the nature of public venture capital, the chapter concentrates on the role played by the Scottish Development Agency (SDA) and the Highlands and Islands Development Board (HIDB) as the two principal providers within Scotland. As befits two organisations very different in size the approach taken in the two cases differs. The divisional structure of the SDA allows us to restrict our comments solely to the investment function. In contrast, given the integrated nature of many of the HIDB's activities, a rather broader approach is required, although again the investment role is singled out for special attention.

The Need for Venture Capital

In recent years the upsurge of interest in the growth and development of small firms in the UK, together with the associated desire to encourage high technology based start-ups, have combined to create renewed, but rather belated, interest in venture capital. There has been a considerable diversity of market response over recent years and the emergence of a genuine venture capital market, serviced by an increasingly wide range of specialised institutions and Business Expansion Scheme (BES) funds. The Scottish financial sector was slow in producing institutions specialising in development or venture capital and in some ways remains relatively underdeveloped. Many of the existing providers would, of course, argue that there has been a consistent problem of the availability of appropriate projects in recent years, rather than of appropriate funds. Indeed, it is acknowledged that the lack of suitable indigenous businesses is one part of the problem. At the very least, however, there is some question about the range and quantity of genuine venture capital sources available within Scotland. Moreover, partly because of the relative scale of many of the funds and their limited experience by US standards, there is a fear of high technology and perhaps, also, of early commitment. There has also been a distinct lack of interest in extensive aftercare involvement in most forms of venture capital management, a reflection of the absence of both knowledge and experience.

Most of these observations could equally be levelled at the venture capital industry in the UK as a whole, especially when it is compared with the much more mature markets of the United States. For the Scottish economy, however, these weaknesses in the financial infrastructure pose serious questions about barriers to entry for innovative projects and it is, therefore, important to consider public sector initiatives which have been designed to bridge some of the observed gaps.

From the perspective taken in this study as a whole, the case for public venture capital largely stems from demonstrated deficiencies within the existing provision from the private sector, from financing problems arising from market imperfections and from differences between the private and social evaluation of the potential costs and benefits of a project. There are a number of circumstances where the overall economic development of the Scottish economy may be hindered through lack of a properly developed venture capital industry. In particular, projects where there is a high risk but potential high reward to the economy, or where the funding required is for a longer term than can be sustained through normal means may both require public sector support. In other circumstances it may be that the project emerges from a relatively unsophisticated management team or there may be a need for significant pre-project investigation and project preparation relative to the size and scale of the project. In some instances the costs of acquiring and processing information for the appraisal may be too high for private sector organisations to bear them alone. Some public sector assistance may be necessary, both to realise the potential of the project and in order to cope with the barriers to entry into the venture capital sector which for small businesses may include the inadequate security against which loans can be guaranteed.

One additional, and often, fundamental problem lies in the distinct lack of familiarity with the technology of potential projects within the highly specialised venture capital institutions. This criticism is of course, one which is often levelled against the UK financial system compared to that of France, Germany and Japan. Thus, it is possible that projects emanating from newer Scottish companies are not readily evaluated by their existing contacts within Scottish financial institutions, or are of too small a scale to be of interest to venture funds at either Scottish or UK level because of the high administrative costs. A minimum institutional investment of between £100000–250000 for equity investments is common. There is limited private sector provision in Scotland for companies wanting to raise less than £50000 of equity. These circumstances, among others, underlie aspects of HIDB investment in fish farming and SDA investment in start-up companies in electronics and health care. There are also cases where a rather longer term view of returns is required than is taken by traditional venture capitalists and where a particular benefit to Scotland as a whole is deemed to accrue.

Clearly, there are few of these circumstances which cannot, with time, be overcome in the private sector, given institutional development and an appropriate view of return on investment. However, in the last ten years or so, there is ample evidence of a number of these factors inhibiting certain types of development. It is therefore largely on such presumptions that the case for public venture capital activity exists in Scotland. The need may be a transitory one and might diminish as sectoral development occurs, but the problems facing the Scottish economy suggest otherwise.

Scottish Development Agency

Investment Philosophy

The initial period of SDA operation in this field was highly controversial and generally ineffective. Broadly speaking, until 1979 the investment function was reactive rather than proactive. It was apparently subject to external influences and this led to investment in a high number of risky and, on occasion, ill-considered projects. Private sector interest in collaborative action was invariably low in the face of an investment philosophy which gave limited attention to normal commercial criteria. While not all negative, nor always regarded by the financial sector in a balanced way, these early years did little to establish sectoral confidence in public venture capital in Scotland.

Faced with a new political environment post 1979, and shortly thereafter with new senior management, the general approach of the SDA over recent years has been quite different. The overall philosophy has been pragmatic, but has operated within more clearly enunciated guidelines. The Agency has, for example, consistently declared that it wishes to encourage the development of the private sector venture capital industry in Scotland, and particularly, of groups who intend to develop an effective after-care capacity within which they undertake to contribute a package of resources other than finance. It has generally been presumed that this additional means of adding value does not exist in sufficient measure within the private sector in Scotland. Yet, the need for technological, market and managerial knowledge to be added to venture capital projects in Scotland is vital. It is, therefore, in the filling of this gap that the SDA has seen its role in the investment function. Much of the capability to provide such a width of support comes from the range of its functions outwith investment and can be provided at marginal or no additional cost in sharp contrast to many private sector players. In consequence, the capability of the SDA to provide both finance and advice (in technology, management services, market research and product development) allows it to operate squarely as a venture capital provider.

In the specific pursuit of its investment function, the Agency has a financial duty, which is guided by the aim of achieving, over a rolling five-year period, a cash return at least equal to the cost of government borrowing over the same period. The financial duty is determined annually by the Scottish Office. Unrealised capital gains are not included in this financial return and the base on which it is measured does not exclude investments which have been written off in previous periods. In making loans, the SDA is required to charge a rate of interest not less than that paid by firms of the highest standing when raising finance. In short, it is not in the 'soft' money business. Central to the SDA philosophy has been the aim of maximising the involvement of private sector capital in its investment activities. Not only is this regarded as critical in terms of the joint development of the venture capital sector and in pursuit of 'gap filling', but it is also consistent with the Agency securing its objectives with a minimum level of involvement. The SDA is expected to dispose of investments when its continued involvement is no longer deemed necessary and as a public agency, its investment decisions are constrained by the need to prevent the generation of unfair effects on competitive firms and a normal requirement to restrict its shareholding to less than 30 per cent of voting rights.

The investment activity of the SDA does not, of course, operate in isolation from the other parts of its mission. In recent years therefore, a significant part of the investment function has been actively directed towards priority areas, which are regarded as having particular potential for generating growth in the Scottish economy. These include, for example, support for the major sectoral initiatives in electronics, health care, advanced engineering and energy related services, as well as in support of the development of technology transfer, indigenous enterprise and area development.

Investment Portfolio
For administrative purposes the investment function of the SDA is handled both by the Investment Directorate (ID) and by the Small Business Division (SBD). The exercise of the function as a whole is overseen by Scottish Development Finance Ltd, an SDA subsidiary with both internal and external directors.

The two parts of the portfolio differ in a number of ways. Based on an initial investment outlay value of some £31 million as at December 1985, 79 per cent of investment is in ID. Most of the ID investment is in preference or preferred ordinary shares in contrast to the SBD portfolio the bulk of which is in loans. Moreover, because of their scale and complexity, the majority of ID equity investments are made jointly with, and on the same terms, as private sector institutions. Such syndication is rare in SBD investments. To provide managerial incentive, especially in buyout or major financial reconstruction cases the shares of the ID are normally redeemable after an agreed period. As regards loans, these are normally made on a secured basis for periods of between five and twenty years.

The broad characteristics of the two components of the SDA's investment

Table 9.1. SDA investment profile.[1]

	HOID	SBD
No. of companies	112	621
Initial investment outlay	£22.1m	£8.9m
Employment		
Under 50	45%	—
50–100	42%	—
1–5	—	47%
6–10	—	20%
Sector		
SIC 3	30%	not applicable[2]
SIC 4	41%	
Portfolio (by date of first investment)		
Pre-1980	11%	13%
1980–83	53%	55%
1984–	36%	32%

1. As at 31 December 1985.
2. Measured by distribution of loans the SBD distribution in SIC 3 and SIC 4 is around 51 per cent.
Source: SDA.

portfolio are set out in table 9.1. It will be noted that the greater number of the investments is in smaller companies. The average ID investment is marginally over £0.25 million, while the average SBD investment is just under £15000. The sectoral focus in the ID case reflects in part the SDA's priority sectors (which account for some 30 per cent of the ID companies) as well as the overall industrial base. As the table indicates, the investment portfolio is relatively young. This is not surprising, given the short existence of the ID function and the general philosophy of searching for appropriate entry and exit points.

Impact
Set against this background, the public venture capital role of the SDA could be expected to result in a number of outcomes over the long term in its attempt to counteract market imperfections. It should enable viable projects to proceed where for one reason or another, other financial sources were reluctant to provide support at a particularly critical stage of a project. It might be expected, for example, to succeed in influencing capital markets in Scotland towards the adoption of more flexible and innovative techniques (especially in less conventional forms of equity); in the enhancing of risk management; and in the encouraging of diversification into non-quoted investments. More ambitiously it may, in effect, promote particular projects in view of their development pay-off, although it prefers not to be in the lead in this way. On occasion with larger projects, early Agency involvement is

now regarded as a 'seal of approval'. A further area of benefit arises from improved management performance of the recipient companies, a result of the significant level of after-care and direct interest in their on-going performance. The SDA portfolio is subject to close monitoring at investment executive level and invariably involves a right to nominate a non-executive director. The scale of private sector investment induced by Agency initiative in any given proposal is an important indicator of its success. Agency involvement can be readily calculated and in 1984–85 the ratio of SDA financial contribution to that of the private sector was 1:5. It is impossible to calculate what would have happened in the absence of either Agency initiative or Agency involvement in certain projects. Another vital dimension of investment impact is in the area of additional net effects on employment, output and investment. Although there are no published data to allow a full evaluation of these effects, it appears that the average investment per job created through SDA investment is much lower than through other instruments such as regional policy.

One of the most frequently perpetrated myths in this area is that there are projects which can readily be distinguished as appropriate for public venture capital and those that are not simply because they will succeed in any event. Most investment propositions handled by the SDA are in neither camp, but invariably move from their initial position as a result of the investment of time and funding. Ideally, if initially high risk, they move out of the intensive care phase implied by the presence of public venture capital and its attendant support structures. But even where a project does move and becomes eligible for wider funding interest, it is often necessary for SDA support to continue, alongside other investors. Such practical considerations are not only necessary in order to build sectoral confidence, they are essential for holding together a team of competent investment executives. Moreover, it would frequently be impossible to approach the targets set by financial duty if SDA investment did not stay with projects as the risk diminishes and the actual rewards increase. Again, the management of such companies are frequently keen to have existing investors stay with them. In effect, exit strategies are often difficult to determine and have to remain opportunistic.

In short, therefore, there are some serious doubts whether the measurement of financial duty, as currently practised, is sufficiently sensitive to measure the true effectiveness of SDA investment performance. By existing measures, the returns are modest, although they might be expected to improve as the equity component of the portfolio matures, given that new pressures for earlier realisation of investments are not brought to bear. But the fact that the Agency does not make a commercial return on its investments might suggest that it is not simply taking investment opportunities neglected by the private sector.

Given the declared interest of the SDA in encouraging the development of the venture capital industry in Scotland, it remains a matter of some debate as to how the Agency's investment function differs from that of a rapidly changing private sector and whether, in fact, it continues to add value to the whole. Some of this debate hinges round the alleged distinctiveness of public venture capital. It is, for example, contended that the SDA can afford to give more attention to the evaluation of both the technical and commercial dimensions of a project. Equally, it has been argued that the monitoring and reporting requirements established by the SDA are more extensive and there has been a general endeavour to set new standards within the Scottish financial sector. Like most such investors, the SDA makes widespread use of non-executive directors and insists on the right to make such appointments. In these three areas, however, the difference between the mode of operation of the SDA and other venture capital providers is one of degree. The matter is made more complicated by the fact that many of the investments are, desirably, made within syndications where there is considerable interdependence between the investors. Thus, one of the more telling responsibilities which the SDA can claim to have shouldered in Scotland is the capability to offer a variety of investment financing packages. Such an opportunity arises directly from the range of Agency functions which allow investments to cover the spectrum of loan, equity, property, and leasing where appropriate.

Clearly, all these elements could be combined within the private sector and frequently are, although it is arguable that for companies at particular stages of development, the ability to have these provided through a single channel is a distinct advantage. There are other areas of importance. Not least of these is that the SDA has a unique overview of the Scottish economy and a particular interest in its long term development. The SDA alone has the capacity to take certain types of investment initiatives, such as major restructuring, investment projects that arise from, or are closely related to, sectoral work and in certain management environments. Another area which is potentially distinctive is associated with technology transfer. Given the SDA's involvement in various aspects of the technology transfer process, it has undertaken some creative initiatives in enhancing the capability to commercialise technology emerging from universities and other sources. Evidence to support this lies in the activities of the modest scale investment funds associated with the SDA, its investment role in the Science parks and in the number of inward investment cases. In short, it is possible to identify a number of areas where there is a distinctive investment policy emerging from the SDA. Yet, at the same time, it shares common needs with other venture capital players. Thus, the SDA frequently invests on similar terms along-side private sector funds, has common terms of entry along with common target rates of return and, frequently, common exit terms. Thus, in all these areas, the SDA has to tread a very fine line between public and private sector modes of operation. Otherwise, the desired effect of encouraging private sector development would not be realised. Nor would the exposure of Scottish business to conventional venture capital terms in the medium to long term be realised.

The financial environment within which the SDA exercises these functions has been changing rapidly over recent years. Not only have there been many new players, there has also been considerable growth in the investment activities of major providers such as 3i. The investment role of the Agency has also changed in the directions outlined. But, in addition, it is worth noting that the level of SDA investment, in step with current policy, has not grown in line with these recent trends so that that ratio of SDA to private finance within investment packages has steadily fallen. While there is evidence of very close interaction with the private sector, there are also tensions. On occasion the SDA is criticised for being too commercial, rather risk-averse on some large projects and inclined to favour topping-up deals rather than going for the role of champion for new, difficult projects. These views are, of course, not universally held and a balanced position might lead to the conclusion that there will be a constant need for the SDA to re-examine its position as the events it set out to create actually come to pass in the capital markets. This involves keeping a close eye on the potential displacement of private sources of finance, but also on the new gaps which might be emerging for more risk capital. Inevitably, this raises the question of the nature of the financial duty placed on the SDA investment function. It contains the implicit assumption of an average five-year life for investments which is unrealistic for a portfolio with many small investments and new start-up companies. In such a portfolio, losses will generally come earlier than significant gains. Taken literally, existing duty would encourage investment in low risk projects which would mature quickly – the hunting ground of many private sector investors! A more realistic approach would indicate the use of different target rates of return on different types of investment.

The Highland and Islands Development Board

Context and Philosophy
The Highlands and Islands of Scotland is one of the geographic areas singled out for special treatment through the setting up of the Highlands and Island Development Board (HIDB) in 1965. The area has been subject to depopulation and substantially higher levels of unemployment than the average for the UK although in recent years the average experience is better than for Scotland as a whole. In recognition of the special problems of the area the HIDB has a very wide remit and extensive discretionary powers which encompass both economic and social affairs. This distinguishes the HIDB from the other special credit institutions established by the government such as the Scottish and Welsh Development Agencies. It has powers not only covering agriculture, fisheries, industrial development and tourism but also powers to keep under review matters relating to the social well-being of the region. It is also required by the Act to have regard to the desirability of

preserving the beauty of the scenery of the Highlands and Islands.

In pursuing its objectives the Board agreed a strategy which, within the major objective of supporting the private sector (which accounts for approximately 50 per cent of the Board's expenditure), gives a high ranking to supporting small businesses. In the year 1982–83 some 73 per cent of the cases approved for financial assistance were for £10000 or less. Whilst attracting large-scale projects may bring many jobs there is a recognition that there are few large scale projects which are likely to be attracted and recent experience at Invergordon with the aluminium smelter and Fort William with the pulp mill suggests that this can be a high-risk strategy. Over the past decade the number of footloose projects has been limited and competition for them is both intense and international. Support for indigenous enterprises may offer greater long-term stability of employment. The Board estimates that some 80 per cent of assistance goes to people already resident in its area.

Within the strategy there is a willingness to provide additional support for businesses located in the more remote and socially fragile areas. The Board estimates that the cost of creating jobs in such areas is some 20 per cent higher than for the area as a whole. The Board adopts a strategy of diversifying assistance over all activities in the region, rejecting the option of establishing growth points and concentrating on them. Priority is given to projects which build on the natural resources of the area where a comparative advantage exists which can be exploited in the market place. The provision of goods and services which would otherwise be bought outside the area is also encouraged.

In common with other public sector providers, the Board seeks to concentrate on activities which would not otherwise have gone ahead, thereby hoping to encourage wider participation in their financing. This has had some measurable effect in that there has been a tendency for the contribution of the HIDB to the total cost of a project to fall over the years, as table 9.2 shows.

Table 9.2. HIDB contribution to project cost (%).

1975–76	1977–80	1980–81	1981–82	1982–83	1983–84
42	30	35	32	27	30

Source: HIDB Evidence to Scottish Affairs Committee, HC22 II.

The main determinant in deciding on Board participation is the creation of new jobs or the saving of existing jobs. The Board followed up all the cases assisted in 1974 and their investigation showed that in 1981, 73 per cent of the predicted jobs were still in existence.

In addition to providing direct financial assistance the Board also undertake activities which support firms through the provision of extension services – training, marketing, technical and transportation advice and guidance. These activities are important in an area where professional services are limited and in cases where small firms are involved which are unlikely to be able to bear the cost of such independent professional advice. Private venture capital would be unwilling to sustain the costs of investigation and advice at such a low level of financial involvement. This is a crucial part of the service provided by the HIDB for its clients.

As well as these activities available for individual enterprises the Board also seeks to provide facilities of a public good nature which would otherwise not be provided. These involve capital and current expenditures on tourist information facilities, publicity for the region as a whole and experimental work on fish and deer farming. These research, survey, publicity, and project development expenditures (such as the provision of advance and bespoke factories for lease) accounted for 40 per cent of the Board's expenditure in 1983–84 (table 9.3).

Income and Expenditure

The main source of the board's income is by way of a grant-in-aid from the government amounting to £31.3 million in 1983–84 (table 9.3). The remaining income is derived from rents on leased premises, interest on loans, repayments of loans and profits on the sale of investments. The decision by the government on the size of its contribution is clearly the major determinant of the level of the HIDB's activity and like other government agencies it has been under pressure. The grant-in-aid has in recent years included the government's special contribution to support the Invergordon area and the EEC contribution to the Integrated Programme for the Western Isles. As indicated in table 9.3 the Board's income has grown significantly over the years from £9.5 million in 1976/77 to £38.2 million in 1983/84.

In utilising this income, the Board distinguishes between two categories of financial assistance, namely economic and social development projects. The bulk of the Board's work is in the former category. Assistance is provided to private sector enterprises either as normal assistance which covers loans, interest-relief grants, subscriptions to stock or shares and removal assistance or special grant if normal assistance is regarded as being over burdensome for the project concerned. The Board has discretion as to whether to give assistance and what combination of normal and/or special assistance to approve. This gives the Board useful flexibility within the limits set by the Industry Department for Scotland (IDS) to adjust its contribution to the needs of each venture presented to it.

Under the category of social development projects the Board may give grants and loans towards the capital and recurrent costs of projects which are not commercially viable when they are deemed to meet the social needs and contribute to the social development of an area. The maximum total

Table 9.3. HIDB receipts and payments account, 1976/77 – 1983/84 (£ thousands).

	1976/77	1977/78	1978/79	1979/80	1980/81	1981/82	1982/83	1983/84
Receipts								
Opening balance	103	60	82	9	9	0	14	18
Grant-in-aid	7300	10400	12700	17432	20021	22942	27506	31334
Other receipts	2146	2400	2915	3946	3693	4345	5162	6801
	9548	12861	15697	21387	23722	27287	32681	38153
Expenditures								
Administrative expenses, salaries and wages	1211	1285	1465	1821	2311	2682	2721	3018
General administration and other	496	563	688	782	939	1049	1183	1253
	1707	1848	2153	2603	3250	3731	3904	4271
Development expenditures								
Research, surveys and publicity	757	930	1115	1002	1608	2230	2709	3504
Project development	1459	3140	3471	6259	7396	8014	11023	11590
Grants and loans	5442	6532	8621	11053	11058	12812	13598	17791
Acquisition of shares	124	330	329	463	410	486	1428	965
	7782	10932	13536	18777	20472	23542	28758	33850
Balance	60	82	9	9	—	14	18	32

Source: HIDB Annual Reports.

contribution per year in this category cannot exceed £700000 at the present time. Such expenditures would cover the provision or improvement of village halls, the improvement of TV reception, local museums, community mini-buses, sports facilities, etc. In considering support for the private sector the main tests with regard to the granting of normal assistance relate to the viability of the enterprise and its job creating or job saving potential. Cost per job criteria are also taken into account. Whilst this is always difficult to estimate, the Scottish Affairs Committee (H.C.22.I and 22.II 1984–85) investigation into the HIDB estimated that the HIDB figure was of the order of £9000 per job. This is below the current government ceiling of £10000 per job. Normal assistance permits a combination of one or all of the following components.

First, loans at rates normally 3 per cent below the prevailing commercial rates. The rate is determined by the IDS and is fixed for the duration of the loan. The Board is also able to offer interest-free periods and postponements of capital repayments to provide relief in the difficult early years of a project.

Secondly, interest relief grants are an alternative to loans and provide a grant for approved commercial borrowing which ensures that the same terms apply as would have applied had a direct Board loan been provided. This has the great merit as far as the Board is concerned of reducing its actual commitment of funds which are now provided by some other institution, normally a bank, thus freeing resources for other projects. The Board has made greater use of this facility in recent years and it is one of the reasons for the increased importance of grants in the Board's total expenditure (table 9.4). The involvement of another lender is also seen as useful in itself, providing further evidence of the viability of a project.

Thirdly, the Board is also able to take an equity participation in a project

Table 9.4. Grants and loan assistance approved 1974–83 at 1983 prices.

	Grants	Loans and equity	Grants as % of loans and equity
1974	6515	11403	57
1975	4819	8355	58
1976	4847	8219	59
1977	6176	10949	56
1978	9921	14941	66
1979	8212	8312	99
1980	8273	7793	106
1981	8758	8353	105
1982	10511	6573	160
1983	14864	8029	185

Source: Minutes of Evidence, Scottish Affairs Committee HC 22 II, p.355.

if it feels that this is appropriate, e.g. where the project may be regarded as somewhat risky with short-term cash-flow difficulties but the distinct possibility of long-term and highly profitable viability. The Board would expect to sell its participation after the firm had established itself at a significant profit. The usual method adopted for these participants is preferred ordinary shares. This gives the Board a regular, if limited, return on its investment from an early stage and provides protection as the Board will acquire voting powers if dividend payments are delayed beyond some agreed time period. It is not the Board's intention to get involved in the normal day-to-day operations of the companies in which it invests, although it has a watching brief over all the firms in which it invests. The Board's participation in equity cannot normally exceed one-third of the issued ordinary share capital (as with the SDA) and in practice is substantially less than this. The final element in the normal assistance package is the Relocation Grant but this is hardly, if ever, used.

A private sector project may also be eligible for special assistance. This unique feature of the Board's financial assistance package permits grants to be given when the Board is of the opinion that the project would not prosper on the basis of the normal assistance package alone but where the venture is of particular significance in economic development terms, as for example where the project offers a high potential for creating ancillary enterprises and employment in the area. Grant assistance could also be justified because of the need to train workers to new skills and the high cost of equipping due to remoteness.

The Board therefore has a wide range of instruments through which to assist enterprises in its area and the discretion to combine these in such a way as to encourage the long-term viability of the project and the employment associated with it subject to the guidelines set by the IDS. These set a ceiling on the total grant/loan/share investment in any one project or individual phase of a project of £250000 at the Board's discretion and up to £400000 with the Secretary of State's consent. The maximum total cash contribution which the Board can make towards total project cost is 70 per cent, i.e. at least 30 per cent must come from private or commercial sources. The normal maximum contribution towards total project cost is 50 per cent. With regard to special grants – other than where buildings are involved – the maximum grant is £30000 or 50 per cent of the cost of the project whichever is the lesser, or with larger projects 20 per cent of the total cost of the project.

Despite these limitations, and given the generally small scale of the projects in which the Board is involved there is still significant scope for the Board to adjust its package to the perceived needs of the individual projects. Supplementary assistance has also been provided through special EEC funding for the Integrated Development Programme for the Western Isles which permitted higher levels of grants to be paid during that project so that the private contribution could be reduced to less than 10 per cent of the capital required. Special finance was also provided through the grant-in-aid to finance expenditure in the Invergordon area after the closure of the aluminium smelter. In the period 1976–85 the Board dealt with 9202 cases, made grants of over £107.5 million and loans and equity investments of over £95 million at 1985 prices, so it has been responsible for a large inflow of resources into the area.

Finance can seldom be the constraining factor for well articulated projects in the Board's area. The difficult task facing the Board is the assessment of the entrepreneurial abilities of those seeking assistance. The Board must expect to take on risky projects since, in the nature of the area it serves and the methods of operation laid on the Board, these are the projects which are likely to be brought to it. The fine line between accepting reasonable risk when venturing public money and unreasonable speculation is a difficult one to draw when the imponderables of ability and commitment by the entrepreneur in an uncertain economic environment are assessed. In terms of repayment of debt the Board's record would appear to be sound with some 90 per cent of loans falling due being met. It has indeed been argued that the Board is excessively cautious in making its investments.

Other Board Expenditure
Other significant expenditures incurred by the Board are associated with supporting the activity of the area through, first, research, surveys and marketing and, secondly, through projects and development (table 9.3.). These expenditures of both a current and capital nature are intended to support existing activities and encourage further private investment.

The Board supports Area Tourist Organisations and undertakes publicity on behalf of the area as a whole. It participates in research, for example, in deer and fish farming in the expectation that such activities will be encouraged in the area. It plays a significant role by undertaking the speculative building of advance factories to encourage movement into the area. At present it owns some 400 factory units. Tourist information centres and advance hotels have also been supported. Multifunctional community co-operatives have been encouraged as a means of improving the viability of a community which is prepared to support such an effort by providing some of the finance and harnessing available knowledge and talent, whilst avoiding the possible adverse reactions to excessive individual initiative in a closely knit community (Alexander 1981).

Performance
Measuring the performance of the HIDB presents problems because of the nature of the institution and the area which it serves. Until recently, the Board had no specific financial targets although this has now been amended, as a result of pressure from the Public Accounts Committee, by the setting

of targets for its property division. It is now expected to earn a modest return of 3.5 per cent on new factory building and a surplus on its factory operations of £3.50 per square metre. This is below the comparable figure for the SDA and is calculated before allowing for repairs, maintenance administration and depreciation. The Board's performance may be judged in terms of the attainment of its objectives relating to reversing population decline, reducing the level of unemployment through creating new jobs and retaining others under threat. In terms of population change, there has been a reversal of the population decline in the area, in contrast to a decline in the total population in Scotland.

Similarly, with regard to unemployment in terms of relative performance compared to the rest of Scotland and the rest of the UK, there has been a significant improvement, although levels of unemployment within the HIDB area vary markedly and the absolute level is still high. In the creation of employment, the Board produces figures showing expected jobs created and saved each year. These show that over the years 1976–85 jobs created were 18399 and jobs saved were 5983.

What is impossible to say is to what extent the activities of the HIDB influenced these figures, as there were obviously other factors at work such as oil-related activities and the general decline in the level of economic activity in the country as a whole, which probably discourages emigration from the Highlands. The improvements have not, however, been limited only to those areas obviously benefiting from North Sea Oil work and it does seem likely that the policies of the Board have made a significant contribution. It will also be true that the jobs created and retained by the Board's assistance will not all be additional jobs for the country as a whole. Many of the jobs would have appeared without the Board's activities, but perhaps in other parts of the country. The Board can nevertheless claim some role in attracting jobs to the area which it serves.

Because of the lack of clear-cut financial targets arising from a recognition of the special problems faced in the Highlands from locational difficulties resulting in higher building costs and transport costs, lack of specialist professional advice, the large number of small firms with relatively low management skills and the social responsibilities placed on the Board with regard to sustaining particularly fragile communities, alternative methods of controlling its activities have to be used.

Controls tend to be of an administrative rather than purely financial form. The sponsoring department, in this case the IDS, has an overall but not detailed controlling function and, for larger loans, must be consulted. As a result of weaknesses in the investigative and control procedures highlighted by the Comptroller and Auditor General in the report on the Investment Activities of the Scottish Development Agency, Welsh Development Agency and Highlands and Islands Development Board, the Industry Department Scotland (IDS) now has a more extensive monitoring role than previously, but still allows the Board a substantial degree of autonomy within the agreed guidelines.

The Board has to report to Parliament on its activities, and is subject to scrutiny in that forum, plus occasional investigation undertaken by Parliament on its activities such as the recent Scottish Affairs Committee Report (H.C.22 1984/85). As a public body, the activities of the Board will be subject to scrutiny and comment by local and national politicians. The board cannot but be influenced by the policies and views of the government of the day, given its dependence on public funds voted by Parliament.

There also exists a Highlands and Islands Development Consultative Committee appointed by the Secretary of State, with a membership of around thirty, representative of all shades of opinion in the Board's area. The objective of the Consultative Committee is to provide advice and criticism to the Board of its actvity and lack of it, so that the overall policies will be responsive to the varying needs of the area it serves. The body is currently dominated by local authority representatives, and the Scottish Affairs Committee recommended a reduction in local authority representation and increasing membership from industry with a maximum tenure of office of five years, non-renewable.

The HIDB nevertheless retains a measure of independence because of its long-term involvement with and experience of the problems in the Highlands. One of the functions of the Board is to influence decision takers at the district, regional and national level to pursue policies favourable to the area.

Another measure of efficiency which can be used relates to the administrative costs associated with the activities of the Board. Given the nature of the objectives set for the Board and the large number of cases presented each year (a number which has grown rapidly in recent years, reaching a total of over 2200 in 1984–85), plus the aftercare activities supporting earlier investments through the Board's advisory services, these costs are likely to be higher than those of purely private sector organisations. These expenses have in recent years accounted for around 11 per cent of the Board's expenditures (table 9.3).

Bad debt experience is another possible measure of the Board's effectiveness. Figures presented by the Board to the Scottish Affairs Committee indicate that actual losses and provisions account for 9.15 per cent of the loans advanced to 1983–84. This measure takes no account of grants made to these enterprises. The use of bad debt as a measure of success has to be used with caution. The function of the Board is to accept risks which commercial organisations would not. Bad debt is an inevitable consequence. The optimal level of bad debt, given the objectives of the Board, is difficult to determine. If the Board was to pursue a policy of substantially reducing its bad debt by restricting activities to the economically more attractive areas, it would not be fulfilling its objectives.

Since the Board is restricted in the amount of assistance it can provide for any project, other financial institutions are likely to be involved. The willingness of these institutions to contribute to a project also provides some support for the Board's involvement, since the other contributors are also subject to the risk of loss, although this is mitigated to the extent that the board contributes to the enterprise in the form of grants. It is interesting to note that the banks that submitted evidence to the Scottish Affairs Committee were generally highly supportive of the Board's activities in the area, although since the banks are major beneficiaries of the assumption of risk by the HIDB this should not be taken as an unbiased opinion.

Overall Conclusions

Comment has already been made about the difficulties associated with measuring the contribution made by the two institutions as public venture capital suppliers. Both are subject to increasing scrutiny and the application of more refined performance indicators despite the inherent difficulties in measuring the performance of institutions set up to overcome market imperfections. They have played an important and, on occasion, pioneering role in the market for venture capital in Scotland. This is especially true of the SDA and any claims to shaping the practices of this part of the financial sector can only really be made for the SDA. The HIDB did seek to enter the venture capital market with Highland Venture Capital, set up with the assistance of a successful American venture capital company but only one project was found which met the required standards, suggesting that the HIDB already provides an appropriate range of financial and other services for entrepreneurs within its area of operations. Similarly for the future, there are reasonable expectations for a continued requirement for SDA venture capital associated, for example, with high-technology start ups, corporate and sectoral readjustment, as well as for some inward investment. In all of these there are more distinctive leadership roles for the SDA than for the HIDB. Yet, the role of the Board in using its diverse powers will remain crucial in its area, penetrating both to a micro level of enterprise, while maintaining an overview on the total development of communities. The ability to provide grants as well as concessional finance and its wider social responsibilities make it a unique institution which does not readily fit the profile of a purely financial institution.

10

INNOVATION IN
FINANCIAL MARKETS AND INSTITUTIONS

The process of innovation has been a frequent theme of previous chapters. Concern has been expressed at both the lack of readiness and ability of the Scottish financial sector to spawn new companies, and the skill of Scottish institutions at innovating by producing new products, employing new delivery techniques, or securing competitive advantage by investment in more efficient processes permitting additional economies of scale. Widespread agreement that the process of innovation is vital to the health of the economy since successful innovation results in substantial profits to the innovator as well as wider benefits such as employment creation suggest that the encouragement of innovation must be a major policy goal. For such a policy to be effective it is necessary to understand the process of financial innovation so as to provide a framework against which the recent and potential innovatory ability of Scotland's institutions can be judged.

This chapter then, examines the ability of Scotland's financial institutions to innovate. After an examination of some of the causes of innovation three questions of particular interest are singled out for consideration. The impact of developments in communications on the need for geographical centralisation whether in London or Edinburgh; the impact of increased competition stemming from a reduction in regulatory constraints on both new and existing products and processes; and the impact of technological developments on institutions, particularly the effects on economies of scale and the diversity of services that may be economically offered. In short, are there economic incentives pushing firms into becoming conglomerates? The chapter concludes with an assessment of the ability of Scottish institutions to innovate.

Financial Innovations

There is little doubt that a major force shaping financial markets in the last decade has been financial innovation. Financial innovation is the act of exploiting new ways of doing useful and profitable things.[1] Financial innovations are rarely dramatic technological breakthroughs but rather the modification of an existing idea which leads to a new product such as traded options or a new process such as more efficient funds transfer or more effective marketing to consumers.[2] The distinction between financial innovation and product differentiation is not always one of substance. Product differentiation frequently involves a repackaging of different financial attributes and in so far as it results in a novel product that meets a previously unfilled need, or more effectively meets the needs revealed by an existing security, it might be considered a financial innovation.

To be viable a financial innovation must make financial markets more efficient or more complete.[3] Greater efficiency is secured if an innovation reduces the cost of financial intermediation to consumers by reducing either the spread between borrowing and lending rates for given risk, or the level of search and information costs. The search for increased efficiency is exemplified by the widespread use of computers to document the issue and characteristics of securities such as insurance policies and the spread of computer-based information systems. The completeness of a market is improved whenever new securities are introduced which allow the construction of combinations of risk, return and liquidity to investors which were previously unobtainable. The introduction of index-linked bonds which allow inflation risk to be hedged, or the introduction of zero coupon bonds which permit investors to construct portfolios with greater duration than was previously possible,[4] provide two recent examples. If a market is incomplete a financial intermediary may find it profitable to exploit the opportunity by tailoring security offerings to the unfilled desires of investors whether with regard to maturity, coupon rate, protection, cash flow characteristics or whatever. Many financial innovations result in an increase in efficiency and, in addition, improve the completeness of the market.[5] The computerisation of life assurance administration enabled the companies to restrain the growth in their clerical staff and costs despite an increase in their business, and to repackage the different characteristics of life policies so as to offer a multitude of different life assurance options.

The difference in the form that innovation takes has been characterised by a number of authors as firms following either an 'innovative' or a 'positional' strategy. The innovative strategy emphasises the acquisition of market share by offering new products whilst the positional strategy emphasises profit opportunities achieved by securing improved efficiency by more effective marketing or administration with the current range of products. The advantages of each strategy are not independent of conditions in the economy and the industry, and the payoffs will vary as market conditions change. It is important to recognise that innovation is a multi-faceted concept and that a failure to innovate in the new product area does not necessarily imply a lack of innovation by a company. New ways of marketing existing products or the securing of cost advantages through improved efficiency may be equally effective if somewhat less spectacular. In changing markets, however, where old products are losing their previous importance, failure to innovate new products may indicate a mature product range and possible difficulties for the future.

An alternative framework in which to categorise financial innovation has been proposed by Llewellyn (1985). He suggests a four-fold breakdown consisting of:

(i) Defensive innovations which occur in response to both policy and regulatory changes and competitors' innovations.

(ii) Aggressive innovations which are new products or instruments that financial institutions believe they can successfully market.

(iii) Responsive innovations which meet a new need of customers. Thus, a change in customers' portfolio requirements as the result of the effects of inflation brought forth a variety of new financial services and

(iv) Protective innovations in which institutions adapt techniques because of their own portfolio constraints.

These distinctions are useful in emphasising the alternative causes of financial innovation and, in particular, the need of institutions to make their own portfolio adjustments in changing circumstances.

Financial innovations occur in response to profit opportunities which arise from inefficiencies or incompleteness. Profitable innovations invite others to enter the market place with a similar product or process resulting in reduced profit margins for the institutions and benefits for the consumer. The successful innovator reaps a reward for innovation. The innovator is established in the market and able to secure higher rewards than would otherwise be possible. The innovator takes on risk but, if successful, secures a commensurate reward. Successful innovations enable companies to grow rapidly by securing additional business as a result of new and more attractive products or lower costs. Delayed entry into new markets reduces the risk but misses the high profit and growth opportunities received by early participants. Imitating the successful products of others is a safer but, in general, less rewarding strategy. Early entrants earn exceptional profits and may establish a position in the market place that is difficult to assail. This said, a distinguishing characteristic of financial innovations is the relative ease with which they may be replicated by competing institutions and the difficulties of securing patent protection.[6] The lead over competitors is shorter than for industrial products and requires quick responses. Investment in more advanced computing equipment may be one method of securing longer term advantages, although a recent study indicated the transient advantages of such a strategy. A second alternative is the investment in extensive name and product awareness in order to build up a marketing advantage. This appears to be a favoured method of several of the larger American financial institutions who make losses on some products for a considerable number of years before they become profitable.

The response of companies to the trade-off between risk and return from innovation differs according to the circumstances of the company and its management. The assumption of profit maximising management responsible to shareholders is sometimes inadequate (even if it is adequate elsewhere) in segments of the financial markets because of the significance and importance of mutual companies. Although it is possible to think of life assurance policyholders as being equity holders it is clearly impossible, in conventional terms, to conceive of a fixed interest deposit holder in a bank or building society as having an equity interest since such deposit holders bear no risk. In addition, mutual organisations pose important incentive problems since it may be difficult to adequately motivate and reward management. The discipline of takeovers is absent and the mass of small depositors and policyholders insulate managers from effective control. Such consideration suggest that mutual institutions may have a predilection to caution and be less likely to innovate.

Causes of Innovation

Although considerable effort has been devoted to studying the process of industrial innovation few investigations of the financial innovation process have been completed. A number of important factors have been suggested of which Silber's (1983) Utility Maximisation hypothesis, Greenbaum and Haywood's (1971) real income explanations and Kane's (1980) regulatory theory have probably been most influential. Silber argues that new financial instruments or practices are innovated to lessen the external constraints imposed on firms. The cost of adhering to existing constraints stimulates the search for new financial products and as the cost of satisfying a particular constraint increases, resources are devoted to circumventing or overcoming it so leading to new innovations. In contrast, Greenbaum and Haywood emphasise the role of rising real income and swings in interest rates on innovation. They argue that growth of real income creates a demand for a wider variety of financial claims and the system responds by producing an ever widening array of claims. If we accept their argument that rising real income is an important cause, in itself, of innovation then companies whose main market is Scottish rather than London and the South of England may find themselves at a comparative disadvantage. Remoteness from main markets could result in a slow response to the newly emerging needs of customers. Greenbaum and Haywood also stress the significance of swings in interest rates on financial innovation. There is little disagreement that inflation, a major factor in swings, has induced a host of innovations such as floating rate and index linked loans and cash management accounts which allow businesses to speed payments and reduce cash holdings. The need to speed payments has been linked with developments in communications and resulted in pioneering systems such as the Bank of Scotland Home and Office Banking System which allows switching of funds between accounts as well as the payment of bills from home or even the offices of small businesses. Kane (1980, 1983, 1984) in a number of papers stresses the regulatory and technical factors inducing innovation. He suggests that managers rearrange the institutions' activities, organisation or product lines in order to render regulations obsolete. He argues that innovation is largely a response to regulation. Indeed, the role of regulation with respect to innovation in financial markets is a continuing theme of several authors. Intermediaries are portrayed as struggling to avoid the more onerous effects of regulation. Innovation provides a means of undermining regulation and is therefore actively pursued by severely regulated institutions. This characterisation of the innovation process leaves much unanswered not least since regulators apparently never learn!

The role of regulation in shaping the structure of the financial sector cannot be doubted. The Edinburgh banks in their early years sought preferential treatment from legislation whilst the provincial stock exchanges had a continual battle with the London Stock Exchange on a variety of issues and legislation that were thought to benefit the latter. However, unlike the United States, much regulation dictating the structure of financial industries has now been removed. The current debate in the UK is concerned rather with the solvency and liquidity of institutions.

Technological developments have also had a major influence on financial innovation. It is not too strong to suggest that in the absence of computers the motivation for introducing new products would have been greatly reduced. Computing power and improved communications have provided financial intermediaries with the capability of introducing new products at an acceptable cost. In its absence the rate of financial innovation would have been very much lower. Technological progress in the accessing of remote data bases, the execution of transactions and the delivery of services to customers has been marked. Automated Teller Machines (ATMs), popular in banks and building societies, exemplify this progress since they allow the customer access to details of his account, the possibility of depositing and withdrawing cash and improved convenience. They also reflect the challenge of the new technology to the banks since they radically alter the economics of the branch network and suggest the need for a change of emphasis in the services banks provide to the public. Examples of the benefits of the new technology are also provided by the Scottish life assurance companies where computerisation has reduced costs by replacing routine clerical tasks, and increased the flexibility open to companies selling in mass markets.

More recently commentators on financial innovation have stressed a multiplicity of factors, those of Llewellyn (1985) providing some interesting insights from a market perspective. Llewellyn stresses the response of the institutions to their changing market environment; an environment that reflects a variety of factors such as shifts in interest rates, growth in real income, legislative, policy and tax changes and technological developments. He emphasises financial innovation as occurring in response to profit opportunities and places particular stress on the effects of changes in the environment on institutions' and individuals' portfolios. Thus, as portfolio behaviour and the preferences of ultimate users of financial intermediation services change, institutions seek to provide suitable financial instruments. Llewellyn cites the shift from bond to bank finance as an example. The changing requirements of savers and borrowers led to facilities for offsetting interest rate and exchange rate risks and the provision of long-term finance at changing short-term rates of interest.

Changing market conditions also require the financial institutions to respond to their own portfolio objectives.

> Financial institutions are not passive but have their own portfolio objectives and constraints which change through time . . . financial innovation represents a process whereby the services offered by institutions are designed to tempt customers to use the institutions' services in a way consistent with their own portfolio objectives and constraints. (Llewellyn 1985)

Thus innovation does not always set out to capture existing demand but also induces demand, the asset led growth of the banks and the internationalisation of portfolios providing examples.

Impact of Innovation on Scotland

The impact of developments in communication on the need for geographical centralisation is an important issue for the continued existence of the Scottish financial sector in its present form. It is apparent that improved communication has been a major feature of recent experience and promises to continue to be of great significance. The benefits of improved communication have been most apparent in the provision of information and the execution of transactions allowing institutions access to on-line databases and other sources of information. Access to such data has improved investment decision-making and allowed deposit institutions to develop automated cash withdrawal facilities. Over the next decade, the effects on consumers of further improvements in communication will be substantial allowing the provision of a wider range of facilities in more accessible locations and with much improved information about financial products. In the circumstances it is difficult to believe that most institutions will continue to require to be located in any particular place. It is unlikely that there will be technological reasons for the continued presence of financial institutions and markets in London or, indeed, in Edinburgh. However, the desire of participants in financial markets and institutions for face-to-face contact, the existing financial infra-structure, the presence of trained personnel in London and inertia will almost certainly continue to keep most institutions geographically concentrated even though few, if any, markets will require face-to-face dealing and the majority may use automatic execution programs at least for small orders. Opportunities may be available for individuals and institutions to supply services from remote installations to financial institutions. Database services are the most obvious but scope may also exist for the provision of a variety of administrative and other services. The hiving-off of 'back office' services by a Glasgow stockbroker provides a model of the opportunities that may arise.

The second question of interest posed earlier concerned the impact of increased competition stemming from a reduction in regulatory constraints on both new and existing products and processes. Deregulation has lowered the boundaries that functionally separate financial institutions and the result has been for market participants to innovate and enter new lines of business possessing previously unobtainable profit and/or risk reduction possibilities. There has been an increased concentration and polarisation of financial firms. The need for increased resources and the anticipation of economies of scale, particularly in marketing, has led to the merger and takeover of many firms, events that have been discussed in earlier chapters. At the same time large multi-function firms pose problems of control and potential conflicts of interest that may inhibit their future growth. Increased disclosure of information, regulatory supervision and 'Chinese Walls' separating the activities of different parts of the firm may reassure clients and overcome the problems associated with the conflicts of interest, but there remains the problem of controlling large financial firms with many different activities. Analysis of the problems associated with multi-function organisations has led some firms to espouse the move towards concentration and instead to market themselves as specialist institutions or boutiques involving no potential conflict of interest with the management able to devote themselves wholeheartedly to their specialisms. This policy of specialisation has been the predominant force in Scotland, whether by accident (a lack of suitable partners) or design.

Both policies are fraught with difficulties. Specialism generally implies smaller institutions and potential problems of marketing. A small specialist investment manager does not have the sales force to market directly to the public and their smaller size makes the cost of such marketing prohibitive. The boutique benefits from specialisation and the pursuit of well-known paths but lacks financial and marketing muscle. The larger conglomerates may have difficulties in convincing customers of their integrity but they will have the resources to market directly and aggressively to the public. It has been argued elsewhere in this book (chapters 7 and 8) that marketing is a vital ingredient in the success of investment management and insurance. The argument can be generalised to other financial institutions and suggests that the success of boutiques or conglomerates may depend on their particular target markets. Organisations aimed at consumers require a direct delivery mechanism to the consumer. A branch structure has, in the past, been one method of securing such delivery. The problems of branch structure are discussed elsewhere but it probably remains the most effective method of securing sales of financial services.

Sales aimed at firms and specialist customers do not require the power of a large direct sales force. Boutiques can hope to compete effectively in this market although there may well be benefits even for large firms, of dealing with one financial adviser. The merchant bank to the company may also secure its pension business although the advantages to the industrial firm from such one-stop shopping are probably small. The real advantage of the boutique is its flexibility and speed of response. The real cost is its separation from a large part of the financial market as a result of its inability to effectively meet all the financial needs of the consumer. The growth in unit trust sales can only be exploited with difficulty by the boutiques because of the lack of a direct sales force and the difficulty of persuading agents to sell their product in preference to someone else's.[7]

The third issue which this chapter set out to address is the the impact of technological developments on financial institutions. The importance of electronic data processing (EDP) on reducing costs and increasing the ability of institutions to offer a wide variety of financial instruments has already been remarked upon but two aspects of the mechanisation process may usefully be distinguished: the replacement of existing computers with cheaper, more powerful machines, and an extension of the frontiers of computerisation to encompass activities that were previously impossible or were not cost effective to mechanise. The benefits from replacement expenditure on more powerful machines are probably small given the software costs that may be required to rewrite programs to take advantage of improved performance, although more powerful machines may remove any remaining obstacles to widespread networks. There has, for example, been some concern that the volume of transactions at peak times from ATMs results in slow response times to consumers and might cause delays and irritation. The mechanisation of new activities may be affected by diminishing returns since the easier and most profitable applications are mechanised first. However, increased EDP has released financial institutions from many constraints that were based on the need to keep the administration of issued securities manageable. EDP is allowing institutions to unbundle the different aspects of their products and offer investors as much, or as little of a particular characteristic that they would desire. Several authors have suggested that financial services can be thought of as a series of fundamental building blocks such as transaction services, investment services, savings services, insurance or protection services, borrowing services and information services and that a variety of financial products can be derived by combining these different characteristics.

The nature of EDP in financial services suggests that it may impart a substantial premium to growth. EDP involves not just a substantial investment in hardware but also a large investment in customised software. Increases in business allow the costs to be defrayed across a larger number of customers and suggest the possibility of scale economies. However, software is not always developed in-house and may be commissioned or bought off the shelf from specialist software houses. This may reduce the costs of software and if standard packages are available it may allow even relatively small institutions to benefit from improved EDP. However, the more standard the application the more likely it is that the innovation of others is simply being copied. True software innovation requires high investment in customised, and relatively untested, software but it presents institutions with an opportunity to offer services that others are unable to provide and hence generate new business.

The standardisation of capital equipment in producing financial services has, according to Kane (1984), resulted in the homogenisation of functions across financial institutions. Technological change has increased the role of multi-purpose capital equipment whilst at the same time its cost has increased the desirability of spreading it across additional product lines. The possibility of using multi-purpose equipment has also attracted non-financial firms into financial services and led to the concept of the 'all purpose' financial firm. According to this view scale economies provide the basis for the move to financial conglomerates.

The movement of firms into the industry from a non-financial retailing background may also lead to some interesting marketing innovations. 'Own brand' products supplied by producers of well-known branded products are a well-known retailing strategy for a wide variety of household goods. An extension of the concept to financial products may be expected with retailers selling the policies of an insurance company as their own. Marks and Spencer insurance policies sold through their stores and credit card and using their reputation for quality and value for money could well take a significant share of the market. The public could be offered a range of financial services, much like those proposed by financial conglomerates, but with the integration provided by the retailer who buys in a range of 'own brand' products.

Computerisation is also affecting the delivery mechanism to consumers. Innovation in this area involves a further complication besides the requisite hardware and software investment. Consumers must be educated to accept new delivery systems and there are bound to be difficulties as services become more complex. The offer of one or two financial services on, for example, ATMs allows customers to call up the service they require by use of dedicated buttons and controls. The offer of a range of services will involve consumers in selecting from menus, keying in appropriate codes, pressing a particular part of the screen or some combination of such acts. The scope for difficulties and confusion multiply as the possible services increase. Consumers will have to master the complexities of the machine and have sufficient information and knowledge to choose what is most appropriate for them. It is by no means certain that these problems are trivial and there may be a great deal of investment required before electronic services are accepted and used by the broad mass of the public.

Assessment

Although complete agreement on the precise causes of financial innovation is absent, it is apparent that regulation, technology, tax and policy changes and economic factors such as inflation and growth, all have a part to play. Scotland's financial institutions as part of a monetary, fiscal and political union operate within the same legal and regulatory framework as other UK institutions facing the same incentives for, and difficulties to, innovation. The lower economic growth of Scotland's economy could have had deleterious effects on the innovatory ability of the banks although the reputation of the Bank of Scotland does not support such a hypothesis, and cannot have had a serious influence on the innovatory ability of other Scottish institutions which operate primarily in UK markets. Differences in technology may exist between London and the North as a result of the cost, and perhaps, technical difficulties of accessing more remote areas – the delay in receiving the Stock Exchange Talisman system is sometimes cited – but the differences are small and temporary. There is, therefore, little reason to assume that the innovatory record of Scotland's institutions should be appreciably different from that of institutions in the rest of the UK.

In the past Scotland has played a notable role in new financial product innovation. The overdraft is possibly the most famous example but its prowess in investment through the medium of investment trusts cannot be far behind. It is noticeable, however, that in recent years Scotland has missed out on some of the most important new product innovations. Growth in unit trusts and particularly unit linked assurance are obvious examples although it is in fact difficult to find many areas of the financial service industry where Scotland has made significant innovatory new product contributions. The criticism is not true of Scotland alone. The rest of the UK has also been slow to innovate new products, a reflection perhaps of lower levels of real income and less burdensome regulation than in the United States. Compliant regulation with respect to international trading has allowed London to rebuild its importance in world financial markets although much of the trading is in the hands of the large American and Japanese banks. The growth in new financial services in London has not been matched by a similar growth in Scotland though existing Scottish companies have continued to do well. With the exception of pension business Scotland has largely missed out on most major new areas of financial growth. Scotland has been slow to respond to many new products and recent years have been marked by a loss of personnel and firms to London. It has grown in the traditional segments of the financial services industry and failed to exploit new trends and find new sectors although there are exceptions to this bleak picture, electronic banking providing one such example.

The growth in the traditional segments of the financial services industry is well illustrated by the Scottish life offices. By concentrating on their traditional business they have increased their market share aided by some interesting innovations, notably the introduction of specialist offices offering unitised investment funds for pension schemes, flexible endowment assurance and cluster policies.[8] However, their expansion in other areas of financial markets, particularly unit trusts and unit linked assurance, has until recently been poor and it has been suggested that there are grounds for concern at their apparently slow response to developments elsewhere. The validity of such suggestions is difficult to appraise. The major Scottish institutions in the life sector have performed as well as their major English counterparts but clearly have not demonstrated the growth of some of the more aggressive, younger, linked offices in the South whether because of differences in commission arrangements,[9] a refusal to exploit tax avoidance opportunities or differences in management. A comparison of the record of innovation of the major Scottish financial institutions with their English counterparts would not necessarily be to the disadvantage of Scotland. The problem primarily lies in the low representation of Scottish firms within the ranks of the fast expanding institutions in the less conventional areas of the market.

The Scottish institutions continue to follow well-trodden product paths, in the main, and there are few examples of new firms and institutions. A reversal of the new product trend is to be hoped for but it is made difficult by the drift of manpower south and the increasing size of the players in the market. If new product innovation is the well-spring of industry then the future does not look attractive. The financial services industry record on innovation in Scotland has been patchy and whilst there are signs of improvement and resurgence these are as yet too few to be interpreted with anything but very guarded caution.

Of course, it is important to emphasise that success in innovation does not imply that companies must follow an 'innovative' strategy. There is scope also for a 'positional' strategy in which institutions improve efficiency with their current range of products. Scottish institutions have undoubtedly invested heavily in automation although this has been a common feature of all financial institutions and it is difficult to assess objectively whether Scottish companies have been more effective in this area than other UK or international institutions. A comparison of expense ratios is one possibility, but different product mixes may result in substantial differences between institutions and confound any such comparisons. There is little doubt that the banks have made considerable progress in introducing ATMs and automating the transfer of funds, and the assurance companies in automating their back offices, but there is little reason to believe that they have secured significant competitive advantages, as a whole, from this source although individual companies may have benefited rather more. Scottish institutions have probably been as successful at innovating for the puppose of reducing costs as other large UK institutions but their record in other aspects of innovation has been less successful. Many innovations by Scottish institutions have been 'defensive' and represent a response to changes in policy and regulatory changes. The record of Scottish institutions in 'aggressive' and 'responsive' innovation, financial instruments which institutions feel they can market successfully or which meet a new need of customers, has been less satisfactory.

NOTES
1. Van Horne (1985).
2. Kane (1980) distinguishes between invention and innovation. Invention he argues is the act of finding new ways to do useful or profitable things – usually cheaper and more efficient ways of doing them. Innovation is the act of putting an invention into practice.
3. If a market is complete then every possible security payoff can be constructed from a portfolio of existing securities. (See Copeland and Weston 1984)
4. For a discussion of duration see Van Horne (1984).
5. Market completeness is not necessarily desirable. Tobin (1984) points to the cost of securing such completeness and suggests that many new financial markets and instruments are of limited value except for speculation and financial arbitrage.
6. Merrill Lynch managed to patent their Cash Management Account in the US. This combines many of the financial functions that better-off investors may require into one product. In particular it allows the automatic deposit of idle cash, instant borrowing and account access via cheque or Visa. There is also a brokerage account which allows the customer to buy or sell securities on a cash or credit basis. The patent has not gone unchallenged.
7. For a discussion of some of the issues see Maycock (1986).
8. We are grateful to Mr W. Proudfoot, Chief General Manager of the Scottish Amicable Life Assurance Society, for drawing these to our attention.
9. The Scottish Life Offices have adhered to commission arrangements agreed by the industry as a whole. It has been suggested that the fast growth of some of the newer institutions arose from their refusal to abide by such agreements. It is an interesting question whether industry-wide agreements are in the consumers' best interest. Such agreements remove commission arrangements from the competitive arena. This is desirable if it is believed that commission would otherwise increase to all customers. It is possible, however, that some customers might actively divert business to the companies that paid low commission.

11

SUMMARY

The primary objectives of this study have been to evaluate the significance and importance of the financial institutions as creators of employment and income in Scotland together with assessing the future impact of these institutions on the Scottish economy. Pursuing these aims has required an examination of the historical and locational factors that have dictated the current shape of the sector, in addition to an evaluation of the impact of current trends and conditions that affect its future.

The preceding chapters have provided a detailed discussion of the factors that have moulded the current structure of the individual institutions but by its nature such an approach cannot adequately outline the inter-connecting influences that have affected the sector as a whole. This chapter attempts to summarise these factors and to draw out the common influences with a view to anticipating the direction in which the sector and its constituent institutions must proceed in the future. It contains a summary of the historical and locational factors which have determined the sector's present position and an outline of the key issues that it faces with their implications for its future growth and prosperity.

Reasons for the Existence of a Scottish Financial Sector

The present level of financial activity results from past developments, particularly from a combination of factors encouraging a separate Scottish identity derived from economic forces and distinctive legal, educational and religous institutions. These factors still exist and are to be seen in a vocal Scottish lobby intent on maintaining a distinctive set of Scottish institutions which retain a major decision-taking capacity in the country.

As part of a monetary union, located in a region where the internal sources of growth dependent on domestic wealth and income are not strong, the Scottish financial sector has been subject to considerable external pressure particularly from London. The attraction and importance of London stems primarily from its scale, variety and internationally diversified interests enhanced by improved communications. These factors are reinforced by the tendency to centralisation of control which has been encouraged by a number of important influences: London's position as the centre of government together with its associated mechanisms of monetary and fiscal control; the well-developed financial facilities of London and the attraction of

Summary

established financial and commodity markets, both domestic and international, together with the associated economies of agglomeration which encourage financial innovation in products and markets; and the continuing economic expansion in the South East which has progressively differentiated it from other parts of the UK.

Despite the expense of a London location in terms of occupancy costs and labour, the benefits of London and the South East of England as a financial centre are reinforced by the continuing need for some transfer of paper and the existence of close links between different institutions and their personnel. The influence of London is increased by the movement of the control of companies by merger and takeover from Scotland to London and more importantly by a concentration around London in the growth of new institutions and the development of new innovations (see Ashcroft et al. 1986). This is clearly seen in the dramatic growth of unit trust managers in contrast to the relative contraction of the older investment trust movement.

The oldest element of the Scottish financial sector is the banks. These developed with the expanding regional economy and associated trade. Poor communications, together with an effective network of local connections and knowledge, enabled Scottish banks to emerge. Early banking history was characterised by significant banking innovations. Indeed, such was its strength that around one hundred years ago the total capital of the Scottish banks in Scotland exceeded that of the London banks and average bank assets per head in Scotland were two-and-a-half times greater than in England (Checkland 1975). Jevons wrote 'There is no doubt that Scots bankers are guiding the course of development of the banking system in England, India and the Australian colonies, and elsewhere, with conspicuous success' (Checkland 1975). Unfortunately banking legislation had already started to stifle the spirit of innovation in Scottish banking and the banks, encouraged by such factors as Bank of England policy, substantial shareholdings by holding groups and the difficulty of acquiring a branch network, effectively kept out new players and competition in the following years.

The banks provide a financial nucleus around which other institutions can develop. They provide payments and loan facilities which allow individuals and institutions to organise financial packages for their clients. Merchant banks, for example, frequently rely on the banks to provide the loan element of the financial deals they have put together. Other activities are also encouraged as a result of the presence of suitable personnel, educational facilities, services and information. The economics of third party institutions such as information providers is transformed by the existence of a group of (institutional) consumers.

Life assurance had its origins in middle-class concepts of self help, origins which are still reflected in their mutual structure and which has rendered them largely immune from takeover. These institutions commenced trading as regional organisations protected from competition in their early years by their local knowledge and sales base. The life offices have long outgrown their regional base and sales are UK-wide. Although closeness to major markets has been an important pressure for moving activity towards London, lower costs and the availability of skills in Scotland are a countervailing force. Investment, whilst an important part of their activities, is not the major function in employment terms. Thus the attractions of London as an investment centre have been outweighed by the advantages of Scotland for the recruitment of personnel. In addition, improved communications have made it easier for both investment and sales facilities to be located outside of London.

Investment firms emerged in Scotland from a surplus of local funds and lack of profitable local opportunities coupled with the opportunities revealed by Scottish emigration and travel. The institutions developed a characteristic investment policy with strong emphasis on overseas investment for which a London location offered smaller advantages than for institutions which invested primarily in UK markets. The appeal of a Scottish base with its perceived marketing strength, together with the predominantly partnership structure of the management groups, maintained the presence of the investment institutions in Scotland. This occurred despite a declining regional economy and the diminution of local stockmarkets and local investment centres. Dundee, for example, was for many years a major trading centre for investment trust shares whilst Glasgow specialised in mining and other overseas speculative ventures.

The attractions of the region have, however, been less effective in retaining the presence of other types of financial institutions. In particular, there has been a decline in the general insurance sector. Scale economies and access to short-term money markets appear to have been an important motivating force in general insurance and, in consequence, led to the merger of several Scottish companies with London-based societies such that only one general insurance company still has its headquarters in Scotland. In merchant banking, there has only been a limited development within Scotland. In the post-war period at least, this has not been encouraged by the acceleration of ownership and control moving outwith Scotland nor by distance from the major domestic and international financial markets. On the other hand, opportunities were lost in that period by the slow movement of Scottish banks into the development and venture capital markets.

In other areas, Scotland's role has either diminished or remained minor. In the former category lies the decline of the Scottish Stock Exchange as it battled unsuccessfully with the strong centralising force exerted by the London markets. Meanwhile Scotland has not been a force in many of the new financial markets while in some areas local characteristics have mitigated against development. The high proportions of public sector home ownership must, for example, have hindered the emergence of indigenous building societies.

Summary

Scottish Financial Institutions

Financial institutions combine a variety of financial functions notably those of a money transmission and payments mechanism, the collection and mobilisation of savings and investment, the provision of insurance and risk management, the supply of lending facilities and the provision of financial information and advice. While all of these services are provided by Scotland's financial institutions, their particular strengths lie in the provision of wholesale investment (predominantly investment management for pension funds and investment trusts), in retail savings and investment primarily through insurance, and, within Scotland, in domestic money transmission and payment. The major weaknesses of Scotland's financial institutions lie in the provision of information and advice to the corporate sector together with associated large scale wholesale (including international) lending. In the personal sector the main weakness lies in the lack of control which many Scottish institutions have over delivery mechanisms for savings and investment outside Scotland. Of the three major functions of a financial system Scotland can claim strengths in the collection and accumulation of funds and in their disbursement and investment. It is weak in the provision of markets for the trading of financial instruments. It may be regarded as a specialist financial centre with an emphasis on investment management and insurance and distinguished by its independent banking.

The Scottish Clearing Banks

On any listing of product range and services offered, the Scottish banks would bear comparison with any other banking group. There are few areas of banking in which they do not participate in one way or another. The more open question is whether the range available is provided on an appropriate scale and on competitive terms within a highly competitive market.

The customer base is predominantly Scottish although this is changing, particularly for the Royal Bank of Scotland with the integration of the Williams & Glyn's operations whilst the Bank of Scotland is establishing outlets in England with a view to competing in the small to medium company market and has recently purchased a majority stake in the Commercial Bank of Wales. These developments reflect the limited opportunities in the market in Scotland and the highly competitive nature of that market since the influx of overseas banks in the 1970s. Outwith London, the English banks have not faced the same degree of competition and opportunities for expansion undoubtedly exist. The Scottish banks, in common with others, have lost their dominant position in the retail deposit market to the building societies. In consequence a greater share of their deposit liabilities to finance their asset expansion has been derived from the wholesale market.

The banks have been effective in their application of technology to transactions processing, the development of ATMs, credit cards and, in the case of the Clydesdale Bank, in experimenting with EFTPOS although so far with no major product development. Similar technological innovation has been demonstrated by the Bank of Scotland with its development of home banking. Competition in the sector in Scotland is strong and will clearly increase from sources such as the TSB and the building societies. The TSB, with a different customer base and with expansion plans in the corporate sector, offers strong competition but like the building societies lacks experience particularly in the area of unsecured lending. Other non-traditional sources of credit have also appeared, such as storecards, but they do, at least initially, offer the prospect of management fees to the established banks. In the corporate sector competition is again keen from other domestic banks, overseas banks and from merchant banks.

The banks have the continuing costs of an extensive branch bank network. It is possible that Scotland is over-provided with bank branches but the costs of concentrating business on fewer, larger branches appear to be prohibitive. With changing technology, particularly in the payments mechanism, the economics of branch banking may be in a period of transition, requiring a reorganisation of priorities in terms of the functions of the branches and the activities of branch managers. The range of products and services marketed effectively from branches is likely to increase in order to justify their continued existence. This has implications for the recruitment and training of bank staff. Scotland has in the past been well served by the traditional education and training of bank staff. There may now be a need for a change in the specification, placing a greater emphasis on, and encouragement of, marketing skills together with an ability to develop and effectively service a wide range of products for both retail and corporate customers.

There is continuing speculation on the probable and preferable future development of the two Scottish-owned banks – the Bank of Scotland and the Royal Bank of Scotland. The two banks view themselves as UK banks as much as Scottish banks although the balance of their activities at present is strongly towards Scotland. Both have a limited overseas presence and both would no doubt welcome the extension of this presence most probably through the acquisition in the USA of an appropriate bank at an appropriate price. To the extent that they develop their activities on a UK-wide basis they may still attract predatory bids from foreign banks seeking a foothold in the UK. Such a move would re-open the arguments associated with earlier attempts to take over the Royal Bank. At present the Royal Bank of Scotland has enlarged its headquarters operations in Edinburgh after the merging of its activities with Williams and Glyn's. Any reversal of such corporate policies either from choice or from future takeover would have very serious implications for Scotland as a regional financial centre. What distinguishes it from other UK centres is the existence of clearing bank headquarters in Edinburgh and the activities associated with such location.

Summary

It would be difficult to visualise a Scottish financial sector in their absence.

The Clydesdale Bank, as a subsidiary of the Midland Bank[*], may have suffered in its expansion plans in consequence of the Midland's well publicised problems with its former American subsidiary. There is a perennial fear that the activities of the Clydesdale will be completely integrated with those of the Midland and its headquarter activity in Glasgow be greatly reduced. Recent pronouncements from the Midland Bank concerning the centralisation of functions heighten these fears.

The Trustee Savings Bank

The TSB has attained full banking status free from residual Treasury control and subject, like all other UK banks, to the supervision of the Bank of England. The dependence on government debt is being reduced and this will free more resources for investment in banking activities. The TSB now offers a wide range of banking services with a strong retail base. The extension of its activities in unsecured lending, the provision of finance for the small business sector, mortgage lending (including its recently acquired estate agency business in Scotland), and expansion through the TSB Group of its unit trust activities, insurance services and instalment credit is likely to place a heavy burden on its headquarters management resources even where it is supplemented by the use of outside expertise as, for example, in the management of its unit trusts.

The TSB faces strong competition over a wide range of its activities and mere incorporation will not diminish them. Incorporation has provided an injection of capital which presents opportunities to the TSB, if wisely used, to complement and supplement its existing activities. As with the other banks it has an extensive branch network to sustain and faces similar strategic decisions as to how to adjust its activities to make the fullest use of them. Takeovers by other organisations are forbidden at least in the early years following incorporation and the TSB is more likely to appear as the bidder, given the capital it has at its disposal after the sale of its equity.

Similar problems of training for the skills of the banker of the future face the TSB. They are much more acute in the short to medium term because of its past history of more limited provision of banking services. In this regard, the next few years will be critical if the TSB is to be capable of exploiting some of its advantages as a new entrant.

Merchant Banks

These are institutions about which it is difficult to make general statements because of their diversity. There are few Scottish merchant banks as a result of the small size and slow growth of the Scottish economy and the banks rely, to a greater or lesser extent, on conducting business outside Scotland.

[*] See footnote on p.68.

Within Scotland they are subject to competition from well-established City institutions who market their services through relatively small Scottish regional offices.

The range of products available in Scotland is therefore extensive but the services actually provided in Scotland are somewhat restricted. The Scottish banks, aware of the growing sophistication of the corporate financial sector, all have merchant bank subsidiaries or access to merchant banking services – the Bank of Scotland through the British Linen Bank, the Royal Bank of Scotland through Charterhouse Japhet and Charterhouse Development and the Clydesdale through its own small subsidiary and its parent's merchant banking connections.

The independent Scottish merchant banks, Noble Grossart, Quayle Munro and James Finlay, operate on a much smaller and more specialised scale, particularly the latter two. They are able to operate in sections of the market which are too small for the big players or where local knowledge is of particular significance and cost advantages may be crucial.

The major problem which these organisations face is the inability of the Scottish economy to generate a large number of new companies growing at a sufficient rate to require the continuing services of a corporate adviser, although the venture capital arm of the merchant banks encourage the development of such companies. The competition for large business is intense and the Scottish institutions may not always have the connections, skills and resources to be effective on the infrequent occasions when such business arises. Even where the Scottish providers meet all these conditions, fears of parochialism and on occasions, misplaced expectations of better service elsewhere, result in high entry barriers being faced. It has to be borne in mind also that some of the Scottish institutions are of recent origin and that reputations and connections take time to establish. It is encouraging that they have been looking outside Scotland as a means of expanding their market.

Life Assurance Companies
The Scottish life assurance companies provide an extensive range of products. The traditional range has been supplemented in recent years by an expansion into unit linked and unit trust activities. They now also have extensive involvement in single premium business, investment management and pensions business. The companies have enjoyed considerable success in extending their share of the life assurance market in recent years. One worrying feature of the market, however, is its sensitivity to government changes in tax treatment. Moreover, the large proportion of the life assurance market which is mortgage related business leaves the companies open to changes in fashion or tax regulation. Both of these issues provide a strong argument for diversification and a continuing search for new products.

The customer base of the assurance companies is UK- wide with not much

Summary

more than 10 per cent of the business of Scottish origin. The base has been widened by the extension of the range of products based on the investment skills which the assurance companies possess. There is little dependence on overseas markets and this may well prove to be a long-term weakness in the context of harmonisation of insurance regulation within the EEC where there is an ageing population enjoying higher levels of income.

The companies have applied their extensive computing skills to the improvement of their traditional products and this has enhanced their market appeal. These skills may have to be developed further as changes in the marketing of insurance take place particularly with the arrival of other institutions offering 'own brand' savings contracts.

Competition, already acute, is likely to become more intense as barriers between financial services are broken down and entry becomes easier and attractive to other potential players. Again marketing skills are likely to determine the beneficiaries. An ability to anticipate the market and respond to change will become even more important under the new regulatory environment. One beneficial effect of the Financial Services Act is that it has forced the assurance companies to consider alternative delivery systems and the prospect of other entrants to an already competitive field.

The costs of the Scottish life offices are generally less than the UK average for life contracts although cost comparisons are difficult because of the differing size of the institutions. Technology has made a significant contribution with costs staying static as output has increased. Marketing costs are, however, likely to become a more important component as frequent adjustment to changing circumstances in the field of personal savings is required.

The mutual companies are largely immune from unwelcome takeovers. It has been suggested that this immunity from continuous market assessment may discourage innovative activity. Equally, however, the absence of shareholders requiring short-term returns could provide a more stable background for such risky activity given management's desire to innovate. The companies are, of course, not immune from competition from other assurance companies or other organisations offering savings contracts. The competition is based on past performance as reflected in the realised values of contracts and from predictions of future performance as reflected in future bonus predictions. Changes in the Financial Services Bill regarding bonus predictions may strengthen the position of assurance companies with already existing successful track records.

The upper echelons of the life offices are dominated by actuaries. This may not necessarily be the best background for meeting current challenges which are largely, and likely to remain, of a marketing nature. Enhanced marketing capability has to be cited as a key determinant of the future of this part of the Scottish financial sector.

Investment Management
Scotland's independent investment managers market their services through two main vehicles; investment trusts and pension funds. Their total investment business is in the region of £11000 million encompassing more than a third of the declining UK investment trust industry, but only a small share of the UK pension fund market (non-insurance based). Two other areas in which the managers are represented are unit trusts and investment management for overseas institutions, but in both areas total business is small. The management of unit trusts is becoming increasingly important as the Scottish life offices set up subsidiaries but the independent fund managers, with one or two exceptions, are not well represented.

A minority of the investment managers stress their regional origins and aim to encourage Scottish and local investment. In general, however, the investment market is UK-wide with increasing effort directed towards recruiting customers from North America and Japan as well as from Europe and Asia. Investment selection is highly international with several managers specialising in the Far East and Japan as well as the traditional orientation to the United States. The independent fund managers have not, in the past, been strongly marketing oriented. The pension fund business is largely dominated by consulting actuaries or pension consultants who appraise the needs of their pension fund clients and then advise accordingly. The advertising of investment trusts has been constrained by law although there is little evidence of significant marketing effort even within the constraints of these restrictions. Unit trusts, one of the more heavily promoted investment vehicles, were largely ignored as a business opportunity, reflecting perhaps the lack of marketing skills and interest within the Scottish investment community but still offer scope for diversification and growth. Emphasis has been upon performance despite the difficulty of either securing or measuring above average risk-adjusted performance. Costs are in general low, a factor that may provide protection from any further increases in competition despite the low barriers to entry and the threat from international competitors. The recent changes in the City and the possibilities of substantial conflicts of interest within competing institutions may indeed emphasise the advantages of independence and aid the competitive position of Scottish fund managers.

The main problem of the Scottish investment managers has been their limited size and cautious investment policy and strategy. This policy coupled with increased resources, particularly for marketing, could be a major selling point for the independent managers. Many investors are looking for caution coupled with low fees and satisfactory performance. The Scottish investment managers are in a good position to meet this need.

Summary

Key Issues for the Future

In this section a number of major issues are examined which can be expected to play a significant role in shaping the Scottish financial sector and in determining its future prosperity. Six issues are identified as of particular importance: international influences; deregulation; technology; marketing; performance and competition; intra-sectoral links; and education and training. Each of these issues is considered and the implications for the Scottish institutions assessed.

International Influences

International pressures have contributed much to the current changes in financial markets. As soon as foreign banks were allowed to operate in a relatively free way it was to be expected that they would attack sectors of the UK market where restrictive practices made it relatively easy to earn profits. In the corporate market the increase in the number of foreign banks in London made it inevitable that they would endeavour to attract domestic business. Regulations could not keep them out of the financial markets since there was considerable profit to be made by designing packages that enabled them to avoid such regulations.

International influences have expanded competition. The path that the UK is currently pursuing is resulting in a more competitive environment and, in particular, one in which international competition is an important element. American and other overseas banks have become an established part of the UK financial scene and their influence is likely to extend beyond the wholesale banking level in the future. It is unlikely, however, that mass penetration of the retail consumer banking and allied services market will take place. The lack of a branch network and the difficulties of acquiring adequate market penetration will be major obstacles to their personal sector expansion, but forays into particularly attractive areas cannot be ruled out.

Because of the relative freedom from regulation and the resulting keen competition, international markets are often a proving ground for financial innovations. The securitisation of international financial lending, the re-allocation of the risks inherent in financial transactions through unbundling and the development of off-balance sheet commitments are among the recent developments in the international markets which are likely to produce spin-offs in domestic banking. International banking involvement provides an exposure to new processes and products which are in turn valuable in the domestic market. The Scottish banks may lack some of these accruing advantages because of their peripheral involvement in wholesale international banking.

Scottish institutions are involved in overseas markets. Investment management is highly international in terms of its investment strategy. A great deal of Scottish portfolio investment is orientated to overseas and Scottish managers have recognised skills in these areas. In addition, many of the larger Scottish investment houses have subsidiaries or joint ventures overseas formed for the purpose of gaining foreign business. They appear to have been at best moderately successful in the past but may be expected to increase their presence in overseas markets in the future. It should be remarked, however, that the orientation of the institutions is predominantly towards America or Japan, despite EEC moves to allow the sale of investment funds throughout the Community by 1989. The lack of initiatives directed towards exploiting the market opportunities offered by the EEC is of some concern. The Scottish banks have limited overseas representation and have shown signs of moderate expansion. There are obvious constraints with regard to TSB Scotland and the Clydesdale Bank. On the other hand, General Accident is an international insurer with the majority of its business carried out overseas and is therefore subject to and responds to international pressures.

The Life Offices represent the most insular of the Scottish institutions although historically Standard Life has links with the Commonwealth and the Scottish Amicable with Australia. The mutual structure of the offices has been used as an argument to stop expansion overseas. It is claimed that expansion in Europe, for example, would not benefit current policy holders and hence should not be carried out. The argument is unanswerable. The interests of current and future policyholders cannot be accurately measured. It has been suggested that the concern about current policyholders is merely a cloak to justify the forces of conservatism and caution. Certainly, if concern for current policy holders was truly the major concern of the life offices few of them would be issuing new business. Most policy holders would be better off with a closed fund from which they received the benefit. The balance between current and future policy holders is, of course, a difficult issue but its use as a stock reply to explain an institution's inaction is unhelpful and leaves obscure both the process by which decisions are reached and the reasoning. It might be expected, in view of European Community aims to secure harmonisation, that the life offices would be establishing subsidiaries or links in Europe if only to secure experience for the future. The ultimate gain stems from the possibility of securing the economies of scale that would be possible if the institution offered policies across the whole Community. Although one would be reluctant to suggest that all companies should be gaining European experience it is worrying that few of the offices are actively pursuing projects in this area.

Deregulation
In some senses deregulation is a misnomer since the current deregulatory process is one of replacing old regulations with new more suitable regulations. The old system was one in which individual institutions were regulated

separately. The system of regulation had no clear objectives and was essentially a response to real or perceived inadequacies in the protection of investors; the need for control of economic variables imposed by the requirements of government policy; a desire to direct funds in particular directions or as a matter of historical accident. The essence of the system was one in which sectors of the market were rigidly segmented. The clearest evidence of this is provided by the building societies which were protected from competition from the banks by the Government's desire to control bank lending. Deregulation is a move away from a restrictive policy based on institutional characteristics to one based on competition between institutions. It does not imply the removal of regulations but rather the implementation of a more rational and fairer basis for regulation. The proposals to date represent a move to more equal treatment in marketing terms. There continue to be significant differences in prudential regulations, namely those aimed at protecting investors which involve balance sheet controls to ensure capital adequacy, liquidity and solvency.

A number of consequences of the deregulation process have become apparent. Firms have, for example, been forced to consider their competitive response to actual or potential changes in competition. Deregulation has lowered the boundaries that previously separated financial institutions with the result that market participants can now enter new lines of business if they are attracted by higher profits. The law of one price implies that lending of equal risk, term and cost of administration should have the same interest rate irrespective of the purpose of the loan. Deregulation, when complete, should remove differences between segments of the financial markets. The result will be that some financial activities will be subject to price competition in a way that has previously been unusual. Mortgages provide a ready example with banks forcing interest rate reductions on the building societies as well as new innovations designed to improve, simplify and cheapen the mortgage granting process.

Given the increase in competition and the expansion of existing firms into new activities it is clear that there may be a trend towards larger firms since such firms may be able to secure economies of scale. However, a countervailing force is the problem of control and potential conflicts of interest posed by large firms as well as the unwillingness of some financial institutions to use the services of financial conglomerates where part of the conglomerate is seen as a competitor. Increased polarisation is probable with at the one extreme large firms looking for marketing and other scale economies and at the other extreme specialist firms aiming to prosper on the basis of service, flexibility, confidentiality and production economies.

Scottish institutions, in as much as they have made conscious decisions of any kind, have followed the second route with the possible exception of the Royal Bank of Scotland and the Standard Life's acquisition of shares in the Bank of Scotland. They have not tried to emulate the London clearers and put together a comprehensive network of financial services under one ownership. Many will have to remember, however, that the deregulation process will also challenge specialisms. In short, there is no ready solution in either extreme, but only in the most careful consideration of where a desirable, competitive advantage lies for each institution.

Technology
Changes in technology have had a major impact on both the financial sector as a whole, and on individual institutions. Among its more significant consequences are improved communications, lower costs, the ability to provide a wider product range and to handle greater volumes of business. Improved communications have made available to both consumers and institutions alike a more extensive range of facilities in more accessible locations as well as improved information systems both for management control and decision making. Improved communication links and the availability of low cost computing facilities is also making possible the automated execution of transactions. For the institutions the improved information is both a benefit and a cost. A benefit because of its ability to improve decision making and control which may, in itself, lead to market growth. A cost since it places consumers in a better position to evaluate alternatives and select the one which is most cost effective for their needs. Moreover, competitors may have ready access to the same data base on which to take competitive decisions and the marketing of financial products thereby acquires greater significance.

The benefits of data processing and the reduction in paper production has resulted in a fall in the cost of servicing accounts; a consequent lowering of charges; and an increase in facilities, with a likely benefit to turnover. The mass processing facilities have enabled institutions to offer a wider range of products which combine different financial functions in a much more effective manner than was previously possible. Computer technology has meant that it is no longer necessary for institutions to offer only contracts that are administratively simple but instead has placed them in a position to offer contracts that meet customers' needs.

This enhanced capability has profound implications for the structure of financial organisations. They are no longer selling a product which, out of administrative necessity, provides individuals with limited scope to exercise choice. Instead the product can be easily altered to meet consumers' needs and to satisfy any requirements that successful marketing may require. The characteristics of financial products may be unbundled and then repackaged in whatever way is most satisfactory. The production of the product has become secondary to a requirement to find out and indeed anticipate the needs of consumers, needs that will vary from simplicity and convenience to requirements for tax efficient packages combining a variety of financial services. The ability to offer a wide range of products has been accompanied

Summary

by an ability to handle a greater volume of business than formerly and allowed the institutions to introduce products and delivery systems that were previously impossible. All institutions have access to the same developments in processing technology. The creative use of the technology for marketing purposes reflects an institution's commitment to meeting customer requirements through research and development to that end.

On the basis of existing technology the Scottish financial institutions appear as well placed as any financial institutions to benefit from it. There is no evidence of technological backwardness and there have been significant innovations in a few areas. However, the nature of technological innovations suggest that benefits in financial markets are at best short-lived and do not provide a permanent basis for fast rates of growth relative to competitors, although technical infrastructure may be a necessary condition for such growth. Of more concern is whether the consequent changes in organisation which enable the effective exploitation of improved technology have occurred or are occurring. In this regard there is little evidence to indicate that the Scottish institutions have moved from being predominantly production-led to being marketing-led.

One issue much discussed has been the relationship between technological advance and jobs. From the statistics in chapter 2 it is clear that the rapid adoption of electronic data processing has not resulted in job losses in total. What it has allowed is an improvement in labour productivity. This outcome has been the result of a number of influences. The improvements in technology have given rise to an increase in the demand for financial services as their provision has more closely accorded with the requirements of customers. This influence has been enhanced by increases in income and wealth which result in further demands for the services of the financial sector. Reduced costs for the services consequent upon computerisation also increase the demand for financial services. Further, the new technology increases employment during research, testing and installation of new applications and technology.

The continuing growth in activity levels has softened the employment impact of changes wrought by computerisation. As growth rates decline the scope for such amelioration is reduced and further advances in electronic data processing may have a more marked effect on employment. The pace of change will also be moderated by agreements within firms as to the immediate impact on employment, the capacity, particularly of branches to accommodate changes and the willingness of customers to adopt the new technology as it becomes available, a function to some extent of the design and marketing of the new products arising from the improved technology.

The effects on employment as Gaskin (1981) notes have been 'evolutionary not revolutionary' and the process is likely to continue. The Scottish institutions appear to have managed the adaptation to new processes well while the skill composition of the staff has been adjusted without excessive disruption.

Marketing
The impact of technology has been to radically change both the opportunities and the problems facing financial institutions. A number of these changes have already been documented including the emphasis that needs to be placed on both satisfying and generating consumer needs and the move towards designing products comprising a collection of financial attributes that can be moulded to suit consumer requirements. Old financial contracts may have to be unbundled and attributes repackaged to meet new needs.

Many changes have been initiated in response to the dramatic changes in competition within financial markets (see next section). More radical changes, however, will yet come in the role and status of marketing skills within the sector. The changes will occur in every element of the marketing mix and at all levels within organisations as product development systems and delivery mechanisms come under new pressures. As part of this process the identification of the marketing characteristics of particular financial products and the methods by which alternative channels of distribution can be employed have become key variables. In the short term the branch network will continue to provide the most satisfactory method of distributing products but as electronic fund transfer becomes more prevalent and acceptable, the need for large branch networks will be reduced and the consequent difficulties of entry even into retail banking will fall. In the short term, the Scottish banks will be protected by their branch networks but in the longer term their future lies in the penetration of a marketing philosophy to the core of their organisations. There appear to be signs that they now attach increased importance to marketing but it is too early to assess their probable success.

It is a common axiom that life assurance is sold and not bought. Yet the dramatic rise of unit linked insurance companies suggests that there may have been a lag in the adoption of market-led management strategies in Scottish life assurance companies. The unitary training associated with the upper echelons of the industry has possibly inhibited the development of a number of business specialists most obviously in the marketing area. Marketing managers must emerge in more central and strategic positions, since marketing is itself about the totality of the business and cannot be seen as a subservient function however actively encouraged.

The suggestion that life assurance is sold and not bought also implies that it is somehow different from other financial products. It is difficult to see why this should be the case in the future even if it has been true in the past. Life assurance is in essence a savings contract and as such is likely to encounter the same difficulties as other such products. Unit trusts must also be sold and the difficulty of selling direct investment in shares, largely for legislative and tax reasons, may explain in part the withdrawal of the personal sector from the stock market. Personal Equity Plans (PEPS) and the increase in competition in stockbroking and allied areas suggest that there will be increased marketing efforts in the savings-investment market in the future. On the loan side bank and mortgage loans have at times been rationed by quantity rather than by price, leading to an important difference between them and other financial products. However, this is rarely the case today. The mortgage market, for example, is witnessing strong competition as indeed is retail lending so that consumers are, in general, in a stronger position than in the past to discriminate between sellers. Attracting and retaining customers becomes a much more important function.

Successful customer relations requires the organisation to build on its strengths and meet consumer needs. A strength of many Scottish investment managers is that they pursue conservative investment policies. It is possible, indeed we are told the evidence is strong, that many investors want conservative investment policies. There may well be an opportunity to continue to pursue a marketing policy based on this coincidence of views. It is unlikely that Scottish investment managers can establish a dominating position in selling investment expertise in international markets. Their international spread of portfolio investment provides investors with additional diversification but it is an industry with few barriers to entry for existing financial institutions and fierce and increasing competition from the large investment houses that can afford to maintain extensive information-gathering services throughout the world seeking early access to new information. The most likely opportunity for the independent investment houses is as low cost providers of expertise for the smaller funds. Their small size, low costs and flexibility should provide opportunities but it would be wrong to believe that they will ever be large players in the financial services market although they may be very important in the independent fund management market.

Performance and Competition
The discussion of deregulation and international influences emphasises the increased competition, both actual and potential, that is emerging in financial markets. A question mark hangs over the most appropriate response to this competition. Throughout the international financial system there has been a tendency for regulatory barriers to be reduced thus removing restrictions on the range of financial products which may be provided by organisations under one ownership. The willingness and ability to take advantage of these regulatory changes has been encouraged by improvements in computer, communications and software technology. The cost of providing for these improvements and the specialist staff to operate these sophisticated systems encourage the growth of international conglomerate organisations operating in a range of currencies in all the major international centres

providing facilities for the large non-financial corporations.

These large conglomerate organisations bring with them their own problems. The issue of potential conflicts of interest arising within an organisation providing both retail and commercial banking, insurance, commodities and securities trading and investment management are frequently commented upon. Questions remain as to the impartiality of advice offered by organisations with interests on both sides of a transaction.

The international market will be able to support only a few major international players and the competition to remain a force in the market will be keen providing some protection for clients against exploitation. Large organisations, although able to reap economies of scale, can also make expensive mistakes as well as suffer from bureaucratic inertia. Supervisory intervention to provide protection to the clients of conglomerates and to regulate the acceptance of risk by the conglomerates cannot be ruled out. These factors may limit the expansion of the financial conglomerates.

The Scottish institutions have not sought to follow the international conglomerate route. Their approach has been to follow the traditional specialist route expecting to benefit from specialisation by concentrating on a narrow range of products where some comparative advantage lies and where conflicts of interest can be avoided. This approach may prove to be attractive to customers seeking independent advice and wishing to avoid dependence on any one institution.

There are also several intermediate positions between specialisation and conglomeration which may offer a perfectly feasible option for a wide range of existing and potential customers. The Scottish banks appear to have opted for such an approach, by developing their own customer base and tapping into the expertise of others by specific agreement. Other institutions are relying on co-operation or joint ventures to extend their range of activities whilst retaining their independence. Access to competitive services, nationally and internationally, may prove to be a more appropriate route than relying on the internalisation of transactions.

As mutual organisations the major Scottish life offices are not subject to shareholder and stock market assessment as are public limited companies. Nor, on the other hand, can they tap the capital markets for finance to undertake expansion. They are nevertheless subject to competitive pressures from other institutions, mutual and public, in all the markets in which they operate. Actual or potential returns on contracts for insurance, investment management and pension business form the basis of these comparisons. Since they do not pay dividends directly to shareholders, but only indirectly to their 'with profits' policy holders, the mutual companies may have a cost advantage which should increase their appeal to potential customers. On the basis of past performance the Scottish mutuals are performing well. Their major weakness appears to have been a possible over-concentration in specific products in the insurance market and in-

Summary

adequate diversification into other fast growing markets. Their record of innovation outside of the traditional areas of the market has been poor. A continuing unwillingness to initiate innovation or even to be effective imitators of successful innovation would prove to be a long-term handicap for the continuing growth of the Scottish mutual assurance companies.

It is particularly difficult to assess the performance of the public sector financial institutions. They too are not directly subject to market appraisal. The SDA has a financial target to meet which is apparently of modest proportions. The question must be asked, however, if such targets are appropriate for a public sector institution set up to fill a gap in the provision of financial services which the private sector was unable or certainly unwilling to fill on its own. The acceptance of greater information costs and higher risk makes direct comparison with the private sector institutions inappropriate and, on occasions, potentially misleading. The HIDB has for the most part no financial target to meet. It is probably best regarded as a mechanism for distributing aid to meet a particular regional weakness. Like the SDA, its operations are subject to government control through the Scottish Office and it also faces external assessment through the political process. The future development and expansion of these institutions will be more dependent on government policy than on profitability and competitive considerations.

Intra-Sectoral Links

Financial flows in Scotland were considered in chapter 2. Although it was found impossible to fully quantify the size of financial flows within the Scottish sector it was shown that the flows were substantial and the role of the banks was emphasised. The importance of the banks for the UK system as a whole can be seen by considering the sources of funds of the non-bank financial institutions as shown in table 11.1. In 1975 the banks were of little significance in providing funds to the financial sector as a whole. By 1985 this position had been completely reversed. Bank borrowing is now a major source of funds for other financial institutions reflecting both the significant changes that have taken place in the security markets and the importance of the banks to the financial system. Building societies, for example, now borrow in the wholesale markets from both banks and industrial and commercial companies, often for the long term. Changes are also evident in the banking institutions. It is increasingly argued that the banks are now asset driven rather than liability led, a reflection of the role of the capital markets in allowing them to match their assets and liabilities. Over the counter deposits now account for less than a half of the liabilities of the Scottish banks. Other deposits, such as from companies, are very volatile and emphasise the banks' need for, and use of, funds from the inter-bank and other markets. In short, there has been a significant increase in the inter-dependence between financial institutions, and the Scottish institutions are no

Table 11.1. Other financial institutions' sources of funds (£ million).

	1975	%	1980	1985	%	% change 1975-85
Building society deposits	4172	44	7002	13736	31	329
Unit trusts	190	2	77	2386	5	1256
Property units	81	1	105	11	0	−87
Capital issues	317	3	20	1678	4	529
Bank borrowing	35	0	628	6514	15	18611
Life assurance and pensions (net inflow)	4162	44	10425	16823	38	404
Other	500	6	2085	2457	7	—
Total	9459		20342	43695		465

Source: Financial Statistics.

different in this respect from other institutions. They are increasingly intertwined with the UK financial system. There can be no separate independent Scottish financial sector, certainly in the present financial environment.

The components of the Scottish financial sector are competitive as well as complementary. Many Scottish institutions appear to have a preference for London based brokers and markets even where a Scottish based alternative is available. Some such business relationships are indicative of the fact that Scotland is part of the total UK market and operates in that total market. Other relationships are designed to avoid competitors and claims of parochialism. Scottish based activities are used because they are as efficient and cheap as competing services elsewhere and not because they are Scottish. A fear of helping an actual or potential regional competitor may drive some institutions to London based companies. However, there is also a strong, regional financial establishment with many and complex links which may lead to a pooling of information and some informal co-operation. This co-operation is most obvious at board level where there are a considerable number of directors who serve on the boards of several financial institutions. However, doubts have been raised as to how far this improves co-operation at executive level. There are undoubtedly close associations between executives in different firms derived from educational and professional links but these connections often stress competition rather than co-operation. This is reflected in intense inter-firm rivalry which bears little reference to competition alone. It is at least an open question as to whether the future of the Scottish sector can be shaped by a more considered development of trading links. Joint products and joint marketing activities are relatively underdeveloped although there have been recent signs of change. Moreover, it is possible that niche activities and particular gap filling specialisms would emerge if joint marketing strategies were developed by some of the leading institutions.

However, there is also a need to be aware that the market is international and not Scottish. Scottish firms are often fond of claiming that they are the largest in Scotland thereby taking a small market as their reference standard. It would be more satisfactory if they took the UK or a wider international framework as their arena. The willingness to co-operate in 'Scottish Financial Enterprise' at least shows an awareness of the potential gains from a joint approach to marketing Scotland as a financial centre, although in itself it does not tackle the specific problem discussed in this section. It is possible to have an apparently co-operative external image without ever exploiting new opportunities at the operational level.

As the second most important financial centre in the UK the attraction of Edinburgh is considerable providing as it does a pool of skilled talent in the financial, accounting, legal and other related areas backed by the appropriate communications and technical skills to provide all the relevant information and services required. The role of Scottish Financial Enterprise is to give these undoubted attractions prominence and publicise them, both as a unified whole and as separate components to potential users both in this country and abroad.

Within this framework it is the responsibility of the individual institutions to develop their strengths as they see fit either on their own or in association with others in the financial centre or outside it. Many of the institutions are small in both absolute and relative terms. There are several areas where critical and non-competitive skills could be transferred between them. For example, the international experience of some investment managers in high technology industries in the US and Japan is directly relevant to merchant bankers supporting similar firms in the UK. Equally, more joint international activity between the clearing banks might be desirable.

Collectively the sector faces major market changes within which institutional boundaries are being redrawn and against which they will have to form new relationships, both within and outwith Scotland. Moreover, there are many areas where the financial services industry has joint interests, for example, in educational, legal and fiscal matters. From a Scottish economic development perspective, there are also important reasons for recognising a centre, not least because it provides a focus for potential policy initiatives as well as highlighting both problems and opportunities. The provision of national and international visibility through concerted action are among the other reasons for identifying inter-sectoral links as an important element for the future. The sector has an underdeveloped potential which appropriate marketing and support could exploit with benefit.

Education and Training
The size and diversity of the labour force in the Scottish financial sector make it difficult to generalise on the exact way in which educational provision will impinge in the future. We found much evidence of the major

firms citing the quality, cost and flexibility of labour being a significant asset arising from their Scottish location. At the same time, consistent shortages in specialised areas are evidenced throughout the UK and particularly in Scotland. However, the trends in the market observed throughout this study would point to a need to recognise the limitations of rather narrow training programmes and of recruitment policies which perpetuate uniform approaches to problems.

Since many of the leading organisations constitute tight internal labour markets, mobility and skill transference is not readily achieved. The signals from the market would tend to suggest an increasing need for more systematic post-experience training which brought together members of staff from different parts of the sector. For example, given the convergence of financial markets and the premium on new approaches to marketing, ways have to be found for large scale quality training in these areas. While there is already evidence of more flexible policies of recruitment in banking and insurance, these largely remain at the margin, whereas the educational challenge undoubtedly lies in achieving high levels of penetration in training in new products and delivery systems.

The case for more joint action within the sector on employee development would seem to be a strong one. It rests on the increasing levels of common interests in staff grounded in finance, marketing and general management skill, as well as offsetting the career pull of London. Both these factors point to considerable emphasis being placed on the development of existing and younger staff, rather than a resort to recruitment at senior levels. Again, in the international arena, there is little evidence of, although much scope for, joint action in the overseas placing and training of staff from Scottish institutions. The total network of contacts known to the sector as a whole could probably readily provide for such schemes. Going further, the promotion of Scotland as a centre for financial training through the support of existing, or the development of new provisions, has also considerable merits, not least because it would help to remove the insularity from some of the existing programmes.

It is acknowledged that the relevant Scottish professional institutions have recognised the need for both broader initial and greater volumes of subsequent training. But they have generally acted individually and show insufficient signs of an integrated approach to the problems outlined.

Conclusions

We have attempted in this chapter to summarise the major factors that have influenced the development of the Scottish financial sector. We have also outlined the key issues that the sector faces. The list is not exhaustive but it is enough to indicate some of the opportunities and indeed some of the difficulties that the institutions will encounter in the coming years.

12

CONCLUSIONS

The previous chapter summarised the development of the Scottish financial system and set out a number of major issues considered to be of particular significance to the sector. Based on that discussion a number of conclusions about the present and future prospects of the Scottish institutions may be drawn and it is the task of this chapter to outline these views. The chapter is divided into three sections. The first sets out our conclusions for three major groups of institutions in the sector, the Scottish clearing banks, the Life Assurance companies and Investment Management firms. Section two considers the possibilities for expansion and growth in the sector whilst section three sets out a suggested Programme for Action. Part three is deliberately different from the rest of the book. It reflects a view of the sector that we believe is supported by the rest of the book and proposes measures that could be taken to improve its viability, growth and prospects. Our intention is to promote deliberation and discussion which examines alternative courses of action and promotes an informed choice of strategies for the future.

Existing Institutions and Markets

Clearing Banks

As a result of the lack of scope for extensive domestic expansion the Scottish clearing banks must, if they are to grow rapidly, follow the assurance companies and increase their dependence on markets outside Scotland whilst changing to meet domestic competition. As the pressure for universal financial institutions develops, and we assume it will, the Scottish banks have a choice of either linking with other institutions to provide adequate coverage or concentrating on particular areas where scale is not of crucial importance. The two major Scottish banks are somewhere in the middle – not big enough to be players in the big league of UK clearers or international banks, but providing a wide range of services although perhaps not on a large enough scale to be completely effective in some market segments. Clearly there are pressures to grow and expand demonstrated by the national integration of its branch network by the Royal Bank of Scotland and the significant holding in the Bank of Scotland owned by Standard Life although this has not, to date, led to integration.

For all banks technology developments in the payments system make cash handling of less significance for the branch network. In the longer term this will also reduce the heavy costs of the money transmission mechanism. To justify their present branch network the banks require to undertake the marketing of a wide range of financial services generating income for the bank. This will require a change in the orientation of management at the centre and at the branches with a major training task to reorientate the branch to new priorities. The banks have a need to reduce the number of branches they have in the slower growing and less profitable markets in Scotland and to increase the number in the faster growing markets of the South.

In the highly competitive corporate finance sector with competition from domestic and international institutions and the growth of new markets, such as that in corporate paper, the banks face increasingly sophisticated competitors and financial managers. Undoubtedly specialist bankers are necessary in this area.

The banks have a reasonable record of adjustment and appear willing to meet changing circumstances. They face increased competition from both existing and new providers in the market although their branch network and skill base currently provides them with opportunities to both retain existing clients and, by selective marketing, to increase their UK penetration. The key to their future success is a clear post-deregulation strategy that recognises their strengths: an established delivery mechanism which is capable of handling new product ranges and serves an established customer base which has in the past exhibited strong customer loyalty; strong balance sheets with a diversified portfolio and a competent corporate performance record. Against these strengths must be balanced their weaknesses: their lack of experience in the large corporate financial advisory sector of the market; their relative size and their over-concentrated branch network in Scotland.

Assurance Companies

Assurance companies have been adept at applying the new technologies to their traditional business and have secured a growing share of the life market although this raises fears about a possible excessive dependence on mature products and particularly mortgage-related products. Significant changes in the types of policies sold from year to year have, however, enabled them to maintain a balanced long-term portfolio of policies. The companies have been less willing to extend their skills to other sectors of the market. Their success in attracting business in the rapidly growing pensions market is, however, encouraging and hopefully provides a prelude to more innovation as needs change. Their belated entry to the unit trust market has been in many cases a spectacular success.

The incentive for change and innovation are possibly reduced with a mutual organisation. The possibility of detrimental effects on policy holders may have acted as a brake on a number of new developments. The Financial

Conclusions

Services Act may, in turn, provide a major spur to innovation as the relative positions of brokers and other institutions with interests in the insurance market are changed as a result of its provisions.

The assurance companies report that they find no great disadvantage in having their headquarters in Scotland, and indeed see advantages in terms of staffing and distance from the financial markets which some contend are excessively driven by short-term influences. Their continued location in Scotland seems assured since they have successfully serviced the 90 per cent of their non-Scottish members for many years and have acquired a reputation for prudence. A major problem of the life companies is their lack of control over fiscal and regulatory changes, changes which in the past have provided them with both short-term boosts and reductions of business in consequence of particular regulatory changes.

This lack of control is also apparent in their product delivery systems. As previously noted the new financial services legislation may require the companies to innovate and explore new distribution systems as well as increasing the emphasis on marketing and the development of new products both within and outside existing markets. Deregulated product markets give the Scottish life companies the opportunity to mobilise their investment management resources and marketing expertise and apply them to new areas outside the traditional life sector. At the same time however, other firms will find it easier to compete in the life sector and the continued success of the Scottish life offices is far from guaranteed.

Investment Management

The investment sector has suffered from a continuing loyalty to investment trusts rather than moving to newer products such as unit trusts which have been the source of major expansion for other groups. Scope for expansion may arise from the expected introduction of PEPs and the continuing tax advantages in favour of pension funds together with the possibility of legislation allowing personal pensions. The Financial Services Act should improve the competitiveness of the independent Scottish investment houses since stockbrokers and merchant banks will find it increasingly difficult to cross-subsidise their investment activities. The investment houses may also gain from fears over the 'impartiality' of some of their conglomerate competitors. The majority of the companies are characterised by high quality staff and have been able to exploit their small size by rapid response and by displaying a high degree of flexibility to new situations. However, most of the Scottish investment managers have only a limited capital base and have found it difficult to exploit innovations and actively market their products in the past. Opportunities exist for developing new outlets for their existing products related to their long-term investment skills as well as developing new products. The key to their success will be in finding, retaining and motivating key staff together with a satisfactory level of product innovation and marketing. Their experience of foreign investment should be helpful in attracting domestic and overseas business, although international investment is a much more competitive arena than in the past.

Other Financial Activities
From the fund of skills and experience existing in the Scottish financial sector, combined with lower operating costs, progress might be possible in a number of areas, three examples of which are cited below.
Information and Computing Services. The restructuring of the UK capital markets will provide a growing requirement for independent and effective research. The assimilation and processing of information for analytical purposes will be a much sought-after skill. These research and computing skills can readily be provided away from the major financial markets. WM Company, originally part of the stockbrokers Wood Mackenzie, provides an interesting illustration of the demand for such services. WM Company is the foremost UK company in the assessment of portfolio performance and provides a management information service to a large number of clients. The business has grown rapidly and employs more than 300 staff, many of them graduates and highly trained. As a measure of its importance and the significance of information provision, it is worth noting that the firm employs a similar number to the entire independent fund management business in Scotland. The setting up of Broker Services Limited, a joint venture between Barclays Bank and NMW Computers (which is to be staffed, in the first instance, by the backroom team from Penney Easton, the Glasgow stockbroker), provides another example of possible developments. Broker Services Limited is an independent clearing firm providing dealing, settlement and computer facilities for brokers. These facilities will be attractive to small- to medium-sized brokers and to foreign securities firms who want to expand in London without the expense of a dealing room. Staff in user firms will be freed to concentrate on cultivating customers.
Share Registration and Credit Card Operations. The banks and other financial institutions are a repository of skills in processing large quantities of routine but crucial information. These skills are already applied by the banks in areas outside banking such as share registration and related activities. Credit card operations require similar skills attached in many cases to financial provision, and as well as their own credit card operations the Scottish banks provide such services to other organisations, such as Marks and Spencer, the AA and Stylecard. These arrangements provide the banks with access to the customer base of other institutions, access to which would otherwise be both difficult and expensive.
Merchant Banking. The strengths of Scottish merchant banks are their small size and specialist nature but they suffer from a corresponding weakness in their capital base and the perception that they lack experience and are essentially serving the small local corporate market. The reality is, of course,

Conclusions

often different and several provide niche services at national and international level. Merchant banking sets a premium on size and tradition although the whole industry is currently undergoing substantial change and increased competition. Because of the increasing institutionalisation of UK merchant banks opportunities may exist in specialist niches but it is important that the Scottish competitors provide corporate clients with ideas and ingenuity in a range of products and services as a credible alternative to the major players in the market.

Expansion and Growth

Ignoring the growth that would result from a general expansion of the domestic Scottish economy, new growth or contraction in the Scottish financial sector is the result of the interaction of two main sets of forces. The first of these forces is a result of the takeover mechanism and induces the movement of management control activities out of Scotland. It has not, in general, benefited Scotland although on the plus side General Accident has acquired a variety of insurance and investment activities whilst the Royal Bank, due to its earlier takeover activities, has been able to extend its branch activities throughout Great Britain. Its recent acquisitions have also greatly improved its presence in corporate markets. A number of individuals have stressed to us the benefits of the merger of the bank's activities in a number of different areas but especially through its effects on management thinking.

On the negative side takeovers have resulted in the loss of business from Edinburgh, particularly in general insurance. Other changes in management control have resulted in the gain of the National Savings Bank and the partial loss of the TSB. Centralisation pressures within the Midland Bank are likely to result in at least a downgrading of decision-making power in the Clydesdale Bank.

Outside of the financial sector there has been a progressive loss of management control from formerly Scottish controlled firms. This loss of control has important effects on the demand for the services of the Scottish banks and specialist financial institutions. The movement of head offices to London or abroad results in a reduction of contact with local financial firms and an inevitable decline in demand for their services (Ashcroft *et al.* 1986).

The second force is the growth of new firms. Scotland has had a low birth rate of new firms in the financial sector and those which have appeared have remained small. It has been relatively poor at new product innovation and in particular in recognising new financial products and markets. It appears to be successful at organic growth although there may at times be a tendency to concentrate on old, mature products. This is not to say that operating effectively in mature markets cannot be highly profitable, but a balance has to be struck in the portfolio of products.

A number of personnel from Scottish firms have started financial enterprises in London and elsewhere. This suggests that the relatively few start-ups in Scotland may not result from a lack of entrepreneurship, although relatively low Scottish salaries and hence opportunities to accumulate capital may deter some personnel from starting on their own. The opportunities are greater in London because of the size of that market and a more open attitude to innovation. Setting up in London is a method of minimising risk. It is not clear that existing UK institutions or individuals, in general, have been particularly innovatory in new product markets and hence it is difficult to judge the record of the Scottish institutions. However, the Scottish institutions largely missed out on the growth of the unit trust market and the number of institutions pioneering new techniques of investment has been proportionately smaller in Scotland.

Future expansion in the Scottish financial sector will primarily be based on the ability of existing financial institutions to meet competition in the domestic market from other national and foreign firms attempting to encroach and, more importantly, to compete successfully in markets outside Scotland. The development of new firms providing new services and products and serving new markets could also be an important source of expansion. Existing relationships and the attractions of the existing sector, particularly the availability of skilled and trained personnel; the existence of appropriate programmes providing education and training; the existence of related outside accounting, legal, computing and other services; cost economies in terms of staff and occupancy costs; and the possibility of aid and assistance from the SDA could provide a basis for future developments. The benefits of a Scottish location require to be broadcast to attract the attention of financial entrepreneurs seeking a base for expansion.

The future expansion of the sector is not assured. The rapidly changing environment does not favour caution. There is a need for frequent reappraisal of strategies and action at the company level to ensure that firms are positioned in expanding areas of the market.

Programme for Action

In analysing the Scottish financial sector, this project has attempted throughout to take a balanced view of its overall economic condition. The general tenor of the findings is cautious optimism, but with a considerable number of reservations. Many of these are related to the perceived strategies of some of the key players. Clearly, however, there is no simple view of what the shape of the Scottish financial sector should be, and this study can only reflect a considered view of actions which might enhance the prosperity of the sector and ensure that it makes a growing contribution towards the Scottish economy.

Even with these qualifications however, there are a number of critical areas which have been identified for both the sector as a whole and its prime-moving institutions. A long-term programme of action is required.

Conclusions

The purpose of this final section is to identify these in the light of the changes anticipated in the capital markets.

Sectoral Development

It is encouraging that the sector has recently recognised the importance of institutional action to promote its interests through the medium of Scottish Financial Enterprise (SFE). Ideally, SFE will open up opportunities for joint activity in many other areas including technology sharing, international networking and building data bases. Many parts of the sector remain complacent about the future and about joint action, and are not apparently implementing development strategies which will maintain their competitive advantage either as specialist or conglomerate institutions. Many institutions have been found to have a real understanding of the opportunities and threats facing them, and the sector as a whole, but are unsure of the appropriate response.

Some companies, including institutions in life assurance and investment management, continue to place too much confidence in mature products and existing delivery systems.

To assess the threats and develop an effective response each board within this sector, and especially in the areas mentioned, should call their executives to account to ensure that radical reappraisals of future options become a way of life in this rapidly changing sector. We found no strong evidence that this was taking place.

In some instances there is a need for a reassessment of executive and board responsibilities to ensure that strategy is effectively developed and monitored. This could involve some board reconstruction and making more effective use of interlocking directorships.

Inter-firm linkages

Although not a uniquely Scottish problem, there are notably few linkages between some of the principal actors in the sector. This is at least, in part, because of the UK and international orientation of some of these institutions and because of their implicit lack of recognition of a sector or centre as such. Fear of parochialism and ignorance of opportunities however, also rank as factors, as do policies of maintaining separate fiefdoms.

At a time when there is much strategic repositioning within financial markets, there are *prima facie* grounds for expecting comprehensive re-assessments of opportunities for collaboration, both within Scotland and beyond. We found little evidence of either existing interaction (in joint products or joint ventures) outwith investment management or of the recognition that there might be scope for building such commercial relationships within the sector.

It is reasonable to hypothesise that, within the constraints of prudence, some increasing interaction would result in the spawning of new initiatives, the emergence of complementary demands for services and the filling of gaps in the sector. This, in turn, might result in significant improvement in the new firm starts within the sector.

Marketing
While we recognise the importance of the SFE initiative to promote the sector, the marketing problem goes much deeper. Several parts of the sector are not yet market driven, even though they show extensive signs of recognising the need to be more marketing orientated.

There are signs that the new competitive environment will reduce brand loyalty, shorten product cycles and take some aspects of financial services closer to 'commodity' products, so that new products and markets must continuously be developed.

We would recommend wide-ranging research as well as individual and collaborative management development initiatives to improve the marketing capability of the Scottish sector as a whole.

In our view increased attention is required in order to equip the sector with the quantity and quality of marketing expertise which will be required for the development of both product and delivery systems as market boundaries are eroded.

There is little evidence that marketing training on an appropriate scale is taking place in many of the institutions. Indeed, the infra-structure to cope with this requirement does not exist within Scotland.

The perceived needs span the whole area of marketing from market research, product development, pricing, distribution systems, logistics, marketing management to advertising and promotion. These requirements call for a concerted Scottish effort to develop the necessary skill base for providing quality training on the marketing of financial services.

Education
In addition to the specific references made above in the marketing context, we recommend a major review of the total educational provision for the finance sector and an audit of the emerging skill requirements in order to ensure that it can respond to the challenges of the 1990s.

Some of the features of employment and training emerging from the study would suggest certain questions which should be borne in mind. These include the relative lack of knowledge and, on occasion, the shortage of systematic planning for manpower development for the future; the tightness of some internal labour markets which work against the generation of general and strategic management skills; the relative inflexibilities of many of the professional training programmes and in particular their failure to develop general financial skills applicable across the sector; and the lack of inter-company mobility and external recruitment.

The future health of the sector in our view will be strongly determined by imaginative and decisive action in the educational field over the next decade.

Government Support

Acknowledging the weight given in this study to the prime moving role of the Scottish banks within the Scottish financial sector, continued vigilance about their ownership, strategies and the location of management functions will be a key contribution to the sector.

The low level of new starts in financial services in Scotland is a cause for concern and efforts might be made through the SDA to identify areas of opportunity and contribute support assistance in a manner which would suit the particular needs of the sector.

There may be a continuing role for sector 'gap filling' by encouraging, through 'Locate in Scotland', the entry of specialist service companies for the UK market.

Both these objectives might require the consideration of the provision of specific types of high quality office space in both Edinburgh and Glasgow, with again the SDA acting as a catalyst.

Closely related is the encouragement which might be given to further state-of-the-art technological developments in Scotland, possibly through joint public and private sector sponsoring of demonstration projects.

One of the most important government contributions is in encouraging a reappraisal of the provision of education and training for the sector.

The Scottish Office should develop a stronger interest in the Scottish financial sector as part of its objective to strengthen the Scottish economy. Local authority attitudes to financial sector development might be improved as a means of attracting employment in areas where growth has been apparent and where Scotland has a comparative advantage.

Central government and the Bank of England might redress their overwhelming concern with the City as the major financial centre and express more interest and involvement with the second financial centre in the country.

The distinctive Scottish financial sector operating within the independent UK and, indeed, international market has many features working in its favour. It does not however, have a pre-ordained right to succeed or survive and in an increasingly complex and competitive environment continuing innovation must be the hallmark of its successful participants. Institutions geared to change and welcoming innovation are a *sine qua non* of future expansion and prosperity. Creating the infra-structure for change provides a positive contribution, ensuring that the employment-creating potential is realised.

BIBLIOGRAPHY

Aaronovitch, S. & M. Sawyer (1982) *A study of the evolution of concentration in the UK Insurance Industry with special reference to life assurance* Evolution of Concentration and Competition Series: Working Papers (44), Commission of the European Communities.

Alexander, K.J.W. (1981) Developing the Highlands and Islands *Dundee School of Economics* (ed. Lythe, S.G.E. & Blake, C.) Gee London.

Arnaud, A.A. (1977) (1st. edn.) (1983) (2nd. edn.) *Investment Trusts Explained* Woodhead-Faulkner in co-operation with the Association of Investment Trust Companies.

Ashcroft, B.K., Love, J.H. & Scouller, J. (1986) *The Economic Effects of the Inward Acquisition of Scottish Manufacturing Companies 1965 to 1980* Submitted to Industry Department for Scotland.

Association of Investment Trust Companies (AITC) (1978-1985) *Yearbooks* AITC and The Macmillan Co.

Bain, A.D. (1981) *The Economics of the Financial System* Martin Robertson.

Bain, A.D. & R.G. Reid (1984) The Finance Sector *Industry, Policy and the Scottish Economy* (ed. Hood, N. & Young, S.) Edinburgh University Press.

Banz, R.W. (1981) The Relationship between Return and Market Value of Common Stocks *Journal of Financial Economics 9,* March 3-18.

Barnes, P. & Dodds, J. (1983) The structure and performance of the U.K. building society industry 1970-78 *Journal of Business, Finance and Accounting 10,* 37-56.

Benston, G.J. (1973) The optimal banking structure: theory and evidence *Journal of Bank Research 3,* No.4 Winter 220-237.

Blyth, S. (1985) Scottish Insurance Broking *The British Insurance Broker* September 23-26.

Boreham, G.F. (1984) *Financial Innovation in Canada* Societé Universitaire Européene des Recherches Financières.

The Building Societies Association (BSA) (1980) *Studies in Building Society Activity 1974-79* BSA January.

—— (1984) Staff and productivity in building societies *BSA Bulletin* No.40 October 7-10.

—— (1984) *Building Societies: A New Framework* Response by the BSA, October.

—— (1985) Building Societies Year Book 1985 Franey & Co.

Button, K.J. (1985) New approaches to the regulation of industry *The Royal Bank of Scotland Review* December 18-34.

Carmichael, W.B. (1985) Glasgow "the most vigorous floor outside London" *Scottish Development Agency 120.*

Carter, R.L. (1979) *Economics and Insurance* 2nd Edition, PH Press.

Carter, R.L. & A.H. Godden (1984) *The British Insurance Industry; A Statistical Review (1984/85 ed.)* Insurance Week Kluwer Publishing Ltd.

Checkland, S.G. (1975) *Scottish Banking A History, 1695-1973* Collins.

Cockerell, H.A.L. & Green E. (1976) *The British Insurance Business 1547-1970* Heineman Educational Books.

Committee of the Edinburgh Stock Exchange (1944) *The Edinburgh Stock Exchange 1844-1944.*

Bibliography

Committee of London Clearing Bankers (1977) *Evidence to the Committee to Review the Functioning of Financial Institutions (hereafter Wilson Committee)* November.

The Committee of Scottish Clearing Bankers (1977) *Evidence to the Wilson Committee, Memorandums 1 and 2* June.

Copeland, T. E. & Weston, J. F. (1983) *Financial Theory and Corporate Policy* 2nd edn. Addison-Wesley.

Crawfords (1986) *Directory of City Connections* 8th edn. Crawford Publications Ltd.

Cucksey, J. & Medland, D. (1984) *The Unlisted Securities Market: A Review* Waterlow Executive Bulletin Waterlow Publishers Ltd.

Davies, G. (1981) *Building Societies and Their Branches - A Regional Economic Survey* Franey & Co.

Davies, P.L. & Canes, M. (1978) Stock Prices and the Publication of Second Hand Information *Journal of Business 51*, No.1 Jan. 43-56.

Davis, E.W. & Yeomans, K.A. (1974) *Company Finance and the Capital Market: A Study of the Effects of Firm Size* Cambridge University Press Occ. Paper 39 Department of Applied Economics Cambridge.

Dimson, E., Hodges, S. & Marsh, P. (1980) *International Diversification* Presented at seminar on The Coming Revolution in Investment Management, London Business School.

Dodds, J.C. (1979) *The Investment Behaviour of British Life Insurance Companies* Croom Helm.

Draper, P.R. (1984) Competition or control: the Green Paper on building societies *The Fraser of Allander Quarterly Economic Commentary 10*, August 56-59.

Draper, P.R. & Stevens, J. (1984) *The Efficiency of the UK Investment Trust Market* Discussion Paper, Department of Economics University of Strathclyde.

Draper, P.R. Gibson, H. & Stevens, J. (1985) *UK Closed End Funds, Liquidation Costs and Market Efficiency* Paper presented to the Western Finance Association Conference Arizona.

Draper, P.R. (1986) The Advantages of Diversification through UK Equities *The Investment Analyst* No. 79 January 23-25.

Draper, P.R.(1986) Unit Trust Objectives and Investor Choice *Applied Economics* 18 157-172.

Dundas Hamilton, J. (1986) *Stockbroking Tomorrow* The Macmillan Press.

Economists Advisory Group (1984) *City 2000 - The Future of London as an International Financial Centre* Lafferty Publications Ltd.

Fama, E.F. (1970) Efficient Capital Markets: A Review of Theory and Empirical Work *Journal of Finance XXV*, No.2 March 383-417.

Fforde, J.S. (1983) Competition, innovation and regulation in British banking *Bank of England Quarterly Bulletin 23*, 3 September 363-376.

Franklin, P.J. (1978) Acquisition and mergers of U.K. insurance institutions 1966-1975 *Journal of Risk and Insurance* September 413-429.

Franklin, P.J. & Woodhead, C. (1980) *The U.K. Life Assurance Industry: A study in applied economics* Croom Helm.

Fullerton, M.J. (1986) *Structural and Competitive Changes in the Scottish Banking Industry* Unpublished MBA Thesis, University of Strathclyde.

Gaskin, M. (1965) *The Scottish Banks: A Modern Survey* George Allen & Unwin Ltd.

Gaskin, M. (1980) *Report on Employment in Insurance, Banking and Finance in Scotland* ESU Research Paper No.2, Scottish Economic Planning Department.

Greenbaum, S.I. & Haywood, C.F. (1971) Secular Change in the Financial Services Industry *Journal of Money, Credit and Banking 3*, May 570-589.

Bibliography

Guy, J. (1978) The Performance of the British Investment Trust Industry *Journal of Finance XXXIII*, No.2 May 443-455.

Havrilesky, T.M. & Boorman, J.T. (1980) *Current Perspectives In Banking* 2nd edn. AHM Publishing.

HM Treasury (1984) *Building Societies: A New Framework* July Cmnd 9316, London: HMSO.

HM Treasury (1984) *Trustee Savings Banks* Cmnd 9415, London: HMSO.

Howcroft, J.B. & Lavis, J. (1986) A strategic profile of the payments systems of London Clearing Banks *Research Papers in Banking and Finance* (eds. Revell, J. & Gardner, E.P.M.) Institute of European Finance, University College of North Wales.

Industry Department for Scotland *Scottish Input-Output Tables for 1979.*

Jensen, M.C. (1968) The Performance of Mutual Funds in the Period 1945-1964 *Journal of Finance XXIII*, No.2 May 389-415.

Jensen, M.C. (1969) Risk, the Pricing of Capital Assets, and the Evaluation of Investment Portfolios *Journal of Business 42*, No.2 April 167-247.

Kane, E.J. (1980) Accelerating Inflation, Regulation and Banking Innovation *Issues in Bank Regulation* Summer 7-14.

Kane, E.J. (1983) Policy Implications of Structural Changes in Financial Markets *American Economic Association Papers and Proceedings 73*, No.2 96-100.

Kane, E.J. (1984) Technological and Regulating Forces in the Developing Fusion of Financial Services Competition *Journal of Finance XXXIX*, 3 July 759-772.

Kerr, D.P. (1965) Some aspects of the geography of finance in Canada *Canadian Geographer 9*, 175-192

Kindleberger, C.P. (1974) *Development of Financial Centres* Princeton Study No. 36.

Leslie, J. (1982) The Trustee Savings Banks: Part 1 *Scottish Bankers Magazine 74*, 295 November 89-96.

Leslie, J. (1983) The Trustee Savings Banks: Part 2 *Scottish Bankers Magazine 74*, 296 February 121-128.

Llewellyn, D.T. (1985) *The Evolution of the British Financial System* Gilbert Lectures on Banking, The Institute of Bankers.

Lyall, K. (1983) *Investment Trust Companies 1971-1980* Ph.D Dissertation University of Edinburgh.

Maycock, J. (1986) *Financial Conglomerates: The New Phenomenon* Gower Publishing Co. Ltd.

Mayers, D. & C.W. Smith, Jr. (1986) The Mutualization of Stock Life Insurance Companies *Journal of Financial Economics 16*, 73-98.

Maxwell, H. (Sir) (1914) *Annals of the Scottish Widows Fund 1815-1914* R & R Clark Ltd.

Merrett, A.J., Howe, M. & Newbould, G.D. (1967) *Equity Issues and the London Capital Market* Longmans.

Mitchie, R.C. (1981) *Money, Mania and Markets* John Donald Publishers Edinburgh.

The Monopolies and Mergers Commission (1982) *The Hongkong and Shanghai Banking Corporation, Standard Chartered Bank Ltd, The Royal Bank of Scotland Group Ltd - A Report on the Proposed Mergers* Cmnd 8472, London: HMSO.

Munn, C.W. (1981) *The Scottish Provincial Banking Companies 1747-1864* John Donald Publishers Ltd.

Munn, C.W. (1982) *Banking in Scotland* Handbooks on Scottish Banking Practice, No.1 (2nd Ed.), The Institute of Bankers in Scotland, William Blackwood & Sons.

Bibliography

National Association of Pension Funds (1985) Year Book

National Audit Office (1985) Report by the Comptroller and Auditor General *Investment Activities of the Scottish Development Agency, Welsh Development Agency and the Highlands and Islands Development Board* House of Commons 230 1984/85.

Paltzer, E.F. (1977) Internationalization of Banking by Foreign Bases and Addresses *The Development of Financial Institutions in Europe, 1956-1976.* Wadsworth, (eds. Wilson & Fournier) A.W. Sijthoff - Leyden.

Pensions (1985,86) Fund Managers Survey, May.

Perez, R.C. (1983) *Marketing Financial Services* Praeger Publishers.

Perman, R. (1986) The mists begin to clear as Big Bang approaches *Scottish Business Insider* July.

Philipp, A.P. (1985) *Pension Funds and their Advisers* Eighth ed. AP Information Services Ltd.

Raynes, H.E. (1964) *A History of British Insurance* 2nd edn. Pitman & Sons.

Read, C. (1982) *The implications of technological change* The Diversification of Banking - Papers and Group Discussions from the 35th International Banking Summer School, June. The Institute of Bankers in Scotland.

Revell, J. (1973) *The British Financial System* Macmillan.

Revell, J. undated *The Complementary Nature of Competition and Regulation in the Financial Sector* Institute of European Finance, University College of North Wales.

Richards, K. & Colenutt, D.W. (1975) Concentration in the U.K. Ordinary Life Assurance Market *Journal of Industrial Economics* December.

Robbins, S.M. & Terleckyj, N.S. (1960) *Money Metropolis: Locational Study of Financial Activities in New York Region* Harvard University Press.

Scottish Affairs Committee. *Report on the Highlands and Islands Development Board* House of Commons 22I & 22II 1984/85

Shawky, H. (1982) An update on Mutual Funds: Better Grades *Journal of Portfolio Management* Winter.

Shiller, R.J. (1981) Do Stock Prices Move too Much to be Justified by Subsequent Changes in Dividends? *American Economic Review 71*, 421-436.

Short, J. (1984) Public Finance and Devolution: Money Flows between Government and Regions in the UK *Scottish Journal of Political Economy 31* No.2.

Silber, W. (1983) The Process of Financial Innovation *American Economic Association Papers and Proceedings 73,* No.2 May 89-95.

Smidt, S. (1981) Economic Efficiency and Financial Reform in Securities Markets *Financial Institutions and Markets* (eds. Polakoff, M.E. & Dukin, T.A.) 2nd edn. Wadsworth.

Smith, C. (1977) Alternative Methods For Raising Capital : Rights Versus Underwritten Offerings *Journal of Financial Economics 5,* 273-307.

Spicer & Pegler Associates (1985) *Future of Stockbroking in Scotland* Briefing Paper for the Scottish Development Agency May.

Stewart, W. (1984) Full Banking Status for the TSB *The Fraser of Allander Institute Quarterly Economic Commentary 10,* 4 August 63-65.

Technical Change Centre (1984) *The Adoption and Impact of Information Technology in the U.K. Insurance Industry* Second ed. May.

Thomas, W.A. (1973) *The Provincial Stock Exchanges* Frank Cass & Co. Ltd London.

Tobin, J. (1984) On the Efficiency of the Financial System *Lloyds Bank Review* July 1-15.

Travers, N. (1986) Winter's daunting tasks at Royal Bank of Scotland *The Banker* January 16-23.

Treynor, J.L. & Black, F. (1973) How to use Security Analysis to Improve Portfolio Selection *Journal of Business 46,* 66-86.

Bibliography

Unit Trust Association (1975-1985) Year Books
Van Horne, J.C. (1984) *Financial Market Rates and Flows* 2nd edn. Prentice Hall.
Van Horne, J.C. (1985) Of Financial Innovations and Excesses *Journal of Finance* 40, July No.3 621-631.
Weyer, D.W. (1982) *The economics of retail banking in the future* The Diversification of Banking, Institute of Bankers in Scotland.
Wilmot, T. (1985) *Inside the Over-The-Counter Market* Woodhead-Faulkner Cambridge.

INDEX

Abbey National Building Society, 151
Adam & Co., 178-9
Agriculture Securities Corporation Ltd, 124
Airdrie Savings Bank, 2, 142-3
Aitken Campbell & Co., 51-3, 171
Alliance Trust, 13, 264
Allied Irish Bank, 178
Allied Provincial Securities, 54
American Depositary Receipts, 59
assurance companies, see Scottish life offices

Bank Acts, 7-8, 14-15, 16
bank notes, 5, 7-8, 15, 24, 76-7
Bank of England, 76-7
   foundation, 3, 14, 15, 16
Bank of Ireland, 178
Bank of Scotland, 100 (tab.4.8), 102, 106, 107, 139
   branches, 95
   expansion, 310-11
   foundation, 3, 5, 7
   Home and Office Banking System, 82, 105, 110, 233, 298, 311
   management, 88
   merchant banking operations, 166-7
   North West Securities, 182
   overseas representation, 89-91, 90 (tab.4.6)
   ownership, 93-5, 95 (fig.4.2), 328
   staffing, 42, 83; training, 87, 326-7, 335-6
   see also Scottish clearing banks
banks
   employment; growth rates, 36 (tabs 2.6-2.7); regional location quotients, 34 (tab.2.5); see also Scottish clearing banks, staffing
   ethnic banks, 178
   international banks, 2, 91-2, 128n27, n28, 173-7; competition, 316
   specialist retail banks, 177-80, 329
   see also under specific names of banks; Scottish clearing banks
Bell, Lawrie, MacGregor, 52, 54, 55, 64

British Institute of Dealers in Securities, 57
British Linen Bank, 7, 166-70, 173, 313
Broker Services Ltd, 55, 331
building societies, 2, 21, 29, 96-7
   branches, 127n14, 151-3, 152 tab.5.10), 158, 160n19
   flow of funds in Scotland, 144 (tab.5.4)
   history, 143-5
   housing sector, 146 (tab.5.5), 147 (tab.5.6), 154 (tab.5.11), 322
   and insurance, 158
   networks, 19
   number, 149 (tab.5.7)
   operations, 145-8, 156, 157-8, 160n22-3
   personal sector, 160n20: competition, 73, 82, 142, 145, 153-8, 154 (tab.5.11), 311; deposits, 138, 153-6, 158; financial services, 157; liquid assets, 155-6, 155 (tab.5.12)
   regional concentration, 149 (tab.5.8)
   representation in Scotland, 150 (tab.5.9), 309
   staffing, 40-1, 41 (tab.2.9), 152-3
   structure and organisation, 148-53
   wholesale business, 145
Building Societies Act, 1986, 157-8, 161n26
Building Societies Commission, 161n24
business expansion schemes, 50, 63-4, 278
business start-up schemes, 167

capital markets, 1, 30, 32, 283
   decline, 10
   international, 47, 162, 164
   primary, 46, 50
   secondary, 46, 50, 64
   see also Eurobond markets, Eurocurrency market, Eurodollar market, Over the Counter market, Stock Exchange
Charterhouse Development Holdings Ltd, 167-9, 173, 313

Index

Clarke Farquharson & Partners, 57
clearing banks
  assets, 68
  sources and distribution of funds, 78 (tab.4.3)
  see also Scottish clearing banks
Clydesdale Bank, 68, 102, 107, 110
  branches, 81, 95
  electronic funds transfer at point of sale, 105, 311
  merchant banking operations, 165-6
  money transmission, 70-3
  overseas activity, 89, 93
  ownership, 93, 95, 312, 332
  staffing, 42
  see also Scottish clearing banks, deposit-taking and lending
Co-operative Bank, 180
Committee of London and Scottish Clearing Bankers, 30
competition among Scottish financial institutions, 322-4
  branches, 82
  building societies, 145, 153-8, 154 (tab.5.11), 187
  deregulation, 317-19
  international banks, 91-2, 176-7, 304
  life office products, 209, 228, 233-4
  merchant banking operations, 310-11, 313
  National Girobank, 180
  retail business, 73, 96-8
  Trustee Savings Bank, 142, 311
credit cards, 71-2, 73, 136, 159n6, n7, 311

Dunfermline Building Society, 145, 151, 158

employment, *see* staffing *under* building societies; financial sector; Scottish clearing banks; Scottish life offices
English merchant banks, 171
Eurobond markets, 65, 91, 174, 176
Eurocurrency market, 88-9, 91, 162, 174
Eurodollar market, 47
expenditure, household, on financial services, 32-3, 32 (tab.2.4)

factoring companies, staffing, 40-1
Faculty of Actuaries, 14
finance houses, 180-3
  marketing, 183

  staffing, 40-1
  technology applications, 183
Finance Houses Association, 181
financial centres, 6, 8, 13-23, 24-7, 307-8
  see also Scotland as base for financial institutions
financial intermediaries, 1, 3, 47, 50, 68
  cost reduction, 296
  development, 4-5, 9, 14-15, 23
financial sector
  central financing, 24-7
  employment, 33-7, 42-4, 43 (tab.2.10): growth rates, 36 (tabs 2.6-7); regional location quotients 34 (tab. 2.5)
  innovation, 295-306, 308: causes, 298-300; framework, 296-7; protection, 297, 306n6; strategy, type of, 296
  inter-sectoral links, 324-6, 334-5
  international trading, 304, 316
  multi-functional organisations, 107, 301-2, 322-3
  Scotland, 24-33: flow of funds, 28-33, 44, 324-5; growth potential, 33, 332-3; links with Scottish economy, 27-8, 44; regional financing, 24-33
  specialisation, 301-2, 323
foreign currency dealings, *see* banks, international
futures, 65

General Accident, 195-202, 196 (tab.7.2), 202 (tab.7.6), 223, 332
gilts, 51, 60
government/regional fiscal transfers, 26 (tab.2.1), 44

Halifax Building Society, 151
Highlands and Islands Development Board, 2, 278-9, 285-94
  financial activity, 286-91
  interest relief grants, 289
  performance, 291-4, 324
  socially fragile areas, support, 286, 286 (tab.9.2), 287, 288 (tab.9.3), 289 (tab.9.4), 291, 292
housing sector, 29-30, 32-3, 44, 309, 322
  average weekly payment table, 30 (tab.2.2)
  insurance, 208, 213, 228, 230-1, 234
  see also building societies

343

income, household, 31 (tab.2.3)
innovation, *see* financial sector, innovation
Institute of Bankers, 14
Institute of Bankers in Scotland, 85-7
insurance, 2, 11, 191-5, 193 (fig.7.1), 194 (tab.7.1)
 general insurance, 191-2, 195-202, 196 (tab.7.2), 198 (tabs 7.3-4), 200 (tab.7.5), 309, 332: performance, 197-201
 household expenditure, 32-3, 32 (tab.2.4)
 international banks, business with, 174-5
 long-term insurance, 191-2, 239n2
 staffing, 37-8, 42, 44, 45n4: changes in male and female staffing, 39 (tab.2.8); growth rates, 36 (tabs 2.6-7); regional location quotients, 34 (tab.2.5)
 see also Scottish life offices, life assurance
insurance broking, 235-9
 competition from Scottish clearing banks and building societies, 237
 technology applications, 238
investment fund management groups, 2, 245-52, 273, 309, 315, 330-1
 activity, 249 (tab.8.3), 250, 322
 assets, 247 (tab.8.1)
 funds under management, 248 (tab.8.2), 250: composition, 251 (tab.8.4)
 innovation, 255-6
 investment performance, 252-6
 marketing, 254-5, 255 (tab.8.5), 301, 315
 new teams, 249, 332-3, 335
 overseas links, 255-6, 273, 309, 315, 317, 331
 ownership, 246-9, 246 (fig.8.1)
 pension fund management, 245-7, 249-51, 266, 274n5, n7, 315, 330
 portfolio management costs, 252-3, 254, 260
 risk, 254, 256
 size, 249
 target for loans, 175
 unit trust marketing, 245, 260, 315
investment trusts, 9, 12-13, 260-5, 273, 276n21, 277n29
 asset spread, 263, 263 (tab.8.8)

 charges, 262-3, 277n26, n32, 315
 future, 264-5, 308
 management groups, 262
 marketing, 265
 overseas investment, 263, 317
 performance, 264-5, 264 (tab.8.9), 275n12-13, 330
 servicing, 272
 staffing, 40-1
Investors in Industry Group plc (3i), 124, 172, 285
Ivory & Sime, 12, 249, 255, 256, 261, 266-7, 270

James Finlay Corporation, 164, 168-9, 313
jobbers, *see* market makers

licensed dealers, 56-7
Life Association of Scotland, 212
life assurance, 11-12, 194, 201, 203-35, 321, *see also* Scottish life offices
Lloyds Bowmaker Ltd, 183
London clearing banks, assets, 68
London Stock Exchange, 9-11, 48-50
 see also Stock Exchange

Maclean, R. A. & Co., 51
market makers, 67n22
 London, 9, 47, 58-60, 66n6
 OTC market, 56-7
 regional (Scotland), 50-3, 64, 65, 66n8
marketing, of products and services, 32, 64-5, 296, 297, 321, 335
 'own brand' products, 303
Martin Currie Investment Management Ltd, 255, 267, 269
merchant banks, 2, 162-73, 308
 fund management, 248, 266, 268, 302
 see also names of specific banks
Murray Johnstone, 249, 255, 256, 266-7, 269

National Commercial and Glyn's Bank, 167-9
National Girobank, 180
National Savings Bank, 2, 39, 180, 184-8, 186 (tab.6.2), 332
 operations, 185-7
 performance, 153
 staffing, 37, 42, 187-8
new issues, *see* securities, new issues
new technology, *see* technology

344

Index

Noble Grossart, 164-5, 167-70, 173, 313
North West Securities, 182

options, 65
Over the Counter market, 48, 56-8, 63-4

Parsons & Co., 52, 54, 64
payments mechanisms, 30, 68-70, 108, 126n2, 162, 328-9
  see also Scottish clearing banks, money transmissions
Penney Easton & Co., 52, 54, 55, 57, 331
pension funds, 267-71, 302, 304
  managed by investment managers, *see* investment fund management groups, pension fund management
  management, 266-70, 267 (tab.8.10), 273
  management charges, 268-9, 269 (tab.8.11)
  overseas funds, 270-1
  performance, 269-70
  servicing, 272
  target for loans, 175
Personal Equity Plans, 62, 157, 265, 322, 330
privatisation of nationalised bodies, 258-9
Public Sector Borrowing Requirement, 27, 184-5

Quayle Munro, 169, 313

Reed Stenhouse, 236-7, 272
risks, 9, 109, 259, 264, 279, 285, 286, 294, 296, 297
Robert Fleming, 59, 249, 260, 264-5
Royal Bank of Scotland, 42, 68, 102, 110, 328
  branches, 81, 82, 332
  Business Development Workshop, 106
  expansion, 310-11
  history, 5
  merchant banking operations, 167-8, 182
  money transmissions, 70-3, 104, 178
  overseas links, 89-90
  ownership, 8, 93-5, 128n31, 129n32
  performance, 139
  senior management structure, 86 (fig.4.1)
  staffing, 83: training, 85-7

  see also Scottish clearing banks

savings banks, 8-9
  see also names of individual banks
Scotland as base for financial institutions, 23, 109, 207-9, 300, 326
  employment, 41-2, 41 (tab.2.9)
  Government support, 336
  history, 22 (tab.1.2)
  see also financial centres
Scottish American Investment Trust, 260
Scottish Amicable, 12, 208, 212-14, 219, 225, 317
Scottish banks, 29-30
  Edinburgh's relationship with London, 16-17
  history, 5-9, 14-17, 308: early innovations, 15 (tab.1.1)
  see also Scottish clearing banks
Scottish clearing banks, 1-2, 68-130, 127n8, n9, 308, 332
  assets, 68
  branch network, 18-19, 29, 68, 80-3, 127n12-14, 329: marketing of products and services, 105-7, 110, 300-1, 311, 321; number, 80 (tab.4.4)
  competition, *see* competition among Scottish financial institutions
  complementary and ancillary services, 709, 108
  deposit-taking and lending, 73-86, 111-15, 112 (tab.4.10), 114 (tabs 4.11-12), 122 (tab.4.16), 129-30n46: balances, 74 (tab.4.1); maturity structure, 109, 115-17, 116 (tab.4.13); number of accounts, 75 (tab.4.2); performance and profitability, 98-104, 99-101 (tabs 4.7-9), 129n35-9
  flow of funds, 69, 324-5
  head office location, 311-12
  interest rates, 125-6, 130n58-9, 300
  international banking operations, 88-93, 128n22, 316-17: competition, 91-2, 304; overseas representation, 90 (tab.4.6), 128n26, 311
  lending, 77-81, 78 (tab.4.3), 108-9, 117-25, 119 (tab.4.15), 130n48: early history, 6, 14, 304; marketing, 322; non-commercial, 18-19; overseas, 91

345

Index

Scottish clearing banks—*contd*
  money transmission, 70-3, 108, 126n6, 128n29, 302-5
  ownership, 93-6, 95 (fig.4.2), 128n31, 129n32
  pension funds, 266
  personal sector, *see* retail business
  retail business, 69, 76-81, 128n20, 1533-6, 158: influences on future development, 104-6, 110
  Scottish economy, relationship, 109, 123-4, 332
  staffing, 39-40, 43, 83-8, 84 (tab.4.5), 108: changes in male and female employment, 39 (tab.2.8); management structures, 86-8, 111; marketing skills, 87; number, 68, 127n15, n16; training, 85-7, 326-7, 335-6
  technology, applications, 104-5, 108, 129n41, 310-11; *see also* money transmission
  venture capital, 125, 309
  wholesale business, 69, 76-81, 109-10, 129n41, n44
  see also banknotes
Scottish Development Agency, 2, 278-85, 294, 324, 333, 336
  investment portfolio, 281-2, 282 (tab.9.1)
  management assistance, 280, 283-4
Scottish economy, 24-33, 44
  financial innovation, 304
  imbalances, 185, 336
  and Scottish clearing banks, 09, 123-4, 332
  venture capital, 279
Scottish Equitable, 209, 233
Scottish Financial Enterprise, 326, 334
Scottish Life, 233
Scottish life offices, 2, 203-235, 304-5, 308-9, 313-14, 329-30
  balance sheet, 206 (tab.7.8)
  cluster policies, 305
  commissions, 231-2, 233 (tab.7.15), 235, 238, 244n66, 305, 306n9
  competition from other financial institutions, 225-8, 225 (tab.7.12), 226 (tab.7.13), 314
  housing sector, 208, 213, 228, 230-1, 234
  innovation, 298, 329
  international banks, business with, 174-5

  investment, 214-18, 216 (tab.7.10), 235, 241-2n32
  life assurance policies, 203-8, 240-1n18, 313, 329
  links with building societies, 233
  marketing, 211-13, 212 (tab.7.9), 241n24, 243-4n59, 314, 330
  overseas business, 213-14, 234, 317
  ownership, 20-4, 234
  pension schemes, 204, 208-9, 230-1, 234, 241n21, 266
  performance, 228-30, 229 (tab.7.14), 322-3
  revenue account, 206 (tab.7.7)
  staffing, 38, 218-20, 219 (tab.7.11), 309, 314: changes in male and female employment, 39 (tab.2.8), 296; management, 219-20
  technology applications, 232-4, 296, 314, 329
  unit trusts, 257, 259, 264, 329
  unit-linked business, 209-11, 227-8, 231-2, 241n22, 243n58, 259-60
Scottish merchant banks, 165-71, 168 (tab.6.1), 309, 312-13, 331-2
  history, 6
  see also merchant banks, names of specific banks
Scottish Mutual, 209, 212, 233, 267, 269
Scottish Provident, 212-13
Scottish Stock Exchanges, 9-11, 47, 309
  see also Stock Exchange, Scottish floor
Scottish Venture Fund, 166
Scottish Widows, 11, 209, 212, 225-6, 267, 269
securities, 47, 48
  dealing, 50: merchant banks, 164
  Government, 47-8
  innovation, 296
  large issues, 9-10, 170
  new issues, 10, 557-7, 62-3, 164, 170
  Public Limited Companies, 47
  rights issues, 67n23
  see also Stock Exchange
settlement, 48-9, 70, 71, 185
  see also Scottish clearing banks, money transmission
small firms, start-ups, 278
Speirs & Jeffrey, 52, 54
Standard Life, 12, 208-9, 212-14, 225-6, 233, 256, 267, 269, 317-18
Stenhouse Holdings, 236-7

Index

Stock Exchange, 9, 46, 47-8, 57-62, 66n19
   quotations, 10, 49, 55-7
   regional Exchanges, 47-50, 65n1, n3
   Scottish floor, 48-9, 50, 51, 65n4-5: decline, 64-5, 67n25; effect of 'Big Bang' changes, 60-2; effect of change in commission scales, 57-60, 268, 270, 273; new issues market, 63
   Scottish members, 52 (tab.3.1)
   see also London Stock Exchange, Scottish Stock Exchanges
stockbrokers, 331
   competition, 64, 322
   effect of 'Big Bang' changes, 60-2, 66-7n20
   effect of change in commission scales, 57-60
   marketing of services, 64-5, 67n25
   new issues market, 63
   pension funds, 266, 268
   private client networks, 51-5, 54 (tab.3.2), 64
   regional (Scotland), 50-1, 53-5, 66n10, n11
   Scottish members of the Stock Exchange, 52 (tab.3.1)
   services in Scotland, 54 (tab.3.2)
   staffing, 40-1

technology, applications, 104-5, 183, 232-4, 238, 319-21
   databases, 300-1
   efficiency improvement, 296, 297
   and financial innovation, 299
   information processing, 331
   new activities, 302-3: consumer reaction, 303
   new ventures, 278, 284, 294, 304, 305
   staffing trends, 38, 40, 85, 187-8, 218-19, 320
   see also Scottish clearing banks, money transmission
telecommunications, 295, 298, 300
   international markets, 46-7
   Stock Exchange dealing, 49-51, 57-62, 67n22
   see also Bank of Scotland, Home and Office Banking System; Scottish clearing banks, money transmission

Trustee Savings Bank, 39, 107, 113, 232-3, 312
   branches, 82, 127n14, 137, 301, 135 (tab.5.2)
   competition, *see* competition among Scottish financial institutions
   future, 139-42
   head office: TSB Scotland, 42
   history, 131-5
   lending, 138
   marketing, 141
   operations, 135-7, 135 (tab.5.2), 153-5, 158
   performance and profitability, 137-9, 138 (tab.5.3)
   principal subsidiaries, 132 (tab.5.1)
   staff training, 128n21, 141, 326-7, 335-6
   structure prior to incorporation, 134 (fig.5.1)

unit trusts, 256-60, 302, 304-5, 330, 333
   charges, 257-8, 262, 275n10, 276n19
   commission, 258-9
   competition, 258, 265, 308
   marketing, 256, 258, 259, 265, 321: by investment managers, 245, 247, 255, 273
   offshore funds, 275n15
   performance table, 257 (tab.8.6)
   profitability, 260
   trustees: Scottish institutions, 271-2
United Dominions Trust, 182
Unlisted Securities Market, 10-11, 49, 53, 55-6, 64, 66n14

venture capital, 170, 172
   public, 278-94
   Scottish clearing banks, 125, 309
   Scottish Venture Fund, 166

Walter Scott & Partners, 267, 270
wholesale banking, *see* Merchant Banks, Scottish Clearing Banks, wholesale business, Scottish Merchant Banks
WM Company, 272, 331
Wood Mackenzie, 52, 53, 61, 63, 64-5, 272, 331